MULTINATIONALS AND POLITICAL CONTROL

MULTINATIONALS AND POLITICAL CONTROL

John Robinson

St. Martin's Press   New York

Printed in Great Britain
First published in the United States of America in 1983

ISBN 0-312-55262-9

Library of Congress Cataloging in Publication Data

Robinson, John.
   Multinationals and political control.

   Includes index.
   1. International business enterprises — Political
aspects.
   I. Title.
   HD2755.5.R62   322'.3   81-23342
   ISBN 0-312-55262-9   AACR2

Contents

List of tables   xiii

The Author   xiv

Foreword by Etienne Davignon, Vice President,
European Commission   xv

Acknowledgements   xvii

List of abbreviations   xviii

PART I   INTRODUCTION AND SUMMARY

1   Introduction   3

2   Summary and outlook   6

     OECD Guidelines for MNCs: pre-emptive Western
     strike emphasises business responsibility   7

     The UN: towards a 'comprehensive' — but
     voluntary — code of conduct   8

     The European Economic Community: a special
     approach to MNC control   9

     Negotiations on multinationals; the conflicting
     forces   10

     Trend analysis of MNC policy outlook 1980—85:
     key pointers   11

PART II   THE EUROPEAN COMMUNITY: THE
BINDING IMPACT OF LEGISLATED
CONTROL

3   European multinationals' policy: the roots   19

    Europe's post-war tradition, national frustration
and the multinational enterprise   20

    Factors conditioning EEC policy towards multi-
nationals   22

4   European multinationals' policy: from conception to
impact   35

    Key characteristics of European MNC policy   36

    Conclusion and outlook   44

5   Europe's democratic challenge to multinationals   46

    Multinationals, European industrial relations –
and the erosion of capitalism   47

    European industrial democracy: the burgeoning
mosaic   50

    Democratic control: EEC labour law and MNC
hostility   56

    Corporate responsibility: emerging European
trends   64

    Conclusion and outlook   68

6   Europe's capitalist challenge to multinationals   73

    Introduction   73

    Focus on multinationals as EEC policy strengthens   75

    Independence and rapidity of EEC anti-trust   76

    Private monopolies: the EEC's emerging power   79

    The battle against size: outlook 1990   82

    Crackdown against cartels: the EECs mailed fist   89

    Nationalised industries: EEC shirks responsibility   90

    EEC control of state aids: MNCs bear the brunt   93

    Conclusion and outlook   93

7   International competitivity: Europe on the defence   98
           Free trade is dead! Long live organised liberalism!   99
           EEC attitude to international business codes   100
           The EEC and South Africa   101
           The EEC, the US and international anti-trust   102
           Conclusion and outlook   104

     EEC legislative check-list for multinational companies   106

PART III   THE OECD GUIDELINES FOR MULTI-
             NATIONAL ENTERPRISES: THE
             POLITICISATION OF INTERNATIONAL
             BUSINESS

     The hard fact of 'soft law'   111

8   Towards a political framework for Western business   113
           The Guidelines' paternity: the UN connection   115
           The Guidelines' paternity: internal pressure in the
           West   118

9   The OECD Guidelines in action: 15 multinational
     'cases'   122
           (i)   Badger Company: parent company liability,
                  employee consultation and compensation
                  (Belgium)   125
           (ii)   Hertz Rentacar: transfer of workers to
                  influence collective bargaining (Denmark)   129
           (iii) Massey Ferguson: Motor Ibericq: trade union
                  recognition (Spain)   129
           (iv)   Black and Decker: trade union recognition
                  (UK)   130
           (v)   Siemens: employment protection (Belgium)   130
           (vi)   Warner Lambert: closure, employment pro-
                  tection and wage level maintenance
                  (Sweden)   131

(vii) Litton Industries: production transfer and plant closure (Sweden)   132

(viii) Philips: trade union information and co-operation on plant closures (Germany)   132

(ix) International Telephone and Telegraph: worker representation and union information (Germany)   133

(x) Citibank–Citicorp: trade union formation and recognition (UK)   134

(xi) European Airlines Groupings: definition of a multinational (Europe-wide)   135

(xii) & (xiii) Firestone (Switzerland) and BATCO (Netherlands): do the Guidelines restrict business relocation? – No, but ...   136

(xiv) & (xv) British Oxygen (Sweden) and Philips (Finland): access to authorised decision-makers   137

10 Political and business impact of the OECD code   141

Greater impact for the OECD code – outlook for implementation of the Guidelines   142

From MNC control to investor encouragement?   146

The OECD: the industrialised world's lobby on MNC issues   150

Assessment of the OECD Guidelines: a general code with selective impact   152

PART IV   MULTINATIONALS AND THE UN SYSTEM: TOWARDS VOLUNTARY BUT EFFECTIVE CODES

11 The UN code of conduct for transnational corporations   163

The roots of the UN code of conduct   163

Negotiations: the forces in conflict   167

The major issues – agreed and outstanding   168

12   Sectoral codes for international business   171

The ILO's 'Tripartite Declaration of Principles concerning Multinationals and Social Policy'   171

Anti-trust: applying Western rules to MNCs in the developing countries   176

Transfer of technology: major unresolved issues   178

Bribery and corruption: UN Treaty delayed despite US pressure   182

Other UN activities on MNCs: focus on information and advice   184

13   Embryonic business control in the UN system; medium-term perspectives   189

Implementation: the key to effective codes   190

PART V   CONTROL OF INTERNATIONAL BUSINESS: THE STRUGGLE FOR INFLUENCE

14   The war of the lobbies   195

European unions versus Western multinationals   195

At the EEC: trade unions' collective impact versus multi-faceted business pressure   198

At the OECD: the institutionalisation of business and union lobbies   204

At the UN: the international dimension of union/ business conflict   212

PART VI   CONCLUSION

15   The political constraint and the business response   223

Capitalism in decline and accountability on the rise   224

Business and the politics of rejection   226

An alternative strategy for the company   228

APPENDICES

I — Relating to Part II (EEC policy on MNCs)   231

   I(a) 'Multinational Undertakings and the Com-
       munity': Communication of the European
       Commission to the Council of Ministers,
       8 November 1973, followed by text of
       EEC draft resolution on MNCs   231

   I(b) Interview with Etienne Davignon, EEC
       Commissioner for industrial affairs, on EEC
       policy towards multinational companies   245

   I(c) 'Community law and codes of conduct for
       multinational enterprises' (EEC Commission
       policy paper, January 1979)   250

   I(d) 'Companies which are members of a group'
       (Appendix to EEC's 'Green Paper' on
       'Employee participation and Company Struc-
       ture', November 1975)   263

   I(e) Code of conduct for companies with sub-
       sidiaries, branches or representation in South
       Africa (adopted by EEC Foreign Ministers,
       September 1977)   269

   I(f) European Parliament resolution on MNCs
       (16 April 1977) — Draft code of principles
       for multinational enterprises (US Congress/
       European Parliament, September 1976)   272

   I(g) Countries of origin of the 200 multinationals
       with the highest turnovers (EEC Commission
       survey on MNCs, July 1976)   283

   I(h) EEC proposals for worker information and
       consultation in MNCs (October 1980)   285

II — Relating to Part III (OECD Guidelines)   294

   II(a) Declaration on international investment and
       multinational enterprises (21 June 1976)   294

   II(b) Annex to Declaration on international
       investment and multinational enterprises
       (21 June 1976)   296

II(c) Decision of the Council on inter-governmental consultation procedures on the Guidelines for multinational enterprises (21 June 1976)   304

II(d) Decision of the Council on national treatment (21 June 1976)   306

II(e) Decision of the Council on international investment incentives and disincentives (21 June 1976)   308

II(f) Recommendation of the Council on the determination of transfer prices between associated enterprises (16 May 1979)   309

II(g) Recommendation of the Council concerning action against restrictive business practices affecting international trade including those involving multinational enterprises (adopted on 20 July 1978)   311

II(h) Review of the OECD Guidelines on multinational enterprises (as agreed by OECD Ministers meeting in Council, Paris, 13–14 June 1979)   314

II(i) TUAC statement for the mid-term report on the OECD Guidelines for multinational enterprises submitted to Governments (14 October 1981)   337

III — Principally relating to Part IV (multinationals and the UN system: towards voluntary but effective codes)   350

III(a) International Labour Organisation: Tripartite declaration of principles concerning multinational enterprises and social policy (adopted by the Governing Body of the International Labour Office, November 1977)   350

III(b) Restrictive business practices: a set of multilaterally agreed equitable principles and rules for the control of restrictive business practices (22 April 1979)   365

III(c) Draft international code of conduct on the transfer of technology   378

III(d) Draft international agreement to prevent and eliminate illicit payments in international commercial transactions   404

III(e) Concluded provisions of a UN code of conduct   411

III(f) Chairman's formulations on the parts of the UN code not yet concluded   424

IV —Relating to Part V: control of international business — the struggle for influence   433

IV(a) European Action Programme — Multinational Groups of Companies (European Trades Union Confederation, June 1977)   433

IV(b) A checklist for trade unionists (November 1979)   448

IV(c) The OECD Guidelines: Trade Union Demands (TUAC, November 1978)   455

IV(d) International Business' Policy Position on the OECD Guidelines on Multinational Enterprises (BIAC, January 1979)   462

IV(e) Guidelines for International Investment (International Chamber of Commerce, November 1972)   466

IV(f) Extortion and Bribery in Business Transactions (International Chamber of Commerce, November 1977)   477

IV(g) Multinational Charter (International Confederation of Free Trade Unions, October 1975)   484

Index   498

Tables

3.1 Number of multinationals by country of origin   24

4.1 Turnover and assets totals of multinationals surveyed, by country of origin   40

6.1 List of EEC markets where the market leader holds 45 per cent or more of the total national market   84

10.1 Outward direct investment flows in the OECD countries   149

10.2 Inward direct investment flows in the OECD countries   149

The author

John Robinson was educated at St Bees School, Cumberland, and at Manchester University where he read French and then completed an MA in Government. Following jobs in Canada, first at Montreal University and then as an investment analyst in a major brokerage house, Mr Robinson worked in Brussels as a journalist throughout the 1970s. During this period, he was founding editor of both *European Report* and *Multinational Service*, a director of European Information Service, and a contributor to *The Economist*. From 1977 to 1980, he was special EEC correspondent of the *Washington Post* and also EEC correspondent of *Business Europe* and *Business International*. Since April 1981, he has been a member of the Spokesman's Group of the European Commission.

Foreword

The interlocking nature of private enterprise and public responsibility is a phenomenon which in recent years has assumed greater acuity. This interface between business activity and the public interest has been dramatically reinforced as an issue by the worldwide economic crisis. Among its other consequences, the prolonged period of uncertainty provoked by the sharp oil price rises of the 1970s has narrowed the distance between business decisions and their social and political impact, and thus between private economic decision-makers and their public, political counterparts. The crisis, leading to low investment and high unemployment, has crowded the politician and company executive together in a shrunken economic canvas. From this narrowing context has gradually emerged the notion of broader, public responsibility directly accruing to 'private' business.

Pressure for wider corporate responsibility, bringing with it an extension of the company's environment beyond strictly business factors, has tended to focus on the multinational corporation. At the same time, the nation state, beyond whose bounds multinationals naturally overspill in their search for resource optimisation, has proved neither appropriate nor able to provide the legal framework within which such companies operate.

It is against this background that John Robinson's book serves a most valuable dual purpose. First, it guides the reader, particularly the business reader, through the complex labyrinth of issues affecting multinational companies that are now the subject of negotiation in the

European Community and leading international organisations, and thus it identifies the key areas for policy development for the 1980s. Second, it sets the whole multinationals issue against the broader backdrop of post-war developments in European history and in international capitalism. Mr Robinson's work can thus be used both by the generalist for its insights into the tightening link between government and enterprise, and by corporate management as an aid for developing business responses in areas of public policy.

Indeed, the author ends his book with an implicit challenge to business to give greater emphasis to the role of public affairs both in the overall conduct of company strategy and in corporate organisation. It is of course up to individual companies to respond to that challenge as they see fit. However, in view of the welter of issues identified in the following pages as affecting the business environment of tomorrow, it is clearly not a challenge to be dismissed lightly. Mr Robinson's book can contribute to generalising amongst the international business world a sensitivity to the public policy issues that will increasingly shape the business decisions of the future.

Etienne Davignon,
Brussels, August 1982

Acknowledgements

This book attempts to describe the emerging and tangled skein of international law and business codes within which the multinational corporation is increasingly being forced to operate. This attempt has only been possible thanks to the help and guidance generously afforded me in particular by officials at the European Community institutions, the Organisation for Economic Co-operation and Development, and the United Nations and its specialised agencies. In addition, I am indebted to representatives of business and trade union organisations, and indeed to those in individual companies whose assistance has been most valuable. I should like especially to thank Robert Coleman and John Temple-Lang whose invaluable assistance in no way renders them responsible for the views set out in the following pages. Taken together, these people — civil servants, politicians, lobbyists, trade unionists and company officials — have provided the vast majority of my source material for this book.

My acknowledgements must also extend to various international organisations — the EEC institutions, the UN and its specialised agencies, the OECD and its business and union bodies, BIAC and TUAC, the international trade union centres and the International Chamber of Commerce (ICC) — which have authorised the reproduction of the documents set out in the Appendices. OECD documentation is available from the Director of Information, 2 Rue André Pascal, 75775 Paris Cedex 16. The ICC publishes a number of documents on questions of international trade, a catalogue of which is available at no charge from ICC Publishing S.A., 38 Cours Albert 1er, 75008 Paris.

Thanks are also due to my erstwhile colleagues at European Information Service, and in particular to its managing director, Gérard Rousselot-Pailley, who was an unstinting source of encouragement and support.

Lastly, I should emphasize that the views expressed in this book are entirely my own responsibility, and in no way are intended to represent those of my current employer, the European Commission.

J.R.

Abbreviations

Throughout the book, the author has been forced to use a series of abbreviations which, while generally explained in the text itself, are clarified here for the reader's benefit:

ACP   African, Caribbean and Pacific states associated with the EEC

AFL/CIO   American Federation of Labor/Congress of Industrial Organisations

Benelux   (Economic Union of) Belgium, Netherlands and Luxembourg

BIAC   Business and Industry Advisory Committee (to the OECD)

BIFU   Banks, Insurance and Finance Union (British)

CBI   Confederation of British Industry

CEEP   (French acronym for) European Centre for Public Enterprises

CGT   Confédération Générale du Travail (French Communist trade union centre)

CIME   Committee on International Investment and Multi-national Enterprises (of the OECD)

CIS   Comprehensive Information System on Transnational Corporations (of the UN)

CTC	Centre on Transnational Corporations (at the UN)
	Commission on Transnational Corporations (at the UN)
DGB	Deutscher Gewerkschaftsbund (German trade union centre)
EC or EEC	European (Economic) Community
ECOSOC	Economic and Social Council (of the UN)
EFTA	European Free Trade Association
ELEC	European League for Economic Co-operation
ETUC	European Trade Union Confederation
FAO	Food and Agriculture Organisation (of the UN)
FIET	(French acronym for) International Federation of Commercial, Clerical and Technical Employees
FNV	Federatie Nederlandse Vakbeweging (Dutch trade union centre)
GATT	General Agreement on Tariffs and Trade
GDP	Gross Domestic Product
GNP	Gross National Product
Group B	The grouping of the industrialised countries at the UN
Group D	The grouping of communist countries at the UN
Group-77 or G-77	The grouping of developing countries at the UN
GSP	Generalised system of tariff preferences
ICC	International Chamber of Commerce
ICFTU	International Confederation of Free Trade Unions
ICP	Industry Co-operative Programme (of the FAO)
ICSID	International Centre for the Settlement of Industrial Disputes
ILO	International Labour Organisation
	International Labour Office
IME Committee	See CIME (above)
IMF	International Metalworkers' Federation
IOE	International Organisation of Employers
ITF	International Transport Workers' Federation

ITGLWF	International Textile, Garment and Leather Workers' Federation
ITS	International trade secretariat(s)
LDCs	Lesser developed countries
LO	Landsorganisationen (the name for trade union centres in the Scandinavian countries)
MITI	Ministry of Trade and Industry (Japan)
MNC	Multinational company – this is the basic abbreviation used for simplicity's sake through the majority of the text, although other abbreviations (see below) are occasionally used
MNE	Multinational Enterprise (OECD usage)
NICs	Newly industrialised countries
NUBE	National union of Bank Employees (British)
OATUU	Organisation of African Trade Union Unity
OECD	Organisation for Economic Co-operation and Development
SOHYO	the main Japanese socialist trade union centre
TNC	Transnational corporation (UN usage)
TNE	Transnational enterprise (Latin American usage)
TUAC	Trade Union Advisory Committee (to the OECD)
TUC	Trade Union Congress (British)
UA	Unit of Account ($1 US = 0.99 ua on 30 March 1982)
UN	United Nations
UNCTAD	United Nations Committee on Trade and Development
UNCTC	United Nations Centre on Transnational Corporations United Nations Commission on Transnational Corporations
UNICE	(French acronym for) Union of Industries of the European Community
WCL	World Confederation of Labour
WFTU	World Federation of Trade Unions

PART I

INTRODUCTION AND SUMMARY

1 Introduction

Multinational business is now international politics. Multinational companies are increasingly being forced to operate in a framework not just determined by the laws of supply and demand albeit tempered by growing national interventionism and governmental response to the economic crisis, but also by a proliferating set of intergovernmental arrangements specifically targeted at them. This book attempts a predictive outline of the development of these arrangements for multinational company control in the 1980s, based on a detailed examination of the present situation in three key areas: the ten-nation European Economic Community (EEC), the Western political establishment operating through the Organisation for Economic Co-operation and Development (OECD), and the international community meeting in the United Nations system.

The early 1970s saw the real beginning of this trend towards international control of multinational companies (MNCs), but the first five years of the 1980s should see it enter a more operational phase already partially begun in the later years of the last decade. As a result, international management will more and more have to perceive itself as it is itself perceived by governments — as much a political as an economic operator, with responsibilities to match. Politically-inspired constraints, in the form of the bewildering mish-mash of European directives, OECD guidelines and UN codes of conduct are, taken together, fast becoming as real a factor in forward corporate planning as traditional economic considerations. The distance between business and international politics, already substantially narrowed, will further fore-shorten dramatically in the coming years. The following pages focus on that trend. The aim of this book is to offer a comprehensive guide through the complex labyrinth of these often interlocking arrangements. Its first chapter provides top management, trade union leaders and economic policy-makers with a succinct 10-page summary of medium-term developments whose detailed monitoring is the task of their public affairs departments and professional consultants. For the latter, the following chapters provide an in-depth analysis of trends in MNC-targeted policy in respectively the Common Market, the Paris-based OECD, and in UN organisations. The more general reader, meanwhile, may distinguish the converging strands of the emerging intermesh between multinational business and international political concern primarily articulated through these three institutions.

The priority issues being considered for legislation or codes in these three arenas are often similar — corporate disclosure, taxation, anti-trust, employment protection and industrial relations etc. — but their treatment is markedly different. The EEC's main impact on inter-national business is and will continue to be via legally-binding directives, rather than sweeping codes of conduct. By and large, precisely the opposite is true for measures impacting on MNCs being developed at the OECD and the UN — two bodies, however, which are in permanent conflict over MNC issues. These distinctions and conflicts are central to the dynamics and results of international negotiations on multinational companies.

In all three of these arenas, as debate on MNCs increasingly gives way to negotiations and policy action, so the conflict of interests, eager to inflect measures in a direction favourable to them, intensifies. Part V of the book deals with the 'war of the lobbies', a conflict led respectively by international business and trade union organisations — an aspect of the process of policy formulation towards MNCs which is critical to an understanding of the issues involved.

A unique collection of source documents is appended and classified by reference to the Part to which they correspond or whose arguments they illustrate. The appendices — including both basic policy texts and confidential memos, interviews and internal negotiating documents — are thus an integral part of the study. The chapters and the appendices are mutually supportive, and combined are intended to provide a basic reference work for those monitoring MNC policy issues in the 1980s.

A final note to the reader: this book, while comprehensive insofar as it provides an overview of the major initiatives on MNCs emerging from the three arenas in question, is clearly not exhaustive in the sense that it seeks to examine all public policy developments (e.g. EEC environmental legislation) which might possibly affect MNCs in common with other firms. Instead, it deals with arrangements or laws directed at MNCs qua MNCs.

2 Summary and outlook

Multinational companies face the prospect in the 1980s of the increased impact of burgeoning regional regulations and intergovernmental codes of conduct aimed at controlling their activities.

This expanding web of constraints targeted on international business, both in the ten-country European Community and at the broader international level, is the outcome of a variety of pressures which fed into the 'multinationals' debate that reached its climax in the confrontation between developing and industrialised countries in the early 1970s. Since then, the debate has made way for action, reflecting a move from the rhetoric of the spoken word to the process of negotiating the written texts of international arrangements or laws affecting multinationals (MNCs).

In parallel with this change, there has been a shift in the attitudes among negotiators, which in turn is being reflected by changes in the scope and nature of the arrangements under discussion. The initial impulse favouring binding control of MNCs fuelled by the political ambitions of recently enfranchised developing countries (LDCs), now appears to have been decisively tempered by the economic stagnation which has gripped the world since the 1974 oil crisis and by the correspondingly heightened need for foreign investment felt in particular by the LDCs. The upshot is that the demands made on multinational business in the international arrangements now under negotiation will be more flexible than they otherwise would have been, but at the same time they may also be more realistically achievable in negotiating terms.

The first five years of the 1980s should see conclusion of many of these agreements and the strengthened enforcement of those whose beginning was in the late 1970s.

OECD Guidelines for MNCs: pre-emptive Western strike emphasises business responsibility

The 'multinationals' issue is no longer a debate, it is a negotiation. Or, rather, a series of intergovernmental negotiations set in different arenas but all pitched at the international level. Some indeed have already given way to agreed measures, the first being the Guidelines for Multinational Enterprises adopted by the Paris-based OECD. Accurately sensing the post-colonial offensive aimed by the developing world at the West's international companies, the industrialised market economy countries were quick to respond when in June 1976 the OECD Council approved the Guidelines. Voluntary in nature, the Guidelines are a calculated compromise by Western governments between, on the one hand, the need to sensitise firms to their social, economic and political responsibilities and, on the other, the need to make the rest of the world aware, and in particular the LDCs negotiating a UN code of conduct for transnational corporations, that the West is not prepared to see excessive constraints imposed on their major creators of wealth: the MNCs. Nonetheless, the West's trade unions — much to the alarm of the international business world — have succeeded in using the leverage inherent in the OECD Guidelines as a platform for presenting a series of specific complaints against individual companies (outlined in detail in Part III). This pressure will almost certainly continue over the next five years, which will be a test period for the success of the OECD model for multinationals' control as the more ambitious UN code of conduct and related UN arrangements either conclude or swing into full operation. Conscious of the immediacy of this threat, policy-makers in OECD countries decided in June 1979 to make improved implementation of the Guidelines on MNCs the key priority for the 1979–84 period. The centre-piece of this strategy is the call on multinationals to show clear compliance in all areas of their activities with the OECD arrangement (corporate disclosure, competition, financing, taxation, employment and industrial relations, science and technology).

The Geneva-based International Labour Organisation (ILO) was in fact the first UN specialised agency to adopt an international instrument on multinationals, when in November 1977 it agreed a Declaration of Principles concerning Multinational Enterprises and Social Policy. Aimed particularly at controlling the impact of MNCs on employment and industrial relations in the LDCs, this Tripartite

Declaration (so-called because it was negotiated by and is addressed to trade unions, employers and governments) will probably only begin to enter its operational phase in 1982—83. Here again, then, the key phase for the implementation of the Declaration — voluntary, like the OECD Guidelines, but containing more detailed standards than the Guidelines on employment and industrial relations — will be the next few years. The ILO initiative could, in addition, be given greater limelight because its key theme — industrial relations in the MNC — is precisely the area of greatest concern with international business both in the EEC and the international labour movement.

The UN: towards a 'comprehensive' — but voluntary — code of conduct

The highlight of international public policy towards MNCs in the period 1980—85, centres on the prospects for the gradual finalisation of a comprehensive code of conduct for transnational corporations by the UN in New York. Called for back in 1974, substantive drafting on a common text did not in fact really begin until 1979. Despite many problems, prospects for concluding at negotiating level by 1982 and thence working out how the code is to be enforced seem better than even. Already there has emerged a clear idea of the profile of the code, which in all probability will bring within its umbrella other intergovernmental arrangements on 'sectoral' MNC issues, and will be largely or totally voluntary in nature. These other arrangements, besides the ILO Declaration mentioned above, are codes of conduct sponsored by the United Nations Conference on Trade and Development (UNCTAD) dealing respectively with anti-trust (or 'restrictive business practices' as it is officially known) and technology transfer. To this should be added a UN agreement under negotiation on ethical practices in international business transactions. Other key issues to be covered by the code include corporate disclosure, taxation, MNC impact on balance of payments and financing, together with the political demands of non-interference by MNCs in internal or inter-governmental affairs, respect for national sovereignty, etc. These and other issues are treated in detail in Part IV.

Despite initial pressure by developing countries backed by Western trade unions in favour of legally binding international instruments, the UN arrangements will be voluntary in nature. But, as at the OECD, MNC management should not be lulled into false security by the trend towards voluntary codes, since they will be accompanied by vigorous demands for effective implementation. The business world already knows what this has meant in the comparatively congenial framework of the OECD Guidelines, where so-called 'soft law' can have rough edges. By 1985, companies will know for certain what demands they are to be specifically subjected to in the framework of the UN.

The European Economic Community: a special approach to MNC control

In this general trend towards greater control of MNCs, the European Economic Community presents a special case. Not for the EEC comprehensive codes of conduct, binding or otherwise, despite any impressions given by the draft code of principles for MNCs jointly agreed in 1977 by representatives of the European Parliament and the US Congress. This code, if for no other reason than the subordinate role played by the European Parliament in the EEC's decision-making process and the economic realities facing the EEC authorities who would have to implement it, is long on ideas but will continue to be short on impact. The same analysis does not apply to the EEC's code of conduct for European business in South Africa (September 1977), but that is to be seen as an exceptional measure taken for exceptional reasons of high international policy.

More usually, EEC strategy towards multinational company issues is typified by a series of specific measures legally binding in nature because they are applicable directly or indirectly into the national laws of its ten member countries. For international management, the EEC presents a challenging input to forward planning only to be ignored at its peril. This challenge, which has been gradually unfolding since the European Commission adopted its programme on multinationals back in November 1973, is now making itself felt in four key business sectors: corporate disclosure, taxation, anti-trust and employment protection (and especially the latter two). More difficult to chart than the global international arrangements under discussion elsewhere, the EEC's often two-edged strategy reflects the differing policy stances of ten sovereign countries, and more particularly the Community's continued soul-searching over the option between economic liberalism and interventionism. Yet despite these factors, there is little doubt that the 1980s will see the growing impact of Common Market policies aimed at multinationals, which already began to 'bite' significantly in selected areas in the late 1970s. These areas are analysed in detail in Part II.

Negotiations on multinationals: the conflicting forces

The past decade has witnessed a clear affirmation by all key governments — both of OECD countries, where the vast majority of MNCs are headquartered, and of LDCs — that control of multinationals must be partially or totally carried out at the international level. Even the USA Administration, the sternest Western defender of the free market economy, has supported the OECD Guidelines and likewise a voluntary UN code of conduct — if for no other reason than the need to create a more stable international investment climate. At the other end of the diplomatic spectrum, the developing countries, grouped together in the so-called Group of 77, have traditionally seen international arrangements restricting MNCs as a direct method of asserting their economic sovereignty, an objective not usually achievable via independent national action. Some groups of developing countries have prepared their own intra-regional responses, e.g. the 1978 Resolution on Transnational Enterprises agreed by the Organisation of American States.

In between the two extremes of the USA and the developing countries, the EEC states, which are both home and host countries to multinational investors, tend to occupy the middle ground. At the same time, within the Community there are important divergences — Germany and the United Kingdom tending more towards the American position, while Denmark and the Netherlands can be regarded as the EEC's 'left-wingers' on MNC policy issues. Elsewhere, Switzerland's emphasis on the positive role of multinationals assigns it to the former group. Meanwhile, to the Danish/Dutch camp should be added the Nordic bloc (Finland, Sweden and Norway, particularly the first two). It is no coincidence that the two key officials in the drafting of a UN code of conduct — Dr Klaus Sahlgren, the executive director of the UN Centre on Transnational Corporations in New York, and Mr Sten Niklasson, the chairman of the code's drafting group — are respectively a Finn and a Swede. The general consensus that international action is needed to cope with the activities of MNCs should not obscure the importance of national measures, e.g., the inward-investment controls and codes in force in countries like Sweden, Canada and Australia. But international action on multinationals is now the accepted policy basis on which the decade of the 1980s started.

No clear picture of the international policy developments affecting MNCs can be given without reference to the part played in the process by the world's two major lobbies: Western business and the international trade union movement likewise centred in the West. Both make a strong impact on the preparation and implementation of international arrangements on MNCs. Their positions, not surprisingly, are diametrically opposed. The trades unions, whose motive force often appears to be the major ideological union centres of Western Europe, have traditionally been the strongest supporters of mandatory international arrangements restricting MNC activity and so have naturally lined up with the developing countries in international negotiations, while at the same time exerting pressure on certain European governments. However, both at the ILO and the OECD they have shown themselves willing to give voluntary 'codes' a try.

Business organisations, by contrast, are, like the MNCs they represent, on the defensive. They tend to identify with the negotiating positions adopted by the 'conservatives' in the Western bloc. But being on the defensive does not mean they lack impact. On the contrary, they have proved a strong counterweight to unions in the war of influence which surrounds the negotiation of MNC codes and their application. Moreover, in two important cases, they have turned defence into attack: in 1972 and again in 1977, when the International Chamber of Commerce respectively adopted 'Guidelines for International Investment' and created an 'International Panel on Extortion and Bribery in International Transactions'.

Both unions and business, which have played major roles in the development and follow-through of the OECD Guidelines and the ILO Declaration on multinationals, can be expected to continue flexing their muscles as the UN and UNCTAD codes begin or conclude the substantive phase of negotiation in the first years of the coming decade.

Trend analysis of MNC policy outlook 1980–85: key pointers

With political constraints on multinational business planning now gradually edging onto a par with more traditional economic factors, it becomes important for management to identify the major components of the emerging framework within which they are to operate in the coming years. The components of the medium-term perspective facing those responsible for corporate strategy in the field of international MNC regulation include the following:

General trends

Barring major surprises, 1980–85 will see the final negotiating phase and probable conclusion of a series of interlocking international codes of conduct on multinationals, all or mostly voluntary in nature. They include the UN code of conduct on transnational corporations, an international agreement on illicit practices, and UNCTAD codes on technology transfer and restrictive business practices. This prospect has been made realistic by

11

progress towards compromise between industrialised and developing country governments in the last few years, a process which has gradually emerged since the confrontation of the early 1970s.

Enforcement, or implementation, of these codes will be the key theme for governmental negotiators and a focal concern for multinationals. Western governments and MNCs will be under built-in pressure to show that negotiated arrangements, far from being diplomatic cosmometry, have real ability to change or inflect corporate behaviour. To assist in this process, a series of intergovernmental 'monitoring committees' will be set up, mirroring the MNC policy body (the so-called 'IME' Committee) already created at the OECD. The emphasis on effective implementation will be the key factor in the development of the OECD's Guidelines on multinationals in the medium term. The same applies to the ILO's Declaration on MNCs and social policy, which should become operational by the mid-1980s.

The EEC will continue to shun the use of global codes of conduct as a policy strategy for controlling MNCs, but the constraints it imposes on international business will nonetheless have an impact. Enactment of legislative proposals and enforcement of binding legislation in key business areas will characterise the early 1980s. The scope and thrust of such schemes will reflect the conflicting pressures in the European Community respectively supporting interventionism and economic liberalism.

Business awareness of the political pressures operating against MNCs will increase, particularly at the level of the individual company, as codes and regulations move from negotiation to implementation in the coming years. Management, while preferring perhaps to operate as a strictly non-political animal, will increasingly find that international business is now international politics. Reacting to the trade unions' avowedly political role of influencing governments, many individual companies will create or expand their government affairs' departments monitoring developments at the EEC, the OECD, the UN and its specialised agencies. They will do so in the knowledge that they are themselves being monitored by these bodies.

Specific trends at a glance

At the EEC

The early and mid-1980s will witness gradual enactment and/or implementation of binding measures particularly in the following areas of the EEC's multinationals' policy programme: corporate disclosure and parent/subsidiary liability; international tax evasion; anti-trust; employment protection and industrial democracy. Other sectors to watch include environmental and consumer protection policies, although these are not so distinctively impactful or targeted on MNCs.

Corporate disclosure: MNC management faces the implementation phase of new EEC rules for subsidiary accounts in the Common Market 'ten', and the enactment of pioneering legislation on group reporting. To this should be added the prospect of policy negotiations on a Community proposal, backed by the European trade unions, which would erode the traditional concept of limited liability.

Tax evasion and transfer pricing: national revenue authorities in the EEC have at their disposal a strengthened co-operation procedure aimed against corporate tax evasion and avoidance, whose initial impact will be gauged during the mid-1980s. This results from an EEC directive which came on line early 1979 and provides for the possibility of establishing EEC rules on transfer pricing.

Anti-trust: the increased use and extended scope of EEC rules against market dominance will characterise the short to medium term, while arrangements concluded by MNCs on trade-mark and patent licensing are certain to come under new regulation and closer scrutiny.

Employment protection and industrial democracy: progressive European philosophy on labour market policy will be reflected by EEC enforcement of directives on employment protection and proposals for new measures in this field — most notably the famous 'Vredeling' initiative on worker information and consultation in MNCs. But a persistent economic slowdown and low investment levels might moderate policy extremes. An effect of such moderation might be to increase the attractiveness of EEC policy on worker participation, as a less confrontational alternative expression of industrial democracy.

More generally, European 'macro-policy' in areas affecting business will continue to mirror continuing differences between EEC Member States over interventionism in industrial and investment policy. This ambiguity, compounded by the Community's dual role as both host and home territory to some of the world's major foreign investors, will become more pronounced as a politically-motivated and well-organised European trade union movement vies for influence with business organisations and expanding numbers of MNC lobbyists, for whom a new pressure point will be the directly-elected European Parliament.

Beyond the EEC's borders, the European position on international codes of conduct will be one of strong support of voluntary arrangements, reflecting the desire to maintain an apparently progressive development policy, offset by concern at protecting the foreign investments of domestic multinationals. At the same time, EEC attitude to foreign competition could increasingly tighten as protectionist pressures, particularly directed at Japan and the newly industrialised countries (NICs), increase.

At the OECD

Multinationals will face increased pressure to make public the conformity of their activities with the Guidelines on Multinational Enterprises adopted in 1976 by the OECD Council, which in June 1979 called for greater effect to be given to the arrangement in the coming five years. Governments will in turn come under pressure from organised labour to prove that they are pressurising MNCs.

The guidelines on employment and corporate disclosure, particularly the former, will be the areas which reflect most the demand for more rigorous implementation of the OECD 'code of conduct'. This will confirm the trend already established by international trade union organisations who have used the OECD Guidelines as a point of specific leverage against MNCs by filing complaints against individual companies.

Governments could themselves seek to give greater effect to the Guidelines via measures in areas like taxation, where a code on transfer pricing was adopted in 1979.

Offsetting this push for greater control of MNCs and under pressure from the US Administration, the OECD countries will likely seek to emphasise the positive contribution of multinational investment to the world economy. Greater effect may be given to twin decisions taken by the OECD Council in June 1976 on respectively 'International Investment Incentives and Disincentives', and 'National Treatment' for foreign investors.

The OECD, revitalised in the mid-1970s following the confrontation between the industrialised and developing countries immediately following the oil crisis, will continue to be the major forum for the 'rich world' to iron out its own position on the codes of conduct for MNCs being prepared in the UN and its specialised agencies like UNCTAD. A relatively homogeneous group of countries, hosting the vast majority of the world's MNC headquarters, it will continue to press — with success — for voluntary arrangements at the UN, in line with the status of the OECD model for control of multinationals.

The trade unions will continue to use their position in the OECD's consultative structure (TUAC) as a basis for their role as Guidelines' watchdog. Business, similarly represented (BIAC), will urge governments to stress MNCs' positive impact. As a result, unions may switch some of their effort aimed at increased MNC control to the UN code of conduct when it becomes operational, or alternatively to more direct confrontation with MNCs.

At the United Nations and its specialised agencies

Multinationals face the prospect of a 'comprehensive' code of conduct which, while almost certain to be voluntary, seems likely to boast a scope much broader than that of the OECD Guidelines when it is finally negotiated. In addition to ranging over the specific areas of taxation, corporate disclosure, anti-trust, etc., and linking in with other UN-related arrangements (at UNCTAD, the ILO), the code in its present form contains provisions calling on MNCs to respect national sovereignty and LDC economic objectives, and not to interfere in internal political affairs. Among the hot political issues to be resolved are the controversial questions of nationalisation, compensation and investments in South Africa.

Acceptance by the developing countries of a non-binding code will have its price. This price will be a commitment by industrialised countries to ensure effective implementation, involving pressure for greater 'enforcement' than at the OECD. If this scenario prevails, the UN code would appear to pose a greater threat to MNC freedom than any existing international arrangement.

A key period in the enforcement of the ILO's Declaration of Principles on Multinational Enterprises and Social Policy, adopted in November 1977, should begin by 1982 following decisions on the setting up of machinery giving effect to the principles outlined in the Declaration.

An international arrangement on restrictive business practices (anti-trust), listing a series of MNC activities incompatible with good corporate behaviour and certain economic development goals, was adopted in 1980. Implementation of this code, which provides a model for strengthening the anti-trust laws of developing countries, will begin in the early 1980s.

Attempts will be made to settle the major outstanding differences between industrialised and developing countries on a code of conduct for the international transfer of MNC technology, in particular to third world countries.

An international agreement against corrupt practices in business transactions has been strongly supported at the UN by the US Administration in the late 1970s. Its successful negotiation, however, could be linked to finalisation of the general UN code of conduct, on which the American administration under Reagan, continues to be the major sticking point.

The impact of the UN code and its related arrangements could well be felt by changes in national practices and laws either in anticipation or as a result of its conclusion. The UN code itself, while voluntary in nature, could be seen by developing countries, socialist states and the international trade union movement, as the first step towards a subsequent mandatory arrangement.

PART II

THE EUROPEAN COMMUNITY: THE BINDING IMPACT OF LEGISLATED CONTROL

3 European multinationals' policy: the roots

Europe, and particularly the EEC, is now the fulcrum of international attempts to exert control over multinational companies. This is hardly a development which could have been foreseen in the immediate post-war phase of economic reconstruction followed by the boom years of the 1960s, the major beneficiaries of which were American multinationals. Indeed, the contrast between the attitudes towards big business held by European public authorities in 1970 and 1980 – respectively a pinnacle of growth and a trough of recession – could not be more dramatic. The decade separating these milestone years has seen the gestation and initial application of a package of measures specifically designed to regulate the activities of international big business. The twin thrusts of this European Community multinationals policy – both in its 'democratic' and 'capitalist' challenges to big business[1] – are likely to be the key characteristics of EEC company policy between now and 1990.

By 1970, Europe had experienced a decade of unparalleled growth, having formed 12 years earlier the six-nation Common Market, an embryonic economic and political unit guided by its apparently free market bible, the Treaty of Rome.[2] Its initial priority goals were multinationalisation of the continental economy at home, and un-fettered free trade in the broader international context. But from being a haven of economic growth, buttressed by a common currency (the US dollar) and articulated largely by US companies, the EEC has changed significantly. Ten years of monetary confusion, economic uncertainty and rising unemployment later, the policy towards big business pursued by a ten-nation EEC[3]— much less economically coherent than its streamlined predecessor of the 1960s — bears the stamp of emergent company regulation and embryonic trade protectionism. Companies are now being asked to pay for the transnational opportunities created by the Common Market via acceptance of new responsibilities, when necessary enforced by new legal requirements. These requirements, by their nature and motivation, call for a change in the legal basis on which capitalism has traditionally flourished.

Small wonder, then, that such a sea-change has made international business, not just European, but American and Japanese also, sit up and take notice. The passing of the golden age of European multinational capitalism, 1958—70, when its practice dovetailed with the dominant continental policy trend of market integration, has led to a major switch in business attitudes towards the European Community. The disenchantment of multinationals with recent policies emerging from the Brussels headquarters of the EEC has led to charges of bureaucratic 'mental pollution'[4] spilling unwanted into the market place via a series of Community proposals, directives and regulations. Big business, it would seem, can live more easily with a Common Market than with the European Community.

As a result, the monitoring of political developments through the decade ending 1990 is becoming a top priority for international management, which finds its activities in Europe and beyond influenced by an emerging framework for MNC control spearheaded by the EEC and buttressed by an ideologically-motivated and well-organised trade union lobby, centred in Europe but with far-reaching international political connections. The influence of both European political thinking and of organised labour on the OECD and United Nations' multinationals' codes is a clear example of this.

These two forces, the EEC and the European unions, are perceived by corporate watchdogs as the principal agents, not just in Western Europe but also beyond its borders, for spinning a web of containment around the activities of international big business. The reality to which this business perception corresponds is somewhat more complex, rooted as it is in the ambiguities of the European political tradition. That tradition is often misunderstood, not least by American viewers of European developments.

Europe's post-war tradition, national frustration
and the multinational enterprise

The belief that the countries making up the European Community can somehow be considered an economically liberal society in the sense of the continental American market, is one that dies hard. It dies hard, because it is a belief that the Anglo-Saxon business world, and in particular its North American component, wants to hold. Moreover, it is a belief specifically encouraged by the free market provisions of the Rome Treaty, and reinforced by the parenthesis of freak economic growth between 1958–73. But it needs a hasty or wishful reading of these events, and an American reading of the Rome Treaty, to equate the EEC with the US market as a framework for economic liberalism à l'américaine. The development of the European Community is rather to be seen against the background of the post-war tradition of progressive European politics — not a tradition shared by the USA or, indeed, by any of the EEC's industrial rivals outside Europe.

A major upshot of this post-war European tradition has been the gradual socialisation of the economy, the attainment throughout Western Europe of a high degree of national welfare, and the acceptance — thirty-five years after the end of the war — by virtually all major European political parties of post-1945 attainments in the field of social democracy. Such economic socialisation, whether it takes the form of progressive taxation redistributing national resources, or the 'democratic imperative' of industrial democracy,[5] or, more generally, greater government regulation of the market place, is a far cry from the American tradition of pioneering economic liberalism, of which the multinational company is indeed a logical product.

Yet, at the same time — strange paradox — the multinational company also appears to be the logical and desired consequence of the transnational market arrangements spelt out in the Rome Treaty. But what many in international business have failed to realise is that economic multinationalisation in Europe is set within — or rather offset by — the framework of a European political tradition quite distinct from the North American counterpart. And among the contemporary expressions of this tradition is the call for a redefinition of the company's place in society.

Redefining business' links with its social and political constituencies — a major aim of changes in both national and European company law — reflects and reinforces the undoubted erosion of the capitalist ethic in the old Continent. That is because the capitalist ethic, in its pure traditional form, has proved too narrow to accommodate responses to problems created by the sheer size — economic in nature but social and political in consequence — of the large international enterprise. Such problems are not limited to the relationship between the shareholder and corporate management, as traditional company laws would make believe. They extend quite clearly to the relationship between the company and its workforce, the company and governments, the company and the general public. The field of corporate responsibility has broadened, *de facto* if not *de jure*, just as the democratic impulse has gradually spilled over from the formal political framework into everyday economic life. And the impact on economic life of the strategic decisions taken by international business, particularly in times of widespread uncertainty, rising unemployment and technological change, has made the multinational company a logical focus of this broadened democratic reflex. Thus the multinational company, however natural an economic expression of the interrelated American traditions of democracy and private enterprise, finds itself the target of those forces in Europe calling for a major overhaul of the legal framework in which business is conducted. Principle among these are the EEC and organised European labour, but the need for a fundamental revamping of the international company's links with the broader social framework is a much more widely-held perception.[6]

Need for European public control of multinational companies is further reinforced by the perception that the nation state, itself the traditional centrepoint of the democratic process, is an inadequate framework for responding to the impact of multinational companies. The conflict multinationals find themselves in in Europe is thus not just with a continental political tradition but also with national sovereignty, economically outmoded but politically alive. The large corporate grouping, while perhaps well-suited to a national continental market such as the USA, can and does arouse adverse feelings among local groups, trade unions and governments, when it operates in Europe's more geographically limited but historically deeper national framework. Frustration at the ineffectiveness of existing national laws, particularly those dealing with industrial relations and corporate disclosure, has thus become a major impulse behind efforts to build an international legal framework in Europe to match the dimension of multinational business activity.

Factors conditioning EEC policy towards multinationals

The background to European community efforts to develop a cogent policy to deal with multinational companies is further conditioned by a variety of factors, in particular:

    (a) economically, the importance of Europe as both home and host region to multinational companies;

    (b) institutionally, the fact that the EEC represents the first attempt both to devise a transnational market framework for MNCs and simultaneously a legal framework for their behaviour within this framework;

(c) politically, the gradual politicisation of the MNC issue — not just by European bureaucrats, but by groups operating at a European level, notably the trade unions and political parties;

(d) nationally, the shifting mosaic of governmental attitudes within individual EEC member states towards business regulation;

(e) diplomatically, the importance of European countries, acting individually and through the EEC, in transferring their experience of MNC control via negotiations to the broader international framework.

(a) Being both host and home-base for international enterprise makes for an even-handed approach to the question of legislating for MNCs. At the same time it makes for ambivalence in the EEC's attitude towards big business — an ambivalence which also reflects the see-saw between the liberal and interventionist protagonists of Europe's mixed economy. Such ambivalence has been peerlessly embodied in the elusive political pronouncements of Viscount Etienne Davignon, the European commissioner for industrial affairs since 1977, the man directly responsible for shaping EEC multinationals policy from then until 1981.[7]

The Community's consumer market of 260 million, to increase further in the coming years with Spanish and Portuguese entry into the EEC, provides obvious attractions to non-European enterprise. Meanwhile, Europe's home-grown business community has traditionally had a strong profile of direct investment in non-European countries — initially with French and British stakes in their respective commonwealths, and more recently with the growing German and French presence in North America, a trend encouraged by the dollar's nosedive during the 1970s. The importance of control measures for MNCs worked out in Europe is that they make a direct impact on a large section of international companies, either at the headquarters or subsidiary level.

Around half the world's total of industrial MNCs have headquarters in the ten-nation EEC, according to figures provided by the European Commission in Brussels.[8] Although this statistic — 4,500 of the world's 9,500 MNCs are EEC-based — is crude, it does provide a yardstick, not just of the scope of the impact of Community regulation on international business, but also of the need for such major European bread-winners to be free to operate successfully. Refining these figures somewhat, 70 of the world's 200 largest MNCs (by turnover) were shown to have their headquarters in the EEC, as against 103 in the USA and 20 in Japan. It is worth noting that the majority of the non-EEC companies in table 3.1 have subsidiaries in one or other Common Market country.

Table 3.1
Number of multinationals by country of origin

Country of origin	Number of enterprises surveyed	Per cent of total	Number of enterprises with at least two links in at least two foreign countries	Per cent of total
France	565	6.0	398	6.8
Belgium	252	2.7	161	2.8
Netherlands	467	4.9	238	4.0
Germany	1,222	12.9	803	13.6
Italy	213	2.2	112	1.9
United Kingdom	1,588	16.7	1,130	19.3
Ireland	32	0.4	19	0.3
Denmark	137	1.4	95	1.6
Luxembourg	56	0.6	26	0.5
Total EEC	4,532	47.8	2,982	50.8
Norway	130	1.4	66	1.1
Sweden	301	3.2	210	3.6
Finland	51	0.5	23	0.4
Switzerland	756	8.0	372	6.3
Lichtenstein	89	0.9	28	0.5
Austria	52	0.5	26	0.4
Portugal	10	0.1	6	0.1
Spain	35	0.4	18	0.3
United States	2,567	27.1	1,582	27.0
Canada	268	2.8	154	2.6
Mexico	5	0.1	3	0.1
Indonesia	2	—	—	—
Malaysia	17	0.2	12	0.2
Singapore	67	0.7	38	0.7
Philippines	4	—	2	—
Japan	211	2.2	132	2.3
Taiwan	15	0.2	4	0.1
Hong Kong	24	0.3	19	0.3
Australia	228	2.4	134	2.3
New Zealand	117	1.2	54	0.9
Total non-member countries	4,949	52.2	2.883	49.2
GRAND TOTAL	9,481	100.0	5,865	100.0

Source: EEC: Survey of Multinational Enterprises, European Commission, July 1976. Figures for 9-country EEC (prior to Greece's entry January 1981).

24

(b) Breakding down national trade barriers — be they tariffs, discriminatory product specifications or national procurement rules — has always been a key EEC priority, reflecting the aim of building a multinational market for trade and enterprise from scratch. Yet juxtaposed to this objective, itself alternately decried as a free-market sell-out and applauded for its furtherance of consumer interests, is the very existence of the European Community as an institution. If the EEC is not to intervene in the steering and shaping of the 'common' transnational market it was established to create, just what is the point of its existence, other than to administer and possibly improve existing market freedoms?

The inevitably interventionist vocation of the EEC's major policy-proposing institution, the European Commission, is a factor insufficiently understood by those, like international business, which are the targets of its legislative measures. Of course, in the period 1958—70 this interventionist vocation took the shape of the dismantlement of obstacles to market freedom. The paradox of political intrusion in the name of European economic liberalism may have escaped the multinational business community — but not its beneficial effects: from 1958 to 1973, intra-Community trade outpaced handsomely even the buoyant growth rates achieved internationally (1000 per cent versus 450 per cent in that fifteen year period).[9]

But by 1970, when the EEC had completed elimination of internal trade barriers while fixing a common outer economic frontier, circumstances and objectives began to change. Its initial task accomplished, the six-nation EEC sought a new *raison d'être*, and in so doing proceeded to draw up a comprehensive programme for the transition from Common Market to Community, involving in particular interventionist social and regional policies. Barely had this programme been drafted — at the Paris European summit in late 1972 — when two seminal events occurring in the space of ten months, were to inflect decisively the climate for future EEC policy. The Arab—Israeli conflict of October 1973, and the developments it spawned, tore the heart out of Western Europe's post-war economic confidence, creating a new and damper climate for EEC policy — more defensive, protective and interventionist in posture if not always in accomplishment. Meanwhile, in January of the same year, enlargement of the EEC to include Britain ensured a slow-down in political integration, undermining the achievement of grandiose supranational ambitions but not of EEC activities in more directly business-targeted areas like anti-trust policy and company and labour laws. Indeed, by the end of the 1970s, European integration had, from a business standpoint, become equatable less with transnational market freedoms as with a framework for imposing new transnational business responsibilities.

(c) Mirroring the strong MNC presence in the Common Market, and the existence of the EEC itself as a source of regulatory intervention — two factors in latent or overt conflict — is the gradual politicisation of the whole 'multinationals' issue. This is not just a result of the haphazard meanderings of armchair intellectuals, as some would have it, but of a confluence of factors. First and foremost, there is the strong ideological opposition to international business of the European trade union movement — a body with the political clout to make its views felt. The multinationals issue also reflects the inevitable politicisation of business decision-making in an economy where a company's relations with government can be as important as its traditional relations with the market place — in which governments are in any case increasingly intervening. Corporate strategy, particularly in the field of investment and disinvestment, is now perceived as political as well as economic, especially by governments, for whom investments mean jobs, jobs votes and votes power — and disinvestment can contribute to a process leading in the opposite direction. Companies themselves have come to act as political animals, stepping up their governmental affairs departments. In Brussels, as in no other city outside Washington DC, political intelligence-gathering has become a refined and spreading function of the international corporation and of representative business organisations with American companies such as IBM, United Brands and Ford vying with European rivals like Siemens, Unilever and Fiat for the ear of the Eurocrat (see chapter 14). Company lobbying of the EEC headquarters in Brussels, reflecting the expanding of the public affairs function and prefiguring its growing importance in the corporate structure, is implicit admission by the business world itself that the conduct of international business now is politics.

Unquestionably the major force behind the political activation of the MNC issue, and not just in Europe, is the powerful trade union movement based in the Common Market countries and, to a lesser but significant extent, in Scandinavia. European trade union influence on arrangements designed to exert greater public control over the West's major private operators is profiled in detail in chapter 14. Suffice it to say here that in countries such as Britain, West Germany, Belgium, the Netherlands and Sweden, union influence is built into national power structures. Moreover, the collective strength of national unions is brought to bear on the EEC via the European Trade Union Confederation which, like the Common Market, is headquartered in Brussels. Almost from the moment of its inception in 1973, the ETUC has been the strongest non-governmental supporter of EEC measures designed to curb international business. Often considered the most forceful single lobby in the EEC — unsurprisingly, perhaps, since organised labour shares the EEC's own view of itself as a regulatory body — the ETUC is also linked closely to the international union movement's attempts to foster MNC-targeted control measures in other arenas. The ETUC's international brother, the International Confederation of Free Trade Unions (ICFTU), shares both the ETUC's policy towards business and also, significantly, the same office block in central Brussels. From there, the impact of European unions on the emerging framework for big business control fans out beyond the EEC to Paris,[10] where the OECD's *Guidelines for Multinational Enterprises* were adopted in 1976, to Geneva, where the International Labour Organisation's *Declaration on Multinational Enterprises and Social Policy* was agreed in 1977 and, last but far from least, to New York, where the UN's code of conduct for transnational corporations could reach conclusion and implementation by the mid-1980s. Not without reason do leading members of the international business community identify European-based trade union pressure as 'the real enemy of multinationals' — much more so than the attempts of third world governments to clip the wings of MNCs.[11]

By the priority they have given the MNC control issue, and by the practical steps they have taken to exert greater direct control themselves over multinationals[12] the unions have moved to fill a political vacuum so far left by the formal political process, at least until the end of the 1970s. Certainly there are examples of political parties whose manifestos address the problem of MNCs but, as in the case of the British Labour Party, national action can seem difficult to implement when its result may be to present a neighbouring country with a much-needed foreign investment.[13] But the fact that national measures seem singularly inappropriate for dealing with multinationals has sparked an interest in EEC-wide political groupings, centred on the directly-elected European Parliament in Strasbourg. Besides the European Socialist Group's explicit commitment to MNC control, the principle of legally-enforceable containment of international business activities has achieved much wider backing among Western European political forces. The principle of mandatory rules for MNCs is contained in the approach being pursued by the European Parliament report, being drawn up by Mr Tom Spencer (UK, Conservative), on EEC proposals on worker information and consultation in multinationals — the so-called 'Vredeling initiative'.[14] Meanwhile, the European Parliament report drawn up by Mr Richard Caborn (UK, Socialist), achieved the remarkable result of getting a fundamentally right-wing Parliament to agree to demands for increased control of MNCs in three key areas.[15]

Paralleling the emergence in the mid-1970s of the ETUC as a major EEC lobby and the embryonic interest shown by the European outposts of national political parties, the business world itself has responded in kind. By the end of the 1970s, a host of international companies were following the lead of firms like IBM, Ford, Union Carbide and CPC in setting up high-level 'watchdog' offices in Brussels to monitor Community policy-making. Not to be forgotten is the splendid diplomatic presence of 'the permanent representative of FIAT to the European Communities', a diplomatic title which captures well the growing convergence of public policy and economic practice in the mind of the business world itself.

(d) Varying national attitudes to business control, and more particularly the fluctuating views of EEC member governments to the issue, clearly condition the framework for MNC regulation being built up in the European Community. The 'issue' is in fact multi-faceted, breaking down into areas like worker participation, MNC employee information, corporate disclosure, job protection — items which are also key policy focuses in other arenas like the United Nations and the OECD. EEC governments, whose say is final on policy formulated by the European Commission in these and most other areas,[16] differ quite markedly in their assessment of the role of government in the market place. But confusing simplifications should be avoided. Countries favouring interventionist policies may be philosophically predisposed to business regulation, as in the case of the socialist government elected in France in 1981, but there is certainly no hard and fast rule that the more free market proponents of the mixed economy, such as Chancellor Helmut Schmidt of West Germany, are necessarily opposed to building progressive frameworks revamping the responsibilities of the company to society at large. On the contrary — German post-war practice in the field of company and labour laws is often perceived as the catalyst for similar efforts on the European level.

At the same time, the two-edged nature of EEC policy towards international business — encouraging multinationalisation via the creation of a common European market while seeking to impose legal constraints on companies thus encouraged — also mirrors the diverging economic interests of member states as well as their legal traditions. A rapid sketch of these national characteristics follows.

Belgium: a traditionally exposed economy relying heavily on external trade, Belgium is predominantly a host country to foreign multinationals, although its own enterprises, particularly its major financial and industrial holding companies, are active abroad. The Left is influential, in particular the FGTB union confederation, its strength paradoxically being concentrated in the French-speaking economic problem areas badly in need of foreign investment. Host country status and union pressure combine to make Belgium a supporter of regulation of foreign company behaviour where necessary, as witnessed by governmental action invoking the OECD Guidelines for multinationals in the Badger case (see chapter 9). At the same time, the government, aware of the country's international economic dependence, seeks to avoid being too much out of line with its EEC and Western partners, for fear of prejudicing its international competitive position. But business critics feel that its highly progressive stance on employment security — also a key area of EEC policy on multinationals — in fact justifies this fear. By the early 1980s, some leading MNCs had cut back European headquarter operations located in Belgium.

Denmark: both home and host country to multinationals, but less reliant on foreign capital than Belgium. Importantly influenced by the traditionally progressive stance of its Scandinavian partners on socioeconomic policy, the Danish government has shown that it is prepared to bring national and international political pressure to bear on multinationals not observing what it judges as good corporate practice. It submitted the activities of Hertz Rentacar to the attention of EEC foreign ministers and pursued the case in the OECD (see chapter 9). The government has traditionally supported EEC moves against international tax evasion and is reliably understood to be sympathetic to the controversial EEC proposals for worker information and consultation in multinationals.[17]

Federal Republic of Germany: the Federal Republic's two-edged attitude to control of multinational business is almost a microcosm of the European Community's as a whole. On the one hand, the Bonn government has been a consistent supporter of increased EEC regulation in the key MNC policy area of European company law; by contrast, the German economics ministry has always embodied a commitment to *laissez-faire* and the market economy. So while many of the major legislative planks of the Community's MNC policy are German-inspired (e.g. corporate disclosure, worker participation), in the international arena, Germany tends to line up with the USA, the UK and Switzerland as a staunch supporter of international arrangements which will enable the positive impact of its increasingly successful multinational companies to make itself felt. Internationally, Germany favours a UN code on MNCs which 'should encourage the positive role played by transnational corporations'.[18]

France: ambiguity also typifies the French approach to MNCs, but it differs from the two-edged nature of the German attitude. National economic planning is an accepted fact in France, even under rightist governments, so by extension the authorities are not philosphically opposed to the notion of international regulation of MNCs, either in the framework of the EEC or the UN. At the same time, tempering this, is the concern that France's expanding breed of home-grown multinationals should be able to compete effectively in international markets. However, this latter concern may now be muted with the arrival in June 1981 of the Mitterrand/Mauroy socialist tandem, strongly likely to reinforce the case of stepped-up business regulation both at home and abroad. Committed to a widespread programme of nationalisation at home, from which foreign multinationals are largely exempted, the Mitterrand administration can be expected in the coming years to be a strong backer of the principles embodied in the Vredeling proposal. Equally certain is the commitment of the socialist government to worker participation in corporate decision-making structures, a policy far removed from the hesitant flirtation with company law reform practised under Giscard d'Estaing. Strong support for EEC proposals for enterprise-level industrial democracy, as indeed for other planks of the EEC's MNC control programme, may be expected in the coming years.

Greece: despite a traditionally restrictive attitude to foreign investment, the evidence of recent years suggests a more liberal attitude. However, the extent to which such a policy could be implemented depends on a variety of factors, not least the polarisation of Greek political attitudes toward the American presence — military or economic. A European framework for legal control of MNCs could have its attraction as an offsetting accompaniment to a relaxation of investment controls nationally, or alternatively, could serve to reinforce greater national controls possibly sought by the Socialist government elected in October 1981.

Ireland: a predominant economic interest of any Irish government is the promotion of a highly favourable foreign investment climate. Indeed, Ireland has arguably been the most proportionately successful of EEC countries in attracting foreign multinationals. As a host country to MNCs, Ireland has never been enthusiastic about excessive public controls against multinationals.

Italy: the apparent political importance of the Left in Italy does not seem to filter through to positions adopted by the Rome government in the European or international arenas. Italy is perceived at EEC headquarters in Brussels as very investment-conscious, its authorities reluctant to subscribe to arrangements which could injure its chances of increasing national economic activity via the attraction of international business. Industry representatives often play key roles in negotiating MNC-related legislation being prepared by the EEC.

Luxembourg: like Ireland, a major Luxembourg priority is the encouragement of foreign investment, on which, together with the open economic policy the government pursues, the Grand Duchy's prosperity crucially depends. In the past, Luxembourg has shown itself less than keen to accept EEC measures against international tax evasion and has made little secret of its opposition to measures to increase corporate group disclosure.

Netherlands: definitely one of the EEC's 'progressives', despite the fact that the six of its companies (or part-Dutch companies) in the world's top 200 by turnover — amongst them Royal Dutch Shell, Unilever and Philips — have combined sales equal to 68.8 per cent of Dutch gross domestic product.[19] However, the major Dutch MNCs are sheltered from the impact of laws on worker participation at board level, since more than half their employees are employed outside the country. At the same time, the Dutch government is a positive supporter of EEC initiatives on employment security and company law, while it has taken a tough line on British American Tobacco Co. (BAT) in the context of the OECD Guidelines on MNCs (see chapter 9). Internationally, the government's position on the UN code of conduct is that it 'should be comprehensive' and 'should contain rules applying to transnational corporations and to governments'.[20]

United Kingdom: basically displays a cautious attitude in the EEC and other international organisations dealing with MNCs, reflecting Britain's heavy economic stake in overseas private investment. As with the FGR, a supporter along with the USA of a voluntarist approach to international regulation; unlike the FGR, however, has little enthusiasm for the type of legislative constraints being worked out in the context of EEC company law, although this reluctance has been less forcibly expressed of late. However, sharp swings in the UK's stance on international business policy are likely to characterise an increasingly polarised British political scene. Thus, while in 1977 the British Government was the prime mover behind the EEC's code of conduct for European multinationals operating in South Africa, a measure adopted by the Nine in September 1977 (see chapter 7), the Conservative government of the early 1980s is likely to continue to oppose adoption of EEC measures specifically targeted at MNCs, particularly in the field of industrial relations.

(e) No picture of Europe's growing influence on the establishment of a new framework for international business would be complete if restricted to the EEC. Certainly, the EEC's prime concern is with the preparation of legally binding measures affecting the conduct of business within the Community's ten member countries. But not to be ignored is the extraterritorial impact of EEC policy in areas like industrial relations, anti-trust and corporate disclosure, not to mention European diplomacy and the presence of European officials in key positions affecting international arrangements for multinational companies.

The EEC's crusade for greater *corporate disclosure*, for instance, is carried beyond the 'ten's' borders into the broader range of the OECD world — including countries like the USA, Japan and Canada. So, negotiations in the OECD aimed at strengthening demands on multinationals for fuller and more coherent information on their activities — a key focus of the OECD's *Guidelines for Multinational Enterprises*[21] — bear the stamp of EEC measures being implemented or likely to be adopted in the early 1980s. The same could be said of the much more controversial issue of industrial relations in MNCs, provoked first by the OECD Guidelines and then by the 'Vredeling initiative', the latter move drawing a sharp riposte from the USA in mid-1981 precisely for its extraterritoriality.[22] Not to be forgotten either is the part played by European officials in the Trade Union Advisory Committee (TUAC), a body which enjoys quasi-diplomatic status at the Paris headquarters of the OECD and serves to articulate European pressure against multinationals in governmental negotiations on the OECD Guidelines. The same remark applies to European officials working in the International Confederation of Free Trade Unions, which plays a key lobbying role at the UN, whose code of conduct for transnational corporations is being piloted by two Scandinavians, Klaus Sahlgren (Finland) and Sten Niklasson (Sweden).

Notes and references

1   Respectively treated in chapters 5 and 6.
2   The Rome Treaty, in force since 1 January 1958, is the EEC's basic constitution.
3   Enlarged from its six member composition on 1 January 1973 to include the UK, Ireland and Denmark, and from 'Nine' to 'Ten' with the inclusion of Greece on 1 January 1981.
4   The description is that of Mr Carl Nisser, European governmental affairs director of Goodyear during the late 1970s.

5   See the European Commission's 'Green Paper' on Employee Participation and Company Structure, November 1975; also chapter 5.

6   The French, Dutch and Danish governments, all of which have reacted favourably to EEC proposals for enhanced public control of multinationals, may be counted in this category. In addition, political parties of the European Centre-right, notably the Christian Democrats, have shown in favour of new legal controls of international business. See p.27 of this chapter.

7   Although changing his portfolio responsibilities in early 1981 following the appointment of the new Commission under President Gaston Thorn, Davignon remains a key arbiter of MNC policy. The two EEC Commissioners directly responsible for MNC policy since 1981 are Karl-Heinz Narjes, a man from the right of the German political spectrum (in charge of company law), and Ivor Richard, a British socialist (labour law).

8   *Survey of Multinational Enterprises*, European Commission, July 1976. See also Appendix I(g).

9   EEC figures.

10   Via TUAC, the Trade Union Advisory Committee to the OECD.

11   Working group on economic multinationality, the European Management Symposium, Davos, Switzerland, 1979.

12   Circulation to TU membership of *Trade Unions and the Transnationals – a Handbook for Negotiators* (ICFTU, Belgium, 1979).

13   *Viz.*, the sharp contrast between Labour Party support for MNC control and the efforts of Mr James Callaghan, then Prime Minister, to secure a Ford Motor Company investment in S.Wales.

14   *Procedures for informing and consulting the employees of undertakings with complex structures, in particular transnational undertakings* – official name of EEC proposals, otherwise known as the 'Vredeling initiative', made 1 October 1980. See also Appendix 1(h).

15   Information disclosure, merger control and worker consultation rights.

16   The key exception to this is anti-trust policy, where decisions are taken by two Bodies – the European Commission in Brussels and the Court of Justice in Luxembourg – not directly influenced by national European governments. See chapter 6.

17   The so-called 'Vredeling initiative', see note 14.

18   *Transnational Corporations: Views and Proposals of States on a Code of Conduct*, UN, 30 December 1976 (E/C. 10/19), p.7.

19   Figures established on basis of early version of EEC Commission's *Survey of Multinational Companies* (final version, July 1976). For details see *Multinational Service* (fortnightly), no.3, Background Document, 16 February 1977. Also Appendix I (g).

20 *Transnational Corporations: Views and Proposals of States on a Code of Conduct*, p.11.

21 See the *Guidelines for Multinational Enterprises*, Appendix IIb.

22 Bills tabled in the US Congress (H.R.4339 and S.1592) which seek to block demands made by a foreign nation requiring an American company to supply confidential information to a foreign affiliate.

4 European multinationals' policy: from conception to impact

Given the conflicting trends behind EEC business policy,[1] a global European policy exclusively addressed to multinationals *per se* does not exist, never has and, short of unforeseeable political earthquakes, never will. There is no prospect of a European Community code of conduct for multinationals — not at least in the sense of the OECD Guidelines adopted in 1976 or the United Nations code under negotiation since January 1977. The European Community deals not with general voluntary statements, but with specific statutory law. To the extent that there is a European multinationals' code, it is the relevant constitutional provisions of the EEC's Treaty of Rome.

Code or no code, however, there has been plenty of action on the multinationals front at EEC headquarters in Brussels throughout the 1970s, and more can be expected in the 1980s. During the last decade, Community authorities have been involved in carrying out a policy schedule for dealing with the economic and social problems posed by the progressive integration of the Community, problems which may be particularly exacerbated by the operations of multinationals. This has led to the pinpointing of measures for MNC containment in a variety of specific sectors, rather than the creation of a specific, readily identifiable European philosophy on MNCs from which all truth flows. But it is policy not philosophy which impacts on the real world, and the measures identified earlier in the 1970s are now being enacted at a steady and even accelerating rate, as firms themselves are the first to admit.

EEC policy towards MNCs has followed a three-fold development during the 1970s, when work on the subject first seriously started:

1970–73: gestation – the gradual preparation under Commissioner Altiero Spinelli, now a left-wing MP in the European Parliament, of a general policy paper entitled 'Multinational Undertakings and the Community', approved by the European Commission in November 1973 and submitted to the Council of Ministers. This identified key sectors for EEC measures[2] and, more formalistically, called on member governments to approve an EEC resolution of policy towards multinationals. It remains an important reference point for MNC policy at the EEC.

1974–76: slowdown – during the period of economic and political uncertainty imposed on the EEC by the oil crisis, the 'nine's' ministers refused to act on the formalistic ambitions of the Spinelli resolution. More significantly, however, work on implementing MNC legislation in the specific sectors mentioned in the resolution nevertheless gradually started.

1977: impact – renewed vigour has characterised EEC work, perhaps partially encouraged by the adoption in June 1976 of the OECD *Guidelines for Multinational Enterprise*, in the last years of the 1970s. Rules and decisions affecting MNCs in a wide variety of sectors (employment protection, anti-trust and information disclosure, particularly) have been adopted, and in other areas the enactment process is well underway. Heightened activity during the present period reflects disparate causes. These include external political pressures for MNC control exerted on the EEC, such as the start of UN negotiations for a Code of Conduct in 1977, UNCTAD IV's resolution on MNCs (transfer of technology, etc.) in May 1976;[3] the arrival of pragmatist Etienne Davignon to head up EEC industrial policy (and create a small MNC policy office at Community headquarters in Brussels); and the increasingly successful drive of European anti-trust officials against big business abuses (through the creation of precedents based on Article 86 of the Rome Treaty).

Key characteristics of European MNC policy

The paradoxical nature of EEC policy on MNCs – encouraging the creation of European transnationals while limiting the abuses to which this process may give rise – has clearly been fostered by the conflicting influences on its development as outlined in the preceding chapter. European policy towards big business was conceived in the pre-crisis boom of the early 1970s by a left-wing European ideologue, Altiero Spinelli, while its subsequent development and gradual implementation in a period of protracted economic uncertainty has responded instead to the ministrations of the expert centre-right tactician that is Commission Vice-President Etienne Davignon.

Nonetheless, certain general motivations activating European MNC policy today are identifiable:

(a) It favours a series of specific measures of containment in sectors where multinational activity gives rise to particularly sharp anxiety, rather than the development of a global EEC code of conduct.

(b) It is set in a European industrial policy framework which steers not always predictably between economic dirigisme and a more liberal approach, and is now characterised by an approach best described as corporatist.

(c) It seeks to encourage European multinational companies via removing residual obstacles to a single EEC market, an aim which leads to lingering suspicions of anti-American bias.

(d) It claims non-discrimination between multinational and national companies, but the EEC's choice of legislation often determines that the impact will be greater on MNCs.

(a) *Political option: selective measures for MNC containment*

Retaining the priority sectors for action outlined by Spinelli in 1973, the EEC has pushed ahead with policy measures in selective areas, while publicly rejecting any idea of a witch-hunt against big business. 'Multinationals is now a slogan and we are not that interested in slogans', Viscount Davignon told the author soon after assuming control of EEC policy towards multinationals in early 1977.[4] While reflecting the EEC's rejection of the idea of a Community code of conduct specifically directed at multinationals, Davignon's view also shows that the Community is interested in legally binding measures rather than general voluntary guidelines which so far has been the unfailing result of the 'code' approach to MNCs. Paradoxically, this is the opposite of the EEC position adopted in external negotiations on MNCs, where Europeans favour voluntary rather than binding codes of conduct.

The present EEC line thus appears close to that initially spelt out in 1973 when the Commission stated that problems raised by MNCs 'could not be solved by adopting a few spectacular measures or a code of good conduct which by definition would be binding only on undertakings of good will. Indeed, the size of certain problems, in particular relating to security of employment, tax avoidance or disturbing capital movements, justifies the adoption of measures of greater restraint'.[5]

Since 1973, the EEC has concentrated with most success in the following areas — corporate disclosure and taxation, anti-trust, employment protection and development policy. In fact, the 1973 EEC statement outlined the need for specific measures in a variety of areas, thus providing a framework which still appears to activate EEC policy-making. These areas are:

- protection of the general public;
- protection of workers' interests;
- maintenance of competition;
- take-over methods (although this is one area where the vital impetus given by the 1973 programme has not been maintained);
- equality of conditions of reception;
- protection of developing countries;
- improvement of information.

Moreover, the considerations lying behind the choice of these action areas, and the further choice of particularly priority sectors for EEC measures, still appear to provide much of the rationale for MNC policy being conducted today from Brussels. For this reason, the full text of the 1973 draft EEC resolution on MNCs is still required reading, and is reproduced at Appendix I(a).

A measure of the operational significance of the 1973 resolution is that, of the priority areas outlined in it, by early 1979 the EEC had adopted measures which now have changed national legislation, or are in the process of doing so, in the following areas: large-scale dismissals, employee protection in the case of mergers, internal company mergers, international assistance between tax authorities on corporate tax evasion (particularly via transfer pricing). In addition, proposals in virtually all other areas are now being actively pursued, with particular emphasis being put on corporate disclosure via the creation of a European body of company law. A succinct analysis of the state of EEC legislation on MNC-related issues is given on pages 106–7.

(b) *Dirigisme or liberalism — the middle way*

'Both thorough-going dirigisme and total freedom are equally exaggerated postures in today's world, and we in the Commission want to be between the two extremes', says Davignon,[6] reflecting the EEC's desire to strike a bargain with big business. The European Commission's part of this bargain is that it will strive to create free European market conditions, and use its good offices with the ten European member governments to create 'framework economic conditions' conducive to profitable business activity, provided that business fulfils its part of the bargain.

What is business's part of the bargain? In a word: *transparency*. 'In return', says Davignon, 'we're entitled to some consistency in the way in which multinationals react to the needs of the market . . . you can't pursue this sort of policy without a minimum of transparency. And to be sure of this transparency, there must be rules — not more in the EEC than in the USA and Japan or elsewhere, but not less either.' These rules — on corporate disclosure, competition, taxation, etc. — are needed because 'obviously when operating within a multi-state framework, there are more loopholes in legislation'.

Davignon's highly individual approach to industrial policy is characterised not just by persistent diplomatic pressure exerted on the 'ten's' ministerial representatives, but also by a special brand of corporatism in the Commission's relation with big business. Describing his industrial department as 'an open shop for consultations with industrialists' — clearly not to the exclusion of the trades unions, however — Davignon stresses the need for investment co-ordination between businesses and the EEC authorities. 'Some sort of harmonisation of investments' is described as one of 'the main focuses of our policy on multinationals'. Needless to say this trend has disturbed US multinationals, who feel unable to fully participate in what they perceive as a sort of cosy Commission-sponsored corporate co-operation for fear of the long extra-territorial arm of American anti-trust law. This concern reached its height in 1978 with the strange history of the EEC fibres cartel, where neither Dupont nor Monsanto felt able to join in a Davignon-promoted arrangement for reducing sectoral capacity between major European manufacturers.

(c) *Pro European multinationals — or against American business?*

A clear aim of the EEC is the fostering of European transnationals, capable of taking advantage of the single European market that is gradually being developed, and thus of competing with non-EEC rivals more effectively both at home in Europe and on extra-EEC markets. The major planks of this 'positive' dimension to European policy on multinationals are measures designed to remove the non-tariff barriers still existing between the ten national territories making up the 'common market'. Notable among measures in this category are a comprehensive EEC programme for eliminating technical barriers to trade[7]

39

Table 4.1
Turnover and assets totals of the multinationals surveyed, by country of origin
(Figures in units of account)*

Country of origin	TURNOVER				ASSETS			
	Number of enterprises for which information is available	Percentage of total number of enterprises surveyed	Amounts (thousand u.a.)	Percentage	Number of enterprises for which information is available	Percentage of total number of enterprises surveyed	Amounts (thousand u.a.)	Percentage
France	394	80.8	80,665,049	5.1	40	52.6	87,519,010	6.2
Belgium	91	51.7	9,987,447	0.6	55	72.4	18,600,274	1.3
Netherlands	196	48.3	56,781,889	3.5	21	33.9	30,414,602	2.2
F R Germany	674	63.4	148,171,661	9.4	64	39.5	173,752,039	12.3
Italy	75	41.4	40,147,279	2.6	20	62.5	65,160,530	4.6
United Kingdom	958	70.8	181,573,972	11.5	120	51.1	210,606,244	14.9
Ireland	25	89.2	1,492,032	0.1	4	100.0	5,704,481	0.4
Denmark	72	60.0	6,020,060	0.4	4	23.5	7,396,768	0.5
Luxembourg	6	17.6	2,550,774	0.2	1	4.5	446,358	–
TOTAL EEC	2,491	64.7	527,390,163	33.4	329	48.8	599,600,306	42.4
Norway	79	68.7	3,051,645	0.2	5	33.3	3,041,189	0.2
Sweden	203	92.8	27,691,549	1.7	25	30.4	21,232,326	1.5
Finland	38	88.4	2,590,884	0.2	2	25.0	2,944,184	0.2
Switzerland	116	18.6	20,231,310	1.3	30	22.7	23,615,803	1.7
Lichtenstein	1	33.3	65,700	–	–	–	–	–
Austria	20	50.6	2,125,708	0.1	6	50.0	7,259,281	0.5

Portugal	3	42.9	923,117	0.1	2	66.7	6,772,336	0.5
Spain	5	23.8	917,637	0.1	9	64.3	9,551,993	0.7
United States	1,199	49.4	738,394,412	46.7	87	61.7	406,734,986	28.7
Canada	136	58.9	24,748,810	1.6	23	63.9	72,072,047	5.1
Malaysia	2	16.7	9,292	–	1	20.0	11,404	–
Singapore	6	12.0	235,028	–	–	–	–	–
Philippines	2	50.0	432,917	–	–	–	–	–
Japan	149	86.1	219,495,879	–	18	47.4	225,587,641	15.9
Taiwan	1	6.7	2,763	–	–	–	–	–
Hong Kong	4	8.0	270,315	–	4	44.4	6,099,983	0.4
Australia	56	31.1	9,132,494	0.6	25	52.1	29,165,133	2.1
New Zealand	20	20.0	2,077,395	0.1	5	29.4	1,857,463	0.1
TOTAL NON-MEMBER COUNTRIES	2,040	47.7	1,052,396,855	66.6	242	36.5	815,945,769	57.6
GRAND TOTAL	4,531	55.8	1,579,787,018	100.0	571	42.3	1,415,546,075	100.0

*1 unit of account (u.a.) = approximately 1.23 US dollars in 1973, the period to which the EEC Survey refers.

Source: European Commission Survey on Multinational Enterprises, July 1976, p.31.

41

and an EEC directive, now in force nationally, for opening up public procurement contract awards in the 'ten'.[8]

This drive to aid the multinationalisation of European business has left the suspicion that EEC MNC policy is anti-American. Such suspicions, perhaps somewhat exaggerated, are not without foundation and were voiced strongly in mid-1981 by the US Congress.[9] In mid-1976, an EEC study on multinational companies asserted that since

> European multinationals are both more numerous and weaker than their American counterparts, is not this a clear pointer as to what approach to adopt to the formation of multinationals in Europe? The figures [contained in the EEC study, see table 4.1] would certainly appear to lend support to an idea frequently expressed in Community circles — that the development of European transnational companies should be promoted, in order to counterbalance multinationals based outside the Community.[10]

comment the authors of the study, officials working in Davignon's industrial policy directorate at EEC headquarters.

The figures referred to in the EEC study, at 1973 dollar/u.a. conversion rates, reveal that in 1973 2,491 EEC-based multinationals generated a turnover of 524 billion units of account (around 645 billion dollars) on assets of 600 billion units of account (around 740 billion dollars). The comparable statistics for the USA show that 1,199 MNCs created 738 billion units of account (around 900 billion dollars) on assets of 407 billion units of account (around 460 billion dollars). Certainly, objective analysis would seem to show that on a crude turnover/asset ratio comparison, American multinational capital is being much more profitably employed than European capital — or for that matter than Japanese capital, where assets as in the case of EEC multinationals exceed annual sales. Differences in size — and thus in economies of scale — are clearly profiled by the European Commission's statistics.

Davignon himself appears to lend weight to those believing in a degree of anti-American bias inherent in European policy towards big business when, in talking of the advantages enjoyed by US companies as a result of the vast American market for public procurement (Defence Department programmes, the Buy America Act, etc.) he stresses that 'of course we've got to pursue a policy of public purchasing just like the US does', which means that 'Europe must try to give the same type of guarantees to our own companies as other big companies have'.[11] This message has since been reinforced, notably by the EEC's plans, revealed late 1981,[12] for Community preference within the context of a revamped industrial policy. Just how this policy can be carried out in the framework of EEC liberalisation of public procurement, ensured by a directive adopted by the Community's Council of Ministers in December 1976 is unclear. The public procurement legislation should legally benefit any company established within the Common Market irrespective of the country from which it is ultimately controlled. But American companies, among them in particular IBM, fear that the Commission is developing a definition of a European company which would effectively prejudice their ability to compete on an equal footing in European public purchasing markets with their EEC rivals. This fear, which is worrying US companies other than IBM, and extends to policy areas other than public purchasing[13] leaves a decided rift in approaches as between US and European MNCs towards the EEC authorities.

(d)   *Discrimination against multinationals: small is beautiful*

The EEC's claim not to discriminate between MNCs and national companies may hold good in an abstract legal sense, but there is little doubt that policy measures are chosen by the EEC which have greatest if not exclusive impact on MNCs (e.g. rules on Europe-wide corporate disclosure, anti-monopoly legislation, international tax evasion controls, and most recently the Vredeling measure on worker consultation). In addition to this *de facto* focus on MNCs, there is the political impact of their economic power, to which the 1973 memorandum eloquently testified. That policy statement reflected the belief that multinationals were, at least politically, a brand apart from national companies, when it talked of 'the growing hold of multinational undertakings on the economic, social and even political life of the countries in which they operate'.[14]

A further if less direct component of the EEC's discretionary policy towards multinationals is its championing of the cause of small and medium-sized businesses, particularly for the positive role the latter play in the creation of employment.[15] The 'jobs' factor, as unemployment moves to the centre of EEC economic policy priorities in the 1980s, should not be underrated as a touchstone in the formulation of Community business policy. The greater the emphasis of economic policy on unemployment, the greater scrutiny likely to be directed at the contribution made by multinationals, more often seen as technological innovators than labour creators, to limiting its impact. Even now, there is a tendency among those committed to the private enterprise system to buttress their support by reference to the smaller, more locally identifiable company, rather than to its massive international relation. This is a factor that could subtly tilt and differentiate public and governmental perceptions of the private sector of the economy, eventually making an impact on policy.

Conclusion and outlook

European policy towards multinationals is set in a climate often favourable to interventionism and regulation offset, however, by constitutional EEC provisions and attitudes supporting a more liberal approach. As a result, the European Community's policy towards big business is two-edged, encouraging multinational activity in a transnational European market, while seeking to remedy the concerns caused by this activity by specific binding measures of containment, rather than a single voluntary EEC code of conduct. Paradoxically the EEC, concerned at the phenomenon of multinational size, is also worried that European multinationals are not big enough to compete with their American and Japanese counterparts. Against this somewhat bizarre background, specific measures, developed gradually throughout the 1970s, are now beginning to make an impact on multinational companies, particularly in the following areas: corporate disclosure and legal responsibilities, employment and industrial relations, and anti trust. Lumped together, these policy items constitute the guts of the 'democratic' and 'capitalist' challenges outlined in the following two chapters.

Notes and references

1   Outlined in detail in preceding chapter.
2   For list of such measures, see p. 38 of this chapter and also Appendix I(a) for further details.
3   See Part IV for further details on UN and UN-related developments.
4   'Multinational Service' (fortnightly report), Brussels, no.10, 25 May 1977. For full text of Davignon interview, see Appendix I(b).
5   'Multinational Undertakings and the Community', Commission Communication to the Council of 8 November 1973. See Appendix I(a).
6   Interview quoted above from 'Multinational Service', Appendix I(b).
7   General programme approved 28 May 1969. See EEC Official Journal C 76 of 17 June 1969.
8   Council decision of 21 December 1976, EEC Official Journal L13 of 15 January 1977.

9   See chapter 3, note 22.

10   'Survey of Multinational Enterprises', European Commission, July 1976, vol.I, p.6.

11   Davignon interview from 'Multinational Service'.

12   *A Community Strategy to Develop Europe's Industry*, Brussels, 23 October 1981.

13   E.g. Company law and anti-trust, see chapters 5 and 6.

14   *Multinational Undertakings and the Community*, p.4 *et seq.*

15   It is estimated by EEC officials that some 70 per cent of all employment in the European Community outside agriculture and the public service is in small and medium-sized firms.

5 Europe's democratic challenge to multinationals

Multinational company management, scanning the European panorama on the threshold of the 1980s with its sights on the 1990 horizon, faces a reality and perspective dramatically contrasting with the attractions — political cohesion, economic growth and transnational market liberalism — that made the European Community the prime post-war target for the international investor up until the early 1970s. Now the tables have turned. It is the international investor, the multinational corporation, which sees itself as the prime target of Europe's emerging business control policy. And for business, the most disturbing silhouette of all on that none-too-distant horizon is the spectre of radically revamped European rules and national practice redefining the company's relations with society in general and, more particularly, with the various local cells of its international workforce.

Prefiguring this prospect is the reality of new departures in European industrial relations' practice, reinforced by growing EEC legislative support, not to mention parallel progress called for by intergovernmental codes directed at multinational business. Common Market measures, drawing on the pioneering experience of countries like Germany and Holland in the key area of enterprise-level industrial democracy, are distinguished by their explicit attempt to convert national labour and company laws into a coherent body of EEC legislation principally directed at international companies. This chapter deals with the social and economic background to these measures, their actual substance, and an assessment of their medium-term impact.

Multinationals, European industrial relations — and the erosion of capitalism

The European Community's programme in the labour and company law field seeks to impose 'local' European constraints on the global planning reflex of transnational firms, notably by demanding greater accountability to national governments, the general public and, most controversially, to the local workforce. Chief components of this integrated EEC policy are the famous so-called 'Vredeling initiative',[1] whose demands that key corporate decisions should be subject to prior trade union control caused a shock from which MNCs have yet to recover; and moves to legislate for worker participation in company boards,[2] multinational information[3] and stepped-up international legal liability.[4]

Combined, these measures form a democratic challenge to some major tenets of traditional capitalism. Amongst the assumptions so challenged are: management's decision-making autonomy; the primacy of shareholder control and of company policy oriented to serve shareholder interests; and the treatment of labour simply as a variable cost and a factor of production. By querying the absoluteness of these assumptions, the Common Market's programme constitutes a quiet revolution in the values of traditional capitalism.

However, in throwing down the gauntlet, the EEC — in common with others, notably Western governments as a whole[5] and particularly European trade unions — is also responding to changes in the capitalist system which the multinational company itself, wittingly or unwittingly, has wrought. Amongst these is the actual subservience of notionally independent companies, in key areas of business strategy, to central management authority, and thus the erosion of local management decision-making autonomy. Another is the upthrust of central management at the expense of effective shareholder control. A third is the increasing separation of employee interests from those of the multinational employer, whose aim of optimising worldwide resources does not necessarily — indeed in many cases cannot — mean optimising the welfare of local workforces.

In other words, traditional free enterprise, and the capitalist legal system which grew up in the confines of the nation state, is under attack both from within and without. In Europe it is challenged both by specifically European trends in industrial democracy, and from within its own ranks by the growth of the multinational company whose operations have outstripped the capacity of national company laws to effectively control it. It is the convergence of these two initially independent trends that provides the ideological momentum behind the EEC's programme in the field of company law and industrial relations — also, indeed, behind initiatives in the broader international context.

An introductory word about each of these trends

Pressure for industrial democracy, increasingly finding expression at the level of the individual company, has been one of the key trends in the contemporary history of European industrial relations. The emerging mosaic of national laws and practices in this field[6] expanded significantly during the 1970s and reflects a shift in the focus of democratic rights from the formal political process to the everyday economic framework and, more particularly, to the decision-making structures of the company. Of course, this trend may take different shapes in different European countries. But it is nonetheless widespread for that — be it expressed via laws on worker participation as in Germany, Denmark and the Netherlands, by the increasing importance of local shop stewards in the UK and the *consigli di fabbrica* in Italy, or again by the action of international trade unions in forming 'world councils' in companies like Philips, Volkswagen and Renault. Such an extension of the democratic franchise, vigorously supported by an active and influential European trade union movement, has in any case been strengthened by the employment impact of an economic crisis likely to persist well into the 1980s,[7] and by the parallel fact that the subject-matter of the formal political process in European democracies is now in any case primarily economic. The heightened democratic impulse given to European industrial relations, complete with an ideological dimension not found in the USA and coupled with a focus on the local subsidiary, has placed many multinationals in a particularly vulnerable position. This is especially true at a time when central management, often from distant foreign headquarters, has reacted to the new competitive constraints of a troubled world economy by internationally re-allocating investments — and jobs. The natural focus of European pressures for more meaningful industrial democracy — of which the problems faced by Firestone, Badger International and Siemens are three recent salient examples — has thus become the multinational company. These examples are detailed in chapter 9. With its impact on investment and indeed on the economy in general, the multinational company has, in turn, begun to be perceived less as a private organisation and more as a quasi-public international institution, but one operating largely free of public controls.

At this point, Europe's domestic challenge to the multinational dovetails with the multinational's own — if unintentional — challenge to the unreconstructed basis for Western free enterprise found in existing company laws. It takes no great imagination to see that such laws, territorially limited to the nation-state and vesting control of management decisions in the hands of the shareholder and ultimately the stock market, are not ideally suited to ensuring the accountability of multinationals in the traditional area of economic performance, let alone to their new social and political constituencies. Indeed, the large multinational through its complex organisation, international operations and the primacy it gives headquarter's management in controlling group decisions, has effectively transferred authority from the owners to the executives and, as J.K. Galbraith has noted, has left 'the shareholders without powers'.[8] Thus the idea that 'the discipline of the marketplace checks and ultimately destroys those who are irrational in the exercise of corporate power . . . has lost most of its vitality — at least for the largest corporations'.[9] Moreover, from the standpoint of public control, multinationals are in the awkward and paradoxical situation of being both the strongest economic proponents of capitalism and, at the same time, the form of free enterprise with the weakest link to capitalism's ideological — even democratic — base, namely the individual shareholders. The MNC is capitalism's star performer — but also its Achilles' heel.

These misgivings, already strong when applied to the multinational group as a whole, become much more acute at the level of the individual MNC subsidiary. For the local subsidiary, the parent company is the sole, or solely important, shareholder. Corporate decision-making and control have thus become merged in a single, and often distant, executive board, and power has become or at the very least is seen to have become, unaccountable to the society in which the subsidiary operates. The retreat of capitalist forms of democratic control, a process indissociable from the multinational, has led to demands in Europe, centred on the EEC and the OECD, and again supported by the trade union lobby for a major overhaul of laws governing companies. Their dual thrust is to 'unlimit' the liability of central management for the activities of the subsidiary, and to offset executive power by the democratic authority of a supervisory board of directors.

The multinational business community's response to these new trends and embryonic legislation in the area of European corporate accountability has been unwaveringly hostile, and shows little sign of moderating during the coming years. Greatest hostility is reserved for the idea of any dilution of management prerogatives to the profit of organised labour — indeed EEC proposals on worker consultation in multinationals have united the international business world as never before. The imprecations of the Confederation of British Industry, the Patronat Français and European employers in general[10] have been answered by equally resonant echoes of shocked surprise from

49

American multinational interests, notably the American Chamber of Commerce and the National Foreign Trade Council.[11] With equally vociferous support coming from the trade unions, what has occurred is not just a deepening of business/labour polarisation in Europe, but also a substantial reversal in the attitudes of Europe's major interest groups towards the European Community and, beyond that, to the very idea of European integration. Business, which favours market liberalism and was the main beneficiary of the Common Market's creation between 1958–70, sees as a political threat any extension of the European Community's powers which could involve restrictions on corporate freedom. Exactly the opposite is true of the trade unions and, more generally, Europe's political left.

European industrial democracy: the burgeoning mosaic

Pressure for enterprise-level worker involvement in European countries has grown up out of, and alongside, broader expressions of industrial democracy, notably collective bargaining which in many EEC countries is still its dominant channel. However, mechanisms for employee participation and consultation within individual companies and plants, or serious policy discussions aiming at such innovations, have in recent years so developed as to create a specifically Western European brand of industrial democracy. This development has, moreover, been aided by the tendency of more traditional forms of collective bargaining, including in those countries like Italy and the UK where employee representation has been most resisted, to localise its focus on the individual company, particularly the large and in many cases multi-national enterprise.

For international business, the key decade has undoubtedly been the 1970s when, following the expansion of European economic multi-nationalism 1950–70, national collective bargainers and legislators alike found themselves having to deal increasingly with employers whose activities were often transnational in dimension and foreign-controlled. This realisation provided a major impulse to EEC efforts, begun in the 1960s and given greater acuity by the rising social concerns sparked by the still-persisting economic crisis of the 1970s, to introduce proposals which would provide a transnational political response to the multi-national economic phenomenon. Meanwhile, employee participation and worker consultation machinery which had been pioneered in West Germany in the 1950s was paralleled throughout the 1970s by similar developments in other EEC countries and spectacularly reinforced in the Federal Republic by company law reform voted for controversially by the Bunderstag in 1976 and since confirmed, in the face of united business opposition, by the German constitutional court in March 1979. The symbiosis between EEC proposals and legislative initiatives in individual European countries has provided a special political impetus to new trends in European industrial democracy, mutually reinforcing Europe-wide debate and national laws.

At the same time, and as part of the broader canvas of industrial relations, employment protection rules[12] were being introduced for the Common Market as a whole. Hastened by the onset of Europe's economic slowdown following the oil crisis, these rules tend to make labour less a variable and more a fixed cost, leading either to reduced company mobility or at least rendering it much more costly. Unhindered capital mobility, one of the Common Market's most sacred shibboleths, quickly ran into conflict with actual labour immobility, and many multinationals, seeking to relocate investment, had to pay a heavy price for the privilege. Instances of this include massive compensation payments paid by ITT as it trimmed down its Brussels' European headquarters, Monsanto's pull-back from Luxembourg, and the contraction of ICI's European operations. Meanwhile the pull-back of American MNC regional headquarters from Brussels has been a permanent factor of business life in 'Europe's capital' in the latter half of the 1970s.[13]

Against this backcloth, the centre-stage of Europe's push for enterprise-level democracy is unquestionably occupied by West Germany's integrated system of worker participation and consultation. Prefigured by the 1951 Codetermination Law which stipulated parity between worker and shareholder representation on the supervisory boards of large coal and steel companies, the German model has been gradually extended, initially only partially, to all large publicly-held companies.[14] In fact, the 1976 law falls a hair's breadth short of full parity in board representation, but is still ambitious enough to cause the German employers' federations to question whether its implementation would not upset the social balance necessary for company activity in a free society, by giving too much power to the unions. The testing time for this view, shared by the multinational business community as a whole,[15] will be the decade of the 1980s as the law is gradually implemented, but at least one company, ITT (Graetz), chose the moment to make controversial adjustments in its corporate operations. The trade unions referred to the OECD's Guidelines for Multinationals to complain to Western governments that this subsidiary of the US conglomerate had restructured its operations so as not to be covered by the 1976 law which extended to joint stock companies employing more than 2000 workers; see p.133 for union complaint and OECD reaction.

Yet although worker participation rules are a key part of German enterprise-level democracy, and an important model for EEC proposals in this field, they should not be seen in isolation from other components of the German system, in particular the works councils. Indeed, in many respects, the works councils, together with the consultation and information rights they grant employees on a whole range of corporate decision-making, are more important as a model for other European countries, where there is resistance to board-level participation but equal if not greater pressure by unions for gaining knowledge of and influence over management decisions and strategy 'from the outside'. Indeed, EEC proposals calling for revamped worker information and consultation rights in multinational companies, authored by Dutch trade unionist Henk Vredeling, are related, not to the board-level participation mechanism, but rather to the functions increasingly assumed by the works councils. And works councils are by no means a purely German phenomenon.

In the Netherlands, the Dutch equivalent of the German works council, the enterprise council, saw its powers of consultation and information significantly strengthened by a 1971 law which also legislated for the creation of employee participation in the appointment of members of the supervisory board. The Netherlands' law, since strengthened by a further amendment in 1979, forces all company establishments employing more than 100 employees to set up enterprise councils which, besides enjoying co-decision with management on a number of strictly 'social' matters, also have the right to prior consultation on key strategic decisions, such as divestment and change of ownership. Moreover, the 1979 amendment removed management from membership of these committees, reinforced their information rights and added the right to appeal against inequitable decisions by management. Meanwhile, board-level involvement of employee interests is ensured by the peculiarly Dutch system of 'co-optation', whose application has resulted, by the end of the 1970s, in 'a gradual decline in the number of supervisory board members coming from private industry in favour of people from the universities, the public sector and politics'.[16] In other words, control over company decisions is gradually passing from the shareholder to the company's social and political constituencies.

A point worth mentioning in this context is that the Dutch system, perhaps more than any other in Europe, reflects some of the priorities for management supervision also felt by business policy thinkers in the USA. A strong case for the need for large corporations to have 'independent directors — men and women whose perspective goes beyond the parochial concerns of the particular corporation' was made by the Chairman of the American Securities and Exchange Commission in a speech addressing the theme 'Free Enterprise in a Free Society'.[17] Indeed, passing from words to action, a series of American multinationals have formed international advisory councils — IBM, General

Motors, Ford, amongst others — which, while not linked organically into the corporation's legal structure, as in the case of Dutch law, nevertheless reflect the concern that management must be aware of the political and social implications of what have traditionally been considered purely economic decisions.

Coupled with sophisticated machinery for collective bargaining, Dutch rules on worker consultation and participation make up a comprehensive system of industrial democracy which has significantly influenced EEC thinking, particularly on the issue of multinational control, in two ways. First, the consultation rights of the enterprise council in Holland again lend further 'grass roots' support to the Vredeling initiative. Second, the fact that leading Dutch multinationals — Royal Dutch Shell, Unilever, Philips, AKZO (whose combined turnover is around 60 per cent of Dutch GDP[18]) — have successfully lobbied for exemption from the co-optation system of worker participation in their central boards has stiffened the EEC argument that, only at a wider international level, can adequate legislative measures be taken to ensure that MNCs are subject to the same democratic constraints as other companies.

Germany and Holland, while undoubtedly the torch-bearers of European enterprise-level industrial democracy, are no longer alone. Further momentum to this general trend has been supplied in recent years in most other European countries, either by new legislation, practices or policy debate.

Thus in Denmark, by the mid-1970s, national collective agreements had set up employee/management works councils with extensive rights to information on corporate strategy. In addition, by 1980 Denmark, which can be seen as a protuberance into the EEC of the progressive social systems of its Scandinavian partners, had upgraded its embryonic attempts at worker participation in management control. As of early 1981, a third of all board directors must now be employee representatives.

Meanwhile, other north European countries have begun tinkering with worker participation, even if more tentatively. Luxembourg's 1974 law on minority employee representation on boards of companies employing more than 2,000 in practice only applies to Radio Luxembourg, the national railway company and the Grand Duchy's one major industrial company, Arbed — the steel-making giant whose multinational turnover has been reported as exceeding Luxembourg's gross national product by 50 per cent.[19] Ireland, also, has introduced board-level participation for workers in six state-controlled companies, including for example Aer Lingus, and in 1980 a conservative Irish government proposed an extension of this system and consideration of worker democracy in the private sector.

In other EEC countries like Britain, Italy and France, the traditional emphasis has tended to be less on the integration of worker influence into the decision-making structure as on the exercise of worker control on companies from outside the structure. All of these countries have traditions of adversary industrial relations. However, some important qualifications need to be made to this simplistic picture.

In Britain and Italy, for example, where industrial democracy has been mainly articulated through collective bargaining, a significant development has been the trend towards its expression at plant level. The drift away from centralised collective bargaining in Britain coincides with the growth of local shop steward organisations, a trend paralleled in Italy by the rising importance of the *consigli di fabbrica*, a plant-level workers' council which, in cases like Fiat, almost is the functional equivalent of board-level participation in Germany. In addition, in the UK, debate on worker participation has been fuelled throughout the 1970s by the Bullock Report, not to mention the TUC's explicit support for parity shareholder/worker participation after many years of reticence towards a formula for industrial demo-cracy that seemed to British trade unions to bear the stamp of class collaboration. Of course, by the end of the 1970s the chill wind of radical Thatcherite conservatism had frozen active discussion of employee board-level representation — conveniently stigmatised by its opponents as 'a Trojan bullock' within the walls of free enterprise. Yet, even in Britain, opposition to worker participation is far from monolithic. A British Institute of Management survey in 1981 found an absolute majority of its respondents accepted some form of worker participation.[20] UK personnel managers,[21] meanwhile, have expressed interest in greater employee involvement in business activity. At the same time the emergence post-1980 of a British political force of the centre brings with it a commitment to consensual industrial relations foreign to the UK's two traditional political parties.

In France, another country with a tradition of adversary industrial relations and sharing with Britain hierarchical decision-making structures, the wind of participation which has blown with varying degrees of force since the watershed events of 1968, is likely to increase following the election of a socialist administration in 1981. Until then, debate on participation has been focused on the report of the Sudreau Commission,[22] set up by ex-President Valéry Giscard d'Estaing to discuss overall reform of French company structure. Although it has yet to be answered by legislative action of any consequence, the report concluded in favour of minority worker representation on the boards of large corporations and, in the area of worker consultation machinery, had a particularly direct message for foreign multinational groups operating in France. This was the recommendation that non-French multinationals should be forced to nominate a representative in each of their French subsidiaries who would be answerable to local workforces for the multinationals' overall policy — a demand which appears to be paralleled by requirements asked of international business in the OECD's code on multinationals,[23] and at the same time a direct fore-runner of EEC proposals for MNC control contained in the Vredeling proposals.

The advent of Mitterrand and Mauroy at the head of a thorough-going socialist government in mid-1981 casts the development of French labour law and industrial relations in the 1980s in a radically new light. The systematically rejectionist attitude of the French Patronat (employers' organisation) to the gradualist types of reforms contained in the Sudreau Report may now simply be swept aside by legislation. Immediately following their 1981 electoral triumphs, the socialists made clear their intention to introduce board-level partici-pation into the nationalised industries, and could well enact similar schemes for economic democracy in the private sector. Further, by bringing the Communists into government, the socialists may have done much to defuse the traditional opposition by the Confédération Générale du Travail[24] to board-level worker representation, seen traditionally by the CGT as a form of class collaboration.

Paralleling the French experience of union/business hostility, the traditionally conflictual nature of industrial relations in countries like Britain and Italy, while likely to hinder any rapid move towards board-level employee representation, also argues in favour of it as an objective need. This is perhaps particularly true in Britain and Italy, two countries whose demonstrably blocked political systems apparently mirror their adversary systems of industrial relations. Yet, as suggested above, cracks are appearing in traditional mutual antagonism, just as with Italy's 'compromesso storico' and Britain's embryonic political realignments,[25] the demarcation lines of traditional political rivalry are also being fudged.

Even the traditional situation in France, where both the Patronat Français and the CGT have habitually snubbed enterprise-level represen-tation, is not without its impact on trends in European industrial democracy. The aversion of French unions, shared by their Belgian counterparts, to the class collaboration they have tended to feel is inherent in employee membership of company boards, actually in-creases the pressure for extending the consultative powers of existing works councils which, set up outside the corporate decision-making structure, are a natural bridgehead to the goal of worker control. And it is precisely on extended employee information and consultation rights in multinationals that the EEC's industrial relations policy, following the Vredeling proposals of October 1980, is in large part focused.

Democratic control: EEC labour law and MNC hostility

Multinationals, with few exceptions, view this emerging mosaic with concern, and its extrapolation on the European level with antagonism. They dislike the proposition, inherent to the whole philosophy behind company-level industrial democracy, namely that workers are to have an increasingly greater say in the conduct of a company's activities. Their anxiety and opposition are further heightened by the fact that industrial democracy targeted directly at the enterprise is not just a philosophical abstract, or the product of EEC wishful thinking, but increasingly impinges on company structures and economic reality.

Thus the extension of German codetermination laws in 1976 has enabled international trade union officials like Charles Levinson, secretary-general of the International Federation of Chemical, General and Energy Workers, and a famed critic of multinationals,[26] together with Herman Rebhan of the powerful International Metalworkers unions, to sit respectively on the boards of the German subsidiaries of Dupont and Ford. The same German law, according to the trade unions, prompted another leading US multinational, ITT, to take action allegedly to avoid similar consequences. In addition, since 1977, a series of 'cases' involving the industrial relations' practices of individual multinational companies — Philips, Siemens, Hertz Rentacar, British Oxygen and BAT, amongst others — has been the focus of European trade union complaints to Western governments, and has thus aggravated MNC concern with European trends in industrial democracy, see chapter 9. The prospect of the conversion of these national laws and international guidelines into a full-blown body of European law on multinationals' labour relations is what the international business world cannot stomach. Multinationalisation of economic activity is one thing. Multinationalisation of labour relations is another.

So it is that MNC antipathy reaches its apex when focused on EEC business control measures. Internationalisation of industrial democracy is absolutely opposed. Resistance is strongest amongst American companies, with no indigenous experience of employee representation, let alone of worker directors who are also members of politically powerful trades unions. If industrial democracy can be isolated in a variety of national contexts, it can, with difficulty, be managed, contained or, with a little legal ingenuity, avoided. But its extension onto the international level is feared both in itself as a restriction to central management's decision-making freedom and, beyond that, because it seems another step towards that horror of horrors for the multinational community: international collective bargaining, and ultimately the prospect of worldwide union action on pay and other disputes with management.

This prospect, while not for tomorrow, is clearly one which the EEC, and particularly its policy-making body the European Commission, has given business every reason to suppose it is encouraging, both by general policy statements and specific proposals. The resulting close link between EEC and trade union policies on business control is a matter of continuing anxiety for multinationals. The call for 'a trade union counterweight' to multinationals, and indeed for European collective agreements[27] was thus made not by the trades unions themselves, but by the Commission in its programme on multinational control. In addition, active encouragement has been given by EEC leaders throughout the 1970s to the Europeanisation of the trade union movement in response to the transnational market liberalisation of the first twenty-five post-war years. The European Trade Union Confederation was in fact set up in 1973 and since then has come to be regarded as one of the foremost pressure groups on EEC policy formation — a development which Mr Roy Jenkins, for one, strongly supported when president of the EEC Commission.[28] European unions, responding to these official proddings, have naturally laid special stress on policy areas most directly affecting their membership, and in the ETUC's own programme for multinational control,[29] industrial relations has pride of place. The ETUC has thus been a permanent factor continually bringing back European policy attention to what for it is a central issue. This state of affairs has acted as a final exacerbating factor for MNCs who detect, not very far behind EEC business control policy what for them is the sinister shape of their real enemy, the Western trade union movement ideologically centred in the European Community. It's strongest individual components are the British TUC, the German Deutscher Gewerkschafts Bund, and the Scandinavian Lands Organisationen.

The climate of business/union hostility is a strange monument to EEC legislative efforts in the field of labour law, whose aim is to achieve more harmonious industrial relations between what Eurojargon has euphemistically dubbed 'the social partners'. Such hostility has increased as the Community's labour law programme, after a period of painful gestation, has gradually begun to be enacted in the late 1970s. First successes were employment protection rules designed to limit the employment consequences of excessive capital mobility in a structurally changing European economy. But by the early 1980s the focus of the EEC programme had gradually shifted onto measures more specifically targeted at multinationals' labour relations practice, and thus much more controversial. An outline of the European Community's labour law programme as it relates to multinationals follows.

(i) Europe-wide employment protection

The emphasis put by the European Commission's 1973 multinationals programme on employment protection found its initial expression in the adoption by the Council of Ministers of two EEC directives[30] respectively aligning the laws of Common Market member states on company responsibilities in the event of mass dismissals (February 1975) and employee rights in cases of changes in company ownership or control (February 1977). Common to both these rules, which even at the beginning of the 1980s have yet to be fully implemented into national European laws, is the requirement that companies envisaging redundancies or acquisition should engage in prior consultations with workforce representatives prior to, and with the aim of affecting, final management decisions. A central aim of these rules is to ensure that multinationals do not select investment sites in the EEC out of preference for countries with relatively lax labour legislation. They set a minimum standard below which national laws may under no circumstance fall.

The importance of these measures, moreover, has increased with the onset of generalised economic uncertainty and the resultant cut-back in European investments undertaken by many multinationals who, during the late 1970s and early 1980s have begun to switch capital expenditure to areas like the United States and the advanced developing countries. The existence of the two EEC directives, by setting minimum Europe-wide standards, acts as a European brake on the speed with which investment reallocation can take place. Perhaps just as significant for the multinational investor is the fact that such minimum legal standards, which may mean little change in practice from labour laws prevalent in advanced European countries like Germany and the Netherlands, could entail quite radical adjustments in the newly-democratised countries like Greece, Spain and Portugal, all states whose membership of the EEC will mean adoption of employee protection rules more progressive than hitherto practised.[31] The same may be said for Ireland, a country which traditionally has gone out of its way to encourage inward international investment, while in the case of the United Kingdom, where implementation procedures are dragging, the acquired rights directive will mean a new legal departure.

(ii) Employee consultation in multinational companies

The establishment by the EEC of minimum protection standards for local European workforces of multinational companies is one thing, the creation of bold new information and consultation rights, open-ended in scope, extra-territorial in application and aimed ultimately at central management, is quite another. This, however, is precisely the controversial goal of the Vredeling initiative – 'Proposal for a Council directive on procedures for informing and consulting the employees of undertakings with complex structures, in particular transnational under-takings – more usually known simply as the EEC's 'multinationals directive', full details of which are given in Appendix I(h).

Proposed by the European Commission in October 1980 and likely to run the gauntlet of governmental and business/union discussions throughout the 1980s, the Vredeling initiative constitutes the first legislative attempt by the EEC to implement the aim of international collective bargaining urged by the Community's 1973 programme for multinational control, see Appendix I(a). Equally worrying for inter-national business, it is also a direct response by the EEC to the urgings of industrialised governments, to strengthen the effectiveness of the West's own multinationals' code, the OECD Guidelines for Multi-national Enterprises. By extending the demands made by the OECD's voluntary code and converting them into legally compulsory obli-gations, the EEC multinationals' directive would indeed achieve that. Hence the consternation of the business world which with the excep-tion of some large and leading international businesses, is reluctant enough to give public support even to voluntary guidelines for multi-national behaviour.

The Commission's scheme would make multinational company decisions on key general issues like investment planning, divestment and diversification subject to advance consultations, if not the prior say-so, of employee representatives in European subsidiaries, that is, to all intents and purposes, the trade unions. Greater acuity is given to this objective by the fact that it brings the two great barons of the inter-national private sector – the multinationals and the trade unions – into direct confrontation. The intensity of this confrontation is heightened by two mutually incompatible anxieties. First, there is the concern of international business that fundamental changes in economic con-ditions – notably the economic crisis, the opportunities provided by the industrialisation of the advanced developing countries, the challenge of Japan to Western competitivity, and the technological revolution in the West – require the utmost flexibility in decision-making if manage-ment is to respond successfully. This flexibility, maintains business, is directly threatened by the type of control envisaged by the EEC. Paradoxically, the second anxiety, that of European organised labour, starts from an identical awareness of fundamental economic changes, but comes up with exactly the opposite response. Given such radical shifts in international economic structures, the trade unions — and the EEC Commission — demand that greater information and consultation rights must be given local workforces if they are to be expected to 'play ball' in this process of economic reorganisation. The anxiety of organised labour is moreover, enlivened by the fact that its membership is increasingly composed of workers who are employees of multinational concerns while affiliated to national trade unions. Without such increased information and consultation rights, unions claim that the type of economic reorganisation which Europe must undergo — indeed, as the European Community's ten million dole queue shows, is in fact undergoing — will take place in unacceptable conditions, unilaterally decided by an often far-away central management and without the necessary social consensus.

The Vredeling initiative, which is certain to be the subject of lively if not acrimonious debate in the 1980—85 period, notably in the European Parliament and the Council of Ministers,[32] seeks to remedy this situation by addressing itself directly to the multinational undertaking as a single legal entity. This approach, though apparently justified by the reality of the ultimate control exercised by headquarter management over the decision-making of subsidiary companies, is in fact revolutionary, particularly in its implications for company law. Profiting from the legal fiction that local subsidiaries are operating as independent units, multinationals can accommodate without any great difficulties to the requirements of worker information as fixed by national law, since the key decision-making and thus information centre is located elsewhere, namely at the headquarters. The Vredeling initiative seeks to destroy this legal fiction, at least for the purposes of EEC labour law. The Commission would thus subject MNCs to real exposure on key employment-sensitive issues. Small wonder, then, that it has brought on its head the single-minded opprobrium of the international business community.

In detail, the twin aims of the EEC multinationals directive, corresponding to the information and consultation requirements set out respectively in Articles 5 and 6 of the draft directive, are as follows:

Article 5

1   At least every six months, the management of a dominant undertaking shall forward relevant information to the management of its subsidiaries in the Community giving a clear picture of the activities of the dominant undertaking and its subsidiaries taken as a whole.

2   This information shall relate in particular to:

(a)   structure and manning;

(b)   the economic and financial situation;

(c)   the situation and probable development of the business and of production and sales;

(d)   the employment situation and probable trends;

(e)   production and investment programmes;

(f)   rationalisation plans;

(g)   manufacturing and working methods, in particular the introduction of new working methods;

(h)   all procedures and plans liable to have a substantial effect on employees' interests.

3   The management of each subsidiary shall be required to communicate such information without delay to employees' representatives in each subsidiary.

4   Where the management of the subsidiaries is unable to communicate the information referred to in paragraphs (1) and (2) to employees' representatives, the management of the dominant undertaking must communicate such information to any employees' representatives who have requested it to do so.

5   The Member States shall provide for appropriate penalties for failure to comply with the obligations laid down in this article.

Article 6

1   Where the management of a dominant undertaking proposes to take a decision concerning the whole or a major part of the dominant undertaking or of one of its subsidiaries which is liable to have a substantial effect on the interests of its employees, it shall be required to forward precise information to the management of each of its subsidiaries within the Community not later than forty·days before adopting the decision, giving details of:

—   the grounds for the proposed decision;

—   the legal, economic and social consequences of such decision for the employees concerned;

—   the measures planned in respect of these employees.

2   The decisions referred to in paragraph (1) shall be those relating to:

(a)   the closure or transfer of an establishment or major parts thereof;

(b) restrictions, extensions or substantial modifications to the activities of the undertaking;

(c) major modifications with regard to organisation;

(d) the introduction of long-term cooperation with other undertakings or the cessation of such cooperation.

3   The management of each subsidiary shall be required to communicate this information without delay to its employees' representatives and to ask for their opinion within a period of not less than thirty days.

4   Where, in the opinion of the employees' representatives, the proposed decision is likely to have a direct effect on the employees' terms of employment or working conditions, the management of the subsidiary shall be required to hold consultations with them with a view to reaching agreement on the measures planned in respect of them.

5   Where the management of the subsidiaries does not communicate to the employees' representatives the information required under paragraph (3) or does not arrange consultations as required under paragraph (4), such representatives shall be authorised to open consultations, through authorised delegates, with the management of the dominant undertaking with a view to obtaining such information and, where appropriate to reaching agreement on the measures planned with regard to the employees concerned.

6   The Member States shall provide for appropriate penalties in case of failure to fulfil the obligations laid down in this article. In particular, they shall grant to the employees' representatives concerned by the decision the right of appeal to tribunals or other competent national authorities for measures to be taken to protect their interests.

Moreover, and more controversially, the EEC's multinationals bill would explicitly bring into this web companies controlled from beyond Common Market borders. Accordingly,[33] foreign multinationals would have to ensure the presence in the Community of at least one authorised headquarters' representative 'able to fulfil the requirements as regards disclosure of information and consultation'. The open-ended nature of these requirements, coupled with an implicit extra-territoriality shared by other EEC business legislation, for example, the seventh directive (see pp. 67–8), makes this element of the European business control package particularly indigestible for American-controlled companies.

To grasp the full potential scope of the democratic control sought by the Vredeling initiative, a simple example suffices. The US central management of a multinational controlling, for example, subsidiaries in the UK and West Germany, and intending to open up new operations in, say, Taiwan or Brazil, would be obliged to inform and consult — and the divide between consultation and negotiation is thin — British and German trade union officials in advance of the investment decision being taken. It is the competitive consequences of this process, to say nothing of its confidentiality risk, that both American and European multinationals find so frightening. Equally frightening a prospect for European trade unions, however, is that the allocation of international wealth and employment should be carried out by multinationals without union or public control.

(iii) Employee participation in company boards

By comparison to the furore created by the Vredeling initiative, the third major strand of EEC industrial relations policy — worker participation in company boards — appears to have become less acutely controversial. Yet these appearances, strengthened by the EEC's evident desire to inject greater flexibility into earlier proposals calling for mandatory board-level representation,[34] may prove to be misleading. This is because there is a clear and mutually supportive link between the EEC's new flexibility on worker participation in company activity and the ideas for increased employee involvement contained in the Vredeling initiative. Chief among the forms of industrial democracy, other than board-level worker representation, which the EEC is now supporting, is greater use of enterprise councils and extension of their information and consultation rights. Such structures — be they works councils (Germany), enterprise committees (Netherlands, Belgium) or local shop stewards committees (UK, Italy) — constitute precisely the framework for the channelling of the information and consultation demands encouraged by the Vredeling proposals.

Alongside this perspective, the EEC's ultimate aim nevertheless remains the achievement of board-level participation of company employees in large publicly-held companies, both in EEC-controlled multinationals, and in the subsidiaries of multinationals controlled from beyond the Common Market's borders. Major Community proposals for realising such stepped-up worker control were made or developed in the 1970s. They include the so-called 'fifth' EEC company law directive,[35] whose initial aim was an astute mixture of the German and Dutch systems described above in this chapter; the draft regulation for a European company statute;[36] and the European Commission's 1975 policy paper authored by the late Mr Finn Olav Gundelach, entitled 'Employee Participation and Company Structure'.[37]

In narrow EEC legislative terms, progress to date on these measures has been slow, although the broader impact of ideas contained in EEC proposals on the climate for legislation in individual EEC countries should not be underrated, even in countries hostile to board-level participation. In addition, the debate on the key fifth directive, which has occupied the European Parliament in the last years of the 1970s, should shift to the decision-making framework of the Community's Council of Ministers during the first years of the 1980s. Given the readiness of EEC policy-makers to envisage forms of effective participation lower than board-level, coupled with the sensible abandonment of the aim of imposing outright harmonisation on ten diverse if gradually converging national traditions, the proposal may stand a greater chance of eventual adoption than at one time seemed the case. Certainly support for it is not limited to European 'lefties' — a grotesque caricature which multinationals should only believe at their peril.[38] The more progressive forces in international business, meanwhile, may judge it opportune to channel the pressure for greater employee democracy into the flexible forms of participation contained in the fifth directive, and away from schemes more potentially divisive, such as the Vredeling initiative.

Corporate responsibility: emerging European trends

(i)   The two-tier board structure

No clearer indication of the interlocking nature of the control over management sought by EEC labour and company laws is available than that provided by the European Community's worker participation proposals. The fifth directive is in fact the natural bridgehead between European efforts to legislate for management responsiveness to employee concerns, on the one hand, and on the other, to create within the company an organ of control over executive decisions. Worker participation and the two-tier board system — a management committee whose decisions are controlled by a supervisory board — are the clear expressions of these twin aims. They are fused together in the dominant strand of EEC thinking by the call to incorporate worker participation in the supervisory board. The fifth directive, by embodying these objectives, already practised in many EEC countries, is the meeting point of EEC company law and EEC labour law.

The strengthening within the company's structure of the function of management control, whether it takes the form of a supervisory board (as in Germany, the Netherlands, Denmark) or via adjustments in the single boards found in countries like the UK and France, is one of the key methods backed by the EEC for re-establishing control over management decisions. In traditional company law terms, membership of the supervisory board could be reserved entirely for representatives of the shareholders, providing the latter with the scope to regain the control no longer assured by the general meeting. In fact, the dominant trend of European company law particularly in the case of the Dutch system of co-optation, is to enable participation in this control function of interests other than the company's shareholders, be it those of the workforce or the company's broader social constituencies,and whether they are represented on a supervisory board or via non-executive members of a single board of directors. Moreover, as indicated earlier the spontaneous creation by some leading American multinationals of worldwide regional advisory boards is evidence that trends towards new forms of management control are not exclusively European.

(ii) 'Unlimiting' company liability

The other main thrust behind the attempts of EEC company law to re-vamp the control over management decisions is directed more specifically at multinational concerns. Its aim is to 'unlimit' the liability of the parent company for the subsidiary — in other words, to do for Europe-wide company law what the Vredeling initiative seeks in the field of multinational labour law. This objective enshrined in the European Commission's draft proposal for a 'ninth' directive,[39] is once again opposed by leading representatives of the business world. But business would do well to note that the EEC is not acting in a vacuum. EEC thinking in fact reflects a general feeling of unease among the Western political establishment, also expressed by those responsible for overseeing the application of the OECD 'Guidelines on Multinational Enterprises', that the level of responsibility imposed by national laws on a parent company in its dealings with affiliated companies is insufficient. Factors catalysing this unease have been the Badger Company disinvestment case in Belgium — a *cause célèbre* for the OECD Guidelines — and, once again, the pressure exerted by an active international trade union movement. The West's organised labour, on this as on other issues affecting international business, closely co-ordinates its lobbying efforts between those focused on the European Community and those addressed to Western governments as a whole via the Trade Union Advisory Committee to the OECD in Paris.

Business opposition to the 'ninth' directive reflects the belief that it, like the Vredeling initiative, is evidence of unnecessary EEC tinkering with the existing legal framework which enables firms to make profits in a responsible way. Multinationals claim they are good corporate citizens in the various countries in which they operate; they pay their fair share of taxes in support of local communities; they respect national laws, in particular company laws. No doubt the majority of them do just this, but the laws they respect are national laws which are not framed so as to ensure the responsiveness of a parent company to the foreign local communities where its subsidiaries may be operating.

Thus the total control of a subsidiary guaranteed a parent by a 51 per cent, or indeed minority, shareholding, is not matched by the absolute financial commitment of the multinational group as a whole to the subsidiary. Profits are distributed as the parent decides. Investment strategy is planned as the parent decides. Local employment prospects are ultimately determined by central management. Given such unlimited power, and the unified group management which makes its exercise possible, the EEC Commission is pushing for an offsetting extension of group liability. This, complains the multinational business world, is like driving a coach and horses through the very basis of traditional capitalism, namely limited liability. At the same time, however, the very existence of the multinational has undermined the notion of economic independence for supposedly legally-independent subsidiaries. The parent company is not acting primarily in the interests of the individual subsidiary, and the shareholder of the central company certainly has no illusions about the legal independence of individual member companies. He knows what everyone else knows, but what laws still fail to recognise, that the multinational is a single, unified entity, capable of rapidly switching resources from one foreign affiliate to another — indeed, it is exactly this flexibility which makes the MNC so attractive to the investor.

Throughout the 1980s, companies should expect the EEC to be in the forefront of international attempts to right this judicial omission. The new liabilities which the Commission's draft proposal on corporate groups seeks to assign to the parent company cover guarantees for creditors, workers and minority shareholders of subsidiaries. Minority shareholders, for example, would have the option of being bought out at legally determined 'fair rates', or otherwise be guaranteed a fair dividend return, notably by linking local dividends to consolidated group profits. Local subsidiary creditors should, according to prevalent EEC thinking, have recourse to group assets — in other words multinationals should be ready to cover local foreign debts with central collateral. Meanwhile, employees, who are treated by EEC company law on an equal footing with shareholders and creditors, should also be afforded special protection by increasing the financial liability of the parent to the local workforce, e.g. by setting up a special contingency fund for redundancies. Moreover, a subsidiary possessing a greater degree of employee participation in its decision-making bodies should, maintains the EEC company law department, be legally empowered to refuse the instructions of central management — a notion unlikely to win the EEC many corporate friends in the USA. This confirms once again the close link between EEC company and labour laws — a relationship further exemplified by proposals for a European company statute which, like the themes contained in the 'ninth' directive, will be under debate in the EEC's policy-making institutions in the 1980s.

(iii) Corporate disclosure and tax exposure

The 1980s should also witness the implementation in EEC member states of new measures designed to revamp the public, and particularly the financial, accountability of multinational companies in Europe. Here the leading contenders for corporate attention in the coming years are the EEC's emerging rules on consolidated financial reporting and on tax evasion. And here again, the EEC is driving home a by-now familiar message: governments can no longer treat notionally independent companies as actually independent for reporting purposes or fiscally at 'arm's length' when in fact they are part of a group pursuing a single collective policy, usually multinationally.

The EEC's so-called 'seventh' directive,[40] which should be agreed by 1983 at the latest, is in the forefront of the European charge for greater 'transparency' — a jargon word which has now spread, together with EEC influence, to other arenas seeking to exercise public control of MNCs, notably the OECD and the United Nations. The greatest impact of the measure, on which intergovernmental negotiations first started back in 1978, looks likely to be on multinationals headquartered in mainland Europe, as well as on non-European firms with inadequate or non-existent requirements on consolidated accounts. The directive's major requirement will be worldwide consolidation for any multinational corporation with significant operations in the European Community. In other words, in common with the Vredeling initiative, the new EEC rule on international accounting will be extraterritorial in impact.

European obligations for worldwide consolidation should, paradoxically, work to the advantage of publicly-held American multinationals who already have to meet similar requirements laid down by the US Securities and Exchange Commission. But if there is little change for such firms, the opposite is true for the large privately-held American concerns, sometimes personally and inevitably secretly run. Besides a few American examples of this, Japanese business, with its growing investment stake in the European Community, looks like being much more exposed than hitherto. More importantly, the same applies to German, French and Italian firms and Luxembourg holding companies — indeed companies in virtually all the mainland EEC countries. No great effort, for example, is needed to imagine why Luxembourg, with its concentration of international holding companies, has been an inveterate opponent of the 'seventh' directive. All EEC countries, apart from the UK, Ireland, Denmark and the Netherlands, currently have little or no legal requirements for or practice of consolidation. The impact on companies headquartered in them can thus be expected to be significant.

Another main prong of the EEC's push for greater information on multinationals is taxation policy, including moves to combat abuse of transfer pricing carried out between affiliated companies in different tax territories. 'Tax evaders!' has been a favourite accusation thrown at multinationals by their critics and, indeed, according to the EEC MNC policy programme, 'the area of taxation probably best reveals the inadequacy of nationally-devised systems for tackling the phenomenon of the growth of multinational companies'.[41] That said, the EEC itself, with its collection of different national tax territories, systems and rates, paradoxically provides the major incentive to multinational tax evasion. But removal of these disparities through a tax harmonisation programme initiated by the EEC in the mid-1970s seems a long, long way off. It would be surprising indeed if the continued opposition to such moves both from the European Parliament and jealously sovereign member states allowed any significant progress before the end of the 1980s.

In the meantime, attempts by MNCs to locate profits in the most favourable European tax territories will understandably continue, and the only potential legal constraint on their doing so abusively — apart from an existing network of bilateral agreements between individual EEC countries — is the EEC's 'mutual assistance directive'.[42] This seeks to increase the multilateral flow of information between the tax authorities of EEC member states so as to stop 'the artificial transfer of profits within groups of undertakings', and possibly draw up rules which could ultimately form part of an EEC transfer pricing code.

Conclusion and outlook

'The future of the free enterprise system . . . will be shaped to a significant extent by the public's perception of whether it is accountable to rational, objective decision-makers who are acting according to publicly acceptable norms.'[43] The source of that remark is not Mr Henk Vredeling, the man who gave his name to the controversial EEC proposals on worker consultation in multinationals, but Harold M. Williams, chairman of the American Securities and Exchange Commission. What is true of the need to accommodate public perceptions of big business in the USA is doubly true in Western Europe where the norms, or rules, that are being drawn up reflect political and social traditions quite distinct from those prevalent in North America.

This is particularly true of EEC legislation, proposed or enacted, which seeks to flesh out the skeletal notion of public accountability as it applies to big business. Lumped together, the European Community's proposals and directives detailed earlier in this chapter constitute a democratic challenge which the multinational business world operating in the Community cannot ignore.

There are of course nuances in this challenge, and the challenge itself needs to be put into perspective. In the field of labour law, for example, the EEC authorities may consider whether the democratic control of business is better achieved by the worker participation approach, i.e. by involvement of employees in the decision-making machinery of the corporation, rather than via the Vredeling proposals, which seek such control from outside the company's decision-making structures. During the 1980s, both international business and the European trade union movement may have to trim back the more extreme of their positions on these issues. Just as the trade unions may have to lower their ambitions on EEC-legislated union consultation rights, so multinational business cannot maintain its outright opposition to the Vredeling initiative and at the same time hope to stem the tide flowing in favour of enterprise-level industrial democracy.

The economic crisis, certain to persist throughout the bulk of the 1980s, may brake the over-rapid advance of progress on European Community labour and company legislation, as EEC countries begin to count its cost in investment terms. The same factor, however, could also produce a quite different outcome. Of the four major EEC member states, France appears to be seriously embarked on a socialist experiment for at least half the coming decade; Germany, irrespective of its government, has industrial democracy writ deep into its national legal traditions; the post-war grip of the Christian Democrats in Italy appears to be slackening; while the development in the United Kingdom of centrist politics combined with the generalised unpopularity of strident monetarism could well lead to British governments in the mid-1980s being more favourable to a review of the company's responsibilities to society.

Notes and references

1   Proposal outlined in full, Appendix 1(h).

2   Proposal made 9 October 1972, emerged from consideration by the European Parliament in 1982.
3   Proposal for a seventh directive in the field of EEC company law, May 1976. See this chapter, p.67.
4   Draft proposal, yet to be agreed by the EEC Commission; see this chapter, p.65.
5   The West's governments adopted the OECD Guidelines for Multinational Enterprises in June 1976.
6   See this chapter, p.50.
7   According to the EEC fifth medium-term economic plan (1980–85), annual growth rates of around 2 per cent through the middle of the 1980s are the best that can be hoped for (see *European Economy*, no.9, July 1981). Such rates are insufficient to stem the growth in unemployment let alone cut it back.
8   'Vive les Multinationales' by J.K. Galbraith in *L'Expansion*, January 1979, pp. 71–6.
9   'Free Enterprise in a Free Society', address by Harold M. Williams (Chairman, US Securities and Exchange Commission), 1 February 1980, Dallas, Texas.
10   See UNICE's (the EEC Employers' Organisation) opinion on the 'Vredeling initiative', termed 'totally unacceptable'. (14 January 1981).
11   For the American Chamber of Commerce in Belgium, the 'Vredeling initiative' is 'ill-advised' (letter to EEC Commissioner Etienne Davignon, 23 September 1980). For the NFTC (22 December 1980), the 'Vredeling initiative' would 'impair competitiveness' and 'introduce extraterritorial conflicts between EC Member States and their industrial trading partners'. For other adverse US business reactions, see articles appearing in the American press in October 1981, e.g. *Journal of Commerce*, New York, 28 October 1981 'US Multinational Companies concerned about EC proposals'.
12   (a) EEC directive on worker protection in the case of mass dismissals, adopted February 1975 and scheduled to come into force since 1977; (b) EEC directive on worker protection following changes in company ownership, adopted February 1977, in force since 1979.
13   Source: American Chamber of Commerce in Belgium. NB Pullback of MNC headquarters not to be confused with the continued and rapidly increasing presence in Brussels of American companies' EEC-monitoring operations.
14   Workers having the right to only minority board representation.
15   Clearly expressed by leaders of European business at the European Management Symposium, Davos, February 1980.
16   Source: material made available by EEC company law department.
17   'Free Enterprise in a Free Society', Williams.

18   See Multinational Service, no.3, Background Document, 16 February 1977.
19   Ibid.
20   'Employee Participation', British Institute of Management, May 1981. (The phrase 'Trojan Bullock' is an allusion to the Bullock Report, commissioned by the UK government, on employee participation.)
21   Institute of Personnel Management.
22   Rapport du Comité d'étude pour la réforme de l'entreprise, Paris, February 1975.
23   See OECD Guidelines for Multinational Enterprises, Appendix II(b) — particularly paragraph 9 of guideline on employment and industrial relations.
24   The French Communist labour organisation.
25   The emergence of the Social Democratic Party/Liberal alliance in 1981.
26   See particularly Mr Levinson's 'Vodka–Cola' (Stock, Paris, 1978).
27   'Multinational Undertakings and the European Community', op. cit., p.10.
28   Mr Jenkins' address to the ETUC Congress, Munich, Germany, 15 May 1979.
29   'European Action Programme — Multinational Groups of Companies', ETUC, Brussels, 10 June 1977. See also Appendix I.
30   See note 12.
31   Greece, which joined the EEC 1 January 1981, should be joined by Spain and Portugal in the mid-1980s.
32   Begun in 1981.
33   See Article 8 of Vredeling proposals, Appendix I(h).
34   The so-called 'fifth' company law directive — for details, see note 35.
35   9 October 1972 proposal which emerged in its amended form from consideration by the European Parliament in 1982.
36   Amended proposal for a European Company Statute, May 1975.
37   Published in the 'Bulletin of the European Communities', Supplement 8/75.
38   A major body of Christian Democrat thinking is not inimical to industrial democracy.
39   Yet to be submitted to the Commission.
40   The EEC's 'seventh' directive — on consolidated accounting for groups of companies — is the follow-up to the 'fourth' directive, adopted by the EEC in July 1978, which stipulates harmonised accounts for subsidiary companies.
41   'Multinational Undertakings and the European Community', see Appendix I(a).

42   The EEC directive 'concerning mutual assistance by the competent authorities of the Member States in the field of direct taxation' was adopted 19 December 1977. Also to be mentioned in this context is the EEC Resolution on Tax Evasion, adopted by the Council of Ministers, February 1975.

43   'Free Enterprise in a Free Society', Williams.

6 Europe's capitalist challenge to multinationals

Introduction

Undoubtedly Europe's most incisive cutting-edge for controlling abuses of economic power by international business is vested in the EEC's fast maturing anti-trust policy. Unsurprisingly, it is the area which arouses most concern at least among sophisticated multinationals operating in the EEC because, although not specifically targeted at MNCs, Common Market trust-busters, by the EEC's very transnational nature, find themselves scrutinising allegations of multinational mis-behaviour. Companies like Hoffmann Laroche, United Brands, the Continental Group, not to mention household names from the Japanese industry like Pioneer (hi-fi) and Kawasaki (motor-bikes), have all crossed swords — sometimes at great financial and public relations' expense — with the European Community's small but ambitious and independently-operating team of competition watchdogs. More recently the activities of IBM have come to be a major focus of the European Commission's anti-trust force. Yet, paradoxically, it is a policy area extensively ignored by many in big business who should know better, but which MNCs will only continue to neglect at their peril during the 1980s. There are sure signs now that, as the new decade begins, European anti-trust is poised to move from tentative infancy to aggressive adolescence.

Big business may feel understandably aggrieved that in Europe it faces not just a stepped-up democratic challenge to its freedom of manoeuvre but also the burgeoning power of the classical weapon of good capitalist discipline, namely anti-trust — inspired by American economic practice rather than European social tradition. Business, in a sense, gets the worst of both worlds. Thus, multinationals, peering edgily into the European future, can view with concern the paradox of the twin EEC developments of socially progressive measures which are gradually eroding the traditional basis of capitalist company law and, in strange parallel, the growing assertion of the capitalist market ethic via a no-nonsense Community competition policy coming complete with all the dramatic anti-trust paraphernalia, ranging from dawn raids on company premises to fines, sometimes in the multi-million dollar bracket, for offending companies.

European anti-trust, with its dual thrust against cartelisation and monopolies, is often considered a technical subject of arcane complexity — wrongly so. It is in fact a politically-motivated power-drill forcing business into increased economic accountability. Particularly as it affects multinationals, it starts from the clear assumption that economic power must be subject to economic rules drawn up and executed by political authorities. Nothing controversial, perhaps, in that. More controversial, however, is the way this premise has become politically embroidered by the belief, expressed by the European Commission in its memo on multinationals,[1] in 'the growing hold of multinational undertakings on the economic social and even political life of the countries in which they operate' — a hold which gives rise to 'deep anxieties' in areas like competition. In other words, the European Commission, which in EEC anti-trust matters has a much greater margin of independent power than in other policy areas, sees corporate 'bigness' as a political threat to European society at large via the incidence of its power in the market place. Sheer size, and not just the abuses perpetrated by sizeable companies, is increasingly seen as a no-no by European anti-trusters. And, in the accumulation of size — and power — multinationals are out on their own. As the Commission puts it, 'most multinational undertakings are of considerable size and control substantial sections of markets. They are more able than other companies to restrict competition and to abuse dominant positions'.[2] Moreover, sympathy with this view has also been expressed both by the European Parliament and a delegation of the US Congress which, in jointly calling for 'intensive cooperation between anti-trust authorities of the United States and the European Community', claimed that multinational enterprises 'frequently have technical or financial advantages over their competitors, giving them a certain position of power'.[3]

Focus on multinationals as EEC policy strengthens

Before analysing the EEC's anti-trust crusade against multinational business abuse, and indeed against corporate size itself, it is as well to explain the context in which its emerging power is developing so dramatically. For not only is anti-trust a major spearhead of EEC multinationals' control policy, but its development in the coming decade will outstrip advances in the world's other major anti-trust theatres, notably the USA. In particular, American companies operating in Europe will no longer be able to consider the European Community as a kind of international soft option in the matter of good capitalist discipline. Japanese firms, which operate from a home country where many standard notions of Western anti-trust appear to have little impact, will also find life hard — and increasingly expensive — if they continue to ride roughshod into European markets in the unsophisticated manner shown by some of their leading firms in recent years.[4] EEC companies, meanwhile, have yet to come to terms with the competitive requirements imposed on them by Community anti-trust law — an American invention grafted as late as 1958 onto deep-seated European economic traditions. The same remark applies even more strongly to enterprises from other West European countries, notably Switzerland and Sweden.[5]

Economic accountability required by EEC anti-trust will increase more rapidly than in the USA, as EEC trust-busters use the case law built up in the late 1970s to strengthen their control powers in the 1980s. This emerging power has passed largely unnoticed by international business. EEC policy has started from a much later base than US anti-trust where the first laws were voted in 1890 and begun really to bite post World War I, while European competition policy has been around for only 20 years[6] and, understandably, has a lot of growing up to do quickly. Thus, unlike the USA, where almost a century of anti-trust tradition and practice have done much to eliminate cartels and monopolies, EEC competition watchdogs are only too aware of the leeway to make up in Europe, noting 'the relative abundance in the EEC of cartelisation discovered, under investigation or suspected, as compared to the USA'.[7] Table 6.1 shows the acute nature of concentration prevalent in a variety of European markets.

At the same time, the impact of Europe-wide competition policy has begun to outstrip that of national anti-trust bodies like West Germany's Bundeskartelamt and the UK's Monopolies Commission and Office of Fair Trading. The reasons for this are not difficult to unravel. The massive increases in international economic penetration triggered by the post-war world boom and specifically encouraged in Europe by the signing in 1958 of the Rome Treaty, have increased the number of multinational firms, making the context of their competitive behaviour multinational rather than national. As a result, abuses of economic power tend increasingly to have a multinational dimension, in particular a directly adverse effect on trade between countries — one of the great taboos of Common Market competition policy. To the extent that such abuses lie beyond the scope of purely national anti-trust bodies, the EEC has gradually assumed greater importance as a breaker of trusts and a shield against monopoly sharp practices. Indeed, the primacy of the EEC over national anti-trust authorities is now clearly established. And multinationals, or at least multinationally-rigged abuses, are the *sine qua non* of European anti-trust power. It is not surprising, therefore, that multinationals are its major if not exclusive target.

Independence and rapidity of EEC anti-trust

In assessing the likely impact of the EEC's powers to bring multi-nationals to book for economic wrong-doing, two further factors should be stressed — the European Commission's margin for independent action in the execution of EEC competition policy, and the surprising rapidity of the Community's anti-trust procedure, at least in cases involving private sector firms. The relative speed of action is surprising particularly for those familiar with the usual plodding pace of EEC activity in most other policy areas, where administrative and political delays have been fused into a fine diplomatic art. Indeed, both in terms of its political independence and procedural rapidity, Community anti-trust compares favourably with its counterpart in the USA.

These two characteristics — independence and rapidity — are linked, and in some ways make the EEC, despite its minute enforcement staff, as formidable an adversary to international business as the USA's public watchdogs, the US Department of Justice and the Foreign Trade Commission. Indeed, these American bodies have legal and enforcement staffs which make the small band of EEC anti-trust lawyers appear like the Town Clerk's department of a medium-sized municipality. For all that, European anti-trust power has the advantage of being concentrated exclusively in the hands of a single EEC policy department, and not dispersed in a variety of bodies as in the USA. Beyond that, the comparison with American anti-trust is above all a contrast of systems, the essentially administrative process of EEC anti-trust contrasting sharply — especially in Anglo-Saxon eyes — with the 'due process' (and lengthy delays) in the US system. In addition, for all the much-vaunted independence of American anti-trust, executive control over nominations to the great branches of American government, including the Department of Justice, is such that a pro-business President, such as Ronald Reagan, can appoint high officials likely to be sympathetic to corporate concerns.[8] In other words, the degree of actual impact of public US anti-trust policy on the business world can be politically responsive. That said, a large measure of independence from political influence is ensured in the American system by private plaintiff actions and the inherent threat to offending companies of triple damage suits — a sanction not present in the EEC.

Yet despite this, and the existence of certain conditioning factors, the EEC anti-trust authority, at least in its dealings with private enterprise,[9] enjoys a large measure of operating independence. First, anti-trust decisions, applying the EEC Treaties or their implementing legislation, are taken directly by the European Commission, the EEC's executive authority, or indeed directly by the EEC's competition Commissioner himself. These decisions can only be appealed against in one final tribunal, the EEC's Court of Justice in Luxembourg, and do not have to run the usual Community gauntlet of Common Market member governments sitting in the Council of Ministers. Freed from such political fetters, the European Commission is thus a vastly different proposition in the field of anti-trust than in any other sphere of EEC economic and political activity. True, the personality of the Commissioner in political charge of EEC anti-trust[10] may have its effect on the enforcement and other decisions taken by his department — above all perhaps, on the speed with which they are taken — but, whatever his political persuasion, he can be expected to have a vested interest in developing the application of the policy instruments at his disposal, and making his presence felt on the European scene. His main motivation, and in this he will have the backing of his 13 fellow members of the Commission, is the maintenance of the unity of the 10-nation Common Market against attempts by international business to carve it up into isolate national 'pockets' for reasons of private profit.

At the same time, however, broader political considerations can occasionally dilute the application of EEC anti-trust to the private sector. Thus, in hard-hit sectors like chemicals and steel, economic emergency has pushed the EEC into supporting, or at least tolerating, cartelisation. Davignon's steel plan in the late 1970s and his synthetic fibres cartel (1978) are two good examples of this trend. However, such tampering with normal market rules does not reflect the European Commission's pro-business concern so much as a strategic commitment to buttressing a European industrial base. This strategic aim is not necessarily shared by multinationals who, especially if headquartered outside the Community, often see the 'Europeanist' influence in EEC anti-trust and industrial policies operating against their interests.[11] Moreover, as in the case of the EEC synthetic fibres cartel, US companies, such as Dupont and Monsanto, could not in any case be party to such an arrangement without coming into almost certain conflict with US anti-trust rules.

In other words, EEC anti-trust policy towards the private sector operates by and large free of political conditioning factors or, where such factors do come into play, they tend to be such as to weight it against foreign business, i.e. multinationals controlled from outside the Community, often with no indigenous political protector in the EEC. And a further factor causing frustration among the foreign community doing business in the Common Market is the little that EEC competition policy has done to date — in stark contrast with its posture towards the private sector — to control the competitive sharp practices perpetrated by Europe's member governments in providing discriminatory support of their nationalised enterprises, which are increasingly seen as multinationals as subsidised rivals on national and international markets. This fear of *de facto* discrimination against multinationals increases in direct relation to the steady growth of the public sector of the European economy, and the manifest inclination of the Community's competition watch-dogs to trim private cartels and monopolies rather than act against public trusts or other forms of anti-competitive practices carried out with governmental collusion or as a result of public policy. Signs that this imbalance may be being corrected are not promising.[12]

Companies, particularly foreign multinationals, must expect to bear the brunt of EEC anti-trust policy, and they must also watch out for its relative speed of action. Here the contrast with the long drawn-out and often unwieldy American anti-trust procedure is marked. Not for the EEC the multi-level court structures of the American system, with appeals, counter-appeals, etc., possible at every stage in the judicial process. Once an EEC decision has been taken — an administrative rather than a judicial decision — appeal is possible to one tribunal only: the European Court of Justice in Luxembourg, whose decision is final.

The Court is, in fact, the only real constraint on the European Commission's otherwise independent authority in this highly business-sensitive field, but companies should not derive too much consolation even from this apparent constraint. For although the Court will certainly crack down sharply against the Commission if there are any demonstrable legal flaws in its arguments, its basic commitment is to European integration and to the furtherance and strengthening of policies likely to bolster such integration. Moreover, on occasion,[13] the Court has made clear its intention of actually building up the base from which the Commission can conduct its offensive against big business abuses. Indeed, particularly as regards anti-monopoly legislation, it is not too much to say that, between them, the two EEC institutions, the Commission and the Court, have in the years since 1973 created a framework for combating big business abuses which is even broader than American monopolies legislation.[14]

Private monopolies: the EEC's emerging power

The 1980s promise to be a decade of unprecedented EEC activity against both industrial size and its abuse. European trust-busters will be on the hunt not just for wayward monopolists but also possibly for oligopolists — small numbers of large firms which, between them, dominate specific European markets. With the experience and case law built up in recent years — most spectacularly in the actions against multinationals like American companies United Brands (foodstuffs) and the Continental Group (packaging), and Swiss pharmaceutical giant Hoffmann La Roche — the Community's competition policy staff is now poised for a much more general and confident onslaught against market dominance and its anti-competitive exploitation than it has hitherto been able to undertake. Initial proceedings begun against IBM, the undisputed leader of the strategically key data-processing industry, confirm this new-found determination.[15]

Of importance in assessing the likely scope of this European challenge to big business is the EEC's officially-voiced anxiety at 'the long-term growth of oligopoly: in the various markets, the number of firms operating has shown a steady and striking fall'[16] over the ten years 1970–80. Sectors such as chemicals, oil, aluminium, electronics, motor manufacturing, aircraft and shipbuilding are just a few of the areas identified by anti-trust officials as oligopolies or oligopoly-tending. In addition, firms like Coca Cola, IBM, General Foods, Nestlé, Unilever, Kodak, Thomson-Brandt and H.J. Heinz — to name but a small sample — have all been identified by the EEC Commission as enjoying shares of key European markets above that already identified by the Court of Justice as potentially constituting dominance, and thus are a particular focus of interest for Common Market watchdogs; see table 6.1.

Article 86: the EEC's holy writ on monopolies

The EEC's bible for prospective monopolists and officials of sector-dominant companies is Article 86 of the Rome Treaty, worth quoting in full here because of its brevity and importance:

Any abuse by one or more undertakings of a dominant position within the common market or in a substantial part of it shall be prohibited as incompatible with the common market in so far as it may affect trade between Member States.

Such abuse may, in particular, consist in:

(a) directly or indirectly imposing unfair purchase or selling prices or other unfair trading conditions;

(b) limiting production, markets or technical development to the prejudice of consumers;

(c) applying dissimilar conditions to equivalent transactions with other trading parties, thereby placing them at a competitive disadvantage;

(d) making the conclusion of contracts subject to acceptance by the other parties of supplementary obligations which, by their nature or according to commercial usage, have no connection with the subject of such contracts.

A point of significance is that the EEC Commission — with the Court of Justice as its only ultimate constraint — can prosecute not just abuses by individually dominant companies but also by oligopolies ('one or more undertakings'). The fact that the EEC has yet to use its powers against oligopolies should not be interpreted as an absolute reluctance to do so but rather by reference to the priority put by EEC trust-busters on first establishing the case-law basis for action against individual instances of dominance, a process which has gradually moved towards completion in a very short space of time, namely the eight years since the Continental Can judgement was given in early 1973.

A further point is that, while Article 86 provides the basis for EEC anti-monopoly action, it is not exhaustive. It can be — and has been — built on in the last eight years, thus providing the Commission with a broader base for sanctioning anti-competitive behaviour by large firms in the future. Three developments are particularly important in this respect. Probably the most spectacular is the assertion, backed by the Court, that attainment of dominance — monopolisation in US anti-trust jargon — can itself be considered an abuse if achieved by external growth, i.e. a company achieving monopoly or dominant status via acquisition (merger, take-over, controlling shareholding, etc.). The second is that the level of what, for EEC anti-trust purposes, constitutes dominance has been set as low as 45 per cent of a given market, and could be further lowered. The third is the rapid extension of the types of company behaviour — over and above those mentioned explicitly in Article 86 — which can be considered illegal if carried out by a dominant company.

These three major developments were thrown up by three key anti-monopoly actions undertaken by the EEC in the 1970s, involving respectively the Continental Group, United Brands and Hoffman La Roche — all major multinationals controlled from outside the EEC. A thumbnail sketch of these cases — important for the emerging profile of European anti-trust in the 1980s, is given below. To be noted in particular is the 'creative interpretation' of the Court of the Commission's powers which have been reinforced — rather than restrained — by the Court's exercise of judicial 'control'.

(a) Continental Can

The Court's judgement in February 1973 — the first major one in an Article 86 case — established two main bases for the extension of EEC anti-trust powers, namely:

> — a dominant company commits an abuse if it seeks to extend its dominance by external acquisition (what EEC jargon calls 'structural behaviour') as opposed to internal growth. In deciding this, the Court seemed to edge EEC anti-trust powers towards equality with those traditionally practised in US anti-trust law, namely that the process of monopolisation (as distinct from abuse of a monopoly position) is illegal, i.e. the acquisition of undue corporate size is bad. By pinpointing a type of illegal behaviour not specifically mentioned in Article 86, the Court explicitly broadened its scope. This scope was further to be enlarged by the Hoffman La Roche case (see below) and to a lesser extent in the case against American multinational Commercial Solvents, on which the Court gave judgement in March 1974. In the latter case, the Court declared that a dominant company's refusal to supply a customer also directly contravened Article 86.

> — a dominant company can commit an abuse by behaving in such a way as to restrict competition even if its behaviour has only an indirect effect on competition, and could be legally copied by a firm which was not in a dominant position.

(b) United Brands

The Court upheld in February 1978 the vast majority of the Commission's arguments (and confirmed a fine against the US multinational amounting to approximately one million dollars), and established a definition of dominance as it related to United Brands (the Commission had failed to get Court agreement on this in the Continental Can case), and showed that dominance could be defined at quantitatively lower levels than had previously been thought possible. More particularly, the United Brands judgement made it clear:

— that while there was no simple test of what constituted a dominant position, it could be proved by reference to a variety of factors. In the UB case, the Court outlined three: the characteristics of the allegedly dominant company; the degree of competition in the relevant market by reference to the market share of the company in relation to that of its principal competitors; the behaviour of the allegedly dominant company in relation to the market and its competitors;

— that the threshold of dominance could be as low as 45 per cent of the relevant market, a decision that was greeted with universal (if obviously private) dismay by executives of large MNCs operating in Europe. (For analogous, although not absolutely identical purposes, British legislation has used a 25 per cent threshold.)

(c)   Hoffman La Roche

The new ground broken by the United Brands case in both qualitatively and quantitatively defining a dominant position was matched only a year later in February 1979 when the Hoffman La Roche judgement significantly increased the types of behaviour to be considered illegal by companies so defined. Continuing and vastly expanding the trend begun with Continental Can and Commercial Solvents, the Hoffman judgement:

— specifically condemned fidelity rebates as an abuse under Article 86, which had not explicitly listed this behaviour;

— more generally, however, appeared to extend Article 86's scope on a very broad basis. In a key section of its judgement, the Court stated a position which came close to saying that any anticompetitive or exclusionary practice was indictable under Article 86.[17]

The battle against size: outlook 1990

The upshot of the major developments of the 1970s, especially when taken in conjunction with the high levels of concentrated market power the Commission has identified in many sectors, seems to point in one direction only: acceleration of EEC action against both the attainment and the abuse of corporate size in the coming decade; see table 6.1. This prediction has in fact been buttressed by the announcement in late 1980 that the Commission, after five years of detailed preparation, is embarking on its most testing case yet, that against IBM.

Put simply, the European anti-trust threat to big business, and in particular to big international business, is that the EEC has acquired powers to attack a vastly increased number of firms for types of behaviour which were not considered illegal at the start of the 1970s. For instance, with dominance now set as low as 45 per cent of a given market (United Brands), with the possibility that it could be set even lower, and with attainment of market dominance by acquisition now considered a competitive abuse (Continental Can), the leeway for external growth by a long list of companies in a cross-section of European markets is now virtually nil. From a list drawn up by the Commission in 1977 emerge 112 cases of companies enjoying a more than 45 per cent share of various markets. Moreover the list is far from exhaustive, being only a 'small sample' according to the Commission. But it provides a good outline of the extended scope of the EEC's battle against size, and is reproduced below (table 6.1).

In other words, thanks to the Court's action on Continental Can and United Brands, the EEC now has the basis for an extended merger control authority. The Commission has in fact sought to achieve such powers through new legislation,[18] but its proposals for a new legislated EEC merger control authority — made in 1973 — have run into tough opposition from member state governments, particularly Italy's, ever since. (These proposals seek to compel notification of any mergers or take-overs resulting in a combined turnover in excess of 1,000 million units of account (around 1,250 million US dollars at 1973 US/u.a. conversion rates).) But now the Commission looks set to achieve by case law and precedents supported by the Court what it has failed to do by legislation. The way is now open for EEC control of takeovers which, if not as explicitly founded as its authority over mergers in the coal and steel sectors,[19] could prove to be nonetheless effective for that.

Moreover, following the Hoffman La Roche case, the regulatory web facing companies on the Commission's monopolies' list (see table 6.1) — and others in similar positions of market power — extends beyond merger control to scrutiny of virtually any type of anti-competitive behaviour. Here again, Article 86 has been turned into an incisive weapon for cutting back any form of behaviour likely to restrict competition, not just exploitation of market power. In this important area of business control, the scope of EEC anti-trust extends far beyond that vested in the US competition authorities by the Sherman Act, whose monopolies section is limited to sanctioning the creation of monopolies (monopolisation) rather than the competitive behaviour of firms in monopoly positions. The margin for the slightest deviation from good competitive behaviour by dominant firms in the EEC has,

Table 6.1
List of markets where the market leader holds 45 per cent or more of the total national market
(based on a small sample of the products and countries in these markets)

Ranking	C_1 (%)	Market	Industry	Country	Year	Brand leader or market leader
1	86	Sugar	ALI	DK	1975	De danske sukkerfabrikker
2	> 85	Cola beverages	ALI	B	1976	Coca-Cola
2	> 85	Spirits	ALI	DK	1976	
2	85	Beer	ALI	DK	1975	United Breweries
2	85	Threads for needlework	TEX	F	1973	Dollfus Mieg
2	85	Chewing gum	ALI	F	1972	General Foods
7	84	Electric coffee machines	ELE	F	1975	Moulinex
8	82	Unworked filter paper	PAP	B	1975	Intermills
9	> 80	Refrigerators and freezers	ELE	F	1974	Thomson-Brandt
9	80	Dishwashers	ELE	F	1974	Thomson-Brandt
9	80	Hairdryers	ELE	F	1975	Moulinex
9	80	Cotton sewing threads	TEX	F	1973	Dollfus Mieg
9	80	Automobile ignition systems	TRA	D	1974	Bosch
9	80	Floor detergent powders	CHI	I	1976	Spic-Span (Procter & Gamble)
9	80	White rum	ALI	UK	1974	Bacardi-Bass Charrington
16	75	Jute yarn and fabrics	TEX	F	1972	Agache-Willot
16	75	Concentrated milk, unsweetened	ALI	F	1972	Gloria (Carnation)
16	75	Baby foods	ALI	DK	1975	Nestlé
16	75	Sparking plugs (as originally fitted)	TRA	I	1974	Marelli
20	74	Coffee grinders	ELE	F	1975	Moulinex
21	73	Frozen foods	ALI	I	1973	Sages
22	72	Cine film (8, super 8, etc.)	CHI	UK	1973	Kodak
23	71	Still films	CHI	UK	1973	Kodak
24	> 70	Non-barbiturate sedatives	PHA	UK	1973	Roche
24	70	Chocolate powders	ALI	F	1972	Poulain
24	70	Breakfast cereals (flakes)	ALI	F	1972	Kellogg
24	70	Milk powder	ALI	UK	1973	Cadbury Schweppes
24	70	Dog and cat food	ALI	F	1972	Mars (Unisabi)
24	70	Instant coffee	ALI	F	1972	Nestlé
24	70	Condensed milk	ALI	F	1972	Lait Mont Blanc
24	70	Tranquillisers	PHA	NL	1973	
24	70	Sulphite paper	PAP	B	1974	Denayer
33	69	Detergent for dishwashers	CHI	I	1976	Finish (Soilax)
34	67	Margarine	ALI	UK	1973	Van der Bergh & Jurgens
34	67	Detergent powders	CHI	UK	1975	Unilever
36	66	Canned spaghetti, etc.	ALI	UK	1973	H.J. Heinz
37	65	Kraft paper and the like	PAP	I	1972	Imports
37	65	Newsprint	PAP	B	1975	Imports
37	65	Vermouth	ALI	UK	1974	Martini
37	65	Corrugated board	PAP	B	1974	Imports
37	65	Sparking plugs (replacements market)	TRA	UK	1975	Champion
42	63	Car batteries (as originally fitted)	TRA	I	1972	Marelli
43	61	Frozen foods	ALI	UK	1973	Unilever
44	> 60	Stationery	PAP	UK	1972	Dickinson-Robinson Group
44	> 60	Other hypertensive drugs	PHA	UK	1973	MSD
44	60	Bulbs and lamps for motor vehicles	TRA	D	1974	Osram

Table 6.1 (cont.)

Ranking	C_1 (%)	Market	Industry	Country	Year	Brand leader or market leader
44	60	Margarines, oils & edible fats	ALI	D	1974	Unilever
44	60	Puffed cereals	ALI	F	1972	Kellogg
44	60	Whisky	ALI	UK	1974	Distillers
44	60	Canned soups	ALI	UK	1973	H.J. Heinz
44	60	Dietetic products & baby foods	ALI	F	1972	Fali
44	60	Dried potato powder	ALI	F	1972	Nestlé
44	60	Margarine	ALI	F	1972	Astra-Calvé
44	60	Canned meats	ALI	I	1973	Simmenthal
44	60	Sparking plugs	TRA	D	1974	Bosch
44	60	Malted beverages	ALI	F	1972	Sopad-Nestlé
57	58	Edible oils	ALI	F	1972	Groupe Lesieur
57	58	Processed cheese	ALI	F	1972	Bel
59	57	Prepared potatoes	ALI	D	1974	Pfanni-Werk
59	57	Car tyres	TRA	F	1975	Michelin
59	57	Analgesics	PHA	DK	1972	The Danish Pharmacies
59	57	Powered scythes	MAC	I	1974	BCS
63	56	Board from recycled paper	PAP	B	1975	Imports
63	56	General-purpose computers	MAC	I	1973	IBM
65	55	Soups	ALI	D	1974	Maggi
65	55	Milk powder	ALI	F	1972	France-Lait
65	55	Instant chocolate drinks	ALI	F	1972	Nestlé
65	55	Canned soups	ALI	F	1972	Liebig
65	55	Mustard and condiments	ALI	F	1972	Générale Alimentaire (Cavenham—UK)
65	55	Mopeds and scooters 50 cc	TRA	I	1972	Piaggio
65	55	Canned prepared beans	ALI	UK	1973	Heinz
65	55	Lining materials	TEX	F	1972	Dollfus, Mieg & Cie
65	55	Newsprint	PAP	F	1974	Imports
74	54	Sugar	ALI	UK	1973	Tate & Lyle
75	53	Tranquillisers	PHA	DK	1972	Dumex
76	> 52	General-purpose computers	MAC	UK	1973	IBM
76	> 52	General-purpose computers	MAC	D	1973	IBM
76	52	Car batteries (as originally fitted)	TRA	UK	1975	Lucas
79	51	Electric cookers	ELE	DK	1973	Ernst Voss
80	> 50	Cola beverages	ALI	NL	1974	Coca-Cola
80	> 50	Slimming preparations	PHA	UK	1973	
80	> 50	Refrigerators	ELE	I	1973	Zanussi
80	> 50	Anti-angina drugs	PHA	UK	1973	ICI
80	> 50	'Plain-skin' hormones	PHA	UK	1973	Glaxo
80	> 50	Tranquillisers	PHA	UK	1973	Roche
80	50	Tinned salmon	ALI	UK	1973	John West
80	50	Flax yarn	TEX	F	1972	Agache-Willot
80	50	Dietetic food preparations	ALI	I	1973	Plasmon
80	50	Precooked meals	ALI	F	1972	Buitoni-Perugina
80	50	Chocolate biscuits	ALI	UK	1973	United Biscuits
80	50	Crisps	ALI	F	1972	Flodor
80	50	Ice-cream	ALI	D	1974	Langnese-Iglo
80	50	Printing paper and stationery	PAP	B	1975	Imports
80	50	Electric vacuum cleaners	ELE	F	1975	Moulinex
80	50	Rice	ALI	F	1972	Cofrariz
96	49	Condensed and evaporated milks, sterilised creams	ALI	UK	1973	Carnation Foods
96	49	Vacuum cleaners	ELE	UK	1975	Hoover
98	48	General-purpose computers	MAC	B	1973	IBM
99	47	Dry-cleaning machines	ELE	DK	1973	Fisker og Nielsen
99	47	Biscuits	ALI	F	1972	Aliment Essentiel
99	47	Synthetic detergents	CHI	UK	1975	Unilever

Table 6.1 (cont.)

Ranking	C_1 (%)	Market	Industry	Country	Year	Brand leader or market leader
102	46	Ice-cream	ALI	DK	1975	Frisko
102	46	Canned meat (corned beef)	ALI	UK	1973	Fray Bentos
102	46	General-purpose computers	MAC	F	1973	IBM
105	45	Dried soups	ALI	F	1972	Maggi (Nestlé)
105	45	Spa waters	ALI	F	1972	Groupe Perrier
105	45	Special soups	ALI	UK	1973	Baxters
105	45	Cocoa (butter and powder)	ALI	NL	1973	De Zaan (Grace Cy.)
105	45	Motor vehicle lighting systems	TRA	D	1974	Westfalische Metallindustrie
105	45	Frozen foods	ALI	F	1972	Findus
105	45	Beer	ALI	F	1972	BSN
105	45	Sedatives and hypnotics	PHA	NL	1973	Hoffman-La Roche

Key to abbreviations appearing in above table:

C_1 = Share of market held by company

Industry:
ALI	=	food and foodstuffs
CHI	=	chemicals
ELE	=	electrical consumer goods
MAC	=	machinery, including electronic equipment
PAP	=	paper and board
PHA	=	pharmaceuticals
TRA	=	automobiles, motorbikes, etc.
TEX	=	textiles and clothing

Country:
B	=	Belgium
D	=	Germany (Federal Republic)
DK	=	Denmark
F	=	France
I	=	Italy
NL	=	the Netherlands
UK	=	United Kingdom

Source: EEC's *Seventh Report on Competition Policy*, Brussels and Luxembourg, 1978 (i.e. prior to Greek accession to EEC).

like their potential to expand by acquisition, been drastically reduced.

The *cause célébre* of the 1980s in this area already looks like being the Commission's anti-trust contest with IBM. According to EEC figures, the undisputed world computer industry leader had by the mid-1970s acquired shares of between 46 per cent and 56 per cent of the Italian, German, UK and French markets for general purpose computers. IBM, whose group turnover in 1980 was 26,000 million dollars, with approximately 38 per cent of this worldwide figure being generated via its European-based World Trade Corporation. According to EEC figures, the US multinational has 54 per cent of the European Community market for large mainframe computers, or central processing units. The Commission, which sent its complaint to IBM headquarters in Armonk in December 1980, had earlier produced several data-processing industry analyses highly suggestive of the position of outstanding leadership enjoyed by IBM in European and world markets.[20]

The IBM affair — it is certain to be much more than a simple case — is of major significance for a number of reasons. First, it sees the EEC Commission attempting to do what plaintiffs in the USA, including the Department of Justice, have so far failed to do: nail IBM on an anti-trust rap calling into question the practices of 'bundling' memory and software with the price of the central computer and delaying the release of vital 'interface' information to its competitors. Second, it sees IBM caught for the first time in what is an *administrative* process which it may find less responsive to delays and checks than the US judicial system where legal filibustering has become a widespread art. So despite IBM's attempts to question the procedure by which the Commission is attacking it,[21] the chances are that the pace of the IBM/EEC contest will be dictated much more by the authorities than by the company.

But there are further points arising from the IBM affair which are of importance to the transatlantic business community as a whole. The overlap between some of the European complaints against IBM and the charges it faces in the USA means that it may be hazardous for the company to seek an out-of-court settlement with the EEC, if by so doing it concedes on practices which it is using elsewhere, e.g. the USA. There is a further transatlantic connection, again of significance to companies other than IBM. All of the complainants in the European case are in fact American[22] — a sure sign that international business outside Europe is itself waking up to the potential of EEC anti-trust law as a new weapon for private economic combat.

The IBM affair, however, is not simply economic. It is highly politically charged. For it is difficult to dissociate the European Commission's anti-trust enquiry into the American company's affairs from the EEC's parallel attempts, thus far not spectacularly successful, to lay the basis of a viable European-owned data-processing industry, capable of competing multinationally, i.e. with IBM. EEC officials of course throw up their hands at any suggestion that legal action in the anti-trust field could in any way be flavoured by a politically-motivated industrial policy, encouraging European MNCs as against foreign multinationals. But there is more than the suggestion of such a link. It was in a controversial EEC report[23] on the need for measures to boost the creation of European data-processing multinationals that the Commission first identified IBM with a market position in Western Europe whose level is above that held to provide evidence of 'dominance' (for example in the United Brands case). Also to be mentioned in this context are the strenuous efforts of Mr Christopher Layton, until early 1981 the director of EEC advanced technology policy, to devise a definition of 'European company' which would effectively exclude IBM — which, whatever its presumed aims, is one of Europe's leading taxpayers via the revenue contributions of its immensely profitable German, Italian, UK and French subsidiaries.[24] Such attempts are again symptomatic of the political priorities which sometimes inflect EEC policy towards international business (see chapter 4).

The newfound confidence and strength of EEC competition policy, epitomised by its decision to take on IBM, is not the only trend for the international business community to monitor closely in assessing the development of European anti-trust in the coming decade. Paralleling the expansion of the Community's direct control over big business abuse will be two other developments: private suits by companies which feel they have been damaged by a dominant firm's abusive actions, and increased fines for offenders. Although there is no prospect of a parallel in Europe to the American practice of private triple damage actions — one of the major deterrents to competitive misbehaviour in the USA and encouraged by chunky contingent fees for lawyers — the decade of the 1980s should witness a proliferation of civil actions, with the courts awarding fines corresponding to the actual loss suffered by the plaintiff company. In addition, as EEC jurisprudence on monopolies becomes more firmly established, the EEC itself will start imposing higher fines on the grounds that ignorance of the law is no excuse. Indeed there are now signs that fines not far under the rate of a company's expected return on sales may be under consideration. Such rigour also mirrors its decision to deal harshly with offenders against EEC rules on cartels and restrictive practices. This is the other main area of EEC attempts to control multinational business abuse.

Crackdown against cartels: the EEC's mailed fist

The multi-million dollar fine slapped on the Japanese consumer electronics multinational Pioneer in December 1979 (even if since reduced by the Court from 9.5 million dollars to 'only' 5.5 million), shows beyond doubt that the increased legal impact of EEC anti-trust is now to be matched by tougher financial penalties. The 1980s seems likely to be strewn with cases of international companies parting with large percentages of their annual cash flow as the price for cutting competitive corners.

Restrictive practices (cartels, collusionary activity, price-fixing, market-sharing etc.),[25] especially if their effect is to imperil the unity of Europe's painstakingly built Common Market, are likely to be the most severely sanctioned. Multinational companies which conclude agreements whose effect is to repartition the ten-member EEC market into separate national markets for the purpose of artificially protecting high prices in one or other country, can expect to be confronted head on.

In this respect, the fine against Pioneer, which the Commission charged with rigging an anti-competitive import ban around its high-priced hi-fi goods in France, is illustrative of the shape of fines to come. The penalty fixed by the Commission was just under 5 per cent of Pioneer Europe's annual turnover – equal, indeed superior, to most firms' profit margins. In fact EEC legislation[26] provides for fines of up to 10 per cent of sales and, although it seems hard to imagine such drastic penalties, business should be aware of the Calvinistic rigour with which EEC officials seem resolved to instil the true spirit of capitalism on errant firms. Says one Eurocrat: 'the reasons why we have decided to step up the level of fines is that some companies have been clearly wondering whether it's not more profitable to infringe the Treaty and pay the fine. Obviously we've got to fix fines at a level high enough to discourage this line of reasoning'. In this, the Brussels bureaucracy is not out on a limb, since representatives of cartel offices in EEC member states have agreed 'to render the prohibitions contained in Articles 85 and 86 more effective'.[27]

Firms can expect highest penalties in those fields where EEC jurisprudence is the most clearly established. Chief among these are laws against export bans which trammel so-called 'parallel imports' (into one EEC country from another) – a process of which the Pioneer case is an exemplary illustration. Companies most likely to be tempted into such costly offences are those operating in consumer goods industries characterised by high prices, large price differentials between different national markets, and by products which, because of characteristics such as lightness and thus transportability, can be moved rapidly from one Common Market country to another. In practice, sectors which

EEC officials will be keeping close tabs on in the years ahead are consumer electronics, pharmaceuticals, watches, perfumes, drinks and 'white goods' such as fridges and freezers.

In other areas of EEC jurisprudence on concerted practices, further clarification appears to be needed before such draconian penalties are inflicted. Thus a variety of business arrangements favoured by multinationals, such as selective distribution and exclusive dealerships will be reviewed by the Brussels authorities in the coming years. This reflects the growing feeling that such apparently respectable agreements may, in certain sectors,[28] be nothing more than a cloak for artificially protecting national markets with much the same effect as — if in a less direct way than — the blunter method used by Pioneer. In addition, multinationals should keep a close watch on what promises to be rapid developments throughout the decade of the 1980s in EEC trademark and patent law. Particularly in the case of patents, the Commission is gradually enforcing its restrictive stand against the ability of MNCs to divide up the Common Market by devices limiting the normal flow of competition between patented products.

This picture of the EEC's burgeoning capacity to deal with competitive malpractice in the private sector of the economy would not be complete without one final remark — one which no doubt will chill many MNCs uncomfortably into the 1980s. A vital and — until mid-1980 — contested weapon in the EEC's enforcement armoury is its powers to make unannounced raids on the premises of companies its anti-trust authorities are investigating. Once again the Court, in a judgement involving another Japanese company, National Panasonic (again in the consumer electronics sector), has backed the Commission's rights to make such information swoops.[29]

Nationalised industries: EEC shirks responsibility

The free-market enthusiasm of EEC anti-trust pales into relative insignificance when confronted by the competitive misbehaviour of the publicly-controlled sector of the European economy. Disciplining multinational companies — especially those with no natural political mouthpiece in Europe — is one thing. Attempting to force a philosophy of economic liberalism down the throats of EEC governments committed to a greater or lesser extent to state interventionism or dirigism (and many presiding over large public sectors and nationalised industries) is quite another. Admittedly, in the field of control over public incentives granted to private investment, the Commission does have real impact. But in the key area of supervising the way governments bolster the competitive position of their state-controlled enterprises in open conflict with the EEC's constitutional rules (Rome Treaty, Article 90), little or nothing has been done until a modest attempt at initiating control was made in June 1980; see below for further consideration of this. From a legal standpoint, such inaction is a glaring and serious omission. But from the standpoint of Europe's economic and political traditions, it is less surprising (see chapter 3). In other words, the EEC's constitution, at least on this question, is out of kilter with European economic practice.

The upshot of this state of affairs is to cause apparently justified complaints by multinational companies that EEC anti-trust policy is effectively biased against them and in favour (by omission) of their publicly-run rivals. 'Hard law for us, soft law for them', they grumble. Yet such an implicit anti-business bias is in fact only a logical consequence of the highly socialised nature of the EEC economy (which paradoxically appears in certain instances to be becoming more socialised as a result of the negative impact of monetarist policies in vogue in certain countries on the private sector). It is this political fact that foreign multinationals, looking at the legal provisions of the Rome Treaty on competition, rather than European economic structures, fail fully to realise. The degree of independent control exerted by the Commission over competition in the private sector is drastically reduced when dealing with the giants of the public sector.

There can be little doubt about the sheer size of the problem posed by the activities of state-controlled but competitively-uncontrolled corporations operating in the productive sectors of EEC countries. Although no homogenised statistics are available for Europe as a whole, the few quantitative indications that are available paint a clear picture. In West Germany, for instance, the supposed bastion of market economics in the Community, the shares in national industrial output enjoyed by publicly-owned enterprises are as follows in some selected sectors: aluminium (49 per cent), automobile manufacturing (28 per cent), shipbuilding (19 per cent), iron and steel (76 per cent).[30] Statistics for France, where governmental assistance to public enterprises has risen sharply during the 1970s,[31] show that public undertakings in the aviation supply sector have a 'very important' share in total production (falling into the 40–80 per cent category), while for cars the figure is well over 20 per cent. In Italy the figure for cars is 27 per cent, 49 per cent for metals and 72 per cent for mining, while in sectors such as steel, chemicals, electronics and engineering, subsidiaries of nationalised enterprises are active and significant. With the exception of chemicals, this last remark applies to the UK, where by the mid-1970s nationalised industry output as a share of GDP had reached 11 per cent, while 19 per cent of total national fixed investment was supplied by public companies. Moreover, this picture does not include the significant, dominant or monopoly positions enjoyed by state-controlled corporations in the more traditionally nationalised sectors like banking (e.g. France, Germany, Belgium, Italy), energy and water supply (France, UK, Germany), telecommunications and transport (the vast majority of EEC countries).[32]

Somewhat late in the day, the EEC is attempting to get to grips with this economically sizeable and politically charged problem. This attempt is vested in a new rule adopted in Brussels in mid-1980,[33] intended to come into full legal force in all Community member countries in the early 1980s, and obliging EEC governments to detail just what money they are giving to whom and why. The main inspiration of the move is to ensure a modicum of equal treatment, from a competitive standpoint, between private and public corporations, a strangely American idea for grafting into the European context. Indeed, its aim, if achieved, would do much to quell American criticism, as voiced by a leading US anti-trust official,[34] holding that 'it is neither rational nor, ultimately, possible to have healthy competition in the private sector and pervasive protectionism, favoritism and economic restraints in the public sector. This is especially true as governments themselves increasingly engage in the production and distribution of resources'.

'Amen to that', says private business operating in Europe, particularly American multinationals two of whose most vocal apologists have pointed, perhaps a little dramatically, to the interface between political leftism and public ownership, tracing the impact of anti-business trade union strategy on the European private enterprise system.[35]

Drama or no drama, it is certain that the Commission's aim of imposing financial disclosure requirements[36] on testily sovereign governments, even if backed by the EEC Treaty and the Court of Justice, will lead to political conflict and controversy before Europe's nationalised industries really are put on an equivalent competitive footing to the multinational private sector, which is subject to the increasingly harsh rules outlined earlier in this chapter. Already governments in France, Italy and the UK have lodged formal appeals with the Court against the Commission's new directive.[37] So, on balance, MNCs' expectations of equal treatment will not be quickly achieved, especially since prolonged economic uncertainty may strengthen governmental determination to resist attempts from outside to control national prerogatives. They should also recognise the force of the infrequently-voiced but widely-felt European argument that, while nationalised industries are *ipso facto* subject to national democratic controls, multinational companies are not and thus must bear the brunt of international regulation of economic power.

EEC control of state aids: multinationals bear the brunt

At the same time, multinationals are also in the centre of the firing line of European regulation aimed at curbing national government incentives to private investments. Here the Commission's powers of control, vested in Articles 92–94 of the Rome Treaty and strongly reasserted by the Court in a landmark judgement given against US tobacco multinational Philip Morris in late 1980, fall principally on international companies. It is they that are perceived as seeking to play one government off against another so as to get the best cash grant for investments which, in many cases, would be made without public assistance. Little imagination is needed to surmise that, as economic uncertainty persists and dole queues lengthen, the temptation facing governments to pay MNCs over the odds for the privilege of hosting new plant and thus new jobs will intensify. So, however, will the EEC's determination – and ability – to put a stop to the anti-competitive channelling of taxpayers' money into the cash flow of international companies. The power of European competition authorities to stop misuse of public funds for private investment is again in sharp contrast with their inability, to date, to take similar steps as regards aids to public sector investments.

The Court's judgement in the Philip Morris case, involving an aid provided by the Dutch government, is important because it not only frees the Commission's hands to deal with investment grants, it practically orders the Commission to curb unjustified governmental assistance to private industry. A series of further decisions banning grants intended for MNCs may thus be expected in the coming years – indeed the series already started in late 1980 with a decision against the part-financing by the Belgian government of an Exxon refinery in Antwerp. Belgium and the Netherlands, traditionally prime European locations for the international investor, will most likely attract the brunt of the EEC's scrutiny in an initial phase, while France, Germany and Italy could also follow suit provided that the Commission is prepared to stiffen its sinews for major political rows. Meanwhile, for as long as Thatcherism persists undiluted in the UK, little interference by European watchdogs will be needed, but the return of a Labour government could usher in a new era of EEC interest in British interventionism.

Conclusion and outlook

The European Community practices dual standards in the execution of its competition policy. Private enterprise operating in the Community can expect to be strictly monitored and, in cases of abuse, increasingly severely sanctioned during the coming decade, as the European Commission's competition agency grows in authority. By contrast, past experience – not to mention the bald fact of the persistent economic crisis and its political repercussions in EEC member states – suggests that the EEC will be unable in the 1980s to exert the same control over the Common Market's nationalised industries, the key competitors of multinational private enterprise in certain sectors. Mailed fist for multinationals, kid gloves for governments.

Moreover, a further distinction is to be made. EEC anti-trust policy may well deal more harshly, or at least with less political restraint, with multinationals controlled from outside the EEC than the homegrown variety. The type of industrial policy considerations which have seen a softening of the application of EEC anti-trust to European producers in areas like steel, man-made fibres and even consumer electronics[38] would be unlikely ever to benefit 'foreign' multinationals. Conversely, the vigour with which the Commission is pursuing IBM can be set against an industrial policy priority for creating a viable European computer industry which has seen leading data-processing companies – Siemens, ICL, CII–Honeywell Bull, Nixdorf – foregather regularly with EEC policy officials in meetings which would be improbable under the strict anti-collusionary laws of American anti-trust.

For all this, EEC anti-trust is now a power to be reckoned with – a factor which multinationals, particularly foreign ones, should process into their forward planning for the coming decade. True, by contrast to US anti-trust cases – which can result in the actual break-up of large companies – Europe's anti-trust has more limited ambitions. But within these limits – and the risk of a fine equal to annual profits means these limits are potentially extensive – its power to act is if anything more incisive because it is less cluttered by judicial considerations. Unlike the American model, unlike also virtually every other area of EEC policy-making, European anti-trust is a fast-track administrative process that brooks little opposition and less delay.

Finally, EEC anti-trust is unquestionably on the move, broadening its scope to deal with an increasing range of business abuses. Here the main focus is the pioneering crusade, jointly undertaken by the Community's executive and its Court of Justice, against market dominance. Moreover, as anti-monopoly cases are increasingly prosecuted with success, the possibility that the Commission may have to turn its attention to corporate divestiture procedures cannot be ruled out entirely. At the same time, the Community will strike against cartelisation and trusts more incisively than in the past. All of which means that multinational business in the 1980s will face stepped-up pressures to be good capitalist citizens in an environment which elsewhere calls the capitalist ethic into serious question; see chapter 5 for detailed consideration of this.

Notes and references

1 Multinational Undertakings and the Community, Appendix I(a).

2 Ibid.

3 See Appendix I(f) for this quote from 'A Draft Code of Principles for Multinationals and Governments', Washington DC, 19—23 September 1976.

4 Pioneer and Kawasaki are the two most notable examples of Japanese clashes with EEC anti-trust. More seem likely to follow as Japanese industrial presence in Europe increases. Japanese firms in the consumer electronics industry are under intensive scrutiny.

5 The pulp and paper sector and the pharmaceuticals industry are respectively the key EEC focuses on Scandinavian and Swiss firms.

6 EEC Regulation 17 of 1962 is the key anti-trust instrument, implementing the Rome Treaty (Articles 85 and 86 — see this chapter).

7 Source: EEC officials.

8 See *Business International*, Washington, 2 January 1981, pp. 3—4.

9 Apparently less so with the public sector — see this chapter, pp. 90—2.

10 As of 1981 and for four years, the incumbent is Dutchman Frans Andriessen, generally seen as much more of an activist than his predecessor, Luxembourger Raymond Vouel.

11 IBM has watched the EEC Commission's attempts over the years to concert a European industrial response to its leadership. In the consumer electronics sector, there are plenty of signs pointing to a more rigorous application of EEC anti-trust rules to Japanese companies than to their hard-pressed European competitors.

12 See section on 'Nationalised industries: EEC shirks responsibility', pp. 90—2.

13 The Continental Can case, see this chapter, p.81.

14 As contained in Section 2 of the Sherman Act.

15 EEC complaint ('statement of objections') sent to IBM, December 1980.

16 EEC's Ninth Report on Competition (April 1979), p.142.

17 Consideration no.91 of the Court's judgement in Hoffman La Roche reads (French original): '*La notion d'exploitation abusive qui vise les comportements d'une entreprise en position dominante qui sont de nature à influencer la structure d'un marché où, a la suite précisément de la présence de l'entreprise en question, le degré de concurrence est déjà affaibli et qui ont pour effet de faire obstacle, par le recours à des moyens différents de ceux qui governent une compétition normale des produits ou services sur la base des prestations des opérateurs économiques, au maintien du degré de concurrence existant encore sur le marché ou au développement cette concurrence.*' Translated, this

becomes: 'The concept of abusive exploitation is an objective concept that applies to the behaviour of an undertaking in a dominant position which can influence the structure of a market where, precisely as a result of the presence of the undertaking in question, the degree of competition is already limited, and whose effect is to hinder, by methods distinct from those which govern normal competition for goods and services . . . the maintenance of the degree of competition theretofore existing on the market or the development of competition' (author's unofficial translation).

18   See EEC official Journal C.92 of 31 October 1973. A renewed call for action on merger control was made October 1981 when the European Parliament, in adopting the 'Caborn Report', called for greater public control of multinationals. See also chapter 3.

19   The Paris Treaty setting up the European Coal and Steel Community gave the EEC much greater powers in these two sectors than it enjoys in other areas.

20   *Report Concerning the Developments in the Data-Processing Sector in the Community in relation to the World Situation* (Volume III), EEC Commission, Brussels, 27 October 1976.

21   IBM has questioned EEC procedure on several occasions in 1981.

22   Intersil, Memorex, National Advanced Systems, Amdahl and Itel.

23   *Report Concerning the Developments in the Data-Processing Sector in the Community in relation to the World Situation.*

24   See table 6.1. See also the 'Profitability' League of EEC Companies presented in the EEC's Sixth Report on Competition (1976), p.166, showing IBM Germany to be no.1, IBM Italy no.5 and IBM Britain to be no.11.

25   All practices banned by Article 85 of the Rome Treaty.

26   Regulation 17 of 1962.

27   Minutes of the meeting of the EEC Advisory Committee on Restrictive Practices, 30 October 1979.

28   Consumer electronics, a sector domestically dominated by German firms.

29   Court decision 26 June 1980 (Case no. 136/79).

30   Figures from 'Financial relationships between governments and public enterprises', EEC Budget Committee's report on seminar held in London, 12–13 October 1978.

31   Rising from 12.8 billion FF in 1973 to 29.5 billion FF in 1978 in 14 major state-controlled companies. Source: ibid.

32   Source: ibid.

33   Commission directive (25 June 1980) on 'the transparency of financial relations between Member States and public undertakings'.

34   John Shenefield, assistant attorney-general, US anti-trust, when making this comment, 12 June 1979, Dallas, Texas.

35   Mr Carl Nisser, formerly of Goodyear, and Mr John Alan James, joint authors of 'Trade Union Strategy for the Private Enterprise System in Europe'. See Multinational Service, 17 January 1980, no.75.
36   As set out in the Commission directive cited above, note 30.
37   The three complaints were made in the space of four days, 16–19 September 1980. They have since been rejected (July 1982).
38   A regrouping of domestically-controlled European companies is seen by many EEC officials as the only way of effectively meeting the Japanese challenge in the consumer electronics sector (particularly televisions and television tubes).

7 International competitivity: Europe on the defence

The EEC's duality of purpose — in seeking to organise, across a ten-nation territory, transnational market freedoms within a European framework of business control — is mirrored in its external policy. Habitual EEC support for a liberal economic framework internationally is now being increasingly qualified by two offsetting factors — the Community's flirtation with protectionism, reflecting a need to dilute the freedoms inherent in the post-war economic framework; and its support for greater business regulation worldwide. Both these factors, directly or indirectly, affect multinational companies as they seek to maximise profits within the liberal system set up by the West, institutionally reinforced by GATT and OECD in the post-war years, but by the late 1970s threatened by the spread of defensive economic and business policies.

The EEC's commitment to transnational economic freedom is traditionally expressed, beyond the EEC's borders, in its self-trumpeted devotion to the cause of international free trade. Yet in recent years — characterised by world economic stagnation, declining European competitivity and stepped-up business mobility searching for new profit centres — the trumpeting appears to have assumed greater reality than the actual commitment behind it. Indeed, the best evidence for the EEC's free trade commitment is historical rather than contemporary. Were not European nations great post-war supporters of GATT? Has not the EEC been one of the leading protagonists in each of the last two trade liberalisation negotiations — the Kennedy Round (1962–67) and the Tokyo Round (1973–79)? Is not the EEC's external tariff one of the lowest in the world? All these claims may be true, and they are reinforced by the massive 35 per cent share of world trade taken up by the Community.[1] And yet, and yet . . . .

Free trade is dead! Long live organised liberalism!

More recently, the emphasis of EEC external trade policy has shifted. 'Free trade for free trade's sake' is a posture no longer fashionable, particularly in a European Community embarking on the 1980s with almost 10 million unemployed[2] many in sectors suffering from acute penetration of imports from Japan and the newly industrialised countries. International trade liberalism has in the process become a notion which has outstripped the ability of an increasing number of European nations to live with its social and political consequences. In its stead have emerged the more subtle concepts of 'organised free trade' and 'orderly marketing' — camouflaged catchwords to cushion erstwhile liberals from the shock to their consciences of the transition towards protectionism. West European countries, co-founders of GATT, although still among its principal beneficiaries, have by the early 1980s seen the time arriving when this may no longer be so, and are thus preparing in consequence.

Multinational companies are clearly among the first to be concerned by these developments. Unlike nations, they can handle changes in competitivity as between different regions of the world by their inherent flexibility, switching production to where local costs are most favourable. If having done so, however, they then find themselves facing artificial offsets to such competitive advantages — in the shape of import quotas, emergency tariffs, withdrawal of trade preferences, or anti-dumping action imposed by the outcompeted regions — their multinational world becomes frayed. Such protective measures have multiplied in the European Community in recent years — affecting sectors like textiles, automobiles, and steel, and threatening many others where free trade is no longer working to Europe's advantage.

The measures themselves vary. But notable among them are: much intensified use of a revamped Community anti-dumping machinery;[3] the insidious spread of voluntary restraint arrangements, whether at the level of the Community as a whole or of individual EEC countries, aimed particularly at curbing imports from Japan in certain key sectors; and the gradual toughening of the EEC's generalised system of trade preferences, designed to cut back the preferential access of imports from rapidly industrialising countries — like Hong Kong, Indonesia, Malaysia, Philippines, Singapore, Venezuela, Brazil and Argentina. Such measures are at least partly designed to counter the mobility of multi-national companies, many of whom have invested in the advanced developing countries to benefit from cost advantages. These attempts at trimming the competitive onslaught of the so-called NICs (newly industrialised countries), first implemented by the EEC in its generalised system of preferences for 1981, could well be reinforced during the remainder of the decade.

At the same time, the Community is in the awkward position of having to 'dose' any protectionist reflexes with the knowledge that it exports almost as much of its gross domestic product as Japan and is thus embarrassingly exposed to retaliation — much more, for example, than the USA.[4] The hard truth facing the Community in the early 1980s is that it depends crucially on the maintenance of an open world trading system in which, however, many of its member states are less and less able to compete effectively. EEC trade deficits have moved from 5,800 million dollars in 1978, to 33,000 million in 1979 to a staggering and unprecedented 65,000 million in 1980.

Multinationals thus face the prospect in the coming years of uncertain shifts in the conduct of EEC external trade policy, responding unpredictably now to liberal now to protectionist impulses, and affecting the overall economic framework in which they operate. In the case of Japanese companies, moreover, they will be under added pressure from European authorities to cut back their export-led incursion into sensitive EEC markets and instead invest directly in the Common Market, preferably in joint ventures with erstwhile European rivals.

As regards the EEC's business control efforts in the broader international framework, large companies also must watch a variety of developments. These include European influence on the codes of conduct being worked out at the UN or under implementation at the OECD and the ILO, and also the Community's distinctive contribution to development policy, its initiative on South Africa, and US/EEC co-operation on anti-trust matters.

EEC attitude to international business codes

The EEC's attitude to worldwide codes of conduct for international business is ambiguous. At the fully international level, the EEC seeks to sustain the Community's worldwide economic interests, including those of its firms, while doing so in a way which is consistent both with a moderately progressive European development posture and with the extension into the broader international arena — notably the OECD and the United Nations — of some of the policies developed internally e.g. disclosure rules).

As a result, neither the European Commission nor the Council of Ministers has ever favoured the idea of any binding international (as opposed to Community) legislation on multinationals, preferring instead to use the idea of codes of conduct and moral suasion. Moreover, there has never been any question of the EEC as such being mandated to present a single European position in international negotiations seeking to establish across-the-board behavioural rules for multinationals (with the exception of specific areas on which the Community has binding legislation on its books, e.g. accounting and anti-trust matters). By and large, the European position in arenas like the UN and the OECD is expressed by individual EEC governments, who often approach a given subject from a different standpoint while generally sharing a common belief in the voluntary nature of international arrangements of this kind. This belief is often reinforced by the unstated but typically Europeanist conviction that only a truly supranational authority (such as the EEC) should be in the job of issuing binding international rules. Cocking a snoot at 'international co-operation' in the OECD, as opposed to transnational integration in the Community, is part of a built-in and not always well-placed superiority complex shared by many EEC officials.

The EEC and South Africa

Against the background of a progressive development policy embodied by its multi-billion dollar commitment to African countries in the Lomé Convention, the EEC's most spectacular attempt to influence the behaviour of MNCs beyond Community borders came in September 1977 when EEC foreign ministers, in response to a British foreign office call, adopted a 'Code of Conduct for Companies with Subsidiaries, Branches or Representation in South Africa'.[5] Voluntary in nature but nonetheless benefiting from the cachet of high political support, the code made a coherent set of operational demands on subsidiaries of EEC multinationals operating in South Africa including: promotion of collective bargaining; freedom of black employees to join trade unions; wage minima; black advancement and vocational training; desegregation at the place of work.

The code, received with hostility particularly by German business and perhaps precociously written off as political verbiage both by its convinced opponents and frustrated sympathisers, revived in importance in 1979 when the UK labour government published a report on the state of application by British companies of its major provisions.[6] Released to the House of Commons in February 1979, this report appeared at the time to indicate that Britain was going to pressure its eight EEC partners to follow suit in ensuring implemen tation of the code by the companies involved. The nature of this implementation is spelt out in the code as follows:

— Parent companies to which this code is addressed should publish each year a detailed and fully documented report on the progress made in applying this code.
— The number of black Africans employed in the undertaking should be specified in the report, and progress in each of the six areas indicated above should be fully covered. [These areas are: relations within the undertaking; migrant labour; pay; wage structure and black African advancement; fringe benefits; desegregation at the place of work.]
— The governments of the Nine will review annually progress made in implementing this code. To this end a copy of each company's report should be submitted to their national government.

Pressure for effective implementation of the code throughout Europe depends on a variety of factors, amongst them: changing attitudes in British government circles; developments in Southern Africa; the pressure on European governments by big business which conceives the code of conduct as a 'deplorable' instance of 'the attempts of governments to use MNCs as a means of political pressure on other countries' policies'.[7] Whatever the outcome, the code should not be written off, either as a basis for governmental influence on corporate conduct in Southern Africa or as a precedent demonstrating how political imperatives can condition EEC policy towards big business. Further signs that dismissal of the code as a meaningful instrument may be premature came in late April 1979 when French Secretary of State for foreign affairs indicated to the European Parliament that European governments were serious about giving the code effective follow-up.[8] With the advent of the Mitterrand administration, and its outspokenly progressive development policy, France may be expected to be a key backer of a tougher European line against South Africa — and against European businesses operating there.

The EEC, the US and international anti-trust

A particular context within which in recent years certain MNC-related initiatives have been sponsored by EEC institutions is the US/ Community transatlantic framework. Developments so far have had

102

little measurable direct impact, but nonetheless should be watched as a possible source of future interest.

The Code on Multinationals agreed by a joint European Parliament/US Congress delegation in April 1977 — known more intimately as the Lange-Gibbons code after its two principal co-authors, German socialist Erwin Lange and US democrat Sam Gibbons — falls into this category and is as Appendix I(f). It received a passing show of interest from the European Commission, which muttered some ritualistic phrases of dutiful approval, then appeared to carry on as before. And yet it would be wrong to write off too lightly either its influence or its ideas. From a European standpoint, the Parliament's code did provide some support, however limited in impact, for many of the new legislative proposals which the EEC was considering and in many cases still is. Meanwhile, in the United States, it had direct follow-up when Mr Gibbons subsequently presented his own bill to the House of Representatives on the regulation of multinational companies by American law. In terms of ideas, besides making traditional calls for increased information, the curbing of tax avoidance and investment monitoring, the authors of the code touched a raw nerve in the international business world when it urged much tighter co-operation on anti-trust matters between the EEC and the USA.

The significance of the demand for greater anti-trust co-operation is three-fold: first, it is an area viewed with the greatest sensitivity by all multinationals; second, there already exists a quasi-institutional forum for co-operation between the EEC competition department and the US Department of Justice; third boosting co-operation between these two authorities — in effect the most powerful anti-trust powers in the world — is in any case an issue which has been raised on more than one occasion, particularly by Washington. Whether the Reagan administration will continue activity in this area remains to be seen.

As Mr Lange and Mr Gibbons saw it:

> multinational enterprises, like other large enterprises, frequently have technical or financial advantages over their competitors, giving them a certain position of power. Competition policy should be aimed at checking abuse of this position. To achieve this, much more intensive co-operation is essential between anti-trust authorities of the United States and the European Community. Controlling multinational enterprises is made more difficult by the problems of implementation than by shortcomings in national legislation. The anti-trust bodies are frequently unable to prove abuse by a multinational enterprise because the necessary evidence is in the hands of another of its establishments abroad, creating the need for free access to information.

In fact, the prospects for increased co-operation between the US and the EEC on anti-trust matters remain subdued for the moment. This state of affairs stems mainly from the opposition among European governments to the extra-territorial pretensions of the US anti-trust authority — an antagonism which reached its height in the famous uranium cartel controversy of 1977–78. Against this background, it is clear that the Commission's anti-trust department simply cannot go ahead with more deep-seated co-operation with its American counterpart. For the moment such collaboration takes the form of regular twice-yearly exchanges of non-confidential information between high officials of both sides. However, the forum is there. (So, incidentally, is the dust-covered draft of an EEC/US anti-trust co-operation agreement.) And it seems likely that for as long as that institution exists and the whiff of co-operation remains in the air, the possibility of more far-reaching reciprocal exchanges of information cannot be discounted. Multinationals, in any case, cannot afford to ignore possible developments in this sensitive sector.

Conclusion and outlook

The EEC's external policy will be a priority area for business monitoring in the 1980s. The trend towards protectionism, articulated primarily through anti-dumping action and voluntary restraint measures, will in all probability become more pronounced as the decade proceeds, and will increasingly impact on policy. Also to be included in this picture of European economic defensiveness is the emerging acceptability of the notion that government contract decisions — affecting a greater and greater percentage of national markets — should be openly tilted in favour of European companies; see chapter 4. Pieced together, the mosaic of EEC trade and trade-related policy is much more sombre, particularly for multinationals operating in a framework directly responsive to it, than the optimistic, liberal attitude embodied in EEC trade and economic policy at the outset of the 1970s.

Paralleling its defensive external policy, the EEC will be a continuing supporter of international arrangements stipulating greater control of multinational business — but of a voluntary nature. This at least is true for the OECD and UN codes on multinationals, even if, in the specific and highly political case of the EEC's South Africa code, the division between the voluntary and the mandatory may not always be clear.

Notes and references

1   1979 figures.
2   In September 1981, EEC unemployment stood at 9.4 million, or 8.5 per cent of the Community's working population. This represents a growth of 3 million in 18 months.
3   Adopted by the Council of Ministers, 21 December 1979.
4   Extra-EEC exports as a percentage of GDP (1980) were 11.2 per cent. Comparable figures for Japan and the USA are respectively 12.5 per cent and 8.6 per cent. Source: Directorate for economic and financial affairs, EEC Commission.
5   Adopted by EEC foreign ministers, 20 September 1977. See Appendix I(e).
6   UK Government statement to House of Commons, 15 February 1979. For details see Multinational Service no.54 of 15 March 1979.
7   Statement made by leading MNCs, represented on the European Management Symposium, Davos, Switzerland, February 1979. For full details, see Multinational Service no.52 of 15 February 1979.
8   Statement by M. Bernard-Reymond, to European Parliament session held in Luxembourg, 25 April 1979. See Multinational Service no.58, 10 May 1979.

EEC legislative checklist for multinationals

This is a summary in tabular form of measures distinctively targeted at MNCs. It does not attempt to cover the much broader gamut of other measures affecting the business world, e.g. EEC consumer and environment protection programmes — or indeed measures intended to boost MNC activity in the Common Market (e.g. public procurement liberalisation).

Item	Status	Outlook	Reference
GENERAL			
Memorandum on EEC policy towards MNCs	Approved by Commission November 1973	Never adopted by Council but nevertheless a continuing framework for EEC initiatives	Chapter 4; see also Appendix I(a)
Lange-Gibbons code on MNCs	Approved by European Parliament, April 1977	Impact limited, but could increase following EEC direct elections, June 1979	Chapter 7; see also Appendix I(f)
Caborn Report on Multinationals and Governments	Approved by European Parliament, October 1981	Will provide support for EEC action on MNC consultation and disclosure	Chapter 3
CORPORATE DISCLOSURE AND LIABILITY			
'Fourth' directive: subsidiary accounts	Adopted by Council, July 1978	Implementation by 'ten', early 1980s	Chapter 5
'Seventh' directive: group accounts	Official consideration, begun 1978, continuing	Adoption in early 1980s	Chapter 5
'Ninth' directive: group liability	Proposal yet to be made, but exists in draft form	Proposal being withheld, pending outcome of discussions on the Vredeling initiative	Chapter 5
TAXATION			
Resolution on tax evasion and avoidance	Adopted by Council February 1975	To be implemented via specific measures (see below)	Chapter 5
Directive on 'mutual assistance'	Adopted by Council December 1977	Implementation phase, begun 1979, could lead to scheme on transfer-pricing	Chapter 5

Item	Status	Outlook	Reference
ANTI-TRUST			
Article 86, Rome Treaty	Basic EEC constitutional provision	Extended application, 1980	Chapter 6
Regulation on patent licensing	Published in draft form, February 1979	To be adopted and implemented 1980	
Merger control regulation	Proposed by Commission, July 1973	Adoption unlikely, but offset by extension of Article 86 action (see above)	Chapter 6
LABOUR LAWS			
Directive on worker protection/mass dismissals	Adopted February 1975	Active Commission monitoring of member state application since 1977	Chapter 5
Directive on worker protection/change of ownership	Adopted February 1977	Commission monitoring since 1979	Chapter 5
Employee information and consultation in MNCs (the 'Vredeling initiative')	Proposal made October 1980	Expected to emerge from consideration by European Parliament in 1982. Discussion by government officials already begun; should intensify 1983–85	Chapter 2, Appendix I(h)
'Fifth' directive on worker participation	Proposed October 1972, subsequently amended	Official consideration of amended proposal by governments 1982	Chapter 2 Appendix I(b)
'Green paper' on employee participation/ company structure	Approved by Commission, November 1975	Continued use as spur to participation moves	Appendix I(d)
DEVELOPMENT POLICY			
EEC code on South Africa	Adopted by Nine, September 1977	Pressure for effective implementation to continue in 1980s	Chapter 7; see also Appendix I(f)

PART III

THE OECD GUIDELINES FOR MULTINATIONAL ENTERPRISES: THE POLITICISATION OF INTERNATIONAL BUSINESS

The hard fact of 'soft law'

By comparison to the legislative threat of compulsory control posed to multinational freedom by the European Community, the 'voluntary' code of conduct embodied by the 'Guidelines for Multinational Enterprises' adopted by the OECD in 1976[1] may appear small beer. Appearances, however, deceive. While the OECD Guidelines are indeed voluntary, in the sense that they do not constitute rules whose infringement can lead directly to legal sanction,[2] they have nevertheless developed the status of what has become known as international 'soft law'. Soft law — politically-agreed guidelines for behaviour which cannot be directly legally enforced but cannot either be legitimately infringed — is a new and, for many in international business, a disturbing concept. Soft law is disturbing because of its very open-endedness. For just as with soft law business is safe from legal sanction, so also companies accused by their adversaries — this means above all the international trade union movement — of contravening the OECD code cannot definitely prove their innocence. The price for contravention of the OECD Guidelines, even if it is merely alleged, can thus be high, both in public relations terms and even, indirectly, in business terms. Companies like ITT, Citibank, Hertz, Raytheon, British Oxygen, Philips (Netherlands), British American Tobacco, to cite a random if leading sample have all in recent years been faced with the political yardstick for their economic behaviour. Soft law can have hard consequences.

Moreover, it is with one single area — an area of extreme and growing

111

sensitivity for the multinational business community — that the impact of the OECD's 'soft law' has become predominantly associated: industrial relations. Thanks to the institutionalised presence of the international trade union movement in the application of the OECD code,[3] the guideline dealing with employment and industrial relations has been marked out as the principal lever used to gain greater labour control over management decisions. What is more, single-minded concentration on industrial relations[4] has had its impact way beyond the scope of the OECD Guidelines. The EEC's much-advertised 'Vredeling initiative', detailed in chapter 5, which seeks stronger mandatory information and consultation rights for trade unions in MNCs, is directly related to the OECD Guidelines. Indeed, without the OECD Guidelines, and in particular the industrial relations section, it is more than likely that the Vredeling move would never have seen the light of day. One of the major rationales of the EEC proposal was to give greater legislative follow-up to the Guidelines, as a means of giving greater effectiveness to their principles.

By their emerging status as 'soft law'; by their direct and dual impact on industrial relations and on legislation — particularly but not exclusively in Europe;[5] by the scope they give the international trade union movement for exerting influence with government against multinational business; and lastly by the embryonic actualisation they provide MNCs of the hated spectre of international collective bargaining — for all these reasons, the OECD Guidelines have proved in the few years since their adoption that they are a force that multinationals should reckon with in the coming years.

Notes and references

1   'Guidelines for Multinational Enterprises'; for full text, see Appendix II(b).
2   Indirectly, however, there may be such an impact. See, for example, the BATCO case in Holland, outlined in chapter 9, under BATCO/Firestone title.
3   TUAC, the Trade Union Advisory Committee to the OECD, like its business counterpart, BIAC, enjoys institutionalised consultative status at the OECD.
4   Virtually all of the 'cases' of individual companies brought before the OECD have concerned issues within the scope of the industrial relations guideline; see chapter 9.
5   Australia, for example, has incorporated the 'Guideline on Competition' into its inward investment code; see chapter 10.

8 Towards a political framework for Western business

The 'Guidelines for Multinational Enterprises'[1] adopted on 21 June 1976 by the OECD Council of Ministers, represent, as indicated above, a markedly different approach to the MNC issue to that adopted by the EEC. The Guidelines take the shape of a general code of behaviour for the international business world – a global strategy which the European Community, partly because of its regional character, has avoided for itself while backing it in the OECD. Unlike EEC measures, the Guidelines – as the name suggests and as the OECD text renders explicit – are voluntary recommendations to multinationals, not legislation binding on national governments. These two important distinctions are supported and explained by a third which is crucial to understanding the OECD operation on multinationals: their origin is not the by-product of policies aimed at regional integration as are many of the European Community's MNC-related measures. Instead, the paternity of the OECD Guidelines is to be found in the major international ructions which first shook the confidence and authority of the Western world and its economic system in the mid-1970s. Viewed in terms of contemporary diplomatic history, the Guidelines were – indeed remain – part of the response of the major industrialised countries (all of whom are represented in the OECD, sometimes referred to as 'the rich man's club') to the dramatic political and economic shifts occurring during the past decade and likely to continue through the 1980s.

Of course, the Guidelines represent much more than just the Western position on big business in the global international economic negotiation which has characterised recent years:

> For multinationals themselves, the overwhelming majority of which are headquartered in OECD countries,[2] they are an expression of moral pressure by the Western political establishment which is often viewed by individual companies with resignation tinged with suspicion. At the same time, after the first five years of operation, the Guidelines are finally becoming more widely-known in the business world — a result of a few spectacular cases of their application, the renewed focus conferred on them by the first three-year review process, and of the attempts made by business organisations to sensitise their membership to the demands made by the Guidelines. This process has intensified following the recommendations made by governments in the context of the Guidelines' review, completed in June 1979,[3] and by the follow-up given the review, particularly in the area of industrial relations by the trade unions (e.g. the Philips case in Finland, the British Oxygen case in Sweden, see chapter 9, and by the EEC Commission in proposing its multinationals directive). Few MNCs now ignore the issues underscored by the Vredeling initiative or by the OECD Guidelines in the area of labour/management relations.

> For trade unions, the Guidelines represent a start, but little more, in the process of building public international control over big business. But the downbeat manner in which the unions tend to treat the non-binding recommendations of the OECD on MNCs (they have an understandably strong preference for binding regulations) is deceptive. It has not stopped organised labour from using them to attack specific multinationals' behaviour both directly with governments and indirectly via use of the press. Despite some union disaffection with the results obtained from the application of the Guidelines, active use of the Guidelines is likely on balance to continue to be a hallmark of international trade union strategy in the coming years.

> For Western governments, the Guidelines are part of an overall package of measures adopted in June 1976 and, as events have since proved, clearly the most important component of that package. Yet alongside the Guidelines, which represent official sanctification of the need to control MNCs, governments also adopted decisions accentuating the need to create a positive investment climate within which MNCs could better contribute to international economic development and growth: decisions respectively on 'national treatment' (aiming to ensure that MNCs are not discriminated in relation to national companies by govern-

mental laws and regulations) and on 'international investment incentives and disincentives' (enabling intergovernmental discussions if the interests of one OECD country is threatened by the investment regulations of another.[4] Following the 1979 review of the Guidelines, there is evidence of some pressure from the business world for governments to balance out the emphasis on MNC control inherent in the Guidelines, with greater application of the decisions on national treatment and international investment. Such pressure is supported by the US administration which, under President Reagan, is not over enthusiastic about public control of big business and, at the same time, is concerned at the trend in the European Community to give European multinationals preferences, particularly in government contracts, over their American competitors.

The Guidelines' scope largely corresponds to the key MNC-related issues being debated in other arenas, like the EEC and the UN. Specific areas, aside from the preponderant emphasis on industrial relations, in which behavioural norms are recommended are: disclosure of information, competition, financing, taxation, science and technology. In addition however, a series of general policy guidelines are outlined, whose very existence is a reflection of the shortening distance between the political and business worlds. Just as Western governments are increasingly involving themselves in economic management, so multinational firms are themselves being called upon to consciously inject a measure of political and social responsibility into their corporate strategy. This is not to imply that such considerations would be foreign to all or even the majority of multinationals without the OECD Guidelines. But one of the originalities of the Guidelines is to have put the 'free' world's major economic operators publicly into a political context. By and large it is a framework in which they feel less at ease than the two other major protagonists: governments themselves, and the national and international trade union movements which often have specifically political vocations.

The Guidelines' paternity: the UN connection

How did this curious state of affairs come about? How was it that Western governments suddenly decided to tell their great corporations to 'behave' just as the economic crisis was beginning to take its toll of profits and investments? Why was the whole process forced through at a pace totally uncharacteristic of the normal plodding rhythm of international diplomacy?[5] Without the answers to these questions, understanding present governmental attitudes in the West to big business and their likely development is difficult. Companies, in particular, have a vested interest in understanding why they are considered as political animals and why they will increasingly continue to be as the 1980s progress.

The seeds of the OECD Guidelines on MNCs are to be found, not in the Paris-based headquarters of the organisation, but rather in the diplomatic activity in the United Nations and its specialised agencies in the first years of the 1970s. 'Multinationals' then became an issue for public debate, as the developing countries found that the political independence conferred by the decolonisation of the 1960s was one thing, but economic independence quite another. The word 'multinationals' became amongst other things a rallying cry for those seeking to ensure the economic counterpart to political autonomy. Economic independence appeared to be equated with increased public interventionism and in particular with public control of multinationals.

Prospects of further success of this endeavour seemed slim, since there were no objective factors pushing for any collective change of heart in the countries in which multinationals were headquartered: the West. The industrialised world was living out the last years (as events were to prove) of the post-War boom, and had convinced at least itself that international economic development would progress happily enough if the Western system was freely allowed to radiate its beneficial influence, multinationals and all, throughout the less developed countries. A fair assumption, at least at the time — and one still held apparently by the US administration under President Reagan.[6] Armed with it, the industrialised countries paid scant political attention to early developments on MNCs in the UN, such as the creation in 1972 of a 'Group of Eminent Persons' to report on the impact of MNCs on development and to formulate as necessary recommendations to deal with it.[7] The same could be said for the reaction of the West (i.e. the OECD world) to the beginnings of work in various UN specialised agencies focusing on the international economic imbalance and the role that MNCs played in creating or mitigating it. True, Señor Salvador Allende's speech to the UN General Assembly in 1972[8] made a political mark which more than scratched the surface (as events in the United States, which began enactment of a corrupt practices law finally adopted in 1977, were to show[9]). But what was lacking above all was a real economic dimension to a political argument which appeared to be conducted in a vacuum.

The missing economic dimension was supplied dramatically and suddenly when the oil crisis broke in late 1973. It was to provide developing countries with the belief that they were not after all powerless to alter the balance of world economic power in their favour, a belief reflected by the call for a new international economic order by the United Nations' sixth special session in autumn 1974. In this new economic order, multinationals were to play a strictly defined role, and evidence of the type of controls envisaged was not slow in coming. In late 1974, the UN's Economic and Social Council called for a code of conduct on transnational corporations, while at UNCTAD IV in Nairobi, held in May 1976, demands were forwarded for a code of conduct regulating the conditions under which MNCs transferred their technology and know-how internationally. To this UNCTAD added a call for a code on restrictive business practices. All these instruments, it was hoped both by developing countries and the West's trade unions, would be legally binding on multinational companies.

The world's industrialised countries, rocked by the crisis and recognising the need to respond to the demands triggered by it, acted pre-emptively. Less than a month after the end of UNCTAD IV, and just as the ILO was beginning the drafting of guidelines for MNC 'social' behaviour in the developing countries,[10] OECD ministers, at the urgings of the US government, adopted their own multinationals' package, including a 'code' taking the form of voluntary guidelines addressed to MNCs. The speed with which the Guidelines moved from conception to decision was dramatic, and was a direct product of the rich world's belief that it had to go into the UN negotiations on multinationals with a coherent and apparently progressive position with which to confront the developing countries clamour — articulated by the so-called Group-77 of LDCs — for more radical and compulsory control. Adoption of the OECD Guidelines on MNCs, together with two declarations on national treatment of MNCs and international incentives, had taken only eighteen months to negotiate and adopt.

There can be little doubt that the OECD Guidelines were consciously written as a model which the United Nations, it was hoped, could be persuaded to copy, rather than simply to pursue the more ambitious plans for compulsory regulation which were born of the climate of political confrontation that characterised the first half of the 1970s. The Western gambit, moreover, appears to be paying off. The head of steam behind demands for a binding UN code is now evaporating, despite initial pressure from both the developing countries (LDCs) and the international trades unions, in particular the Brussels-based International Confederation of Free Trades Unions (ICFTU) and the World Confederation of Labour (WCL).

Evidence of this strategic aim behind the OECD initiative is easy to hand. Referring to the Guidelines, OECD Secretary General Emile van Lennep wrote that 'the consensus reached in the OECD represents a joint philosophy and common approach on the part of a group of countries accounting for most international investment. This should have an influence even beyond the OECD area',[11] a point made at greater length in the text of the Guidelines proper:

> Since the operations of multinational enterprises extend throughout the world, including countries that are not Members of the Organisation, international co-operation in this field should extend to all States. Member countries will give their full support to efforts undertaken in co-operation with non-member countries, and in particular with developing countries, with a view to improving the welfare and living standards of all people both by encouraging the positive contributions which multinational enterprises can make and by minimising and resolving the problems which may arise in connection with their activities.[12]

The Guidelines' paternity: internal pressure in the West

But the countries most active in the OECD initiative — basically the North Americans and the northern Europeans — were also responding to increasing concern in their own countries, expressed most vociferously by the trade unions and the press, at the 'power' of multinationals. Indeed, they still are. The need for a countervailing force to multinationals has thus come to be perceived as an urgent need by some powerful domestic lobbies as well as by the developing countries. The OECD initiative had thus an internal spur as well as an external incentive. Indeed, Western unions now seem a more potent force for MNC control than the developing countries. Moreover, the evidence of the early years of the Guidelines' operations indicates clearly that a major concern of governments is to show that the Guidelines do represent a credible platform for clearing up problems associated with MNC activities *within* the OECD world. This concern with the credibility of the OECD exercise has led the trades unions, represented by the Trades Union Advisory Committee to the OECD (TUAC), to call strongly for stronger and broader application of the Guidelines in the 1980s.

At the same time, a basic motivation stated by Western governments and stressed in particular by the US Administration, was and is that demands for voluntary self-discipline by MNCs is only part of the picture. Besides possibly causing problems, MNCs are also the major investment agents[13] in the OECD world and as such demands for their control should be offset by a collective attempt to improve the investment climate in which they operate. This aim is partly sought by the MNC Guidelines but, more importantly, by commitments from OECD member governments 'to strengthen their co-operation in the field of international direct investment'.[14]

The business world, influencing the OECD decision-making process via the Business and Industry Advisory Committee (BIAC), is seeking to channel governmental attention away from an exclusive emphasis on MNC control to giving greater effect to the OECD decision — adopted on the same date as the MNC Guidelines — on international investment and disincentives. Its major governmental supporter in this endeavour is the US Administration — surprisingly described by one leading MNC executive as the 'overriding obstacle to American multi-nationals'[15] a view which hardly seems to be corroborated by Washington's stance in international economic negotiations, or to be shared in Europe.

The genesis and development of the OECD Guidelines on Multi-national Enterprises cannot be fully grasped without reference to TUAC and BIAC, the key and opposing lobbies for trade union and business interests in the OECD. The Guidelines were indeed only finalised after consultations with both these organisations, and as such are in a sense a corporatist initiative. But the Guidelines were a compromise which pleased neither side in 1976. The unions in particular made clear their basic opposition to an exercise in voluntary moral suasion, whose success depended on the goodwill of the companies whose activities it was trying to control, but agreed nevertheless to 'give it a try'. Judging by the numbers of specific cases of complaints against individual MNC actions as being incompatible with the Guidelines, this attempt has not been unsuccessful. Moreover, it could further intensify as the unions continue to seek more effective implementation of the OECD's norms.

BIAC's uneasiness is understandable, since business was suddenly faced with a quite original initiative emanating from the governments of the countries hosting the headquarters of virtually all the world's multinationals. The international business community had no precedent[16] against which to assess the OECD Guidelines, it was uncertain as to how they would be applied, and it perceived them as a potential stick placed by governments in the unions' hands for MNC-beating. It also found itself in the position of having to put to governments the coherent positions of the international business world, when that world was and is heterogeneous, and the issues on which the positions were demanded unclear. These problems still by and large beset business representatives, who have found it a long process to persuade individual companies of the need for a meaningful observance of the Guidelines which, though voluntary, are 'morally binding',[17] according to BIAC.

Finally, a word on the administrative machinery set up by governments to ensure the application of the Guidelines.

The key body in the OECD's MNC exercise is the Committee on International Investment and Multinational Enterprises. The IME Committee, made up of officials from OECD member governments,[18] meets 'periodically', as the June 1976 Decision puts it,[19] holds 'an exchange of views on matters relating to the guidelines and the experience gained in their application'. While 'the Committee shall not reach conclusions on the conduct of individual enterprises', taken together with its subcommittees, it has nonetheless become the central international forum in the Western world for governments and unions to air grievances on particular instances of MNC behaviour, as the following chapter amply demonstrates. The two subcommittees, officially styled ad hoc working groups, that report to the Committee are the Lévy Group and Gauthier Group,[20] which deal respectively with the Guidelines as such and the Committee's activities on national treatment. Of the two, easily the most important to date has been the Lévy Group, which is composed of largely the same officials as sit on the full IME Committee.

Plugged into this committee structure, admittedly on a consultative but nevertheless influential basis, are TUAC and BIAC. Each has several formal meetings with the IME Committee and — probably as important if not more so from the standpoint of the exercise in influence — informal sessions with the Lévy group. These sessions tend to deal with individual complaints raised by TUAC (examined in detail below) and ways of better 'enforcing' the Guidelines. Both TUAC and BIAC also have on-going contacts with the OECD Secretariat.[21]

Notes and references

1   Hereinafter referred to as the Guidelines. See Appendix II(b).
2   An idea of aggregate economic impact can be had from tables 3.1 and 4.1, and from Appendix I(g).
3   For an outline of the review process, see chapter 10. For review Appendix II(h).
4   The whole package of OECD texts on MNCs and investment are outlined in Appendix II(a)—(e).
5   In January 1975 the OECD's Committee on International Investments and Multinational Enterprises was set up to prepare the Guidelines and associated instruments. By June 1976, Ministers had adopted them.
6   See, for example, President Reagan's public remarks to the North/South summit at Cancun, Mexico, October 1981.
7   The so-called 'Eminent Persons' report — 'The Impact of Multinational Corporations on Development and International Relations' was

finally published in 1974 (see also chapter 4). By then the international climate was changing for reasons spelled out below.

8   Señor Allende's speech to the UN General Assembly, 4 December 1972.

9   Foreign Corrupt Practices Act, signed by President Carter, 20 December 1977.

10   The International Labour Office (ILO) gave initial instructions for the drafting of a set of principles to guide MNC behaviour on social policy in May 1976. For further details here, see Part IV.

11   Foreword to the OECD Guidelines, Paris, June 1976.

12   'Guidelines for Multinational Enterprises', Introduction section 3. See Appendix II(b) for full text of Guidelines.

13   The policy emphasis on the positive impact of MNCs via their investment function was most clearly expressed by a US government submission to the IME Committee of the OECD in December 1977 (see Multinational Service no.26, 18 January 1978). This is a permanent thread running through American attitudes to the Guidelines and is likely to strengthen under President Reagan.

14   Declaration on International Investment and Multinational Enterprises, adopted by OECD Council, 21 June 1976. See Appendix II(a) for full text.

15   Statement by Robert H. Malott, chairman of FMC in 1977. See Multinational Service no.4, 2 March 1977. This was before the advent of Ronald Reagan.

16   The 'Guidelines for International Investment' of the International Chamber of Commerce, adopted in November 1972, were not of course governmental. See Appendix IV(e).

17   See Multinational Service no.53, 1 March 1979.

18   The OECD's 24 Member countries, minus Turkey, which abstained from the decision setting up the Guidelines.

19   For full text of Decision, see Appendix II(c).

20   Respectively chaired by Mr Philippe Lévy, a senior Swiss government official, and Drs Aak Gauthier, a similarly placed Dutch representative.

21   A fuller profile of BIAC and TUAC, and the contexts in which they operate is given in Part V.

9 The OECD Guidelines in action: 15 multinational 'cases'

Whatever the shortcomings of the OECD Guidelines perceived by the international trade union movement, European unions in particular have shown themselves energetic in exploring their application to the fullest extent. And whatever the limited nature of the Guidelines' impact, they have certainly been used by labour organisations to achieve as wide an effect as possible. In the years since 1976 their impact has been significant if usually indirect. They now represent a source of moral pressure which, as in the case of Badger International (Belgium), Hertz Rentacar (Denmark), British American Tobacco (Netherlands) and British Oxygen (Sweden), can lead to both political and administrative pressure on the company concerned. Their application, and the discussions between OECD government representatives in the various bodies set up to supervise the Guidelines, have on occasion contributed to changes in the perception of the business/society relationship held by certain public authorities. Thus the debates over parental responsibility for a foreign subsidiary, triggered by the Badger case and continued in cases like BOC and Philips, appear to have reinforced the case for a European law on groups of companies and have certainly stimulated EEC legislative activity on MNCs. Indeed TUAC's demands for greater information, particularly on the employment-oriented activities of MNCs, are directly paralleled by EEC schemes — drafted partly as a result of union pressure — to introduce obligatory consultation machinery for workers at MNC headquarters.

The 'publicity impact' of the Guidelines should also not be under-estimated. Detailed cases involving in total some 20 companies[1] have been claimed by the unions as instances of MNCs breaking the spirit or letter of the Guidelines. They have not necessarily been upheld as such by governments, which in any case — as indicated above — made it clear at the inception of the OECD exercise, that the Committee on International Investments and Multinational Enterprises was not a kangaroo court for censoring business behaviour. However, the names and detailed practices of some large companies have been enumerated to government officials responsible for foreign investment and have also found their way into the international press.

In their complaints, which it is the purpose of this section to analyse, the unions, working through the TUAC, have focused above all on the chapter of the Guidelines entitled 'Employment and Industrial Relations'. Understandably enough. This provides a readily exploitable basis for labour organisations to reinforce their claims on issues such as employee protection, trade union rights, including in particular the right to organise and the right to relevant information, and more recently union access to central management. The vast majority of the complaints brought by the unions have been based on this chapter, which is required reading for the analyst of OECD work on multi-nationals. For this reason, it is reproduced in full below:

Employment and Industrial Relations — OECD Requirements of Multinationals

Enterprises should, within the framework of law, regulations and prevailing labour relations and employment practices, in each of the countries in which they operate,

1. respect the right of their employees to be represented by trade unions and other bona fide organisations of employees, and engage in constructive negotiations, either individually or through employers' associations, with such employee organisations with a view to reaching agreements on employment conditions, which should include provisions for dealing with disputes arising over the interpretation of such agreements, and for ensuring mutually respected rights and responsibilities;

2. a) provide such facilities to representatives of the employees as may be necessary to assist in the development of effective collective agreements;

   b) provide to representatives of employees information which is needed for meaningful negotiations on conditions of employment;

3. provide to representatives of employees where this accords with local law and practice, information which enables them to obtain a true and fair view of the performance of the entity or, where appropriate, the enterprise as a whole;

4. observe standards of employment and industrial relations not less favourable than those observed by comparable employers in the host country;

5. in their operations, to the greatest extent practicable, utilise, train and prepare for upgrading members of the local labour force in co-operation with representatives of their employees and, where appropriate, the relevant governmental authorities;

6. in considering changes in their operations which would have major effects upon the livelihood of their employees, in particular in the case of the closure of an entity involving collective lay-offs or dismissals, provide reasonable notice of such changes to representatives of their employees, and where appropriate to the relevant governmental authorities, and co-operate with the employee representatives and appropriate governmental authorities so as to mitigate to the maximum extent practicable adverse effects;

7. implement their employment policies including hiring, discharge, pay, promotion and training without discrimination unless selectivity in respect of employee characteristics is in furtherance of established governmental policies which specifically promote greater equality of employment opportunity;

8. in the context of bona fide negotiations* with representatives of employees on conditions of employment, or while employees are exercising a right to organise, not threaten to utilise a capacity to transfer the whole or part of an operating unit from the country concerned nor transfer employees from the enterprises' component entities in other countries in order to influence unfairly those negotiations or to hinder the exercise of a right to organise;**

9. enable authorised representatives of their employees to conduct negotiations on collective bargaining or labour management relations issues with representatives of management who are authorised to take decisions on the matters under negotiation.

*Bona fide negotiations may include labour disputes as part of the process of negotiation. Whether or not labour disputes are so included will be determined by the law and prevailing employment practices of particular countries.
**NOTE: This paragraph includes the additional provision adopted by OECD Governments at the meeting of the OECD Council at Ministerial level on 13th and 14th June 1979, in response to the Hertz Rentacar case (see below, p.129).

The first series of 'cases' was presented by TUAC, on behalf of its affiliated organisations, to the IME Committee meeting held in Paris on 30 March 1977. The majority of these,[2] together with subsequent submissions, including the latest ones discussed after the 1979 review of the Guidelines, are analysed below. The purpose of this section is to give a rapid overview of cases brought to date, not to provide exhaustive analysis. The first one is something of a *cause célèbre*: the Badger case.[3] In addition, the Badger case drew the attention of governments, unions, MNCs and the general public, to some of the possibilities inherent in the Guidelines, providing an important initial impetus.

(i) Badger Company: parent company liability, employee consultation and compensation (Belgium)

The first case submitted to the OECD's IME Committee immediately raised the Guidelines from the level of an arcane bureaucratic exercise to the first rank of political and economic reality. Concerning the Badger Co., a wholly-owned Belgian subsidiary of American multinational Raytheon, this case was brought not just by TUAC on behalf of the unions involved but also by the Belgian government in the shape of Minister Mark Eyskens, then Secretary of State for the Regional Economy, and since Belgian Prime Minister.

The situation was triggered when in late 1976 it became clear that the central management of Raytheon was actively considering the close-down of Badger in the absence of a prospective buyer for its unprofitable Belgian subsidiary — which management claimed had in any case been only kept alive by transfer to it of work and orders from other of Raytheon's European subsidiaries. By early February 1977, closure was effected and by the time of the 30 March session of OECD government officials, the following state of affairs had been reached, according to Minister Eyskens' letter to the IME Committee:

> compulsory winding-up of Badger (Belgium) has been ordered and it has not paid its creditors. The compensation owed to members of staff in the case of the closure of an enterprise amounts, according to Belgian law, which makes no distinction here between national and foreign enterprises, to BF 250 million (6.5 million dollars) (compensation for dismissal + additional compensation for workers in the case of the closure of an enterprise). The parent company has refused to intervene to settle the liabilities of its subsidiary not covered by the available assets.[4]

At stake in the Badger case, then, were a variety of issues of seminal interest, including in particular: the application of the Guidelines in bringing about actual changes in corporate behaviour; the issue of parent company responsibility over a foreign subsidiary limited in liability, the question of the notice to workers and public authorities to be given by a company envisaging shutdown and lay-offs and the compatibility of this practice with national laws.

In summary these issues were resolved or debated along the following lines:[5]

> — *the Guidelines and individual MNCs:* as laid down in the 1976 decision of the OECD Council, the IME Committee 'shall not reach conclusions on the conduct of individual enterprises', a point eagerly made by the 30 March 1977 meeting of the Committee. However, there can be no doubt that the Guidelines were used successfully to exert pressure on Raytheon's central management to change its initial position, and in this the use of the Guidelines was not restricted to the forum of the IME Committee. Strong bilateral representations were made by the Belgian government to the American State Department, to say nothing of parallel interventions between Brussels and respectively the Netherlands and Britain where two other subsidiaries of Raytheon were located. Set against the background of these intergovernmental contracts, continued union pressure and IME Committee debate, Raytheon finally agreed a settlement with the Belgian government in April 1977.[6] The Badger case thus contains an important lesson for the future. While there is no question of the OECD governments constituting a court to sit in judgement over individual multinationals, the Guidelines themselves can clearly be used as a strong basis for high-level political and economic leverage outside the formal context of the IME Committee. This lesson was to be reinforced in the Hertz case.

> — *parental responsibility over a foreign wholly-owned subsidiary:* this in many senses is the key issue of the Badger case, since the extent to which Raytheon was to be considered responsible for the activities (or the cessation of those activities) of a subsidiary raised the central question of the legal status of corporate groups, and got the IME Committee willy-nilly into a debate directly associated with this question. Is a parent company liable, beyond its equity stake, for a subsidiary's obligations to its local environment? Considered 'crucial' by government representatives,[7] this issue was given in-depth debate by them in late 1977 when the Badger case continued to smoulder. The confidential report of the Lévy subcommittee of the IME Committee said:

126

It was generally recognized that there was no absolute, unqualified principle of responsibility on the part of the parent company. On the other hand, it was also generally recognized that in some circumstances, which would have to be defined pragmatically, some degree of responsibility on the part of the parent company did exist as a complement to the existing legal provisions . . . . It was suggested that consideration be given to the idea that the responsibility of the parent company might be based on the notion of some behaviour on its part which would lead to its having a responsibility in certain situations. Lastly, it was also suggested that the IME Committee should examine the actual situation as it existed in each Member country as regards the responsibility of parent companies with respect to their subsidiary companies located within the country.

(All of which have proved grist to the mill of EEC company lawyers who are now actively preparing such an initiative on multinational group law.)[8] The report by Mr Levy was in fact in response to the Belgian government memo on Badger which, invoking the introduction to the OECD Guidelines in support of its case, stated baldly that 'a parent company is obliged to help its subsidiaries to fulfil their obligations'. In actual fact, section 8 of the introduction to the Guidelines is provocatively evasive when it states:

the guidelines are addressed to the various entities within the multinational enterprise (parent companies and/or local entities) according to the actual distribution of responsibilities among them on the understanding that they will co-operate and provide assistance to one another as necessary to facilitate observation of the guidelines. The word 'enterprise' as used in these guidelines refers to the various entities in accordance with their responsibilities.

— *company dealings with workers and governments:* the Belgian government referring to section 7 of the introduction to the Guidelines, had made much of the need for Badger to meet its obligation under Belgian law. Section 7 states:

Every State has the right to prescribe the conditions under which multinational enterprises operate within its national jurisdiction, subject to international law and to the international agreements to which it has subscribed. The entities of a multinational enterprise located in various countries are subject to the laws of these countries.

This, together with section 8 of the introduction (see above) was the basis for the Belgian government's contention that Raytheon should be liable for Badger (Belgium's) debts and severance indemnities for its workforce. However, in the view of other OECD governments, 'it would seem to be interpreting the guidelines too broadly' to say on the basis of the Guidelines that 'parent company should be liable for debts of subsidiaries even if the latter has been declared bankrupt unless the law provides for such responsibility'.[9] As against this, said the OECD Committee: 'it must be recognised that section 6 of the Section on Employment and Industrial Relations places termination claims in an exceptional position by virtue of the parent company's responsibility for the livelihood of the employees of its subsidiary when deciding to close down the operations which lead to the collective lay-off or dismissal of labour employed by a subsidiary'.[10] Section 6 of the Guidelines section on Employment and Industrial Relations states:

> in considering changes in their operations which would have major effects upon the livelihood of their employees, in particular in the case of the closure of an entity involving collective lay-offs or dismissals, enterprises should provide reasonable notice of such changes to representatives of their employees, and where appropriate to the relevant governmental authorities, and co-operate with the employee representatives and appropriate governmental authorities so as to mitigate to the maximum extent practicable adverse effects.[11]

So despite the strictures put by the IME Committee on an interpretation of the Guidelines which would offend accepted wisdom on parent company responsibility, 'the Guidelines may, and sometimes do, put obligations on multinational enterprises going beyond what it required from them by law'.[12] More ominous still for MNCs is the assertion made in the closed-door intergovernmental discussion of the Badger case that the Guidelines, while not legally binding, may become *de facto* part of customary international law: *'in the course of time, sections of the Guidelines, although voluntary in their origin and not being sanctioned by law, may pass, by virtue of their general acceptance and frequent application, into the general corpus of customary international law, even for those international enterprises that have never explicitly accepted them'*.[12] So is 'soft law politically hardened.

(ii) Hertz Rentacar: transfer of workers to influence collective bargaining (Denmark)

The issue at stake in the Hertz Rentacar (Denmark) case, brought by TUAC on behalf of the Danish LO union confederation, was whether the temporary transfer of workers from outside Denmark to meet staff shortages caused by a strike at Hertz in Denmark infringed the section of the Guidelines dealing with Employment and Industrial Relations, in particular its section 8, which states:

> Enterprises should, in the context of *bona fide* negotiations with representatives of employees on conditions of employment, or while employees are exercising a right to organise, not threaten to utilise a capacity to transfer the whole or part of an operating unit from the country concerned in order to influence unfairly those negotiations or to hinder the exercise of a right to organise'.[13]

The action by Hertz, bringing in workers from its other operations in a variety of Common Market countries (between which there is free movement of labour), was also condemned by the LO under other paragraphs in the Employment and Industrial Relations section. It was also debated in the European Parliament, and was the subject of discussion in the EEC Council of Ministers,[14] indeed by and large raised such widespread interest as to be a further warning — following the Badger case — to those who considered the OECD Guidelines an esoteric parenthesis.

The OECD itself trod more carefully when it came to analyse the case, maintaining that the company was not in contravention of the Guidelines *per se*, since — in its judgement — section 8 did not apply to temporary transfers of workers as a method of 'influencing unfairly' . . . '*bone fide* negotiations with representatives of employees'. However, the OECD did consider that the Guidelines should perhaps be redrafted to plug this gap — a consideration which was in fact enacted when the review of the Guidelines, completed in June 1979, 'recommended to multinational enterprises to abstain from transferals of personnel as described above'.[15]

(iii) Massey Ferguson : Motor Iberica: trade union recognition (Spain)

It was claimed by TUAC representatives that Motor Iberica, a Spanish subsidiary of Massey Ferguson, had for years 'violated trade union rights' by 'victimising' in Spain alleged actions which according to TUAC were contrary to the Employment Guidelines for MNCs. The terse reply from the OECD was that 'nothing in the Guidelines may be construed as recommending to multinational enterprises to act against the laws and regulations in force in each country in which they operate, including those on the recognition of trade unions, or to disregard court decisions'.[16]

(iv) Black and Decker: trade union recognition (United Kingdom)

The TUAC, representing the British General and Municipal Workers Union, claimed 'lack of management co-operation' in promoting unionisation of company employees at a UK subsidiary and 'refusal to grant recognition' of unions. But according to the OECD verdict, 'the Section on Employment and Industrial Relations does not provide that a multinational enterprise should actively encourage its employees to organise in trade unions or other *bona fide* organisations but to secure for the employees the freedom of choice to organise or not and to be represented by or to become a member of such organisations'.[17] (This is a reference to section 1 of the Employment and Industrial Relations section detailed earlier.) However, the OECD did subsequently make clear, when addressing itself to the Citibank case, that management should not discourage employees from unionising.

(v) Siemens: employment protection (Belgium)

Belgian unions complained, on the basis of the Employment and Industrial Relations section, that Siemens, which had signed a contract with the government allegedly committing itself to create jobs in return for government contracts, had not only failed to meet contractual employment increases but had cut its workforce by some 25—30 per cent. The OECD reply was to the effect that 'the implementation of agreements or contracts, including those between governments and multinational enterprises, is primarily a matter of the applicable law and jurisdiction. The Guidelines do not relate to the implementation of contractual obligations by multinational enterprises'. In addition, the Guidelines point out (said the OECD) that 'Member countries should fulfil their responsibilities to treat multinational enterprises in accordance with the contractual obligations to which they have subscribed, assuming evidently that national law provides the means for making multinational enterprises fulfil their side of the contract', adding: 'The Guidelines, however, may in the event be invoked for the interpretation of contractual provisions, in particular in case a contract refers to the Guidelines or to moral obligations described therein'. The OECD concludes that 'the Guidelines, and in particular section 6 of the Section on Employment and Industrial Relations do not support the view that multinational enterprises should maintain existing employment levels or continue activities they wish to terminate, nor that they should guarantee re-employment for personnel dismissed as a result of closure of an entity'.[18]

(vi) Warner Lambert: closure, employment protection and wage level maintenance (Sweden)

Here the union complaint focused on the intentions of Warner Lambert, an American multinational manufacturing razor blades in a plant in Sweden, to close down the plant and possibly to transfer its operations to Holland. According to the union: 'using the argument of the possible transfer of operations to the Netherlands, the Warner-Lambert subsidiary in Sweden demanded in the course of negotiations that workers should accept a lower wage level than the level of the regional average. Actually, this average for 1976 was more than 12 per cent higher than the wage level of the Warner-Lambert subsidiary'. The unions were thus invoking section 4 of the Employment and Industrial Relations section of the Guidelines which states:

> Enterprises should observe standards of employment and industrial relations not less favourable than those observed by comparable employers in the host country.

The OECD response was that this paragraph,

> although of general application, should not exclude that temporarily and under exceptional circumstances agreements may be reached on wages less favourable than those observed by comparable employers in host countries. The meaning of section 4, in this view, is that a multinational enterprise paying lower wages than section 4 indicates should in good faith aim at restoring wages to the standards referred to in section 4 as soon as the specific circumstances which gave rise to such agreements no longer persist.

But this interpretation, however consistent with the realities of operating an international business, seems somewhat far removed from the actual text of the Guidelines — as the OECD itself recognised when

131

it added: 'in view of the rather categorical wording of section 4, this Guideline may need to be reviewed to provide an element of flexibility for meeting exceptional circumstances, if after further experience it should appear that the present text does not contain flexibility'.[19] However, the 1979 review of the Guidelines omitted any mention of such an amendment to the text.

(vii) Litton Industries: production transfer and plant closure (Sweden)

According to the unions, Litton Industries, the American conglomerate which fully controlled a Swedish subsidiary Sweda, was contravening the OECD Guidelines by progressive reductions in Sweda's workforce leading to intended closure of the operation. This was consistent, said the unions, neither with the General Policy section of the Guidelines nor with (the by now famous) section 6 of the Employment section. According to the General Policy section of the Guidelines, firms were to 'take fully into account established general policy objectives of the Member countries in which they operate' (section 1) and 'in particular give due consideration to these countries' aims and priorities with regard to economic and social progress including industrial and regional development opportunities, the promotion of innovation and the transfer of technology'. The OECD response to the Litton Industries case was to reassert the principle contained in section 1, and to devote the rest of its attention to the mention in section 2 of the 'creation of employment opportunities'. 'In case this latter objective indeed forms part of the host government's objectives' opined the OECD, 'the multinational enterprise should give full weight to it, *inter alia* when it considers closing down an entity or diminishing the number of employees'. 'However', added the OECD secretariat, 'these paragraphs are not meant to prevent a multinational enterprise from closing down an entity.'[20] The OECD opinion then added a reference to the Siemens case discussed above.

(viii) Philips: trade union information and co-operation on plant closures (Germany)

Here the problem called to the OECD's attention by the unions was the closure by Philips of six subsidiary plants in West Germany and the redundancies which ensued, despite strong arguments by the German Metalworkers' Union, IG Metall, and the works councils seeking to defend the job security of the workers in these plants. Again it was section 6 of the Employment and Industrial Relations section, and again, true to its well-established form of nuanced caution, the OECD secretariat made the following careful statements: 'recognizing implicitly that changing operations, including the location of investments, is one of the prerogatives of a multinational enterprise, the Guidelines insist that a satisfactory solution must be found to mitigate adverse effects for employees dismissed as a result of operational changes'. The OECD assessment concluded with a reference to the Litton Industries' case and the sardonic comment that 'once multinational enterprises have made a decision to terminate branch activities, the Guidelines do not require them to solve or improve resulting regional development problems of host countries'.[21]

(ix) International Telephone and Telegraph: worker representation and union information (Germany)

The German unions complained that ITT had decided on 'changes in its legal company structure in the Federal Republic of Germany which obviously were not motivated by business reasons, nor by production, financial commercial or other factors', but rather by 'the possibility of circumventing their obligations to conform with the new German Law on Co-determination of 1976'. The ITT search for new company structures, claimed the union, was simply to avoid the parity union representation on supervisory boards of companies employing more than 2,000 staff. 'ITT's attitude', said the trade union submission to the OECD, 'is to be considered as an infringement of their obligations with regard to representation, direct information and participation of the trade unions'. It concluded that 'the spirit of the OECD Guidelines should commit ITT to recognise the new German legislation. Companies should recognize their moral commitment not to use legal loopholes, particularly in a case where representation of workers and their trade unions — as stipulated by the German law — is to bring about in foreign subsidiaries the greatly needed protection of the workers against the consequences of central management decisions taken abroad'.

The union argument appeared to get short shrift from OECD analysts who examined the ITT case against the general philosophy of the Guidelines and asserted: 'nothing in the Guidelines prevents multinational enterprises from selecting freely the legal form in which to carry out their activities. If there should be loopholes in the law, it is up to the national legislator to complete the law. Furthermore, the Guidelines do not recommend multinational enterprises to introduce co-determination beyond the one provided by law'.[22]

However, in a last delphic statement which could be construed as a warning that MNC activities should come up to national expectations, the OECD added a reference to section 9 of the introduction of the Guidelines, which states:

> The Guidelines are not aimed at introducing differences of treatment between multinational and domestic enterprises; wherever relevant they reflect good practice for all. Accordingly, multinational and domestic enterprises are subject to the same expectations in respect of their conduct wherever the guidelines are relevant to both.

(x) Citibank—Citicorp: trade union formation and recognition (United Kingdom)[23]

> It is the contention of FIET (the International Federation of Employees and Technicians) and NUBE (the UK National Union of Bank Employees) that the international management of Citibank—Citicorp conducts a world wide anti-union policy. Whenever possible, it avoids recognizing trade unions and negotiating with them. To conduct this policy, there is evidence that instructions are given to their local management about the tactics to be used in local situations.

In the submission to the OECD, the unions quoted from a Citicorp 'guide' to managers for handling of labour issues:

> The management of Citibank firmly believes that the best interest of all Citibankers are served without the presence of a union. To that end management commits its efforts to the maintenance of an environment which renders unnecessary the intervention of a third party . . . . It is further the policy of Citibank that only the President or the Chairman of the Board has the authority to recognise or enter into any agreement, verbal or written, with a union, union representatives or group of employees.

Referring to section 1 of the Employment and Industrial Relations section of the Guidelines ('enterprises should respect the right of their employees to be represented by trade unions and other *bona fide* organisations of employees . . .') the OECD responded as follows:

> Respect for the right of employees to be represented by unions implies that multinational enterprises should abstain from discouraging employees to become members of unions. This implies that they should recruit personnel regardless of such membership.

134

The question arises whether the right to be represented implies responsibility of employers to protect their employees or even to facilitate their union organisational activities. This could be an area where the Guidelines could be made more explicit if appropriate [a cross reference is made here to the Massey Ferguson case — see above].

'The Guidelines', concludes the OECD, 'do not indicate which persons or which level should deal with union — or employment — matters. However, negotiations should be conducted on the management side by persons who are authorised to take decisions on matters under negotiation'. This, a reference to section 9 of the Employment and Industrial Relations section of the Guidelines,[24] has since become a crucial issue when the British Oxygen case hit the headlines in 1980 (see below).

(xi) European Airlines Groupings: definition of a multinational (Europe-wide)

The OECD Guidelines contain no definition of a multinational enterprise beyond stating, intriguingly, that:

> A precise legal definition of multinational enterprises is not required for the purposes of the Guidelines. These usually comprise companies or other entities whose ownership is private, state or mixed, established in different countries and so linked that one or more of them may be able to exercise a significant influence over the activities of others, and, in particular, to share knowledge and resources with the others.[25]

At stake in the European Airlines Groupings case was whether such organisations as KSSU (KLM, Swissair, SAS and UTA) and ATLAS (Alitalia, Lufthansa, Air France, and Sabena) could be considered multinational enterprises for the purposes of the application of the Guidelines. The unions, and in particular the International Transport Workers Federation, who had been pressing for negotiations with the groupings on employment-related issues, were met with the argument from the companies that their associations covered co-operation which 'is mainly technical and therefore of no concern to the unions'. According to this argument, the co-operating companies — in a sort of mirror image of the normal subsidiary/parent company relationship — retain their individual autonomy and therefore no useful purpose could be served by international consultation with union representatives. But the OECD considered that KSSU and ATLAS were indeed multinationals from the standpoint of the Guidelines and must therefore enable meaningful negotiations with the unions if appropriate.

(xii) and (xiii) Firestone (Switzerland) and BATCO (Netherlands): do the Guidelines restrict business relocation? — No, but . . .

The last two 'cases' to be considered by the OECD prior to the 1979 review of the Guidelines, those concerning Firestone's Swiss subsidiary at Pratteln and British American Tobacco's cigarette plant in Amsterdam, are generally considered together because they raise similar questions about corporate behaviour. In particular: to what extent do the Guidelines restrict multinationals from relocating as they see fit? Indeed, may a foreign investor close down a profitable subsidiary?

The answer to the second question is affirmative, but with some qualifications important in answering the first. Those qualifications, as was made abundantly clear by the Dutch authorities in the case of BATCO's intention to close its Amsterdam factory, concern a company's industrial relations' obligations to a local workforce in such circumstances. Thus, as a Netherlands government memo to the OECD pointed out in 1980,[26] while the Dutch Companies Chamber 'found no evidence of mismanagement of BATCO in terms of business economics . . . it did find evidence of mismanagement in social terms and therefore annulled BATCO Nederland's decision to close the factory in Amsterdam'. In fact, the company, which had intended to switch its production from Amsterdam to another plant in Brussels, subsequently chose to reinvest in a new plant in Amsterdam, involving trimming 80 off its workforce of 250.

In addition to the use made by the unions in the BATCO case of the industrial relations guidelines, organised labour was also testing the applicability of general policy considerations for MNC behaviour. In the review of the Guidelines in 1979, governments noted that, in cases of intended closure of subsidiaries, 'a prudent company would be well advised to seek any necessary clarification of government policies through advance consultations with the government concerned'.[27]

The case involving Firestone was similar, except that the US tyre company did end up by closing its Swiss factory — but not without special severance costs amounting to 2.5 million Swiss Francs. Here also the unions[28] cited the general policy section of the OECD Guidelines, in particular its paragraph 5:

> Enterprises should allow their component entities freedom to develop their activities and to exploit their competitive advantage

in domestic and foreign markets, consistent with the need for specialisation and sound commercial practice.[29]

Although the OECD did not accept the unions' contention that a profitable subsidiary could not be closed, once again the stress was put on full respect of industrial relations' obligations. This was later confirmed by the decision of the Swiss appellate court in Basel, which found against Firestone.

Finally, a key aspect of the Firestone case was the issue it raised of the access of local workforce representatives to real company decision-makers. Unions claimed that in the process leading to the shut-down of the American company's Swiss subsidiary, they had no access to the people — Firestone's international management in Akron (USA) — actually responsible for the disinvestment decision. That is, they had no access, prior to the decision, to authorised representatives of MNC management — also the key theme of the two major cases which have reached the OECD in Paris after the 1979 review of the Guidelines.[30] These are discussed below.

The 1979 Review of the Guidelines
— National Contact Points —

Following the review of the Guidelines in June 1979,[31] the major innovation in the application of the Guidelines was the creation of the so-called 'national contact points'. This represented an attempt by governments to encourage resolution of MNC/union disputes at the local level. Given this, and the little time that has elapsed since the review, the cases thus brought up for consideration at the intergovernmental level of the OECD have thus been limited in number. However, activity in the national contact points should not be ignored and is considered in chapter 10.

(xiv) and (xv) British Oxygen (Sweden) and
Philips (Finland): access to authorised decision makers

The crucial issue of enabling trade union access to real decision-makers prior to key investment decisions — covered by paragraph 9 of the Guideline on Employment and Industrial Relations — reached a head with the case involving UK-based British Oxygen Corporation International (BOCI) and its Swedish subsidiary Viggo AB located at Helsingborg. As a result of this case, in which the Swedish trade unions alleged BOCI's intention to move the focal point of certain of Viggo's product lines outside Sweden, the OECD delivered a clear 'ruling'[32] to MNCs on union rights to consult with management. Management, if necesary central management, must make itself available for consultation with local unions prior to major investment decisions affecting the local workforce, if local law or practice so decrees. Such consultations with local management are insufficient, says the OECD, if local management is not empowered to take the decision in question and is not effectively informed of decisions taken elsewhere. In other words, the uninformed talking to the uninformed is not a definition of effective consultation. As the OECD put it:[33]

> In carrying out their responsibilities on issues relating to future production and investment plans, management of the enterprise as a whole would seem to have a range of possibilities among which it would choose or that it could combine, taking into full account the need to respect prevailing labour relations practices in the country where the negotiations have been initiated. Its choice depends on various circumstances, such as the matters under discussion, the decision making structure within the enterprise, and the importance of the decisions to be taken. A number of possibilities are open to this end without suggesting any order of preference. Examples of such possibilities include:
>
> — to provide the management of the subsidiary with adequate and timely information and to ensure that it has sufficient powers to conduct meaningful negotiations with representatives of employees;
>
> — to nominate one or more representatives of the decision making centre to the negotiating team of the subsidiary in order to secure the same result as in the preceding example;
>
> — to engage directly in negotiations.[34]

In the most recent Philips' case, sparked by the decision taken in March 1980 to close down a Finnish subsidiary, the unions again complained about lack of meaningful access to management, as well as questioning the compatibility of the Dutch multinational's decision with Finnish policy on research and development. A point of special emphasis for the local trade unions was the company's duty (as the unions saw it) to inform them of corporate decision-making structures. In Paris, where the OECD's ruling on the case has yet to be finally given, the feeling appears to be that it may be legitimate for unions to have such information if it is necessary for specific management/labour negotiations.

Notes and references

1   I.e. cases treated at the OECD intergovernmental level. If cases raised by the so-called 'national contact points' created in 1979 were included, this figure would be much higher. For contact points, see chapter 10.

2   Cases brought by the unions in the initial implementation phase of the Guidelines, but not discussed below, include: Burroughs, Poclain, Bendix, Wasabröd, Bata, and a second case involving Philips.

3   For more detailed analysis of the Badger case, see 'The Badger Case, Dr R. Blanpain, Kluwer, Deventer, the Netherlands, 1977.

4   Belgian government's submission to the IME Committee, reproduced in full in Multinational Service no.7, 13 April 1977 (Background Document).

5   The key paragraphs of reference in the Guidelines, as used by the Belgian government to present its case in Badger are: sections 7 and 8 of the introduction to the Guidelines, and section 6 of the Guideline on Employment and Industrial Relations. These are in fact quoted in the following text, but the reader is recommended to consult them directly at this stage by referring to Appendix II(b).

6   'The Badger Case', Blanpain, pp. 121–6.

7   Confidential report submitted to the IME Committee by Mr Philippe Lévy, chairman of the 'Lévy Group', 7 November 1977.

8   See chapter 5. In addition, the Badger case was the main spark behind the OECD's report, published in June 1980, entitled 'Responsibility of Parent Companies for their Subsidiaries'.

9   IME Committee, internal document 'Considerations on the Badger Case (submitted by TUAC and the Belgian government)', 8 June 1977, pp. 4–5.

10   Ibid. page 5.

11   OECD Guidelines on Multinational Enterprises. See also pp. 123–4.

12   IME Committee, internal document 'Considerations on the Badger Case (submitted by TUAC and the Belgian government)', 8 June 1977, p.5.

13   OECD Guidelines.

14   EEC Foreign Ministers' Meeting, 27 June 1978.

15   Analysis of cases submitted by TUAC in the IME Committee, 30 March 1977, OECD (internal document). Hertz: In fact, following the 14 June 1979 OECD meeting, the text of section 8 was changed as follows: 'enterprises should . . . not threaten to utilise a capacity to transfer the whole or part of an operating unit from the country concerned *nor transfer employees from the enterprises' component entities in other countries . . .* '. See OECD Guidelines (Appendix II(h) and

Employment and Industrial Relations Guideline (Appendix IIb).

16 Ibid.
17 Ibid.
18 Ibid.
19 Ibid.
20 Ibid.
21 Ibid.
22 Ibid.
23 For further consideration of Citibank, see chapter 10.
24 Analyses of cases.
25 Introduction to the Guidelines, paragraph 8, see Appendix II(b).
26 'Memorandum of the Netherlands Delegation concerning the BATCO case', IME (80) 7, 21 April 1980.
27 See Appendix II(h).
28 Submission of the Swiss Trade Union Centre, USS to IME Committee, 1978.
29 See Appendix II(b).
30 And, indeed, of the EEC's multinationals' proposal, see chapter 5.
31 See Appendix II(h).
32 Officially, the OECD does not give rulings but 'clarifications'.
33 'Application of paragraph 9 of the Employment and Industrial Relations Guidelines to Investment Matters', IME (80), 23, 10 December 1980.
34 This is a close parallel to draft provisions of the EEC rule for MNC consultation and information with local workforces. The parallel is no coincidence. See chapter 5.

10 Political and business impact of the OECD code

Of the factors affecting the development of the OECD code on MNCs in the coming years, some relate directly to the code itself while others to the more general economic and political framework within which the Guidelines are set. Thus attempts to give the Guidelines greater practical effect, spearheaded by the trade unions and parried by the international business community, respond to the call made by governments in 1979[1] to improve the Guidelines' implementation.

At the same time, the broader context holds factors which could influence the future of the OECD code and its impact on multinationals. One such factor of particular concern to governments is the need to stimulate economic activity as the world continues in the grips of a recession characterised by lengthening dole queues and contracting investment. As a result, the West's political establishment will likely come under strong pressure from a pro-business US administration to shift the emphasis from MNC control to investment encouragement — in other words, to concentrate on the other parts of the OECD package agreed in June 1976, including the instruments seeking to restrict the power of national governments to discriminate against foreign investors. Business can be expected to encourage sympathetic governments along this path even though the path itself is fraught with many traps which could undermine the unity of the multinational business world — e.g. the American offensive against an emerging EEC policy of industrial preference for European industry could push European and American multinationals to opposite sides of the fence.[2] Meanwhile, the trade unions may be instinctively hanging back from exploring the full potential of the OECD Guidelines as a constraint on MNCs while awaiting what they hope will be a more comprehensive instrument — the UN code of conduct for transnational corporations under negotiation in New York.

Accordingly, this chapter deals with: the outlook for the implementation of the OECD Guidelines in the coming years; the prospect of an accompanying shift from single-minded emphasis on MNC constraint to a policy encouraging investor activity; the OECD as the rich world's lobby in the negotiations for a UN code of conduct for transnational corporations; an assessment of the OECD code.

Greater impact for the OECD code — outlook for implementation of the Guidelines

The issues raised by the initial application of the OECD's multinationals code have almost certainly given it sufficient momentum to continue as a key focus for MNC executives well into the 1980s. The issues are manifold — trade union recognition, access to central management, union information and consultation rights particularly in cases of foreign disinvestment — and are likely to become more acute in the coming years as the world economy stutters uncertainly forward.

The core question is the extent to which governments can steer acceptably between, on the one hand, trade union demands that the Guidelines be more effectively enforced, if necessary by legislation (e.g. the Vredeling initiative in the EEC) and, on the other, business' concern that the very open-endedness of the OECD requirements for MNCs make the Guidelines the maximum tolerable. Western governments have therefore to negotiate a delicate course in applying a business control arrangement which, for the unions, is an absolute minimum, and for the multinational community is an absolute maximum. In their 1979 review of the Guidelines, governments sought to resolve this conundrum by the simple device of calling on all concerned, i.e. both labour and multinationals as well as themselves, to step up implementation of the Guidelines. This they did without giving a simple definition of what was meant by implementation, although they did call on business to better disseminate knowledge of the code, while committing themselves to giving greater force to the code's effectiveness by creating a series of 'national contact points' (as OECD jargon has it) to discuss industrial conflicts.

The *trade unions*, the only party with a clearly perceived and unambiguous interest in giving the Guidelines greater force, have thus been in the forefront of the implementation process. For organised labour, implementation means strong lobbying with governments, particularly at the EEC level, in an attempt to get them to legislate in areas of special concern, like industrial relations, where the Guidelines only provide voluntary recommendations for international business. It also means continued union scrutiny of MNC practice allegedly incompatible with the OECD code. Cases brought up at the inter-governmental level of the IME Committee since the 1979 review include those involving British Oxygen (in Sweden) and Philips (in Finland).[3] Meanwhile, at the national level, the behaviour of many other firms is being scrutinised, following the decision of governments in 1979 to create the contact points as an arena for resolving conflicts between unions and MNCs in their national localities. Among the most notable of these appears to be Ford in the Netherlands, but the behaviour of Japanese and European companies in the United States is also beginning to come under the microscope and this is examined in the section on 'National contact points'.

The trade union position on implementation is well expressed in TUAC's submission to OECD in the framework of the 1979 review of the Guidelines. 'The key question now is their implementation on the everyday working level, in the enterprises themselves' and, 'within this implementation process, the crucial element is the creation of a system of information and consultation at company, national and inter-national levels.' Trade union frustration is never far from the surface: 'for the trade union movement', says the TUAC memo, 'the OECD Guidelines were a first step towards more specific, functioning rules of the game', but 'there has been little progress in making them work, and the follow-up has been largely theoretical'.

Unsurprisingly, *multinationals*, individually and collectively, come to a quite different conclusion and attach a quite different meaning to the notion of effective implementation. Not for MNCs any sharpening of the OECD code. For BIAC, which is the mouthpiece of multinationals at the OECD, implementation means above all reconciling business to the idea of living with the Guidelines — necessary to which aim is opposition to any strengthening of the OECD code's existing provisions. It means keeping its constituent organisations — national business groups — and thus individual multinational companies, abreast of developments in the OECD code. In addition, BIAC has attempted to spur greater knowledge of the Guidelines by encouraging national employer bodies to disseminate the text of the Guidelines with the message that they should be observed. Yet conflicting with this aim is the explicit 'blackballing' by some leading employers' associations of any mention of the code.

Indeed, the MNC community's commitment to the public recom-mendation made by governments in 1979 that 'all enterprises . . .

indicate publicly that their acceptance of the Guidelines, preferably in their annual reports',[4] has been less than total. Certainly some of the multinational giants have openly espoused the OECD code, but the majority have not, and generalised acceptance appears a long way off. The reasons for this may vary. An important cause of business hesitation is the criticism that to publicly embrace the code, including its controversial guideline on employment and industrial relations, is simply to invite trade union harassment. As one governmental relations director of an American MNC operating in Europe told the author: 'if we proclaim to the world in our annual report that we accept the OECD standards, are we not almost legally binding ourselves to observe guidelines which, precisely because of their so-called voluntary nature, are open-ended in their requirements? Are we not giving organised labour the stick with which to beat us?'[5] Multinational companies are caught between on the one hand their fear of a quasi-legal commitment involving exposure to increased union pressure and, on the other, the public perception that they must indeed be reactionary if they cannot even commit themselves to voluntary guidelines recommended by their own governments.

For *governments*, the keynote of implementation of the OECD code, post-1979 and at least up to the mid-1980s when there will be a general revision of the arrangement,[6] is strengthening the application of the Guidelines at the national level. Emphasis on the national framework for implementing what is an international code for multinational companies may seem paradoxical, but the aim of Western governments appears to be to localise union/management disputes in MNCs at the national level — i.e. at the level of the subsidiary in which the conflict has broken out. By and large, this is welcomed by BIAC and multinationals. To achieve this, governments in 1979 recommended the setting up of 'national contact points' — bodies set up within national governments and given the three-fold task of:

— promoting the Guidelines;

— collecting data on the national experience with the Guidelines;

— providing a framework for unions and management to discuss problems with the Guidelines.

National contact points: initial experience uneven

Initial experience with the functioning of the contact points, which have been set up in 21 of the 24 OECD countries,[7] has been varied. The contribution of the contact points to reinforced observance by multinationals of the Guidelines has been enough to keep MNCs on their guard but insufficient to prevent trade unions from asserting that their operation has been a 'disappointment'.[8] The truth of the matter is that there has been little balance in the operation of contact points.

Thus in the Nordic states and the Netherlands and, to a lesser extent, Belgium — small countries with strong trade unions and high levels of foreign investment — the contact points have been used most actively. Even so, it is difficult to make a simple equation between strong unions and active contact points. Little or nothing, for example, has been heard of the contact points in the UK and Germany — two countries with amongst the most powerful national trade union organisations in the West. In the case of the Federal Republic, German trade unions seem to have preferred to rely on their own bargaining strength with multinationals, while in Britain, where both Conoco and Citibank subsidiaries have come under scrutiny, the story is again different. British unions have tried to reactivate with their contact point the allegedly anti-union activities of Citibank[9] but the contact point (set up within the UK Department of Industry) has apparently chosen to act simply as a letter box — delivering union complaints to Citibank management and management responses back to the union.[10] By 1981, the unsatisfactory nature of this 'letter box' arrangement had spurred the British TUC to pursue high-level contacts with ministers in Mrs Thatcher's government.[11]

In most other OECD countries, with one notable exception, the use of national contact points as conflict resolution centres seems to have been severely restricted, their role being limited to urging companies to comply with the Guidelines — the case for example, of Italy and Japan. Aside from the Nordic and Benelux countries, the one main exception is the USA. The American contact point — the Advisory Committee on International Investment, Technology and Development, of the Department of State — appears to have been fairly active in monitoring the behaviour of foreign MNCs in the USA. This has been particularly the case in the field of trade union recognition.

TUAC's submission to the OECD in late 1981[12] claimed that Sharp, an American subsidiary of a Japanese multinational, and an American affiliate of the German-based Bosch 'violated' the right of employees to be represented by trade unions. A further American case concerns another Japanese multinational, Toshiba, which according to the same sources,[13] 'for its operations in the United States hired a local consultant firm specialising in anti-union practice'. The significance of the activity of the US contact point — another function of which appears to be to protect US investment abroad — is that it shows a practical US interest in using the Guidelines that had not been evident in the years from 1976 to 1979. During that period, indeed, all cases brought to the OECD's attention alleging corporate non-compliance with the Guidelines were brought by European trade unions — the majority against the operations of American-owned subsidiaries in Western Europe. The reverse prospect — that of American unions taking stepped-up interest in the activities of the American affiliates of European parent companies is intriguing and is buttressed by the European investment invasion of the USA which reached its peak in the late 1970s as EEC multinationals, egged on by a falling dollar, fled to the 'freer' investment climate of the United States.

Nevertheless, it is primarily in the Scandinavian and Benelux countries that the contact points have been, and will likely remain, most active in the years to come. The case involving British Oxygen's Swedish subsidiary Viggo AB, is a good example of the role played by a national contact point.[14] A Finnish parallel is to be found in the 1980—81 case of Philips.[15] Meanwhile in Belgium, where unions brought an intended divestment by US multinational GTE to the attention of the contact point, and in the Netherlands, labour organisations have been exploring the possibilities of contact points as a ploy to get a better grip on MNCs. The Dutch unions have been both closely monitoring the rationalisation plans of Philips, while the *cause célèbre* for the local contact point is the affair of the Ford Motor Company. Ford, the subject in 1981 of high-level political attacks for its intention to close down its Amsterdam subsidiary,[16] is on the receiving end of trade union complaints focusing on its alleged failure to meet requirements spelt out by the OECD both as regards general policies and its industrial relations practice.[17] In addition, as in the case of BATCO and Firestone,[18] the unions are pursuing the company through the courts.

From MNC control to investor encouragement?

Shifting the emphasis of the OECD exercise from control of multinational companies to encouragement of international investment is now a central part of the strategy of those who, like the US administration, believe that there has been undue stress laid to date, and certainly up until the 1979 review of the Guidelines, on the 'negative' or control aspects of the decisions taken by the OECD Council in June 1976. The Reagan team's espousal of a policy which seeks to dismantle obstacles to foreign investment rather than increased control of MNCs will probably be supported by Mrs Thatcher's Britain and, perhaps in a more qualified way, by countries like Switzerland and West Germany. But European countries in general will oppose American interference with the development of national or EEC industry policies, and some, in particular the French, Scandinavian and Dutch are likely to be more sympathetic to enforcement of the OECD's multinationals code — an emphasis which will be single-mindedly pursued by the trade unions.

The Americans, together with some major business interests, will be pressing for strengthened action in the 1980s on the two 1976 decisions dealing respectively with 'national treatment' and 'international investment incentives and disincentives'.[19] These decisions stress the need for more equitable conditions for MNCs to carry out their international investment programmes. The trade unions, by contrast, fear that such a policy will create greater freedoms for MNCs just when

> the rapid internationalization of production brings about changes which call for increased attention by governments. . . . In the present economic situation trade unions are worried that there would be a shift towards more permissiveness, less monitoring or control, and, in general, away from the need to eliminate the negative consequences of the activities of multinational enterprises.[20]

The main thrust of the OECD decision on national treatment, likely to be the more important of the two, was the recommendation of a series of norms to be observed by governments to ensure that foreign investors were not discriminated against by national rules and procedures — e.g. preferential government procurement or public subsidisation of state-controlled rivals to multinationals competing in the same sector of activity. The recommended norms were to implement the principles whereby

> Member countries should, consistent with their needs to maintain public order, to protect their essential security interests and to fulfil commitments relating to international peace and security, accord to enterprises operating in their territories and owned or controlled directly or indirectly by a national of another Member country (hereinafter referred to as 'Foreign-Controlled Enterprises') treatment under their laws, administrative practices, consistent with international law and no less favourable than that accorded in like situations to domestic enterprises (hereinafter referred to as 'National Treatment').[21]

The OECD's 1976 Decision on Investment Incentives and Disincentives sought to intensify consultations between OECD governments (in the framework of the Committee on International Investment and Multinational Enterprises) aimed at strengthening co-operation on investment conditions, with the principal aim of removing discriminatory use of national measures to aid investments. As the OECD

Declaration June 1976 put it: 'Member countries will endeavour to make such measures as transparent as possible, so that their importance and purpose can be ascertained and that information on them can be readily ascertained'.[22]

These two decisions — on national treatment and investment aids and disincentives — are clearly linked: both seek to put multinational business on an equal footing, from the standpoint of state intervention, with national firms and state-controlled companies.

To date, concern with this two-fold endeavour has fallen into the deep shadow cast by OECD discussion on the stepped-up implementation of the Guidelines for multinationals. Moreover, even given American attempts to right this imbalance, the situation is unlikely to change very easily. The problem is that for the OECD's national treatment and investment instruments to have the apparent cutting-edge of the Guidelines, like the Guidelines they would have to be used specifically — not of course against multinationals, but this time against offending governments. And this is an unlikely scenario. Indeed, should US government pressure be exerted against European governments, individually or at the collective level of the EEC, on issues like aids to industry, on European industrial development programmes or on government contracting, the response is likely to be as frosty as that traditionally given Washington on similar issues by its northern neighbour Canada.

The Euro-American investment switch

Another factor cautioning against any intensifying of US pressure to remove national discrimination — exemplified in 1978 when Washington circulated to its Western partners a major report analysing incentive practices in OECD countries[23] — is recent changes in the traditional profile of the United States as exporter of investment capital. Prior to the late 1970s, in adopting an international business policy seeking to curb state interventionism, Washington was in a no-lose situation since any ensuing advantages to the foreign operations of American multinationals far outweighed any concessions that the US government would have to make domestically to the relatively small band of foreign-controlled enterprises in the USA. But since the end of the 1970s there has been a major reversal in international investment trends which places Western Europe and the USA, not to mention Japan, in a substantially different relation to each other than has been the case in the preceding 30 years.

Graphic illustration of this shifting investment trend is given by the OECD itself in its 1981 report 'Recent International Direct Investment Trends'.[24] The report focuses on the 'major upsurge which has

148

Table 10.1
Outward direct investment flows
Percentage distribution among 13 countries

	1961–67	1968–73	1974–79
Canada	2.3	4.5	6.2
United States	61.1	45.8	29.3
Japan	2.4	6.7	13.0
Australia	0.7	1.4	1.6[1]
Belgium	0.3[2]	1.4	2.5
France	6.9	5.2	7.8
Germany	7.2	12.5	17.0
Italy	3.6	3.3	2.0
Netherlands	4.4	6.8	9.6[3]
Sweden	2.0	2.4	3.7[4]
United Kingdom	8.7	9.1	9.2
Spain	0	0.3	0.6
Norway	0	0.3	0.9

1 From 1974–76
2 From 1965
3 From 1974–78
4 From 1974–77

Source: IMF–OECD Common Reporting System on Balance of Payments Statistics. The UK and US figures do not include reinvested earnings to place the data on a more comparable basis. UK data do not include the petroleum sector.

Table 10.2
Inward direct investment flows
Percentage distribution among 13 countries

	1961–67	1968–73	1974–78
Canada	16.2	12.1	3.2
United States	2.6	11.4	26.7
Japan	2.0	1.7	1.2
Australia	15.6	12.9	9.5[1]
Belgium	4.5[2]	6.1	9.4
France	8.2	8.2	15.2
Germany	21.3	16.4	14.7
Italy	11.5	8.3	5.0
Netherlands	4.7	8.5	6.0[3]
Sweden	2.4	1.7	0.5[4]
United Kingdom	9.7	7.4	6.1
Spain	2.7	3.7	3.7
Norway	0.8	1.4	4.1

1 From 1974–76
2 From 1965
3 From 1974–78
4 From 1974–77

Source: As table 10.1 above.

149

developed in recent years with the United States taking nearly one-quarter of the overall total of foreign direct investment in the period from 1974 to 1979. As a result', continues the OECD analysis, the USA's 'stock of foreign capital . . . rose from 13.6 billion dollars at the end of 1971 to just over 52 billion dollars at the end of 1979. The United States has attracted almost 31 per cent of the net international direct investment flows in the years 1974–79, against about 2.6 per cent in the 1961–67 period'.

The trends outlined in tables 10.1 and 10.2 show that the USA has quite suddenly become as big a factor as an importer of international investment as an exporter. Moreover, as a capital exporter, it had by 1980 become noticeably less significant than the aggregate contribution to foreign investment of the EEC countries, while Japan has also remorselessly increased its presence over the years.

However, just how these statistics translate into policy is less clear than the trends they indicate. But some policy considerations at least are worth pointing out. First, with the increased presence of European investment in the USA, the American administration could also find itself under pressure from European-owned subsidiaries uneasy at preferences granted their US rivals on the American market. Second, as has been pointed out in the preceding section in this chapter, the foreign investment invasion of the US market being led by European and Japanese multinationals could begin to create greater interest among American pressure groups in the potential for control of multinationals inherent in the Guidelines. This could certainly become a factor if, following further switches in international exchange rates or other factors, investors in the United States then decided to trim back operations, thus creating the type of employment-related problems caused by American investment pull-backs from Europe in the late 1970s and thrown into sharp focus by European trade union use of the Guidelines.

The OECD: the industrialised world's lobby on MNC issues

The industrialised world's major economic policy forum, the OECD has during the late 1970s and early 1980s been increasingly used as the mechanism through which Western governments co-ordinate their position for the various international negotiations with the developing countries which have burgeoned over the last decade. Negotiations on multinationals and international investment are no exception to this pattern. The rich countries use OECD institutions – like the IME Committee and its sub-committees – to prepare negotiating postures for discussions in the United Nations in New York, the International

Labour Organisation (ILO) and United Nations Committee on Trade and Development (UNCTAD) in Geneva. In all three of these institutions, moves are afoot which seek to regulate the activities of multinationals, in particular to make them conform to the economic priorities of the developing countries. In all three of these arenas, there is an ongoing confrontation between the so-called 'Group-77' countries (the developing countries) and Group B, virtually a synonym for OECD Member countries.

Faced with these demands for regulation, the immediate OECD reaction was to close ranks (even if they are now not as tight perhaps as once they were). The OECD Guidelines on Multinationals are, as has already been pointed out,[25] a rapid rich world response to the threatened emergence of a much tougher, legally binding code of conduct being negotiated by the United Nations in New York and at the same time a pre-emptive strike against the tougher ILO position on MNCs and social policy. Since 1976, the OECD countries, some (e.g. the USA, West Germany, Switzerland and the UK) with markedly more enthusiasm than others (the Nordics, the Netherlands) have continued to use the OECD code as a model to be copied by organisations such as the UN. The same can be said for the 'sectoral' arrangements affecting MNCs being worked out at UNCTAD on transfer of technology and restricted business practices. Future trends in the application of the OECD guidelines dealing respectively with science and technology, and competition rules, could thus be affected by this constraint external to the OECD world.

The outlook is for a continuation of such efforts, which have already yielded the result of rendering impossible an extensively compulsory code emerging from the UN, when the negotiations on an international code of conduct for transnationals move towards conclusion (probably in the early 1980s.[26]) The OECD countries which come to the UN armed with the Guidelines and secure in the knowledge that they host the vast majority of the world's MNC parent companies, will probably continue to erode the ambitions of the developing countries and the West's trades unions to set dramatic new ground-rules for MNC activities. This international role of the OECD is outlined as follows by official sources:

> Since 1976, other international organisations have taken up various issues related to the activities of MNEs. The International Labour Organisation has agreed to a tripartite Declaration of Principles concerning Multinational Enterprises and Social Policy. In the framework of the United Nations, a Code of Conduct relating to the activities of MNEs is being negotiated whilst, as part of the UNCTAD negotiations, an international Code of

Conduct for the transfer of technology and an international agreement on restrictive business practices are envisaged. In ECOSOC [the Economic and Social Council of the UN] work is underway on an international agreement to prevent illicit payments in connection with international commercial transactions.

There is clearly a link between these negotiations in other international bodies and the OECD Guidelines, although there is no necessary symmetry between them. Thus, the results of the OECD's work, being the first to be made public, have had an impact on work going on elsewhere, either on specific subjects covered by one of the OECD Guidelines or on the general approach adopted. At the same time, the context of negotiations in other fora differs from that which prevails inside the group of OECD countries so that each set of international negotiations has its own specificity.[27]

The work being conducted in the arenas mentioned in the above extract could well reach an advanced phase (or in the case of the ILO Declaration on MNCs a significant phase of practical application) in the early 1980s. Development of these initiatives, together with the influence of the industrialised world on their development, is examined below in Part IV.

Assessment of the OECD Guidelines:
a general code with selective impact

The OECD code for multinationals is neither outstandingly effective nor, at the same time, without its impact in the control of international business. The picture is mixed. The trade unions are disappointed because the Guidelines, both as regards their substance and the vigour with which governments apply them, fall way below their aim of a legally enforceable international instrument.

By contrast, the anxiety of business, which after the intensive information campaign of recent years must now be fairly familiar with the Guidelines, focuses on their gradual emergence as a body of international 'soft law'. Governments, meanwhile, are in the impossible situation of seeking to show that the Guidelines are a credible means of control over unacceptable MNC activity — without which they may face intensified pressure for national (or EEC) legislation — while at the same time attempting to ensure that they do not discourage investors at a time of falling economic activity.

The truth is that OECD Guidelines are restricted both in policy impact and geographical scope — but within these limits are an unavoidable focus in the development of any MNC public affairs programme for the 1980s.

Their prime policy impact is highly selective — focusing above all on the area of employment and industrial relations. This, apart from corporate disclosure and certain parts of the code's general policy requirements, is fundamentally what the OECD code is all about. This reflects the political power of the international trade union movement at a time of world economic crisis — and consequent business relocation. Boiled down to their core, the OECD Guidelines are an Industrial Relations Code for the Disinvestor.

Geographically, too, their application has been selective. The vast majority of 'cases' against individual multinationals so far, have been the work of the politically active trade unions of Northern Europe — the ·Nordic countries, the Netherlands, Belgium, Germany and the UK. The targets of these trade union complaints have also been fairly selective — over 50 per cent have been subsidiaries of American-owned multinationals. There are signs that this state of affairs could change in coming years as shifts in international investment trends mean that European and Japanese companies operating in the USA could come in for similar scrutiny, and for similar reasons. The same, of course, applies to Japanese companies operating in the EEC, but in this respect it should be noted that, by and large, Japanese investors have a predominantly good press for the conduct of their industrial relations.

Despite these limitations, and despite the disappointment of organised labour, business and governments continue to sit up and take notice.

American government miscalculation

The American government, which was in many ways the decisive factor in getting the Guidelines adopted in 1976, must by now be pondering the wisdom of the move. Washington, with no direct experience of an ideologically motivated union movement in the USA, seriously misread — or ignored — the significance of the quasi-'tripartite' nature of the OECD Guidelines, which effectively gives Western European unions an institutionalised influence over their application. Hoisted, as it were, on their own petard, the Americans will strive in the coming years to channel attention into international measures supporting foreign investment rather than MNC control. For reasons stated earlier, they will find this hard to do, while they cannot simply put a stop to the application of the Guidelines. The OECD code thus has a momentum all of its own which should carry it well into the 1980s provided that the unions continue to consider use of the Guidelines actually or potentially effective.

Other governments have paid their own tribute to the influence of the Guidelines. The Swedish government — like, indeed, the US administration — has referred to the Guidelines on competition policy when dealing with restrictive business practices of multinationals in other countries. The Dutch government has stated it takes the Guidelines into account in determining government policy. The Australian government has incorporated the Guidelines as an integral part of its policy on inward foreign investment. Meanwhile, in Brussels, the EEC is considering legislation — the so-called 'Vredeling initiative' (considered in chapter 5) — whose genesis in 1980 was explicitly linked to the OECD's Guideline on industrial relations. Moreover, Mr Ivor Richard, the man responsible for piloting through the EEC proposal, has already made public his concern with the type of industrial relations problems which the OECD Guidelines seek to help to avoid — citing French auto manufacturer Peugeot's closure of its Scottish factory, UK auto manufacturer British Leyland's pull-back from Belgium, and the sale by US oil multinational Atlantic Richfield of its controlling interest in London's *Observer* newspaper to the British multinational conglomerate Lonrho.[28]

Business's own assessment of the OECD code varies. Some individual multinationals have made known their support for the Guidelines, but the majority of companies, and the organisations that represent them are suspicious. Again this suspicion is a tribute to the perceived impact of the Guidelines on corporate behaviour. Indeed, national employers organisations in the United States and in Sweden have gone so far as to warn their affiliated companies of the dangers of signing agreements with the trade unions which included specific reference to the OECD Guidelines — even going as far as banning such references in negotiated agreements.

Meanwhile, the trade unions, the main pressure on Western governments to effectively apply the Guidelines, are unlikely to abandon the OECD code as a lost cause, even though they are presently disillusioned at what they see as its lack of 'bite'. They, in particular the International Confederation of Free Trade Unions and the World Confederation of Labour, will be seeking a good result from the UN code of conduct on transnational corporations, which they see as the real regulatory forum for MNCs — and in future may tend to downplay the OECD Guidelines as a diversionary tactic perpetuated by the rich world on the developing countries. But it would nonetheless be surprising if the unions ignored the fulcrum for leverage over MNCs that the Guidelines provide them with. This would be especially so if the result of the UN talks on a code of conduct were not to come up to trade union expectations — if that happened, a *retour en force* to the OECD code is to be expected from Western labour organisations.

The unions will in any case be seeking to harden as much as possible the 'soft law' status of the Guidelines underlined by the OECD in the Badger case:

> . . . in the course of time sections of the Guidelines, although voluntary in their origin and not being sanctioned by law, may pass, by virtue of their general acceptance and frequent application, into the general corpus of customary international law, even for those multinational enterprises that have never explicitly accepted them.[29]

Externally, the pressure on the industrialised world to prove the Guidelines a credible exercise will stem from negotiations in other fora, notably the UN and its specialised agencies. If the Guidelines cannot be shown to exert sufficient control over MNCs, the pressure for stronger international solutions could increase. This external pressure dovetails with the internal pressure being exerted by the unions noted above.

Prospect for individual guidelines

As for the development of the Guidelines themselves, the 'Employment and Industrial Relations' guideline will continue to be the one most intensively used, since it is the one most accessible to the trade unions. This prediction should be qualified, however, by awareness of the alternative pressure point provided the unions by the ILO Declaration on MNCs and social policy, adopted in November 1977 and now in early stages of implementation.[30] This covers much of the same ground as the OECD's employment guideline but in greater detail. Those responsible for co-ordinating OECD MNC policy realised this when they wrote:

> The ILO Declaration, to which OECD Member countries have subscribed, has a different scope than the Guidelines. The membership of the ILO is worldwide and its Declaration sets out principles in the fields of employment, training, conditions of work and industrial relations which governments, employers' and workers' organisations as well as multinational enterprises are recommended to observe. Where these principles refer to the behaviour expected from enterprises they parallel the OECD Guidelines and do not conflict with them. In this regard the ILO principles may be taken into consideration in situations in which their greater extent of elaboration or scope is useful.[31]

The issue of a multinational company's *parental responsibility* over the actions of its subsidiaries or dependent companies[32] also looks like being a matter of continued controversy and one on which at least one major group of OECD countries — the member countries of the European Community — could actively envisage legislation in the first half of the coming decade.

The OECD's Guideline on *corporate disclosure* — another area where new EEC legislation aimed at MNCs is in the offing[33] — will also be the focus of increased attention as business is urged to include greater information in annual reports and when necessary via contacts with governments. This trend could well be given a greater cutting-edge by the work of the OECD's ad hoc working group on accounting standards, set up in 1978 largely as a result of American government pressure. The ultimate objective of the group could be to work towards aligning corporate reporting requirements in Western countries. For the moment, the accounting group — an intergovernmental body — has conducted a survey of disclosure standards in OECD countries,[34] with the aim of formulating more precise recommendations. These recommendations could give a first glimpse of any new constraints that are being officially considered for companies in this already complex field in the short and medium-term.

Other issues so far given less prominence in the process of implementing the Guidelines could surface with greater impact in the coming years. Principal amongst these are MNC activities in the field of taxation, anti-trust and science and technology. But it is clear that the impulse for action in these areas lies with governments rather than the trades unions. Indeed a common criticisms of the Guidelines heard in trade union circles is that only they have actively sought to translate the OECD's words into action.

Over the next five years, this criticism could be partially answered, at least in the sensitive fields of corporate disclosure (see above) and taxation. On taxation, the OECD secretariat has already completed an international agreement between the OECD's 24 member governments on *transfer pricing*. Termed a 'Recommendation of the Council on the Determination of Transfer Prices between Associated Enterprises', the measure is a direct follow-up to the 1976 Guidelines calling on multinationals to 'refrain from making use of the particular facilities available to them, such as transfer pricing which does not conform to an arm's length standard'.[35] The recommendation calls on Western governments to 'develop further co-operation between their tax administrations on a bilateral or multilateral basis, in matters relating to transfer pricing'.[36]

International exchange of information on MNC activities is also, within certain limits, a hallmark of a measure on *anti-trust policy* adopted by the OECD in July 1978. This OECD policy recommendation, 'concerning action against restrictive business practices affecting trade including those involving multinational enterprises',[37] aims to beef up national anti-trust laws and at the same time strengthen 'mutual administrative or judicial aid'. Also intended as a statement of the Western bloc's position in negotiations for a worldwide agreement on restrictive business practices finalised by UNCTAD in 1980,[38] the OECD anti-trust initiative could in the coming years give rise to inter-governmental activity worthy of close corporate monitoring. In the same way as Western governments, in response to developing country pressure for a strong UN code of conduct, feel the need to take action emphasising the credibility of the OECD Guidelines taken globally, so the same governments may wish to show that the OECD's anti-trust measure is an effective supplementary instrument for containing multi-national company abuses in the field of restrictive business practices.

The *science and technology* guideline addressed to MNCs in 1976 has given rise to several discussions in the IME Committee, and could form the basis for renewed governmental pressure on firms 'to distribute their research and development activities more widely among the countries in which they operate and thereby contribute to the innovative capacity of these countries'.[39] Here again, OECD govern-ments, which are examining the impact of MNCs' technology transfer in particular in the pharmaceuticals, computers and food processing sectors, clearly have one eye firmly fixed on developments in UNCTAD, where an international arrangement setting ground-rules for the transfer of technology is under negotiation.[40] It is to examination of developments affecting MNCs in the fully international arena that we now turn.

Notes and references

1   Review report, see Appendix II(h).
2   EEC proposals for the development of European industry, revealed October 1981.
3   See chapter 9.
4   Contained in Review of OECD Guidelines, see Appendix II(h).
5   A fear reflected by Swedish and US employer organisations, who dispatched circulars to discourage their affiliates from referring to the Guidelines in drawing up collective bargaining accords with the unions. See p.154.
6   The next 5-year review is scheduled for June 1984 (see Appendix II(h).
7   Turkey, Iceland and Luxembourg have no contact point.

8   TUAC submission to IME Committee, 14 October 1981 (IME(81) 16). See also Appendix II(i).
9   See also chapter 9, p.134, for further details.
10   BIFU, the Banks, Insurance and Finance Union – the successor to NUBE.
11   Sources: British and European trade union officials.
12   TUAC submission to the IME Committee, 14 October 1981.
13   Ibid.
14   For the issues at stake, see chapter 9.
15   Ibid.
16   Including those made by Dutch Prime Minister Van Agt.
17   Letter sent by the Dutch trade union centre, FNV, to national contact point, dated 2 November 1981, cited OECD Guidelines' General Policies section, paragraphs 1, 2 and 4, and Employment and Industrial Relations, paras 3, 6 and 9.
18   See chapter 9.
19   For full texts, see Appendix II(d).
20   TUAC submission to the IME Committee, 14 October 1981.
21   See Appendix II(a).
22   Ibid.
23   'Incentives and Performance Requirements for Foreign Direct Investments in Selected Countries', US Department of Commerce, January 1978.
24   OECD, Paris, 1981. See tables 10.1 and 10.2 extracted from this report.
25   See chapter 8.
26   For further details of negotiating trends for the UN code of conduct on transnational corporations, see Part IV.
27   OECD, IME Committee, 1979, Review of Guidelines.
28   Speech to the American–European Community Association, New York, 1 October 1981.
29   See under Badger Co., chapter 9.
30   See Part IV for further consideration of ILO Declaration.
31   OECD IME Committee, Review of the Guidelines.
32   The subject of an OECD Report 'Responsibility of Parent Companies for their subsidiaries', Paris, June 1980.
33   See chapter 5.
34   See Multinational Service nos. 47, 50, 52, 56 and 59.
35   OECD Guidelines, Guideline on taxation. See Appendix II(b) and Appendix II(f).
36   Ibid.

37 See Appendix II(g).
38 See Part IV.
39 OECD, IME Committee, Review of Guidelines.
40 See Part IV.

PART IV

MULTINATIONALS AND THE UN SYSTEM:
TOWARDS VOLUNTARY BUT EFFECTIVE CODES

11 The UN code of conduct for transnational corporations

The roots of the UN code of conduct

In sharp contrast to the piecemeal approach adopted by the EEC to the containment of multinational companies, and to the establishment of voluntary guidelines for business behaviour by the industrialised world in the OECD, the United Nations has throughout the 1970s led the crusade for a comprehensive, legally binding international code of conduct. But by 1981, that prospect had changed in line with the world's altered economic circumstances. The outlook is now for a voluntary code, but companies should note that governments, particularly those of developing countries, may bind it into national legislation.

The history of the UN code reflects the ideological impulse of the world's developing countries to establish a 'new international economic order' and within it a compulsory mechanism for regulating the behaviour of the major economic actors, the MNCs or (as UN phraseology would have it) transnational corporations (TNCs). The developing countries, grouped together in the so-called 'Group of 77' (G-77), have been backed in their attempts by the international trade union movement, in particular the European-dominated International Confederation of Free Trades Unions (ICFTU, socialist union confederation) and the World Confederation of Labour (WCL, Christian unions). The combined G-77/union lobby has been opposed throughout the past decade by some major industrialised countries, with the United

States, West Germany and the United Kingdom to the fore in this respect. Indeed, the American Administration, accurately reading the change in the political weather-vane towards a climate of North/South confrontation, had by 1974 concluded that the best form of defence against the G-77 onslaught on Western economic interests and values was attack: as outlined in the previous chapter, in a period of 18 months it persuaded its OECD partners to negotiate, finalise and adopt the rich world's position on the MNC issue in the shape of the OECD's package on international investment and MNCs.[1]

The United Nations, which in fact only in early 1979 entered the substantive phase of negotiations for drafting a code of conduct for transnational corporations, is thus in the paradoxical situation of having led the call for international containment action in the early 1970s while having fallen far behind some other organisations in turning ideas into action. The OECD, a much more homogeneous group of countries, agreed its Guidelines in June 1976, while the International Labour Office, a UN specialised agency, adopted its 'Declaration of Principles concerning Multinational Enterprises and Social Policy' in November 1977. The first UN meeting with the specific aim of preparing the ground for a code of conduct for TNCs was only held in January 1977. The gestation period has thus been much longer, but its process is revealing for a reasoned assessment of the present situation and future outlook regarding the UN code.

Impregnated with the gathering economic development philosophy which stamped the 1970s, the UN code finds its direct roots in the 28 July 1972 decision of the United Nations Economic and Social Council (ECOSOC) which established the 'group of eminent persons', whose brief was to prepare recommendations for international action on multinational corporations.[2] The next stage was the publication in May 1974 by the eminent persons[3] of a report entitled 'The Impact of Multinational Corporations on Development and International Relations'. Providing much of the philosphic rationale for the subsequent work on the UN code, and unlike the OECD MNC Guidelines placing international business responsibilities fairly and squarely in the context of developing country needs, the eminent persons' report was translated by the end of 1974 into administrative action. On 5 December 1974, ECOSOC resolved to create a Commission and a Centre on Transnational Corporations, the job of the Commission being to aid ECOSOC to draw up 'a set of recommendations which, taken together, would represent the basis for a Code of Conduct dealing with transnational corporations'.[4] The Commission was given a five-part brief:

— to formulate a Code of Conduct (taking into account the work of UNCTAD and the ILO) on transnational corporations;

- to develop a comprehensive information system on transnationals;
- to research into the political, economic and social effects of the activities and practices of transnationals;
- at the request of governments, to organise and co-ordinate technical co-operation programmes on transnationals;
- to undertake studies with a view to defining the concept of transnationals.

The first meeting of the Commission on Transnational Corporations in fact took place in New York in March 1975, a session which was held at a time when criticism of multinationals among the most vocal developing countries had arguably reached its zenith. Spurred no doubt by OPEC's successful challenge to the West, developing countries had shortly before the Commission's meeting adopted the Charter of Economic Rights and Duties of States,[5] which urged radically new economic and political responsibilities on the reluctant leaders of the Western world. The USA and five EEC countries (Belgium, Denmark, Luxembourg, the United Kingdom and West Germany) opposed the Charter, arguing that international economic requirements would not best be served by application of such an arrangement (which in any case had no binding effect). This opposition presaged the attitude of the industrialised world to the debates on the UN code on transnationals, where the USA, West Germany and the UK (which between them are home countries to a good majority of the world's MNCs), supported by Switzerland, have led the West's counter-offensive against G-77 demands for binding regulations for international business.

Seven annual meetings of the Commission on Transnational Corporations have taken place since the first in New York: Lima (March 1976), New York (April/May 1977), Vienna (May 1978), New York (May, 1979), Mexico (July 1980) and Geneva (September/October 1981). The Commission's first meeting was used by each of the main protagonists — the G-77 (developing countries) and Group B (industrialised countries in UN parlance) — to outline their basic, and conflicting, positions. Since those early days, however, both the procedural and ideological focus has changed. The principal forum for negotiations is in fact not the Commission, but the so-called 'intergovernmental working group on a code of conduct', which has met fourteen times since its inaugural session in January 1977 and reports to the Commission. The group, whose membership is split between developing countries, industrialised countries and communist bloc members (so-called group D), is in fact composed largely of the same individuals who represent their country on the Commission. The working group is chaired by a 'progressive' from an industrialised country, Mr Sten Niklasson of Sweden, while secretarial services together with a degree of negotiating strategy are provided by the Centre on Transnational Corporations, whose executive director is another Nordic, Dr Klaus Sahlgren of Finland. Mr Niklasson and Dr Sahlgren, both individually and in tandem, are key personalities in the preparation of the UN code of conduct.[6]

Economic crisis and the mellowing of North/South conflicts

The ideological tenor of the UN multinationals' debate has muted considerably since the days of heady developing/industrialised country confrontation of the mid-1970s. A prolonged economic slump has altered the climate for the UN code, and its purpose.

In terms of negotiating strategy, developing countries have come increasingly to realise that for an international arrangement to be reached which is to have any real credibility — or, for that matter, a chance of success — the need for an equitable compromise with the developed countries is paramount. First and foremost this has meant ruling out a legally binding code as a political non-starter. This growing realism has furthermore been reinforced by — or reflects — an emerging awareness of the risks of alienating the MNCs, the major suppliers of capital, in an international investment climate still suffering from the aftermath of the oil price rise shock. However, it is not possible to rule out an ideological resurgence, given developing country frustration with the industrialised world's performance in other areas of economic diplomacy (e.g. the Tokyo Round of multilateral trade negotiations and the North/South dialogue now being conducted *sotto voce*). The decade of the 1980s could see a rekindling of the crusading impulse of mid-1970s — but if so against a vastly different economic setting.

Nevertheless in the current climate of renewed realism, the prospects that some sort of overall UN code, of a non-binding character, will emerge in the 1980s seem arguably better than they did in the sterile phase of political tub-thumping that characterised the latter part of the last decade. Some key differences remain to be resolved, but by mid-1981 some two-thirds of the text of the UN's international code of conduct for transnational corporations had been agreed.[7]

These outstanding differences are examined later in this chapter. Chapter 12 meanwhile, deals with the efforts of the ILO and UNCTAD to implement or negotiate codes of conduct for multinationals in the areas of social policy, technology transfer and restrictive business practices — arrangements which seem likely to be tied into the UN code of conduct in one form or another. The same is true for the agreement on illicit payments, likewise discussed in chapter 12, which also provides a brief outline of the efforts undertaken by the UN Centre on Transnational Corporations to implement the other areas of the December 1974 ECOSOC decision noted above (a comprehensive information system on TNCs, technical co-operation for developing countries in their dealings with companies, and research on transnational business activities).

Negotiations: the forces in conflict

Not until early 1979 was a single formulation of certain major elements of a UN code of conduct finally presented to governmental negotiators in the ad hoc working group. This represented the first real indication of the shape of the code, the majority of whose clauses have since been successfully negotiated. The code covers a wide variety of key areas affecting MNC behaviour, and attempts a compromise between the interventionist demands of the G-77 and the more conservative stance of the industrialised countries which seek to stress the advantages of a relatively free framework within which MNCs can contribute to the process of international economic development.

The developing country position: the basic G-77 'manifesto' for a UN code on multinationals is to be found in a document agreed by developing countries in March 1976 in Lima.[8] The G-77 paper, largely a compilation of criticisms, took the MNCs to task in a 21-point list of grievances, including notably: the maladjustment of their corporate strategy to the development needs of the host (i.e. developing) country; political interference with the internal affairs of the host country, including the use by MNCs of home country government influence over the host country government; the refusal of MNCs to admit the exclusive jurisdiction of the host country; the support proffered by MNCs to racist régimes; interference from MNCs in the exercise by the host country of its sovereignty over national resources; lack of co-operation by MNCs in supplying host country authorities with the information necessary for appropriate regulation of their activities; drainage of local financial resources by MNCs; domination of local markets and industry by various methods, including dominant technological power; use of restrictive business practices; undermining by MNCs of socio-cultural identity of host countries. In addition to these negative criticisms, the Latin American group of LDCs (less developed countries) presented some concrete proposals for insertion in the code, in particular: MNCs should be subject to laws and regulations of host countries, should not interfere in their internal affairs, should not allow themselves to be used as an instrument of foreign policy of another state, should be subject to the host country's national sovereignty, should aid in the attainment of host country economic development objectives, should provide information required by local authorities, should tailor their own strategies to ensure net contributions to host country financial receipts and know-how, should avoid restrictive business practices and harming the socio-cultural identity of the host country.

The industrialised country position: basically this is contained in the OECD Guidelines on Multinational Enterprises.[9] It revolves around a positive assessment of the contribution of MNCs to the development process, a belief nevertheless that some form of voluntary arrangement agreed internationally is necessary to provide a framework within which MNCs can operate, the need to ensure non-discrimination against foreign investors (as outlined in the OECD's 1976 decision on 'national treatment'[10]), and the emphasis on the necessity of stable conditions if international investment is to play the role it should in economic development.[11] Many of these ideas were outlined in some detail by a paper submitted to the Commission on Transnational Corporations in Lima in March 1976 by the USA, Germany, Britain, France and Italy, which identified 23 areas of particular concern to the industrialised world.[12]

The communist countries: for the Soviet bloc, the key aim has traditionally been to seek a definition of the transnational corporation for the purposes of the code which would apply simply, or at least principally, to the major privately-owned multinational companies — i.e. to Western multinationals. Paralleling this aim is the Soviet Union's defensive concern that its own state-controlled organisations — 'multinationals' in all but name[13] — should be exempted from the requirements of the UN's code for transnational corporations.

The major issues — agreed and outstanding

Progress towards reconciling these conflicting viewpoints, while never rapid, was by mid-1981 substantive. With some 70 per cent of the draft code's text agreed, negotiators from the industrialised, developing and communist countries have been given until late 1982, i.e. the eighth meeting in Manilla, the Philippines, of the Commission on Transnational Corporations, to conclude a complete draft for the UN code. For this goal to be achieved, some of the thorniest problems — e.g. nationalisation and compensation, and the question of applicable jurisdiction in the settling of disputes — have yet to be solved.

At the same time, as can be seen from the latest drafts of the code itself (see Appendix III(e) and (f)), the basis for movement towards such an objective has now been laid. Concluded parts of the code (Appendix III(e)) now cover the vast majority of the requirements to be made of MNCs in their economic and political behaviour — be it worker consultation, tax, environmental requirements, company reporting, anti-trust, on the one hand or, in the political area, respect for national sovereignty, adherence to economic policy goals of developing countries, etc.

The least advanced aspects of the code are precisely those which concern the offsetting requirements to be made of governments — e.g. in the area of nationalisation and compensation, the requirements which stipulate that 'fair and equitable treatment of transnational corporations by the countries in which they operate includes payment of just compensation in the event of nationalisation'. Appendix III(f) entitled 'The Chairman's formulations on the parts of the code not yet concluded',[14] outlines a suggested draft solution to these outstanding issues, which also include the code's preamble, objectives and scope, not to mention the key issue of its effective implementation. Indeed, 'implementation' has become the battle-cry of the trade unions as regards the UN code of conduct, and also for the MNC-targeted codes completed or being negotiated in other UN agencies — on matters like employment policy (the ILO), anti-trust and technology transfer (UNCTAD), and the UN's own efforts to counter bribery and corruption.[15]

All these 'sectoral' codes, or those of them that are finally agreed — the ones on employment and anti-trust already are — will likely come under the umbrella of the UN code, if and when it is completed. This latter prospect must continue uncertain for as long as the developing countries refuse to give any meaningful offsetting concessions to those already made by the industrialised world which, since the election of President Reagan, could well become less responsive to developing country negotiating demands. Without some form of guarantees on compensation for nationalisation, coupled with a less rigid stance particularly by the Latin Americans on jurisdiction, the OECD countries (Group B at the UN) simply cannot be expected to sign a code in respect of which, as they see it, they have already accepted a variety of demands directed at 'their' multinationals.

These demands, and those made on governments, are the two substantive sections of the UN code, the full text of whose 'concluded provisions' is to be found in Appendix III(e).[16] Immediately following this is Appendix III(f) outlining the Chairman's formulations on outstanding issues.

Notes and references

1   The US emphasis was more on standards for international investment, rather than the MNC Guidelines, whose chief supporter was
Sweden. Sweden provides the chairman of the group negotiating a UN
Code of Conduct — Mr Sten Niklasson, a high official in the Swedish
administration.

2   Resolution 1721 (LIII) of the Economic and Social Council of
the UN.

3   Including such figures as the German Finance-Minister Hans
Matthoefer, US Senator Jacob Javits, and ex-EEC President Sicco
Mansholt, in a 20-strong group.

4   Resolution 1913 (LVII) of ECOSOC, 5 December 1974.

5   General Assembly Resolution 3281 (XXIX) adopted 12 December
1974.

6   The Nordic influence on other arrangements for MNCs should by
now be clear — see also p.206.

7   As indicated by Mr Niklasson in his submission to the Seventh
Commission on Transnational Corporations, Geneva, 2 September
1981.

8   At second meeting of UN's Commission on Transnational Corporations.

9.   See Part III and Appendix II for OECD position on MNCs and
international investment.

10   Ibid.

11   Ibid.

12   For further details, see 'Codes of Conduct for Multinational
Companies : Issues and Positions', H. Schwamm and D. Germidis,
ECSIM, Brussels 1977, pp. 9—10.

13   Elizabeth Jaeger, a senior official of the American AFL/CIO, has
been a leading figure in the attack against the Soviet position on the
UN code of conduct for TNCs.

14   See Appendix III(f). The Chairman of the UN's intergovernmental
working group is Mr Sten Niklasson (Sweden).

15   See chapter 12 for consideration of these initiatives.

16   Brackets in text of Appendix III(e) indicate alternative solutions.
The 'shall'/'should' dichotomy running throughout denotes developing/
industrialised country positions.

12 Sectoral codes for international business

In parallel to the negotiation of the general UN code of conduct, work has carried on elsewhere in the UN system towards concluding business codes in areas where specific problems may arise as a result of the activities of multinationals. These efforts have met with varying degrees of success. Codes on MNCs make an impact on social policy and in the area of anti-trust have been respectively agreed in the framework of the Geneva-based International Labour Organisation (ILO) and the United Nations Conference on Trade and Development (UNCTAD). Markedly less successful, however, have been UNCTAD's attempt to forge a code of conduct for the international transfer of technology and the UN's efforts to gain adoption by governments of a treaty on bribery.

The ILO's 'Tripartite Declaration of Principles concerning Multinational Enterprises and Social Policy'

Adoption in November 1977 of the ILO's Declaration of Principles on MNCs and social policy,[1] a voluntary set of guidelines addressed to governments, labour organisations and multinationals, marked the culminating point in a negotiating process which started in 1972 with the first 'Tripartite Meeting on the Relationship between Multinational Enterprises and Social Policy'. The real impact of the ILO code, however, is not expected until the early 1980s.

The preparatory phase proper of the ILO Declaration did not begin until 1976. In May of that year, representatives of workers, employers and governments convened in Geneva in the ILO's 'Tripartite Advisory Meeting on the relationship of Multinational Enterprises and social policy', a session which ended with the recommendation that the ILO draw up a tripartite declaration of principles for MNC behaviour of the following profile: non-mandatory in character; non-discriminatory in its demands as between multinationals and domestic companies, and as between MNCs of public and private ownership; flexible enough to take account of varying situations yet unyielding in its respect of the sovereign rights of states. Following the ILO's World Employment Conference, held in Geneva, 14–17 June 1976, a meeting of the ILO Governing Body later the same year created a tripartite negotiating group, which by April 1977 had finalised its version of the Declaration. Only a year after establishing the negotiating committee, the ILO Governing Body completed the process by adopting the Declaration at its session on 16 November 1977.

The ILO Declaration, which on social policy matters is considerably more detailed and arguably more progressive in its demands on MNCs than the OECD Guidelines, is the result of a conflicting nexus of forces. The developing countries consistently argued strongly for MNCs to use employment-generating technologies, and to train local personnel in the management of technology. The industrialised countries, which are as morally bound by the ILO Declaration as by their own set of OECD Guidelines, urged their companies to stimulate job creation in the developing countries in various ways (local sub-contracting where possible, local raw material processing, local profit re-investment, replacement of expatriates, training and promotion). The employers, represented at the ILO by the International Organi-sation of Employers (IOE), stressed in the negotiations the need for non-mandatory guidelines, non-discriminatory treatment for MNCs, and the positive contribution of MNCs to international development. The trade unions, the third side of the ILO tripartite structure, called for respect by multinationals and governments of union rights to organise, for improved local wage structures, and much greater information on corporate operations. Trade union officials pressed for this on the assumption that, while the ILO Declaration is essentially aimed at improving the social and employment behaviour of MNCs in developing countries, the Declaration's provisions may also apply to the industrialised countries *per se*.

The outcome of these opposing viewpoints, which earlier (in June 1976) the World Employment Conference had failed to reconcile, is a carefully balanced text which nevertheless could well be used to effect in the 1980s by those seeking to impose restraints on the freedom of action of multinational companies. The main principles of the ILO Declaration are contained under 5 headings: general policies, employment, training, conditions of work and life, and industrial relations. They are preceded by a short introduction which outlines both the potential 'substantial benefits' of MNC activity while at the same time recognising the possible 'abuses of concentrations of economic power'. This introduction, which like the UN code firmly places the ILO Declaration in the context of the New International Economic Order, states that the aim of the Declaration is to 'encourage the positive contribution which multinational enterprises can make to economic and social progress and to minimise and resolve the difficulties to which their various operations may give rise'. The essential philosophy behind the Declaration is provided by the first paragraph of the introduction:

> Multinational enterprises play an important part in the economies of most countries and in international economic relations. This is of increasing interest to governments as well as to employers and workers and their respective organisations. Through international direct investment and other means such enterprises can bring substantial benefits to home and host countries by contributing to the more efficient utilisation of capital, technology and labour. Within the framework of development policies established by governments, they can also make an important contribution to the promotion of economic and social welfare; to the improvement of living standards and the satisfaction of basic needs; to the creation of employment opportunities, both directly and indirectly; and to the enjoyment of basic human rights, including freedom of association, throughout the world. On the other hand, the advances made by multinational enterprises in organising their operations beyond the national framework may lead to abuse of concentrations of economic power and to conflicts with national policy objectives and with the interest of the workers. In addition, the complexity of multinational enterprises and the difficulty of clearly perceiving their diverse structures, operations and policies sometimes give rise to concern either in the home or in the host countries, or in both.

Industrial relations — the key issue of the Declaration

Principal elements of the five sections of the ILO Declaration are given in summary below.[2]

General policies: 'All the parties concerned by this Declaration should

173

respect the sovereign rights of States, obey the national laws and regulations, give due consideration to local practices and respect relevant international standards', says the text. The Declaration then goes on to demand all parties concerned respect the Universal Declaration of Human Rights, to urge all governments to ratify ILO Conventions dealing with employment and industrial relations, and to call on MNCs to operate 'in harmony with the development priorities and social aims and structure of the country in which they operate'. However, it is recognised that 'the principles laid down in the Declaration do not aim at introducing or maintaining inequalities of treatment between multinational and national enterprises'.

Employment: governments should pursue employment promotion policies and multinationals, 'particularly when operating in developing countries, should endeavour to increase employment opportunities and standards'. In addition, 'before starting operations, multinationals should, wherever appropriate, consult competent authorities and the national employers' and workers' organisations in order to keep their manpower plans, as far as practicable, in harmony with national social development and advancement of nationals'. In addition they should use 'technologies which generate employment'. Neither governments nor MNCs should discriminate on whatever basis at the work place, and MNCs in particular should pay due attention to security of employment, e.g. by providing 'reasonable notice' of any major changes in their operations to government authorities and worker representatives.

Training: governments should develop national policies for vocational training, and multinational enterprises should promote local personnel to management positions.

Conditions of work and life: 'wages, benefits and conditions of work offered by multinational enterprises should be not less favourable to the workers than those offered by comparable employers in the country concerned', and if no comparable employer exists then wages should be linked to the economic position of the enterprise, 'but should be at least adequate to satisfy basic needs of the workers and their families'. Governments and MNCs should both ensure that the 'highest standards' of safety and health are maintained, and workers should have access to relevant information in this domain.

Industrial relations: the sting of the ILO Declaration lies in its tail. The fifth and final section of the Declaration, that concerning industrial relations, is clearly the one that is likely to provide organised labour with most leverage in its future dealings with MNCs. The first years of

174

application of the ILO Declaration in the early 1980s may thus be similar in this respect to the first three years' application of the OECD Guidelines, during which time the trades unions honed in on the industrial relations guideline for basing many of their 'cases' against individual MNCs. In the ILO text, the section on industrial relations is sub-divided into five parts, the first seeking to guarantee freedom of association and the right to organise; the second the right to free collective bargaining; the third the right to worker/management consultations; the fourth outlining a procedure for examination of worker grievances; and the fifth, a machinery for settlement of industrial disputes.

Implementation: the litmus test for the ILO code in the 1980s

'Implementation' is as much the name of the multinationals' game being played at the ILO as at the United Nations and the OECD. Indeed, the chief characteristic of the ILO's attempts to enforce the code it adopted back in 1977 seems likely to be a procedure for settling disputes between multinationals and the unions which appears potentially stronger than that set up for the OECD code. Also it is certain that there will be a greater emphasis, even than in the implementation of the OECD Guidelines, on industrial relations disputes.

The disputes procedure, described below, is for MNCs the most important part of the code's implementation package agreed by a tripartite meeting held at ILO headquarters in Geneva in September 1980. Two other components of the package aimed at ensuring effective follow-up should also be mentioned. These are, first, periodic reports on the application of the Declaration to be established on the basis of questionnaires sent via governments to unions and business organisations; and, second, a programme of studies on key labour issues — information and consultation rights in MNCs, and safety and health standards, have been amongst the first topics chosen.

But it is the disputes procedure, in which union sources expect the international trade secretariats (ITS)[3] to play an important role, which is certain to be the focus for attention in the 1980s. The procedure, which will be triggered when a union or an ITS protests non-compliance with the ILO code by a multinational, has been mapped in the following phases:

1   Union raises complaint with company.

2   Depending on result of phase 1, union raises complaint with government of country where multinational/subsidiary is operating.

3   Government attempts to settle the dispute through contacts with company and union.

4   Depending on result of phase 3, government raises issue with ILO, i.e. at the intergovernmental level, asking for 'a reply to a request for interpretation' of the Declaration.

5   If phase 4 has not been carried out or, in the unions' view, unsatisfactorily carried out, the unions may then raise the dispute directly with the ILO.

6   The ILO gives its 'reply'.[4]

The key ILO body for handling complaints is to be the ILO's recently created Standing Committee on Multinational Enterprises. This Committee is a parallel in some ways to the OECD's IME Committee,[5] but with at least two important differences. First, the ILO MNC Committee is by nature tripartite — with unions having equal representation with business and governments — as opposed to the exclusively governmental nature of the OECD body. Second, the ILO Committee would appear to be endowed with independent investigative powers, unlike its OECD counterpart. Prior to giving its replies to trade union complaints, it could thus have considerable scope for fact-finding. Its replies — or 'verdicts' — would then be given the official cachet of final approval by the ILO Governing Body.

Trade union sources who have helped in the formulation of the ILO disputes procedure, feel that the first MNC 'cases' brought to governmental or ILO attention will surface in the early 1980s. They recognise that there is a potential for 'overlap' between the ILO and OECD codes, and that trade union complainants would best choose between seeking to apply to a specific MNC one or other code, but not both simultaneously.

Anti-trust: applying Western rules
to MNCs in developing countries

Of the two codes which UNCTAD IV (Nairobi, 1976) requested of the international diplomatic community, one — that on restrictive business practices — was successfully negotiated and adopted in 1980,[6] while the other — on transfer of technology — appears destined to a much more uncertain future following successive snags in the negotiating process.[7]

As with the ILO Declaration, the arrangement on restrictive business practices — or code of conduct on anti-trust matters — is a voluntary package of behavioural norms, not a series of legally enforceable rules.

For similar reasons, the key to its success — i.e. to its actual discouragement of competitive abuses, particularly those committed by Western multinationals in the developing countries — lies thus with the practical implementation of its guidelines in the areas covered by the code.

These areas can hardly be termed radical — in point of fact they are little more than a restatement of the anti-trust laws already in force in many countries of the industrialised world. The code's originality, however, is to extend these norms — albeit on a voluntary basis — to MNCs operating in the developing countries. It was precisely this point that the key figure of the US negotiating team, Mr Joel Davidow of the American Department of Justice, used in his argument in favour of concluding a code: how could the West refuse to the developing countries the protection against big business abuse which it itself enjoyed as a result of legally binding rules? The question, then, as now, was logically unanswerable and, with the USA and the EEC working in close tandem — and despite some heavy business lobbying, largely too late to be effective — the code was duly adopted.

Scope for effective implementation appears uncertain, but not negligible. Already, at an UNCTAD meeting held in November 1981,[8] significant progress was made by governments towards the drafting of a 'model law' on restrictive business practices which, taking its inspiration from the UNCTAD code, could be directly incorporated into the laws of developing countries. It other words, while the code itself is voluntary, its consequences can be legislative, and thus binding on multinationals. More generally, ensuring the code's effective enforcement will be the work of the so-called 'intergovernmental group of experts', an UNCTAD body whose precise functions are detailed in the body of the code.[9] Meanwhile, overall application of the code is to be reviewed in 1985.

Outline of the anti-trust code

The structure of the code — actually rejoicing in the official name of 'the set of multilaterally agreed equitable principles and rules for the control of restrictive business practices' — is as follows:

- Objectives
- Definitions and scope of application
- Multilaterally agreed equitable principles for the control of restrictive business practices
- Principles and rules for enterprises, including transnational corporations

- Principles and rules for States at national, regional and sub-regional levels
- International measures
- International institutional machinery

According to the Objectives, special account should be taken of the interests of developing countries. Indeed, later on in the code (Section C), the industrialised countries are asked to help the LDCs to promote domestic industries. The aim of the code, *inter alia*, is 'to eliminate the disadvantages to trade and development which may result from the restrictive business practices of transnational corporations or other enterprises'. The code is 'to facilitate the adoption and strengthening of laws and policies at the national and regional levels'.

The actual anti-trust rules which MNCs are asked to observe (Section D) are the traditional ones found in European and American statutes, i.e. those aimed respectively against cartels and dominance/monopoly abuse, including:

- agreements fixing prices, including as to exports and imports;
- collusive tendering;
- market or customer allocation arrangements;
- allocation by quota as to sales and production;
- collective action to enforce arrangements, e.g. by concerted refusal to deal;
- concerted refusal of supplies to potential importers;
- collective denial of access to an arrangement, or association, which is crucial to competition;
- predatory behaviour to competitors when in a dominant position;
- discriminatory pricing when in a dominant position; etc. etc. [10]

Transfer of technology: major unresolved issues

By contrast with the success achieved in concluding a restrictive business practices' code, UNCTAD's other code — that dealing with rules for international technology transfer — has run into major difficulties. Only slow progress has been registered since the UN General Assembly Resolution of September 1975, whose text was re-affirmed by UNCTAD IV in Nairobi.[11] Since then, there have been numerous meetings of specialised UNCTAD negotiating groups, while four sessions of a Negotiating Conference were subsequently held, the last being in April 1981. But as yet to no avail.[12]

Negotiations have once again run into the traditional divergence between developing and industrialised countries — in effect between technology importers and exporters — rendered more acute in this case by the fact the subject matter of the code strikes at the very heart of the private sector's process of wealth creation and maintenance: industrial innovation and its commercial exploitation. In fact, technology transfers include a wide variety of operations, e.g. licence agreements relating to patents, inventor's certificates, trade-marks; licence agreements concerning the supply of know-how; agreements relating to the supply of over-all plans for plant installation; purchase of machinery, raw materials, etc., when included in a technology transfer; industrial and technical co-operation agreements of all kinds; and technology transfers relating to the establishment and operation of wholly-owned subsidiaries or other affiliated companies.[13] When the conditions affecting these vital transactions are at stake, it is hardly surprising that both the MNCs and the industrialised countries which derive so much of their wealth from their activities view askance the imposition of a new legally-binding international framework.

For it is precisely such an arrangement that the developing countries, backed by the communists which like Group-77 are technology importers, have traditionally been seeking: 'an internationally legally binding Code of Conduct on the international transfer of technology'.[14] Group B has been quick to point out that 90 per cent of all technology transfers are carried out *between* market economy countries. Their negotiators at UNCTAD in Geneva have stressed, not without a certain sardonic glee, the unreality of a situation where the OECD countries, whose firms as a general rule derive the vast proportion of their wealth from technology transactions *within* the industrialised world, are on the wrong end of a diplomatic offensive conducted by a large group of countries of comparatively minor economic significance. But this line of argument omits the new political imperatives which have crept into international economic negotiations — indeed, which are their source.

Confrontation between the market economy countries and the developing world (frequently supported by the communists) has arguably been strongest in the transfer of technology negotiations. The starting points of the two main protagonists are so widely different as to have led some commentators to suggest that compromise on a common text is impossible, despite limited progress made during the late 1970s. This prediction has probably been reinforced by the expected hardening of the US position under President Reagan.

So far on only three of the ten main chapters of the technology code (a recent version of whose text appears at Appendix III(c)) has agreement been fully reached between the parties involved. The ten chapters are as follows:

- Preamble;
- Definitions and scope of application;
- Objectives and principles;
- National regulation and transfer of technology transactions;
- The regulation of practices and arrangements involving the transfer of technology/restrictive business practices/exclusion of political discrimination and restrictive business practices;
- Guarantees/responsibilities/obligations;
- Special treatment for developing countries;
- International collaboration;
- International institutional machinery;
- Applicable law and settlement of disputes.

The three chapters on which agreement has been substantively reached are: the preamble, special treatment for developing countries, and international collaboration. In some other areas, progress towards agreement is significant. At the same time, there are major outstanding points of discord (the most acute being (b) and (d) below):

(a) *Disagreement on the nature of the code:* legally-binding as sought by the Group-77 or a voluntary set of guidelines as insisted upon by the market economy countries (Group B)? This divergence runs throughout the entire present version of the code and is symbolised by the confrontation throughout that text by the two phrases 'shall' (G-77's position) and 'should' (Group B) in reference to the legal/moral obligations governments and multinational enterprises are to assume by virtue of the code. However, developing countries appear ready to accept a non-compulsory arrangement (while not preferring it) — a reflection both of a newly realistic assessment of Group B's negotiating leeway and of their own needs for investment capital. The hardliners favouring a legally binding instrument have traditionally been the African countries. A key factor buttressing hope for a compromise solution will be the readiness of the market economy countries to countenance a strong and meaningful implementation process for giving effect to the code. This scenario parallels closely the negotiating situation in the UN code of conduct for transnationals, and in the ILO Declaration on MNCs.[15]

180

(b) Divergences over restrictive business practices affecting technology transfers: this is the central and crucial question against which the whole of the code's negotiating process has abortively broken. At issue is the nature of the relationship, from the standpoint of restrictive business practices for the purposes of technology transfers, between a foreign multinational parent and its subsidiary in a developing country. Developing countries are insisting that, for these purposes, a parent and its subsidiary be considered as legally separate entities. The Group-77 position is understandable, given that the vast majority of technology transfers towards the LDCs take place between affiliated companies controlled in the West. However, in order to protect the economic interests inherent in such intra-group transactions, Western governments are in diametric opposition to the LDCs.

(c) Controversy over parent/subsidiary links in the chapter dealing with guarantees and responsibilities: a similar problem to that noted above arises in this chapter, where the Group-77 approach would effectively put greater responsibilities and limitations on the local subsidiary of a foreign-based multinational than on a domestic company. Group B, and in particular the USA, is refusing to accede to a formulation which would carry in it the potential for overt or latent discrimination.

(d) Differences over the chapter on applicable law and dispute settlement: after (b) above, this is the most serious outstanding problem. On the question of laws applying to technology transfers in case of dispute there is an acute divergence between the developing countries and the industrialised nations. The former seek exclusive application of the laws and jurisdiction of the technology-acquiring country, while Group B wants the code to enshrine the possibility that the parties involved in a dispute can choose the law and jurisdiction best suited to the specific transaction (of the acquiring country, supplying country, or a third country). On arbitration, responding to Latin American practices, the G-77 states oppose neutral arbitration, insisting instead on the direct application of national law. But both Groups B and D (the communists) favour recourse to neutral arbitration, e.g. by the International Centre for the Settlement of Industrial Disputes (ICSID). The whole of this section could conceivably be dropped if it proved ultimately to be the only stumbling-block to an otherwise full agreement.

Bribery and corruption: UN Treaty delayed despite US pressure

The international community's response to the major corporate bribery scandals that rocked the business world in the early and mid-1970s[16] was manifold and rapid. In August 1976, the United Nations' Economic and Social Council decided on the creation of an 'ad hoc intergovernmental working group' whose job was to prepare 'the scope and contents of an international agreement to prevent and eliminate illicit payments in connection with international commercial transactions'. Its strongest national backer was the American government, whose president had by December 1977 signed the US Foreign Corrupt Practices Act into law, thus creating effectively stiffer penalties for US-based MNCs than those in force for the rest of American business' competitors in the industrialised world. A month previous to this, the International Chamber of Commerce[17] had pieced together its own 'Rules of Conduct to combat Extortion and Bribery', and in so doing provided the international business community's own response to an issue which had moved rapidly to the forefront of public and governmental attention.

Developing countries stall American call for binding treaty

Work by the UN towards an agreement on illicit practices, which could form part of the overall UN code of conduct on transnational companies, moved initially very quickly and resulted in a single draft text by early 1978. The 14-article treaty[18] was prepared by five meetings of the intergovernmental working group, which has been assisted in its work by the Centre on Transnational Corporations and the UN Commission on International Trade Law (UNCITRAL). Since then, despite strong and persistent pressure exerted by Washington, little progress has been made.

The urgings of the Carter administration, which saw a binding international treaty against bribery and corruption as a means of putting non-American business on the same footing as US corporations already subject to the domestic Foreign Corrupt Practices Act, consistently failed to get agreement from the international community, particularly the LDCs, on any meaningful progress. Meanwhile, under Reagan, Washington appears to have altered course. Instead of simply seeking a UN Treaty against bribery, there appear to be attempts afoot to draw the teeth of the 1977 American law.

Progress on the UN bribery treaty now depends on a variety of factors, most notably on the broader diplomatic advances made in the negotiation of the general UN code. Developing countries[19] have made it clear that if the United States wants faster progress on the illicit practices treaty, then it must show itself more willing than hitherto to promote speedier negotiations on the UN code. The USA is generally perceived by the developing world and by some of its partners in the industrialised world, as the country least enthusiastic for an early conclusion of the UN code of conduct on transnationals. Use by the developing countries of the diplomatic leverage inherent in the illicit payments agreement may alter Washington's attitude to the broader question of international MNC codes.

Twin focus on extortion and bribery

The agreement itself, which unlike other international arrangements affecting multinationals could well be binding and thus change the national legislation of countries party to it, has twin targets: the criminal outlawing of corporate bribery and governmental extortion. The basic aim of the agreement is encapsulated in Article 1, which states:[20]

1. Each Contracting State undertakes to make the following acts punishable by appropriate criminal penalties under its national law:

   (a) The offering, promising or giving of any payment, gift or other advantage by any natural person, on his own behalf or on behalf of any enterprise or any other person whether juridical or natural, to or for the benefit of a public official as undue consideration for performing or refraining from the performance of his duties in connection with an international commercial transaction.

   (b) The soliciting, demanding, accepting or receiving, directly or indirectly, by a public official of any payment, gift or other advantage, as undue consideration for performing or refraining from the performance of his duties in connection with an international commercial transaction.

2. Each Contracting State likewise undertakes to make the acts referred to in paragraph 1 (a) of this article punishable by appropriate criminal penalties under its national law when committed by a juridical person, or, in the case of a State which does not recognise criminal responsibility of juridical persons, to take appropriate measures, according to its national law, with the objective of comparable deterrent effects.

Other key, and often controversial, components of the draft agreement include in particular: provision that contracting States ensure by law that companies maintain accurate records of payments made by them to an intermediary, including specific payments exceeding $50,000; and the demand that

> each contracting State shall prohibit its persons and enterprises of its nationality from making any royalty or tax payments to, or from knowingly transferring any assets or other financial resources in contravention of United Nations resolutions to facilitate trade with or investment in a territory occupied by, an illegal minority régime in southern Africa.

In addition, measures outlined in the illicit payments' agreement for effective implementation include 'mutual assistance' between States in the conduct of criminal investigations, and the classification of the offences outlined in Article 1 (quoted above) as extraditable.

Other UN activities on MNCs:
focus on information and advice

Information and advice are the two key words characterising the activities of the Centre on Transnational Corporations (UNCTC) outside its assistance in preparing a code of conduct on MNCs. These other MNC-related activities undertaken by the Centre are three-fold:

Establishment of a 'Comprehensive Information System' (CIS) on MNCs: a computer-aided system for collecting and analysing data on transnational corporations and the legal and economic environment in which they operate is one of the priority components of the mandate handed down by ECOSOC to the UNCTC in December 1974. Designed to be of assistance above all to host (meaning developing) countries, focal points of the data-collecting and analysis functions assigned to the CIS, which has yet to become fully operational, are the following: policies, laws and regulations pertaining to transnational corporations; industry-by-industry analysis and the sectoral role of transnationals; trends in the activities of MNCs; general corporate information; contracts and agreements between host country entities and MNCs. The Centre, which is mandated to gather information from governmental, non-governmental and corporate sources, as well as from publicly available sources, has come in for some heavy criticism and not a little suspicion from international business as to the initial operating methods of the CIS and its aims. Amongst its apparent objectives are to assist in the formulation of appropriate policies and regulations on TNC-related matters (activities carried out via the Centre's technical co-operation programme, see below) and strengthening the developing countries' negotiating capacities *vis-à-vis* MNCs. By the late 1970s, the design of 'a computerised corporate profile system' had been realised: according to the Centre, 'commercial data tapes containing information on individual transnational corporations have been selected and acquired . . . coding schemes have been devised to permit the use of these bases in an integrated manner'.[21] The role of the CIS, and above all its potential development, has given rise to keen concern in industrialised countries as well as the MNCs headquartered in them. Yet the Commission on Transnational Corporations has continued to give the scheme the cachet of political approval while noting that the CIS should be based on the needs of home and host countries, should ensure accuracy, and should be widely disseminated to governments and, as appropriate, to non-governmental groups such as trades unions and universities.

Technical co-operation programmes on MNCs: the conviction that developing countries are often ill-equipped to bargain effectively with MNCs is at the basis of the mandate given the Centre on technical co-operation. Aims of this aspect of the Centre's activities include: advice to developing countries on conducting relations with MNCs, in particular outlining policy options governments can follow in negotiations with business, assisting in the formulation of legislation on foreign direct investment, and renegotiating MNC accords with local governments. The Centre is developing both a roster of experts to assist governments in an advisory capacity and a training programme designed to beef up the ability of local officials to deal with MNCs. In this context it has organised several workshops for developing country officials, including those held in San José (Costa Rica) for officials from Central American countries (June 1977); Guyana for Caribbean officials (August 1977); Accra (Ghana) for officials from West African countries (November–December 1977); Khartoum for Sudanese officials (December 1977); Kuala Lumpur (Malaysia) for senior government officials dealing with foreign investment (June 1978); and Bangkok (Thailand) for ASEAN country officials (September 1978); and many others since. In addition, under the technical co-operation programme, the Centre responds to specific requests for information or advice from individual countries.

Research into the political, economic and social impact of MNCs: the Centre's activities in the research field have extended to studies in a variety of sectors, including: transnationals in the food and beverage industry; transnational banking; transnationals and insurance; transnationals and tourism; transnationals and raw material processing; transnationals in the pharmaceutical industry. Other research projects have addressed themselves to topics such as MNCs and their linkages with domestic enterprises, the impact of MNCs on balance of payments. A series of studies have also been carried out on the impact of MNCs in South Africa, while a re-examination of the impact of transnationals on world development — a follow-up to the eminent persons' report of 1974 'The Impact of Multinational Corporations on Development and International Relations'[22] was published in early 1978.

In addition to the activities of the Centre outlined above, the UN is also directly involved in the burgeoning issue of international *standards of disclosure for transnational corporations*. In this it shares an interest with both the EEC and the OECD, with whose activities in this field the UN had begun by the early 1980s to catch up. During 1980–81 several meetings of an intergovernmental accounting group[23] had provided UN work in this area with a much more operational focus — the task of making a direct contribution to the disclosure section of the UN code of conduct[24] — than had hitherto been the case. Prior to 1980, the UN's activity on corporate disclosure had been most notable for an ambitious report on world accounting standardisation, finalised in New York in July 1977.

Highlights of the 1977 report, too radical to gain acceptance by the industrialised countries but at the same time an indication of the demands awaiting MNCs in developing states, were:

- the call for MNCs to 'prepare general purpose reports on the enterprise as a whole' while 'separate reports should also be prepared by member companies of the transnational corporation group, including the parent company';

- general purpose reports should contain a series of minimum items of financial and non-financial information. Financial information should include a statement of sources and uses of funds, while non-financial disclosure should extend to labour and employment, production, investment programmes, organisational structure and environmental measures;

- financial and non-financial information should be reported in aggregate, but also broken down 'by geographical area and line of business';

- reporting of transactions among member companies of transnational corporations and description of the basis of accounting for such transactions;

— reporting on associated companies to be done via equity accounting method.

Since the ambitious times of the 1977 report, however, work at the UN on accounting standardisation for international business has mellowed significantly — and with significant success. By mid-1981, the UN's intergovernmental group on accounting standards had succeeded in drafting the basis for the subsequently agreed section of the UN code on disclosure of information. The extent of this achievement has to be judged against the extreme sensitivity with which both developing and industrialised countries, for different reasons, traditionally approach the key question of disclosure of business information.

Notes and references

1   'Tripartite Declaration of Principles Concerning Multinational Enterprises and Social Policy', adopted by ILO Governing Body, 16 November 1977; see Appendix III(a).
2   Ibid.
3   See chapter 14 for further discussion of ITS.
4   In OECD parlance, this would be 'clarification' — see chapters 9 and 10.
5   See Part III for OECD activities on multinationals, and part played by IME Committee.
6   Concluded at negotiating level, 22 April 1980, adopted by the UN, 5 December 1980.
7   See this chapter, pp. 178–82.
8   Multinational Service, no.119, 12 November 1981.
9   See section G of the code, Appendix III(b).
10   For full list, see section D, Appendix III(b).
11   UN General Assembly Resolution 3362 (S–VII) of 16 September 1975, taken over by UNCTAD Resolution 89/IV of 30 May 1976.
12   The possibility that the whole technology negotiating exercise could be 'buried' in some convenient UNCTAD procedural back-alley is not to be excluded.
13   H. Schwamm and D. Germidis, 'Codes of Conduct for Multinational Companies: Issues and Positions', ECSIM, Brussels, 1977, p.17.
14   Draft International Code of Conduct on the Transfer of Technology, preamble, April 1981. See Appendix III(c) for April 1981 version of code's text.
15   See chapter 9 for the UN code, and above in this chapter for the ILO Declaration.

16   Perhaps the most striking examples were those involving International Telephone and Telegraph, and the Lockheed Corporation.
17   See Appendix IV.
18   See Appendix III(d) for 1978 text.
19   Led by Mexico.
20   This is an updated version of the 1978 text which emerged after two meetings of the Committee on an International Agreement on an International Agreement on Illicit Payments in early 1979.
21   *The CTC Reporter*, vol.1, no.4, p.23.
22   See Multinational Service, 17 April 1978.
23   Officially called 'The Intergovernmental Working Group of Experts on International Standards of Accounting and Reporting'. First meeting took place in February 1980.
24   See chapter 11.

13 Embryonic business control in the UN system: medium-term perspectives

The outlook for an effective United Nations code of conduct for transnational corporations emerging in the 1980s is uncertain but not unhealthy. Prospects are similarly uneven for the sectoral business codes which will probably be linked, directly or indirectly, to the application of the general UN 'umbrella' code for multinationals. A particular factor conditioning the negotiations and subsequent impact of all these codes is the diplomatic awareness of the world economic slump, and its possible exacerbation by either excessive business controls or, alternatively, by random reactions against MNC behaviour in the absence of an internationally agreed framework for their activity.

As regards the 'sectoral' codes, in areas like employment and industrial relations and anti-trust, the 'soft law' precedent created by the OECD Guidelines is likely to be repeated as, in the first years of the 1980s, implementation of the ILO and UNCTAD codes begins to 'bite'. Indeed both these codes, although voluntary in nature, may undergo a much greater 'hardening' process than the OECD Guidelines — with indeed the possibility of their conversion into legal obligations. The reason for this is that the developing countries, who are party to the ILO and UNCTAD measures on labour and anti-trust behaviour, may feel more enthusiastic about incorporating into their national legislation the rules contained in these codes than most industrialised states have done in respect of the OECD Guidelines. By contrast, major difficulties cloud the prospect for finalising UNCTAD's code of conduct on transfer of technology and the UN's draft treaty on bribery and corruption.

The UN code itself, barring absolutely unforeseeable circumstances, will be a voluntary code, if it is to gain the agreement of the differing negotiating parties. This racing certainty became cast-iron with the 1981 change of administration in the USA, bringing in a pro-business President in Ronald Regan. The Reagan administration's firm belief in the beneficial development effects of free enterprise operating in a free international environment will likely ensure that the UN code, if and when agreed, will tend to be balanced evenly between demands made on MNCs and requirements that governments do not over-react against foreign-controlled enterprises. In other words, constraints on business must be offset by measures designed to increase the climate of confidence for multinational investors.

Implementation: the key to effective codes

But another balance has to be struck. For developing countries and their (Western) trade union supporters to accept such a rejigging of the UN code, a voluntary code must be endowed with the machinery necessary for its effective implementation. For, as with the OECD Guidelines and the sectoral codes beginning to emerge from the UN specialised agencies, the key issue will be implementation which industrialised countries will be under strong pressure to render as vigorous as possible.

Just what 'effective implementation' means for the trade unions was well summarised by the submission of the ICFTU to the UN in early 1981.[1] In that submission, the union delegate said:

> First and foremost, the Code must be taken fully into account by TNC managements at both the headquarters and subsidiary levels. The Code seeks to influence the behaviour of all TNCs and we must not lose sight of this basic factor when discussing procedures for implementation. The ICFTU believes that it is necessary to engage the corporations themselves in the procedures. And the most effective way to do this in our view is to encourage and facilitate regular discussions between individual TNCs, and the Governments and unions of the various countries in which they operate. Mr Chairman, we firmly believe that the foundation of an effective Code of Conduct is dialogue between the major parties involved, that is, the corporations, the trade union representing the workers of the TNCs and the Governments.
>
> Our second concern is that Governments of all states incorporate the international standards established in the Code fully

into the corpus of their legal and administrative systems. Too often the commitment displayed by Governments during the negotiation of international instruments is quickly forgotten.

Thirdly, we believe that the Commission should continue to act as the guardian of the Code after its adoption. This is necessary in order to ensure consistency in application, the resolution of disputes concerning the meaning of the Code, and that it retains a continued relevance in the evolving world of TNC activities.

My fourth point is that the implementation of the Code should be based on the best available information and research. The Centre should therefore conduct both periodic general surveys of aspects of the Code and be available for more specific fact-finding work on particular problems brought to the attention of the Commission.

The fifth point I wish to stress is the importance of the trade union role in implementation at the company level, the national level, the regional level and the international level. Within the trade union movement there is a body of practical knowledge and experience which can be of tremendous assistance to the UN in making this Code into a workable instrument.

Nevertheless, the developed world, with one or two noticeable exceptions, has attempted to avoid too strong a follow-up procedure being grafted onto the code — in particular to avoid a situation where individual cases of alleged MNC non-compliance with the UN code could be brought to the attention of the world via a body like the Commission on Transnational Corporations. An important exception to this rich country position, however, was provided by the Netherlands, whose government in 1981 proposed a code enforcement procedure of the type already in hand for the ILO code.

Whatever the eventual outcome, the prospect is thus that the UN code could 'become an embryo to a new part of international law, to which internationally operating enterprises are subject'.[2] The timetable of UN work, even if the final negotiations are successful, makes it unlikely that the code would actually be operational before the mid-1980s. That is an eventuality for which MNCs should be planning. The alternative scenario, that of a resounding diplomatic failure to conclude the UN talks, would not necessarily work in big business's favour. Such a failure would probably not improve the international investment climate. It would not stop developing countries from inserting into national legislation the provisions of the draft code — indeed, it might encourage them to do so. In addition, it would in all probability provoke the international trade union movement into pressuring Western governments into more rigorous application of the OECD

Guidelines, and into making intensive use of the ILO code, while at the same time increasing the risk of direct industrial action organised by transnational unions against multinational business.

Notes and references

1   'Implementation of the Code of Conduct', statement by the ICFTU, 9 April 1981.
2   Statement by Mr Sten Niklasson to the Commission on Transnational Corporations, Geneva, 2 September 1981.

PART V

CONTROL OF INTERNATIONAL BUSINESS :
THE STRUGGLE FOR INFLUENCE

14 The war of the lobbies

European unions versus Western multinationals

No picture of the emerging international and regional framework being built up around multinationals would be complete without mention of the two key interest groups which are seeking to influence its development in their favour: the international trade union movement centred in Western Europe and international big business.

The scope and organisation of the influence exerted by these two directly opposed groups differs sharply, both as between each other, and also in relation to the various arenas in which MNC-related measures are being discussed or negotiated. But, whatever the differences, there is no doubt that the war of influence that has engaged the trade unions and multinational business since the start of the MNC debate in the 1960s, has an often determining impact on the measures being drawn up in the three policy forums outlined in the preceding chapters: the European Community, the OECD, and the UN and its specialised agencies. There is no reason to suppose that this impact will diminish in the coming decade as union and MNC lobbies continue to jockey for position.

The scope of conflicting influences

The most fundamental set of differences separating these two lobby groups, while in itself banal, is vital to the dynamics of political influence which inflect negotiations on MNC issues. The trade unions are on the attack, favouring increased regulation of big business, while business itself, opposing this trend, is on the defensive. The trade unions are swimming with the tide of increased international public interventionism, a tide which gathered speed in the 1970s as a variety of strong political and economic currents favourable to it converged, amongst them: developing country demands for economic sovereignty spawned in a residual climate of anti-colonialism; the strengthening of the anti-MNC lobby in the West reinforced by some spectacular though not necessarily typical instances of corporate misbehaviour (Lockheed in Italy, ITT in Chile); and the worldwide economic slowdown which generated a series of interlocking international problems and at the same time fostered the need for intergovernmental co-operation or even rules for their resolution.

Mirroring and profiting from this broad trend, the international trade union movement's posture on MNCs is thus set against a more general policy strategy supportive of attempts to increase public control of the international economy and the large transnational firms which are its major operators. As a result, the scope of trade union influence on MNC-related policy initiatives goes beyond pressuring national and international authorities to adopt specific measures (e.g. on corporate disclosure, transfer pricing, etc.) and extends to a systematic attempt to influence the global context in which such specific measures are set (e.g. via an activist policy on international development which dove-tails with LDC priorities). Moreover, trade union policy is given added edge by its overt anti-capitalist ideology, at least in Europe where the most influential of international trade union centres are headquartered.

Faced with these imposing forces, business has responded, not without some success, through its various representative organisations at the policy arenas discussed earlier in this book. But the scope of business influence tends to be more limited than that of the unions. Given the secular trend to increased interventionism business has not — perhaps understandably — gone about evolving and proclaiming to the powers-that-be an overall economic policy alternative. Collectively it has chosen not to swim against the current. Instead, it has opted for the uneasy alternative of treading water. Both business organisations and individual companies have opted to concentrate their efforts of influence at limiting the impact of measures directed at them.

The basic battle lines: main union and business organisations

Business's task has been uphill, not just because of the general trend towards interventionism, but because of the nature of the adversary organisations. For the trade unions, besides benefiting from a political climate favourable to many of their aims, have a streamlined and interlocking organisation for international policy influence which, for coherence and flexibility, is outstanding.

The ideological and organisational motor of the trade union offensive against MNCs is located in Western Europe, and more particularly in Brussels where, headquartered on the same premises, are the European Trade Union Confederation (ETUC) and the International Confederation of Free Trade Unions (ICFTU), and elsewhere in the same town the World Confederation of Labour (WCL). The ETUC, including in its ambit the politically influential British TUC, German DGB, the Dutch FNV and the Nordic LOs[1], is widely considered the single weightiest non-governmental influence on economic policy formation at the European level. The same membership, together with affiliates from non-European industrialised countries (excluding the USA) and developing countries, makes up the ICFTU, which concentrates its influence on MNC policy formulation at the UN, while at the same time being an important element in the preparation of union strategy on application of the OECD's Guidelines on Multinational Enterprises. At the OECD, union views are expressed through the channel of TUAC, whose membership includes the American AFL/CIO and the Japanese union centre SOHYO as well as the ICFTU and the WCL, and in whose work leading international trade secretariats actively participate. Indeed, the international trade secretariats (ITS) — European-based transnational union organisations organised by sector — are largely responsible for bringing to TUAC's attention specific instances of alleged MNC non-compliance with the Guidelines. Most of the ITS are in addition linked to the ICFTU. Between them, the ETUC, the ICFTU and TUAC with their position at the centre of a complex of union organisations and channels of communication, are an important cohesive force in the conduct of trade union policy on multinationals in the European, OECD and UN contexts. As a result, in addition to the broad scope of policy influence on MNC policy issues, unions have an integrated and fast-track organisation for making their views known to governments and international bodies.

The same cannot be said for the organisation of business influence on the international political process. Whereas the trade unions are a relatively homogeneous group with an organisation to match, 'business' is in fact a collective misnomer for diversified interests with often only a low common denominator. There is no binding ideological force which is such a cohesive element in the trade unions' organisation. Nevertheless, business is relatively united in opposition to measures directly aimed at curtailing its freedom of action. But the channels for expressing this opposition are much more diversified: besides business organisations like UNICE[2] at the EEC, BIAC at the OECD, and employer federations operating at the fully international level — the International Chambers of Commerce (ICC) and the International Organisation of Employers (IOE) — there are also the individual lobby organisations of large multinational corporations. The structural links between the ICC, IOE, BIAC, UNICE and the various national associations affiliated to them appear nothing like as close as the almost organic relationship and high-speed channels of communication which exist between the powerful national union confederations of Western Europe, the ETUC, the ICFTU and TUAC. By contrast, the sophisticated operations of some leading MNCs do appear to possess, on an individual basis, the political and organisational flexibility enjoyed by the trade unions acting collectively.

These, then, are the principal contours of the battle lines drawn up for the war of influence over international economic policy-making towards multinational companies.

At the EEC: trade unions' collective impact versus multi-faceted business pressure

The European Trade Union Confederation: growth of influence reflects nature of EEC

'We in the European Commission greatly welcome the growing influence and the growing confidence of the European Trades Union Confederation.' The words belong to Mr Roy Jenkins,[3] former EEC Commission President and one of the leaders of the politics of re-alignment in Britain. Mr Jenkins' statement of open support for the European unions, recalling the Commission's earlier call for 'a trade union counterweight' to MNCs,[4] is perhaps surprisingly outspoken and suggests some sort of 'special relationship' between those responsible for policies furthering European integration and those leading the push for increased interventionism in the European economy. The suggestion of a special link between EEC policies and European trade unions, while not to be taken out of context, does nonetheless bear examination (see chapter 3). This is particularly so, since there is widespread acceptance at EEC headquarters of the importance of ETUC influence on EEC policy initiatives especially in key MNC areas; corporate disclosure, taxation, labour laws and even anti-trust.

There indeed is a clear if unspoken equation between European integration and European interventionism, a fact singularly strengthening the unions' potential to influence policy. The member countries of the European Community, after the initial period (1958–70) of liberalising intra-Community trade barriers, have throughout the decade of the 1970s been involved in attempts at transnational cohesion which by definition can only be secured by measures of transnational interventionism binding them together: a central plank of this policy is the creation of common rules for the EEC's major economic operators — multinationals, both of the home-grown variety and those operating in the Community via subsidiaries controlled from headquarters beyond its borders.

This trend is naturally reinforced by the fact that the EEC, a supranational bureaucracy, has no obvious *raison d'être* if it does not propose new policies and rules and work towards their adoption. Conversely, if the territory of the community were no more than a canvas for the conduct of Adam Smith economics, the need for a central policy unit would be limited. But in a Europe whose economy is now thoroughly infected by problems caused by the mid-1970s crisis, that is patently not the case. Instead, the attempt is on to find European responses to the Europe-wide problems (unemployment, industrial democracy, worker rights, etc.) that characterise a now highly-interpenetrated economy. Progress towards an increasingly united Europe is predicated on increasing European interventionism organised by a central policy-making institution.

The trades unions feel basically at home working in such a context and with such an institution. They implicitly share many of its aims, and are well prepared to translate to the European level the patterns of political influence that they have traditionally exerted nationally. Business, by contrast, is less enthusiastic. While having been the great supporter — and a principal beneficiary — of the EEC's liberalising push in the 1960s, it has since found itself swimming upstream against the quickening current of European business regulation. Its representative organisations tend to focus their efforts at influence on mitigating the impact on companies of policies and rules which they oppose, rather than generating any fundamental opposition among EEC policy-makers to the overall trend from which such rules and regulations stem.

There are many instances of the clear dovetailing of the policy priorities of the EEC Commission and the ETUC, and the latter's action programme on MNCs, adopted in June 1977,[5] is as good a point as any from which to begin such a comparison. Virtually all the key components of the ETUC's ideologically motivated MNC programme — 'it is the law of democratic reasoning that power of any sort must be controlled in order to prevent its abuse'[6]— are shared by the EEC's progressive MNC policy, both in its existing and emerging components.

EEC company law affecting MNCs is perhaps the most clearcut example of this convergence of ETUC/European Commission policy aims. The unions' call for new European rules for MNC groups, for the formal establishment of worker information and consultation machinery within them,[7] and for direct employee participation in board-level decisions, are all reflected by EEC proposals either already made or in a state of advanced preparation.[8] This is borne out by comparing the EEC policy watch-list[9] with the core demands of the ETUC on MNC company law.

> Standardised regulations governing groups of companies must be based on the following principles:
>
> 1. Precise definition of the status of group of companies (central management, dependence of companies within the group, procedure for the establishment of the status of group of companies);
>
> 2. Protective measures for shareholders and workers in dependent undertakings of the group of companies;
>
> 3. Obligation to prepare and declare consolidated group annual accounts on the basis of standardised rules;
>
> 4. Establishment of an information and consultative body for the representatives of workers in all the companies within the group;
>
> 5. Representation of workers at the level of governing bodies in dominant companies, where a system of worker representation must be established to enable workers and their trade unions to have an influence on the fixing of the group's objectives and policy, especially in the case of multinational groups of companies.[10]

Not that the interface between trade union priorities and actual or envisaged EEC policy stops there. On taxation, the ETUC's 1977 demand for 'a uniform rule for the control of transfer prices within multinational groups of companies' within an overall 'system of international tax supervision and control'[11] was answered in January 1979 when the 'Nine' adopted the first step towards this aim (see chapter 5). On *investment monitoring*, the ETUC urged that 'an office must be set up at the level of EEC and EFTA organs which must be notified of the investments and investment schemes of undertakings in all sectors'.[12] Although nothing so comprehensively interventionist is in fact likely to be established at the EEC level, nevertheless here again the unions' demand appears to have been a forerunner of the priority the EEC industrial affairs commissioner assigns to some sort of investment co-ordination.[13] This is not in any way to imply that Viscount Davignon's moderate conservatism is to be confused with the ETUC's policy priorities — but merely to re-emphasise the striking convergence of European policy towards MNCs, bred out of a desire to move towards progressive Community integration, with trade union policy priorities, independent of their philosophically disparate roots.

Business influence: stepped-up importance of individual MNC lobby operations

Faced with this burgeoning regulatory framework, multinational business has proved to be far from defenceless, if without the monolithic cutting-edge of the trade unions, its principal adversary group. For there are important differences in the MNC fraternity, and these differences, as already suggested above, affect both the scope and organisation of corporate influence at the EEC. For what, in practice, does the term 'multinationals' mean in the European context? Does it signify MNCs which are privately-owned or publicly financed? Are they European-based or headquartered outside the Community? Are they operating in growth areas or in sectors in economic decline? Are they, for instance, strongly unionised or, in contrast (like IBM), non-unionised (and thus, perhaps, possessing a distinctive attitude on the specifically labour-oriented laws being worked out at EEC headquarters)? These are just an illustrative sample of questions pointing to the heterogeneity of the international business world, which is in sharp contrast to the political and organisational homogeneity of the trade unions.

Reflecting these divergences in the MNC world are disparate channels of influence.

UNICE, the Union of Industries of the European Community, is the main official filter of the combined views on European policy of the national employers' confederations of the nine EEC member countries. But UNICE, though often considered the counterpart on industry's side to ETUC as a representative of organised labour, differs in many respects from the union organisation.

First, as already noted, UNICE is officially restricted in membership to the EEC 'ten', although other European countries have associate status. The membership of the ETUC, which from its inception in 1973 has claimed to be representative of Western Europe as a whole, is fully extended to 18 countries.

Second, UNICE, while certainly a major vehicle for expressing business views, does not enjoy the same pre-eminence as a channel of business influence on issues affecting multinational companies as does the ETUC in the union world.[14] Moreover, it has no special brief for multinationals (as opposed to business in the more general sense) and clearly it has no brief at all for the non-EEC multinationals which are among the major economic operators in the Common Market.

Third, and more important perhaps, UNICE's decision-making structure, from which emerges the official views it then submits to the EEC's policy-making institutions, sometimes mirrors the diverging national business interests it represents, and does not appear as streamlined as that of the ETUC. UNICE does not seem to be granted by its national affiliates the same degree of independent action enjoyed by the ETUC, whose leading national constituents (like the TUC's Len Murray and the DGB's Oscar Vetter) play an active and personal part in evolving a distinctively European trade union policy. At the same time, it should be noted that national employers' federations can often exert strong pressure at home on a government whose representatives in Brussels can in turn influence Community decisions. Indeed, on occasion, governmental representatives on EEC policy groups are in fact none other than industry officials.

Meanwhile, UNICE apart, a variety of other channels are in place for influencing EEC policy affecting the business world. CEEP (the French acronym for the Brussels-based European Centre of Public Enterprises) is the specific funnel of influence for state-owned companies and by general consent it has a good track record. Yet its very existence and success also serve to underline the divergences in the business world, since the philosophy of economic interventionism and the growth of state-run industry on which an organisation such as CEEP is predicated, are precisely two of the chief *bêtes noires* in EEC policy identified by some leading multinational enterprises, particularly American, operating in the Common Market.

In addition, there are a host of trade federations and other bodies (e.g. accountants' organisations) through which business in general and multinationals in particular may seek to influence policy affecting them.

However, for a growing number of multinational companies, these channels are insufficient in themselves as vehicles for policy influence, particularly in the legislative areas specifically involving MNCs to which this book is devoted. Increasingly, both European and non-European companies (the latter largely being a euphemism for American MNCs) are finding that their interests, while often broad-ranging, are sufficiently specific to require an individualised European public affairs operation of considerable sophistication, ranging from information-gathering, through active monitoring, up to and including lobbying for specific policy options.

The gradual increase in such *individual corporate affairs' departments* for handling a company's interests in relation to EEC (and often OECD) policy-formation is one of the two striking developments in the war of influence over the last few years (the other being the emergence of the ETUC during the 1970s as a major policy lobby for the trade union movement). The importance of company offices dealing with government affairs, especially if headed by a high-level executive with permanent access to his board and ad hoc access to the EEC power structure, will likely grow in the coming years. Indeed, some believe that, taken collectively, such operations could well be the most effective business counterweight to the influence of trade unions on the development of EEC policy affecting multinationals.

Major companies with strong and relatively sophisticated public affairs departments for managing European policy issues include the following:

Avon	Ford	Philips
Bank of Tokyo	General Dynamics	Plessey
BASF	General Foods	Procter & Gamble
BAT	General Motors	Rank Xerox
Bayer	Goodyear	Reid International
British Petroleum	Hoechst	Royal Dutch Shell
Brown Boveri	IBM	Siemens
Caterpillar	ICI	Sperry
Ciba-Geigy	ITT	Toyota
Continental Group	3M	TRW
CPC	Mars	Unilever
Datsun	Merck Sharp & Dohme	Union Carbide
Dow Chemicals	Monsanto	United Brands
Dupont	National Westminster	Upjohn
Esso Chemicals	Nestlé	UTC
Fiat	Pechiney Ugine Kuhlmann	Volvo
FMC	Pfizer	

This list of companies, some half of which are controlled from head-quarters in the USA, is intended to be extensively illustrative rather than exhaustive. Amongst EEC-based companies, the two Anglo-Dutch giants, Royal Dutch Shell which also has a strong presence at the OECD, and Unilever, are considered among the most influential. (Sources: company executives, industry representatives and European civil servants.)

The governmental affairs' strategies of such companies often require finely-honed co-ordination between action at the international level (EEC, OECD) and intervention with national authorities. Although companies remain naturally guarded about the activities of their monitoring departments, there nevertheless appears to be a growing acknowledgement by EEC officials of the importance of good and quick lines of communication with individual MNCs. This is borne out, amongst other things, by the industrial policy approach of Viscount Davignon,[15] and by the gradual (though far from complete) acceptance of the lobby function as a normal part of the political process — as it most certainly is in the USA. However, European corporate lobbyism still has a long way to go before attaining the level of acceptance afforded it in Washington, the lobby capital of the world.

In addition to the influence brought to bear by individual companies, more or less informal groupings of multinationals also should be noted as channels for expressing private sector views on European policy initiatives. Amongst these are the Brussels-based ELEC (European League for Economic Co-operation), the Paris-based European Foundation for the Economy, and the so-called 'Ad-hoc Council' also co-ordinated from Brussels. Nor should the influential impact of bodies like the EEC Committee of the American Chamber of Commerce in Belgium be neglected. Indeed, by the late 1970s, this Committee had arguably become among the most influential of business bodies on EEC policy towards multinationals.

A recent major development in EEC integration — the inauguration of a *directly-elected European Parliament* in the summer of 1979[16] — has provided another significant battleground for the exercise of conflicting influences on the formulation of EEC policy. Indeed, even before direct elections, the European Parliament has already been used, both by business in attempts to tone down proposed legislation, and more successfully by left-wing interests to reinforce already progressive Commission proposals. With the new legitimacy conferred on Parliament by its democratisation, however, its importance — particularly in the early stage of EEC policy-making — could likewise increase. In areas like company and labour law some multinationals have already begun to use Parliament as a point of influence over Commission business-oriented proposals before they become politically solidified.[17] Another EEC institution whose potential as a forum for both union and company influence on policy-making has yet to be fully realised is the EEC's Economic and Social Committee.

At the OECD: the institutionalisation of business and union lobbies

The special characteristic about business and union links with the economic power structure of the OECD, the Western world's policy forum on MNC issues, is their institutionalisation.[18] The Business and Industry Advisory Committee to the OECD (BIAC) and its trade union equivalent (TUAC), predate by many years the adoption in June 1976 of the OECD's Guidelines on Multinational Enterprises. Both indeed played an active consultative part in the Guidelines' formulation, and they have both had a significant impact on the review of the Guidelines following the first three years of their application June 1976—June 1979. The conduits for union and business influence are thus built into the OECD establishment. As a result, the Guidelines are in a sense a corporatist initiative, inspired by governments but implemented and developed in close formal and informal consultations with union and business organisations, and with little democratic control — parliamentary or otherwise — since the Guidelines are neither implemented by law nor ratified.

At the same time, there have been sharp differences in the roles played by TUAC and BIAC in attempting to influence the contents and application of the package of measures on international investment and multinational companies adopted by OECD governments in the summer of 1976.[19] This is no cause for surprise since, from the outset, union and business attitudes, particularly to the Guidelines, have been both diametrically opposed and ambivalent.

Back in 1976 the unions, while viewing with suspicion the value of a non-mandatory arrangement for 'regulating' MNCs, nevertheless reluctantly agreed to 'play the game' so as to see just how much leverage over corporate behaviour was to be afforded by the Guidelines. In contrast, business's suspicions were emphatically different. For companies, which in 1976 suddenly found themselves the target of a pioneering new government initiative, the worry was that the Guidelines would provide precisely the leverage which the unions sought but felt would be inadequate. Judging by the first years of application of the OECD code, the paradoxical outcome has been to leave unions well short of their ideal of asserting control over individual MNCs while nonetheless fuelling business fears as to its impact on multinational company activities.

The trade unions: coherent strategy and organisation

If the business world — or rather its leading representatives in BIAC — is on red alert over the Guidelines, it is because of the single-minded way in which the international trade union movement has gone about exploring the application of the Guidelines to specific cases of corporate behaviour. Details of such cases, most of which have been covered extensively above,[20] need not be repeated here. However, of direct interest to an assessment of attempts to influence governmental attitudes towards MNC control is the study of the methods used by the unions for organising the exercise of that influence and establishing policy priorities in the OECD context.

The channels of communication leading to TUAC, which formally represents trade union views on the Guidelines to OECD governments are varied. TUAC policy-making on multinationals takes place at sessions of its working party on MNCs which are attended by three major categories of TUAC-affiliated participants: national union confederations (e.g. the TUC, the DGB, the AFL/CIO), the international union centres (the ICFTU, the WCL), and the international trade secretariats (ITS). Among the ITS, the most active in the OECD context have been the Geneva-based International Metalworkers Federation (IMF), the International Federation of Commercial, Clerical and Technical Employees (FIET, likewise based in Geneva), the International Transport Workers' Federation (ITF, London) and the International Textile, Garment and Leather Workers' Federation (ITGLWF, Brussels).

Meeting two to three times annually to decide policy, the TUAC group has in fact since September 1978 tended to meet jointly with the ICFTU working party on multinationals. The result of this stepped-up TUAC/ICFTU co-ordination, achieved shortly after Mr Kari Tapiola took over as TUAC secretary-general earlier in 1978, has been to give greater consistency between the unions' policy stance in the OECD context (TUAC's responsibility) and on the UN code of conduct on transnationals (where the ICFTU has consistently been the most active trade union lobby). Such co-ordination has been deemed necessary by union officials to match that carried out by both business and governments, who both use the OECD as a forum for preparing their respective positions for negotiations on transnationals at the UN. The coherence of union policy in the various international arenas has been given added strength by the appointment to TUAC of Mr Tapiola, who previously was chief executive assistant to Dr Klaus Sahlgren, the director of the UN Centre on Transnational Corporations and thus a central figure in the preparation of the UN code of conduct on transnational corporations. (Like Dr Sahlgren, Mr Tapiola, a Finn, provides further evidence of the influence exerted by the Nordics in international efforts to control MNCs.[21]) A major and worrying result of this co-operation between TUAC and the ICFTU for international business was the publication in late 1979, of the ICFTU's 'Handbook for trade union negotiators in MNCs', which provided a check list for trade union bargainers as to how best to use the OECD and ILO codes in talks with management.[22]

The international trade secretariats, which have been responsible for most of the complaints brought against individual MNCs, have been the key agents in attempting to get the OECD Guidelines effectively applied to particular instances of alleged company misbehaviour. Other cases submitted by TUAC for co-ordination by OECD governments were initially presented by national union confederations. A paradox is that, while most of the unions' specific complaints involved American multinationals, not one single case has yet been instigated by the AFL/CIO — but this may well change in the coming years. International trade union officials explain the absence of US union activity by reference to the contrasting character of European and American labour organisations — to the strength of ideological commitment in the one, and its absence in the other.

There are also distinctions to be made as between the ITS in their attitude to the Guidelines: unlike the ITS actively pursuing application of the Guidelines, the International Union of Food and Allied Workers has tended to view with particular scepticism the value to trade union aims of codes of conduct on MNCs — a view which may now be spreading following general disappointment in the union world with the June 1979 review of the Guidelines. Meanwhile, the International Chemical and Energy Workers Federation has, under the leadership of Mr Charles Levinson,[23] appeared rather to favour international collective bargaining as a means of fighting organised labour's cause with the multinationals. This alternative course of action may indeed be considered more actively in the 1980s if the international trade union movement's disaffection with the Guidelines deepens.

The more immediate prospect is somewhat different. Following the mid-1979 review of the Guidelines, there are strong signs that the prime responsibility for bringing individual MNCs to book — as the unions see it — will fall much more on the national union organisations bodies rather than just the international trade secretariats. This possible shift in the 1976—79 practice would reflect an emerging strategy, influenced among others by Mr David Lea of the British TUC, that the OECD Guidelines should be used as a basis by unions to concentrate their fire power on the national subsidiaries of MNCs. The necessary complement — control of multinationals at the worldwide group level — would according to this notion be achieved via effective implementation of the UN code of conduct on transnationals.[24]

TUAC itself, in the period following the review of the Guidelines, embarked on a policy rethink in readiness for the application of the Guidelines up to 1984, which outlined an upgraded role for national trade union action for giving added impact to the Guidelines. This in any case parallels OECD governments' own priorities — as set out in the 1979 review report — to give greater emphasis to national action (see chapter 10). TUAC's function as an effective channel for conveying union views to governments should be reinforced in the years to come given the greater co-ordination between union policy-makers since 1978. In addition, TUAC's contacts with governments will, like BIAC's, probably be more frequent in the early 1980s following the recommendations of the official review of the Guidelines. A note should also be made of the frequent informal — and ongoing — contacts the TUAC secretariat has with OECD officials on key areas of business policy.

TUAC's policy priorities — beyond the general goal of effective implementation of the Guidelines — focus on a variety of business-sensitive sectors. These are clearly spelt out in a policy paper agreed by the unions in late 1978[25] and cover in particular:

- parent company responsibility for the behaviour of subsidiaries, implying fundamental questioning of the notion of limited liability;[26]
- meaningful observance by MNCs of local laws and regulations;
- unequivocal MNC commitment to recognition of trade unions;
- right to trade union consultation within MNCs;[27]
- improved MNC information to employees;[28]
- obligation on MNCs to negotiate future plans with the unions.

BIAC: multinationals face two main problems

The challenge posed to the international business world by the OECD Guidelines has caused its own peculiar set of problems for BIAC, many of which stem from the very diversity of business interests already alluded to above in this chapter. BIAC's principal problems, as they relate to the OECD Guidelines, are two-fold and interrelated: how to offset the impact of TUAC's influence on OECD governments; and how to ensure meaningful compliance in the multinational business world with the OECD's good conduct principles, without which the credibility of its opposition to union demands may be diminished in governments' eyes.

The key body for evolving international business's policy on the OECD Guidelines and for conveying views to governments is BIAC's Committee on International Investments and Multinational Enterprises — the equivalent of TUAC's working party on multinationals. Appropriately enough, it has been manned in recent years by an impressive roster of senior executives of leading multinationals, as well as containing representatives of employer federations from the OECD area. But representatives of individual multinationals are the preponderant influence in a group which is currently chaired by Mr André Bénard, a senior executive of Royal Dutch Shell, who succeeded in this post a former Shell Chairman, Mr G.A. Wagner.[29]

An illustrative example of the potential for individual MNCs to influence official business policy at the OECD was provided by the important session of the BIAC multinationals' group held to prepare the Western business' position in the period leading up to the review of the OECD Guidelines.[30] Among the 21 participant organisations of the 12 OECD countries represented were the following:

— Exxon (Mr J.G. Clarke, senior vice-president, together with a senior public affairs advisor), General Motors (Mr R. Lockwood, chairman of GM's European Advisory Council) and US Council of the International Chamber of Commerce (Mr R.W. Markley, National Commissioner), representing the USA;

— ICI (Mr J.A.G. Coates, General Manager, International Personnel Co-ordination), representing the United Kingdom;

— Pechiney Ugine Kuhlmann (Mr M. Serpette, Directeur des Affaires Internationales) and the Conseil National du Patronat Français (Mr V. Carbonel, Chef du Service des Affaires Européennes), representing France;

— Siemens AG (Dr G. Tacke,[31] Senior Executive Consultant to the Managing Board) and BASF (Dr F. Dribbusch, former Member of the Executive Board), representing Germany;

— Federation of Danish Industries (Mr P. Kaaris, Director), representing Denmark;

— Inco Ltd (Mr K.H.J. Clarke, Consultant, Corporate Affairs) and Robert Crean & Co. Ltd (Mr J.G. Crean, President), representing Canada;

— Bekaert, S.A. (Mr Y. van der Mensbrugghe, Director, Public Affairs), and Ford of Europe (Mr P. Chaumont, Director, Governmental Affairs), from Belgium;

— FIAT (Dott. V. Sallier de la Tour, public affairs department), representing Italy;

— Bank of Tokyo (Mr K. Furumi, Deputy General Manager, London Office), representing Japan;

— Unilever (Dr M. Weisglas, Economic Advisor), representing the Netherlands;

— Skandinaviska Enskildabanken (Mr H. Lindgren, Senior Vice-President), representing Sweden;

— Sandoz (Dr H. Glättli, Head of Economic Department, and Mr C.K. Preston), representing Switzerland.

A central problem facing BIAC in getting the OECD's good conduct code effectively applied is precisely the enormous diversity of the business world it attempts to represent. It is one thing for the élite group of leading multinationals,[32] many of which are represented on BIAC and are by and large among the progressives of the international business community, to commit themselves to public support of the OECD Guidelines (and even some of them find that risky, fearing the legal implications of such a course of action in some OECD countries). But it is quite another for them to commit the rest of the world's MNCs to so speedy an assimilation of the new moral guidance handed down by Western governments as they may manage to achieve themselves. This difficulty provides BIAC with an argument which is both objectively fairer than the unions may care to recognise and more politically handy than leading MNCs would probably admit. Using it, BIAC and the powerful companies represented in it, have brought their considerable influence to bear on governments, insisting that the OECD Guidelines, as negotiated in 1976, represent the maximum that international business can accept. They have thus directed their efforts at fighting a holding operation[33] and, judging by the outcome of the 1979 review of the Guidelines, have not been without success.

But such success has not been without its drawbacks for the MNCs, who have found themselves ineluctably drawn into an ongoing negotiating process, demanding political give-and-take.

Multinational business, concerned at the use being made by the unions of the Guidelines against specific MNCs, has thus lobbied strongly with Western governments against union attempts to convert the OECD's Committee on International Investment and Multinational Enterprises (the IME Committee) into a quasi-judicial forum for censoring specific instances of MNC misbehaviour. BIAC, which has been largely successful in this, has nevertheless seen this success qualified by the public relations capital made by the unions from the non-judicial assessments given by the OECD on individual MNCs. More generally, BIAC has stressed the non-legal character of the Guidelines, but the suspicion remains among MNC executives that the OECD good conduct code could in fact serve as a spark for increasingly progressive national laws in the 24-country OECD zone.[34] Likewise, business has sought to deflect the attention of OECD governments away from exclusive concentration on the Guidelines, emphasising instead the need to create better conditions for multinational investment. In this it has found ready listeners in several OECD governments, notably the US Administration, who are already looking with consternation to the persistent economic downturn that will likely characterise the first half of the 1980s. But here again there is an implicit *quid pro quo*, clearly enunciated by OECD governments during the review of the Guidelines in the first part of 1979: the Guidelines must be more effectively applied throughout the business world, and must be seen to be so applied.

As a result BIAC, its national affiliated employer organisations, and the leading MNCs themselves, have found themselves having to direct their lobby efforts as much at the business world itself as at governments. The process of sensitising companies to the OECD code's requirements already started in 1978–79, according to BIAC which noted that:

- 14,000 copies of the Guidelines have been distributed in Belgium to company officials and trade associations;
- 6,000 copies have been distributed in Switzerland;
- tens of thousands of circulars giving information on the Guidelines, and encouraging firms to abide by them have been diffused in OECD countries – 20,000 in Canada alone, for example;
- in Sweden, personal letters have been sent to senior officials of large MNCs, while the application of the Guidelines is regularly discussed in business working groups;
- in Germany, Siemens distributed 190,000 examples of an internal company publication designed to acquaint workers with the firm's adherence to the Guidelines;
- in several countries, standing committees have been set up to study the aims and meaning of the Guidelines. (Here Britain and in particular the CBI and the USA were given special mention by BIAC.);
- the American BIAC organisation, meanwhile has sponsored a series of publications on various aspects of the Guidelines (e.g. disclosure of information, competition, employment and industrial relations) which have been circulated in thousands of copies, in the USA and beyond American borders in other countries, such as Switzerland, Norway and the Netherlands;
- in Japan, business has thrown its support behind a MITI (Ministry of Trade and Industry) questionnaire aimed at finding out the strength of adherence by Japanese firms to the Guidelines. Of the 965 firms contacted, 65 per cent replied to the questionnaire, and of these firms, 85 per cent have heard of the Guidelines, 70 per cent refer to them when taking corporate decisions, while 75 per cent of the firms ignorant of the Guidelines have indicated that they would now quickly inform their officials and workers of the need to comply with them.[35]

In addition, BIAC has sought to give particular follow-up to the Guidelines by eliciting from national affiliates a survey of corporate disclosure requirements and practices in OECD member countries. Completed in late 1981, this initiative is partly an attempt to blunt TUAC's offensive aimed at using the Guidelines for extracting increased information from MNCs.[36] The focus on information disclosure, also a sensitive element in the UN's activities on MNCs, will likely continue to be a priority of BIAC policy in the 1980–85 period, especially as the work of the OECD's committee on international accounting standards gathers momentum.

At the UN: the international dimension of union/business conflict

The battle for influence finds its fully international dimension when focusing on the negotiations for the UN code of conduct for transnational corporations being prepared in New York. It is likely to intensify through 1985, as the code moves from negotiation towards its initial implementation. Already the conflict, no longer set in the relatively homogeneous frameworks of the EEC and OECD, has given rise to some acrimonious charges, levelled by the international trade union movement and other groups, alleging abuse by multinationals of positions of power and influence in international negotiations. As against this, international business, acting in UN organisations principally through the International Chamber of Commerce (ICC) and the International Organisation of Employers (IOE), has already approved its own codes on respectively international investment[37] and extortion and bribery.[38]

But such business-sponsored initiatives have in no way reduced the pressure from adversary organisations to MNCs for intergovernmental control of multinational companies. Principal among such organisations is the ICFTU, by common accord the most active of trade union influences at the UN. The ICFTU has outlined its own basic philosophy and demands to be made of MNCs in its 'Multinational Charter'.[39]

Distinctive UN setting for highly-charged conflicts of interest

There are marked differences between the UN, on the one hand, and on the other the EEC and the OECD, as battlegrounds for conflicting influences on the shaping of intergovernmental arrangements for MNC control — differences which go at least part of the way to explaining the occasional bitterness of the lobby war which characterises the UN. Among the more salient distinctions are:

- the links between respectively the major lobbies and the officials negotiating the UN code of conduct appear much less structured than the parallel relations between union and business organisations and public authorities in the EEC and the OECD. The UN's group of expert advisers on transnational corporations, the most prominent channel for non-governmental influence on the code of conduct's preparation, does not compare with the combined impact of TUAC and BIAC on the OECD's Guidelines on Multinational Enterprises, nor with the consistent and established importance of European lobbies for EEC business-oriented legislation. At the UN the lobbies are less built in to the system;

— the UN has not the established reputation possessed by the EEC and the OECD as a policy forum whose activities can actually affect, to a greater or a lesser extent, the daily conduct of business and the economy. In the absence of a well-defined policy focus — an omission only being gradually arighted as the code's conclusion becomes a more realistic prospect — there is a tendency on the part of lobby groups, particularly on the union side, to opt for direct confrontation;

— unlike the EEC and the OECD, the membership of the UN is politically heterogeneous, providing fertile ground for ideological confrontation and polarisation. The trades unions and international business have tended to graft themselves onto this polarisation by identifying themselves respectively with the most 'progressive' governments (the LDCs and the Nordics) and the most 'conservative' (i.e. least interventionist) Western governments (USA, UK, West Germany and Switzerland).

Against this setting, the fight for influence, often ideologically charged, badly structured and not especially operationally directed, is not always conducted according to Queensbury rules. Indeed the very legitimacy of non-governmental influence, especially that exerted by big business, has been called into question, most dramatically by the Berne Declaration published in the Swiss capital in early 1978. The Declaration[40] alleged attempts by leading Swiss multinationals to use their political influence 'to neutralise the UN and the press' and — amongst other things — to physically boycott a leading international trade unionist, Mr Charles Levinson.[41]

The trade unions, galvanised by the ICFTU, have also led a sustained campaign against the allegedly excessive and abusive influence exerted by multinationals at the UN's Rome-based Food and Agricultural Organisation (FAO). The ICFTU, backed by major international trade secretariats, has lobbied strongly since the mid-1970s against the FAO's Industry Co-operative Programme, whose members are representatives of some hundred MNCs. The gist of the trade union charges — also taken up by the Berne Declaration — was that MNCs have been using a 'privileged' position from 'within' the UN agency organisation to 'abusively' influence policy in a direction favourable to them. The fear was also expressed that multinational business was preparing to extend this type of influence into other UN agencies, notably those whose activities directly overlapped with private sector interests — e.g. the Vienna-based United Nations Industrial Development-ment Organisation. As regards the FAO, the ICP was forced to give up its privileged facilities, as a direct result of trade union pressure.

Channels for influence at the UN

Whatever the rights and wrongs of these allegations, they are symptomatic of the highly-charged climate within which the UN code is being prepared and negotiated. At the same time, as indicated above, there are signs that, as the UN code itself becomes a more credible policy focus — less a religious credo for developing countries and more a negotiable medium-term prospect — so the exercise of influence is becoming less flamboyant and more concentrated on getting the best deal possible from the code.

The channels for influence on the UN code of conduct are three-fold. The major institutional conduit is the 16-member group of expert advisers. In addition, leading business organisations — e.g. the ICC and the IOE — and trade union centres — e.g. the ICFTU, the World Federation of Trade Unions (Prague-based, Communist), the World Confederation of Labour, and the Organisation of African Trade Union Unity (OATUU) have 'observer' status in ECOSOC, the UN organ to which the Commission on Transnational Corporations answers. Thirdly, there are ongoing unofficial contacts between, on the one hand, officials of the Centre on Transnational Corporation and individual government negotiators and, on the other, representatives of trade unions, multinationals and other interested parties (e.g. consumer organisations).

Trade union focus on improved MNC
information and consultation

A key source of trade union influence on the substance of the UN code of conduct is the ICFTU, whose spokesman on the expert advisers' group at the end of 1981 was Mr David Lea. The strategy of the ICFTU, which often co-ordinates closely with the OATUU (Mr Dennis Akumu) has been to seek to enlist developing country support for its view of the code, including initially pressure for making the code's provisions legally binding and subsequently for giving the code strong

214

and effective follow-up if it is to be non-binding. Effective implementation of the code has latterly become the major thrust of the unions attempts at policy influence — extending also to the UNCTAD code on restrictive business practices and the ILO Declaration on MNCs and Social Policy — and will likely continue to be the major plank of trade union policy at the UN in the 1980s. Central to this concern with the code's implementation is the call of the ICFTU, where at its headquarters in Brussels Mr Carl Wilms-Wright played a key co-ordinating role,[42] for an 8-point programme for information and consultation arrangements to be made available to unions by multinational companies.[43] The 8-point programme, submitted to the UN authorities late 1978 and for good measure to German Chancellor Helmut Schmidt (then president of the European Community's Council), reads as follows:

(i)   In order to secure greater accountability, all TNCs (i.e. each parent company) should draw up, at least annually, a report on action taken to comply with the UN code of conduct. This report should deal point-by-point with the TNCs compliance with each section of the UN code, and should be both concise and compact: it would not require, necessarily, lengthy documentation. The exact modality whereby the report is made available and to whom it is made available (e.g. as a separate report with limited distribution, or an annex to a publicly available company report required by national legislation) needs to be further explored. As the question under consideration concerns the global operations of each TNC, it is, however, essential that the report is supplied to each of those governments in whose territory the TNC operates.

(ii)   Governments should have the right to discuss any aspects of the report with the TNC, both at the national and international level, as well as being in a position to discuss certain key matters as and when they arise, in particular major plans (e.g. on investment) prior to the implementation of such plans.

(iii)   Further, in order to facilitate international contacts between a group of governments and a particular TNC, as well as discussions on the report, governments in whose territory the TNC operates should, together, have the right (i.e. the option) to establish a global information and consultation body. Where a great number of host countries are involved, these may wish to agree on a smaller group of representatives meeting the TNC on a regular basis, with less frequent meetings of the whole group. Underlying this proposal is, however, an obligation on the part of TNCs to respond positively to any request made by governments in a representative range of countries to discuss company plans on a global basis.

(iv) The need for an international forum for discussion on a company-to-company basis also bears on the role of the trade unions. The trade union representatives in the TNC as a whole should therefore also have the right to discuss the TNC's report. To facilitate this, provision should be made for trade unions in a particular TNC to have the right to the establishment of an information and consultation body at the level of the global corporation between the trade unions and the corporation, similar to the information and consultation bodies between TNCs and governments. The possible relationship, if any, between the governmental and trade union information and consultation bodies is something best left open and will depend upon, *inter alia*, the degree of tripartite (government, employers and trade union) co-operation already in existence.

(v) Some form of conciliation and arbitration is clearly necessary in those cases where it is held that a TNC is not complying with the above provisions for information and consultation. Governments and trade unions should, therefore, both have the right to make a complaint to the UN Commission on TNCs (or a sub-group established by the Commission for that purpose) when they believe there has been a failure to comply with the code of conduct, to supply the necessary information or to discuss a particular problem in a meaningful way. Such a complaints procedure should not, however, be utilised without giving due notice to the TNC concerned.

(vi) Following the initiation of the complaints procedure, the governments and/or the trade unions, as well as the TNC concerned, should each have the opportunity to make a submission to the responsible UN body.

(vii) On the basis of the evidence submitted to it, the UN body would prepare a report containing its findings and conclusions. The TNC concerned would be expected to comply with these conclusions.

(viii) In a case where a TNC failed to comply, the UN body would approach the government of the home country of the TNC to ask it to ensure compliance, as the global headquarters fall under its jurisdiction. This would be a formal obligation on the home government; otherwise it would not be fulfilling its obligations as a member of the UN.

Business seeks backing of leading OECD Governments

In sharp contrast to union policies and political alliances, international business — basically meaning Western business — gives absolute priority to non-binding measures, is markedly unenthusiastic about giving a voluntary code such implementation as may impinge on MNCs' economic flexibility, and identifies with official positions on the code of conduct adopted by the West's staunchest defenders of the market economy system: fundamentally this means the US administration, largely backed by Switzerland, the UK and West Germany (although in the case of the last two, such backing has in recent years been occasionally mitigated following pressure exerted by the trade unions.[44]).

The ICC appears as the principal channel for the exercise of business influence at the central UN organisation, the IOE tending to concentrate its efforts more (though not exclusively) on the ILO. The ICC's lobby is termed 'very effective' by officials at the UN in a position to have experienced it at first hand.

There is clearly close co-ordination between international business as represented in the OECD context (by BIAC) and at the UN. Such co-ordination is hardly surprising since, reflecting the belief of many OECD governments, Western business by and large views the model of the OECD Guidelines transposed onto a fully international level, as the maximum that it can live with at the UN. So BIAC, which also assists in preparations of positions to be adopted by business on the UN code, is in a sense a further source of influence on the UN negotiations affecting transnational corporations — however indirectly so.

The OECD — or minimalist — approach to the UN code is well voiced in a statement by a representative group of senior executives of leading multinational companies in early 1979.[45] In their statement, evolving from a meeting chaired by Mr André Bénard of Royal Dutch Shell, and since chairman of BIAC's multinationals' committee, the companies concerned noted that:

> We give unstinted support to the view that the OECD Guidelines should be the basis of the draft on MNEs now being developed by the United Nations in New York. In addition we would urge that guidelines for business behaviour being developed in different international arenas — OECD, UN, ILO, UNCTAD — be mutually

consistent and *voluntary* in nature. In this respect, we note with favour the emerging trend to establish a voluntary set of UN guidelines for MNEs, convinced as we are that only with voluntary guidelines can a framework be created possessing the flexibility necessary to accommodate the variety of business situations and national legal frameworks, and their interlocking development in the coming decade. We would further urge our governments to insist at the UN on the need for greater investment security than pertains at present. We believe this to be in the interests of the developing countries, industrialised countries and international business.

Notes and references

1   The ETUC's affiliates, representing a collective membership of 40 million members, span 18 European countries: the EEC 'ten', plus Sweden, Norway, Finland, Iceland, Switzerland, Austria, Spain and Malta.

2   UNICE, the Union of Industries of the European Community, is generally considered the ETUC's *vis-à-vis*, but in fact its membership, unlike the ETUC's is officially limited to the ten EEC countries. However, in addition to its formal membership, industry federations in the following countries also have associate status: Sweden, Norway, Finland, Switzerland, Austria, Spain, Portugal and Turkey.

3   Mr Jenkins' address to the ETUC Congress, Munich, 15 May 1979.

4   'Multinational Undertakings and the European Community'. See Appendix IV(a).

5   'European Action Programme – Multinational Groups of Companies', European Trades Union Confederation, Brussels, 10 June 1977. See Appendix I(a).

6   Ibid.

7   Both these demands are repeated in the context of TUAC's demands in the OECD and the ICFTU's in the UN. See below in this chapter.

8   See above, Part II.

9   See above, pp. 106–7.

10   ETUC Action Programme, p.7. See Appendix IV(a).

11   Ibid., pp. 11–12. Appendix IV(a).

12   ETUC Action Programme, p.5. Appendix IV(a).

13   See interview with Viscount Davignon, Appendix I(b).

14   However, this is not to say that the ETUC monopolises channels of union influence: active roles are also played by ITS such as the European Metalworkers Federation and the International Textile Garment

and Leather Workers Federation, whose secretary-general, Mr Charles Ford, is a leading union spokesman on MNC issues.

15　See Appendix I(b).

16　Direct Elections, 7–10 June 1979. First session of directly-elected European Parliament, Strasbourg, 16–20 July 1979.

17　For elaboration of this theme, see Multinational Service, no.61 of 21 June 1979.

18　The OECD structure should not, however, be confused with the fully *tripartite* relationship operating at the ILO in Geneva.

19　See Appendix II(a–e) for details of OECD package.

20　See in particular chapter 9.

21　As noted in chapter 11, another key figure in this context is Mr Sten Niklasson of Sweden.

22　See Appendix IV(b).

23　Mr Charles ('Chip') Levinson tends to be known, even in union circles, for his distinctive views. See Mr Levinson's 'Vodka–Cola', (Stock, Paris, 1978), for a sample of them.

24　See below in this chapter's section on the UN. Mr Lea, besides being a senior TUC official, is the ICFTU's representative on the body of 'expert advisers' set up to help negotiators prepare the UN code of conduct on transnational corporations.

25　'Trade Unions and Multinational Enterprises', an outline of TUAC's demands in the context of the OECD Guidelines, adopted by TUAC 15 November 1978. See Appendix IV(c).

26　Note similarity of TUAC's demands in the OECD framework with ETUC's policy priorities (see above in this chapter) in the EEC.

27　Ibid.

28　Ibid.

29　Prior to Mr Wagner, the incumbent was Sir Michael Clapham (of the Confederation of British Industries).

30　Meeting held at the OECD, Paris, 29 January 1979.

31　Dr Tacke was also a former business representative on the body of expert advisers assisting the UN in its preparation of a code of conduct on transnational corporations.

32　For examples of this group's membership, see list on p.203 above.

33　This holding operation is reflected in the 16-point memo presented by BIAC to OECD governments on 29 January 1979. See Appendix IV(d).

34　E.g. on parental responsibility and worker consultation in the EEC (see chapter 5). See also chapter 10 for the gradual transformation of the OECD Guidelines into international customary law.

35　BIAC papers for meeting with Lévy Group of OECD IME Committee, 29 January 1979.

36 By invoking the Guideline on Employment and Industrial Relations, see chapter 9 above for details.
37 'Guidelines for International Investment', ICC, November 1972. See Appendix IV(e).
38 'Extortion and Bribery in Business Transactions', ICC, November 1977. See Appendix IV(f). A panel to implement this business code was set up by ICC decision on 20 June 1978.
39 'Multinational Charter', ICFTU, Mexico, October 1975. Appendix IV(g).
40 For details, see Multinational Service, no.37, 28 June 1978.
41 General Secretary of the International Chemical and Energy Workers Federation.
42 Until leaving in 1980 to become the Director of the newly-formed Commonwealth Trade Union Council (London).
43 Compare with ETUC's call for similar arrangements at the EEC level.
44 E.g. (a) the ICFTU memo cited above and sent to Chancellor Schmidt and (b) the UK government's backing for ICFTU policy priorities at the UN in the 'Concordat' between the British TUC and Labour government reached in mid-February 1979. See in particular section 18 of this document.
45 The European Management Symposium, Davos, Switzerland, 1979. Report of working group 'Economic and Social Multinationality: Ways and Means'.

PART VI

CONCLUSION

15 The political constraint and the business response

By the early 1980s, the politicisation of international business has become a fact of life for multinational companies. It is not a fact which is liked by MNCs, nor is it one to which the international business community by and large has adjusted.

Nevertheless, as the preceding pages have sought to illustrate, the political constraint on business is there and is likely to intensify throughout the 1980s. A priority point on the long-term agenda of transnational corporations, renowned for their flexibility in responding to economic change, should be consideration of greater flexibility than shown to date in responding to changed political circumstances.

For business, chief among such changed circumstances is the tendency, on the part of governments and trade unions particularly, to redefine the role of the multinational company in political as well as economic terms. This trend, viewed with hostility by MNCs who see a new dangerous and ill-defined dimension of responsibility opening up before them, has in turn been reinforced by the economic turmoil that has wracked the world since the early 1970s. The multinationals' response to this turmoil has been one of increasing flexibility — accelerating the movement of operations to areas of lowest cost, greatest stability and highest profits. In the process, such MNC flexibility has itself aroused anxieties and enlivened demands for business control.

At the same time, the geographical focus of pressures for political control of multinationals has subtly shifted during the decade of the

1970s. The impetus behind control is by the early 1980s coming as much from the industrialised countries of the North and West as the developing countries of the South. The multinationals issue, from being a slogan of the politics of international development in the 1960s and 1970s, has been gradually transformed into practical measures of legislative control in the West.

Principal causes of this gradual shift of business control from South to North are to be found in the social and political consequences of worldwide economic stagnation.

First, the recession has spawned a general move to the right in the developing countries, whose economic vulnerability and investment thirst have tended to reduce the pressure for more excessive forms of business regulation. Second, the world economic crisis of the late 1970s and 1980s has led to increasing concern within the West — spearheaded by the trade unions but shared in varying degrees by Western governments and international bodies like the EEC and the OECD — with the need to set new standards for the conduct of multinational business. A third fact relates to both the preceding ones. The investor attraction of the newly industrialised countries like Brazil, South Korea and Taiwan, has led to a transfer southwards of resources traditionally supporting the now-declining, labour-intensive industries of the developed countries. This has simultaneously exacerbated already severe unemployment problems in the West and intensified the search for new standards of business behaviour which was in any case under way, particularly in Western Europe.

The key notion running through this emerging body of business standards — be they EEC rules for industrial relations and company information, or international codes for corporate behaviour agreed by Western governments in the OECD — is accountability. By accountability is meant the accountability of business to new constituencies — to governments, to the general public and, above all to the workforce And being accountable to such new constituencies, the multinationa company is forced into a new context of political and social responsibility, as well as retaining its legal obligations to its traditiona constituent, the shareholder.

Capitalism in decline and accountability on the rise

The emergence of the political constraint on Western multinationals ha not been sudden. Rather it is the product of a gradual process, which nonetheless amounts to a quiet revolution in the values and rules governing business and its role in society. The development of this external constraint is paralleled by a decline in the capitalist ethic to

224

which big business, paradoxically and certainly unintentionally, has itself contributed.

The individual stockholder, the link to the democratic base from which capitalism emerged, has now been largely effaced in his function of control of business management. He has been effaced not simply or even principally by the large institutional shareholder, but much more by the upsurge of central management at the expense of the owners. This is particularly true in large and internationally complex companies. Ownership, in such companies, no longer carries with it either the cachet or reality of control. The main exception to this statement — and an exception which merely serves to reinforce it — is where the shareholder takes the shape of the multinational corporation itself, or of an anonymous holding company, which can indeed effectively control subsidiaries. Otherwise the shareholder is less effective at controlling the decisions of distant management than are Bagehot's parliamentarians in the control of British cabinet government. Just as the parliamentarians dignified the reality of government power, so the shareholder is used to dignify the process of international capitalism. But invocation by company managements of the alibi of 'shareholder interests' as grounds for resisting pressure for new social responsibilities — 'our first responsibility is to our shareholders' — rings increasingly hollow. It is also damaging to the business cause. Such arguments, sometimes sincere but more often disingenuous, tend to strengthen, rather than weaken, the case for a change in traditional company laws which, under the guise of deifying the shareholder, give worldly powers to management.

The decline of traditional forms of business control is part of a broader picture in which the decline of the capitalist ethic is a recurring leitmotif. Even in America, the notion that 'the market place checks and destroys those who are irrational in the exercise of corporate power has lost most of its vitality, at least for the largest corporations'.[1] This is doubly true for Western Europe where the market place, even in the halcyon years of multinational economic expansion 1950–70, has never enjoyed such influence. Those years saw most nearly the equation of European political democracy and economic liberalism, but since then the two notions — never really at ease with each other — have parted company. Multinational companies, the great exponents and principal beneficiaries of economic liberalism, have gradually come into conflict with mainstream European political ideology, with its increasing emphasis on economic and industrial democracy as well as its political counterpart. The hierarchical and centralised structure of multinational company decision-making has thus come under attack. Gradually and then more rapidly as the chronic downturn starting in the 1970s has gathered force, economic liberalism has become 'unidentified' with the European democratic mainstream. In the process, multinationals, from having initially been an acceptable — even perhaps logical — economic expression of the Western political system, have instead come to be a prime object of democratic criticism.

The gradual erosion of traditional forms of business discipline, coupled with this more general malaise, has led to an upsurge in the demands for alternative forms of control to plug the accountability gap. These demands, which seemed something of a luxury in the boom years of the 1960s and early 1970s, have by the early 1980s come to be perceived as matching the practical needs of new constituencies. European pressure for an effective supervisory power within the company — a supervisory board, independent of the executive directors, which might include representatives of workers and outside interests — reflects one attempt to fill this gap. Others include the EEC's so-called Vredeling proposal on worker information and consultation in multinationals. Some multinationals have themselves sought to respond, forming 'advisory councils', bodies which seek to provide management with independent advice on the politico-economic environment and the critical issues affecting the corporation.

Business and the politics of rejection

Yet business, as a whole, has failed to respond to these new demands. Multinational companies, seeing themselves as sandwiched between a receding market and expanding governmental intrusion into it, prefer by and large to caricature such requirements as a mixture of bureaucratic meddling, left-wing ideology and trade union pressures — bad in themselves, worse in combination, and worst of all when launched in an economic crisis. Business's key function of wealth creation, already compromised by economic stagnation yet rendered more important because of it, should not be further undermined by the imposition of new political and social constraints. So runs the argument, which concludes that greater, not less, freedom is needed for business to operate successfully in the economic bad times likely to characterise the 1980s. Deregulation, not control, should be the order of the day — or rather the order of the decade. The international business programme of the 1980s thus tends to include a position of blanket defence against any new business standards, rather than allowing an appraisal of individual measures on their merits.

Thus in the EEC, a typical response to the Vredeling initiative — which some multinationals privately view as little more than a simple if clumsy statement of good management/employee relations — has been one of ritual horror, both from European and American business organisations. A similar reflex of rejection has been provoked by EEC proposals on corporate disclosure, which are small beer when compared to American information requirements. The same scenario has been played out in the case of European initiatives aimed at greater employee involvement in the control of corporate decision-making, but in West Germany, the country with the most sophisticated version of worker participation, the ability of management to take decisions does not appear to have been paralysed. Meanwhile, Western government standards on industrial relations set out in the OECD's voluntary code are feared by many corporate strategists as the first step towards international union wage bargaining − a prospect for which trade union organisations are manifestly unprepared and which leading analysts have dismissed out of hand. As for the United Nations code on transnationals, considered with mistrust by international business, it appears to offer the multinational company an improved chance of investment security for a price in corporate behaviour which many companies should be able to pay with little effect.

The dangers for business inherent in such defensiveness are two-fold. The first relates to the risks inherent in self-delusion. This is the danger that the international business community, convinced by its own propaganda of the extent of the threats facing it, will become gradually entrenched in rejectionist strategies that project a reactionary image of the multinational company which, in turn, will sharpen the political and social pressures for business control. Excessive constraints may become more likely if moderate demands are themselves caricatured as excessive. A good example of this in the late 1970s and early 1980s was the systematic stonewalling by certain influential sections of the French industrial establishment of attempts by a centre right government to introduce modest company reforms. While successful in the short-term, this strategy of opposition failed to take account of the consequences of such an attitude in the event of a change of government. Those consequences are becoming apparent as the French socialist administration elected in 1981 embarks on much more radical options of company reform. Another scenario business must ponder is whether rejection of international attempts at setting voluntary standards − like the UN code on transnational corporations − may not lead in the long-term to a less secure investment climate characterised by differing national rules and the arbitrary exercise of national government powers. Failure in the negotiations aimed at establishing the UN code could also lead to less accommodating codes of business practice imposed on a regional basis.

A second danger for companies inherent in out-and-out opposition to new business standards is that of weakening business' standing as a source of legitimate influence over the political process. This could be unfortunate, particularly at institutions like the EEC where business, unlike its major rival for influence, the European trade union movement, appears to be coming gradually alienated from the process of European integration, now that that process is no longer simply identified with the creation of transnational market freedoms. If the business community, for its part, allows itself to become identified with claims that politics should keep out of business, then the political process may be increasingly tempted to repay the compliment.

An alternative strategy for the company

Multinational companies, so quick to adapt to economic change, have shown themselves less able to adjust to new political and social developments. Yet the dangers inherent in non-adjustment are apparent. They include the discrediting of international business in the eyes of those involved in the broader political process, and the strengthening of the positions of interests and groups adverse to multinationals. For companies, there is no ready-made formula for coming to terms with public affairs' issues and trends. But the starting point is not to opt out of involvement in the wider environment.

But how to opt in? — that is the difficult question. Any answer must surely start with the individual company. Little can be done, at least initially, at the level of the official business organisation, unless its membership is unusually homogeneous and the issues it is addressing well-defined. The best that such bodies can do, given the multifaceted nature of the companies that are their constituents, is to reproduce positions which inevitably tend to reflect an uninspiring lowest common denominator. Changes — in attitude and structure — must thus start with the individual firm and then filter through to representative organisations.

Upgrading the public affairs function[2] of the multinational company is a necessary first step in the process of business adjustment. It is in itself recognition that the political and social environment, as well as traditional economic factors, is a proper subject for business management. Some large companies have begun this process, but in the vast majority of cases, central management has not even begun to realise the difference between public affairs and public relations. Even when this distinction has been made, there is much hesitation and not enough sophistication. The public affairs function is often attributed a senior executive who already has his hands full in another management area. Where the public affairs function is granted independent status, its integration with — and the feedback of its result to — the 'line' functions of a company's management is often haphazard. Meanwhile, within the area of public affairs itself, there is insufficient distinction between the different sub-functions — e.g. information gathering, legislative monitoring, and lobbying. There is also inadequate understanding as to how best to carry out such tasks. And there is a lack of awareness that one of the key public affairs functions is to educate and sensitise officials within the company on changes in the political and social environment. Issue management has both an outward and inward dimension.

A further structural adjustment which MNCs would do well to consider is the creation of bodies like international advisory councils (IACs) or regional advisory councils (RACs). A typical IAC/RAC is composed of a small group of leading international businessmen and ex-governmental officials who provide the company with a reservoir of impartial knowledge on broad political and social developments. Such bodies should heighten the company's awareness of the importance of public affairs issues, and at least begin to make it more open to interests other than those of the shareholder and management.

There is also scope for improving the existing 'collective' channels for expressing business viewpoints. It is clearly in the interest of individual companies which assess the public affairs function as important to seek to influence the positions taken by business organisations and federations on issues of public policy. There is probably also a case for supplementing such official channels with the creation of more streamlined groups of public affairs officers from like-minded companies.

However, no amount of adjustment of business structures will make any real difference if the basic approach of companies to the political process is wrong. If firms adopted a more open attitude towards that process, the result would be that, in addition to avoiding the self-inflicted dangers described earlier in this chapter, they would discover areas of public policy where their input could well be welcomed. This is particularly true in the EEC for areas like international trade and investment where, in the 1980s, one of the central political battles is certain to be fought around the issue of economic nationalism both within and beyond the Common Market's borders — a phenomenon that is as much a threat to the multinational company as it is to the EEC and an open international economy. Multinational business's traditional claims of political virginity will not help it make the positive contribution it could to this and a wide range of policy issues. Nor, in the field of business regulation policy, are such claims of chastity likely to prove the best defence against rape.

Notes and references

1   'Free Enterprise in a Free Society', Williams.
2   Numerous other titles are used to designate the public affairs function, including: governmental affairs; corporate affairs; corporate communications; international relations; etc.

Appendix I
relating to Part II

I(a) *MULTINATIONAL UNDERTAKINGS AND THE COMMUNITY* COMMUNICATION OF THE EUROPEAN COMMISSION TO THE COUNCIL OF MINISTERS, 8 NOVEMBER 1973, FOLLOWED BY TEXT OF EEC DRAFT RESOLUTION ON MNCs

I Introduction

Economic developments in recent decades have been marked in particular by a very substantial growth of large undertakings which have industrial establishments distributed in a number of countries.

In most cases, the multinational growth of an undertaking satisfies the essential optimal operating requirements of natural economic and social conditions. It also satisfies, to a certain extent, the need to overcome the obstacles to the free interplay of international trade which States have still left in existence. The abolition of these obstacles would therefore eliminate a good many artificial reasons which lead undertakings to 'multinationalize' themselves without, however, properly satisfying real economic and social requirements.

In some cases such a movement can help to promote better distribution of work and knowledge throughout the world, to industrialize developing regions and to harmonize social conditions.

At Community level, as early as 1970, in its industrial policy memorandum, the Commission had already expressed regret that too many European industrial undertakings still retained a national dimension and were slow in adapting themselves, in size and location, to the new European economic area. The Commission found that the many legal and fiscal obstacles still in existence and the present lack of a European capital market serve to restrain this essential transformation of European industry. At the Paris Summit Conference the Heads of State and of Government wrote into their statement their wish to ensure that the Community had the industrial foundation on which its economic and social development depends. The Commission submitted to the Council an action programme capable of covering its initial phase.

With this in mind, the Commission considers that it should endeavour to remove the legal and fiscal obstacles hampering the transnational integration of member countries' industrial structures, which should be able to develop by cooperation projects, by mergers of undertakings and even by the creation of multinational undertakings when they can make a useful contribution to attaining the Community's economic and social objectives.

Nevertheless, the growing hold of multinational undertakings on the economic, social and even political life of the countries in which they operate, gives rise to deep anxieties which are sufficiently divided, particularly in the areas of employment, competition, tax avoidance, disturbing capital movements and the economic independence of developing countries, to demand the attention of the public authorities.

The main reason for this is that these undertakings have reached a size and geographical spread such as to cast doubts on the effectiveness of the traditional measures of the public authorities and the trade unions, which up to now have been unable to achieve an equivalent degree of coherence or international integration. This situation has resulted in particular in inadequate national legal, fiscal, economic and monetary rules, the scope of which is too narrow to grasp the problems raised by the existence of numerous groups of companies legally separate and covered by different national laws.

In practice, problems begin to emerge as soon as an undertaking has production facilities in two or several countries. They obviously grow concurrently with the increase in the activities of the group of companies and their extension to a larger number of countries. Nevertheless the nature of the problems remains the same.

It should be pointed out that almost all the measures briefly analysed below are or will be carried out primarily in order to attain Community objectives which go beyond that of supervising the operations of multinational undertakings: this is particularly true of everything relating to the attainment of economic and monetary union of for example to taxation or social policy. That is to say that virtually all the measures the Community might take with regard to multinational undertakings relate to problems which may equally well be created by national undertakings or even by private individuals.

The Commission therefore believes that it will be impossible to find solutions and allay anxieties in this area unless suitable counterweights are introduced at Community and international level so as to re-establish the conditions for a balance between the parties concerned.

By its very task, which is to coordinate, harmonize and if necessary supplement the policies of Member States whenever it is essential to seek common solutions, the Community presents the degree of effectiveness and cohesiveness necessary to form the framework into which such a counterweight can be introduced, even if still remaining imperfect: for this reason the Commission considers it useful to present the proposals described below to the Council.

Nevertheless, it is quite obvious that the activities of the Community will be fully effective only to the extent that identically inspired rules are imposed at world level with a view to ensuring a homogeneous framework for the operations of multinational undertakings whatever their origin and their geographic field of activity. The Community will work on this both in the appropriate international bodies such as the OECD and the United Nations, and, for certain points, within the framework of any bilateral negotiations.

The Commission realizes that the proposals described below do not solve all the problems. There are still some in the areas of foreign trade, the distribution of the results of research, the position reserved for foreign executives in management bodies, etc. for which the Commission has not at present been able to find a suitable reply. It is however necessary to undertake the implementation of measures which are feasible right away without waiting to find solutions to all the problems which emerge.

In this document, the Commission has therefore set aside the problems for which, for the moment, it has not been possible to define solutions. It should therefore be considered as the starting-point for measures which are about to be undertaken and subsequently finalized and not as an end result.

II General guidelines for proposals

The Commission considers that the measures to be undertaken should not impede the development of a phenomenon with recognized economic and social advantages, but that they should merely aim at guarding the Community against its harmful effects with the help of a suitable legal framework. It also considers that this framework should contain no discriminatory aspect and that it should apply alike to individuals and to undertakings, whether of national, international, Community or extra-Community foundation.

The examination undertaken by the Commission indicated that the problems raised could not be solved by adopting a few spectacular measures or a code of good conduct which by definition would be binding only on undertakings of good will. Indeed, the size of certain problems, in particular relating to security of employment, tax avoidance or disturbing capital movements, justifies the adoption of measures of greater constraint.

Studies have moreover indicated that the range of possibilities which large international undertakings enjoy enables them to find an effective answer to meet specific isolated measures. The inevitable solution is therefore to set up a network of coherent measures ensuring for undertakings the degree of autonomy essential for the pursuit of their economic and social objectives, but sufficiently finely wrought to prohibit operations considered undesirable by the Community.

This has led the Commission to make an index of a certain number of measures, the implementation of which should help to solve a large part of the problems raised. Some of these measures play a decisive role. Others are accompanying measures, each of which is essential only because it helps to ensure the cohesiveness of the system.

III   The measures envisaged

The various problems raised by the growth of multinational undertakings and the measures envisaged for solving them have been collected in seven chapters concerning:

- (i)   protection of the general public
- (ii)   protection of workers' interests
- (iii) maintenance of competition
- (iv)   takeover methods
- (v)   equality of conditions of reception
- (vi)   protection of developing countries
- (vii) improvement of information.

A.   Protection of the general public

The gravity of the problems encountered in this area justify an active search for effective solutions. These problems in fact concern tax avoidance, security of supply, monetary stability, aid from public authorities and the protection of shareholders and of third parties.

(a) *Tax problems*   The area of taxation probably best reveals the inadequacy of nationally-devised systems supplemented by bilateral

234

agreements for tackling the phenomen of the growth of multinational undertakings.

The coexistence of different non-harmonized tax systems complicates and even often penalizes the intcrnational functioning of an undertaking. For this reason the Commission considered it necessary to submit to the Council two draft directives intended not to create tax burdens for operations carried out in several member countries which are greater than for those carried out purely nationally.

Nevertheless, the very existence of disparities in tax systems has inevitably led multinational undertakings to attempt to protect themselves and even to use them in a way considered improper by some.

As regards legal tax avoidance, the Commission intends to follow up, as soon as possible, its work on tax avoidance, in order to improve international assistance and cooperation relating to information, supervision and recovery. Within the framework of this work, special attention will be devoted to the problems of transfer prices and licence fees. The possible adoption of certain tax agreements should, where appropriate, be envisaged in this context.

Moreover, the suggestions made by the Commission in the report on the taxation system of holding companies which it submitted to the Council in June this year also apply to multinational undertakings.

(b) Security of supply In the event of a crisis, it is to be feared that the influence exercised by a non-member State which has jurisdiction over a multinational undertaking would be detrimental to the Community's interests.

In the sphere of energy, the Commission proposed to the Council measures intended to improve the Community's security of supply, in particular the concerting of action between the Member States and with the participation of the undertakings concerned on their hydrocarbons supply policy.

(c) Monetary problems In this area the Commission considers that one of the principal measures should lead to a better knowledge of the financial flows accompanying companies' transnational operations.

It will therefore propose that a system of presentation of data concerning these flows be introduced at the external frontiers of the countries making up the Community.

The Commission has initiated the study of how to create better statistical information in order to show the influence of the multinational phenomenon on the balance of payments of the Community and of its Member States.

Moreover, a solution to the problem of short-term disturbing capital movements, part of which is attributed to the activities of multinational companies, is being sought, particularly within the framework of work on the achievement of economic and monetary union.

(d) The outbidding in aid by public authorities In many cases, international investment plays an important part in the implementation of regional policies developed by public authorities.

Nevertheless, to the extent that Member States have recourse to a certain amount of outbidding in relation to State aid, particularly for regional purposes, in order to attract large new investment, multinational undertakings have been able to benefit more than others from this outbidding. Being among the first to decide on the location of their establishments, not in terms of such or such a national dimension, but in terms of all the possibilities provided in the geographical area of the Common Market, they could in fact place the different Member States in competition to obtain the greatest advantage for these establishments.

In order to eliminate negative effects, the Commission is continuing to develop its efforts as regards the coordination or harmonization of national, and particularly regional aids.

Moreover, in its stance on aid granted by Member States for a certain number of advanced technology sectors, the Commission has shown that it considered it was advantageous for the Community for European undertakings, confronted by the power of certain multinational groups, to increase their efficiency, this increase involving in certain cases cooperation between these undertakings.

(e) Protection of shareholders and of third parties In the near future the Commission will submit to the Council a proposed 'Law on groups of companies' which recognizes, on the legal plane, the subordination of the interests of particular companies to the group interests and which therefore legalizes the application of a uniform management policy for the group in relation to the companies forming part of it. Conditions as regards advertising are required to guarantee the transparency of the group. This draft also makes provision for arrangements intended to protect external shareholders. Creditors benefit from the guarantee of the parent company in the event of the failure of a subsidiary company.

B.   Protection of workers

The opportunities possessed by multinational companies to affect employment in the various countries in which they exercise an activity causes much anxiety among workers. The Commission considers the setting up of a trade union counterweight as essential for a balanced solution to this problem; however that it is not its task to organize this but certainly to encourage it. The creation of Community joint committees or committees set up on a basis of parity by sector can contribute to this. Moreover, the Commission considers that the growth of European collective agreements can also help to solve the problems which the existence of multinational undertakings causes workers.

Adequate guarantees as regards security of employment may be furnished by the adoption of the following measures:

(a) The proposing of Directive on large scale dismissals

(b) The draft already in preparation aiming at the protection of employers' interests, in particular as regards the maintenance of existing rights in the event of mergers or rationalization;

(c) The draft Directive on the harmonization of national laws on mergers between companies.

This last mentioned proposal includes specific rules for the informing and consultation of the employees prior to decisions by general assemblies, and for the negotiation of a 'Social plan' where the merger is likely adversely to affect employees' interests. In the event of disagreement, the public authorities may be asked by either of the parties to act as mediator. This Directive is concerned with mergers between companies in the same country, but the protective measures laid down therein must obviously also be respected in the case of an international merger, and the convention currently in preparation on mergers will have to contain similar provisions albeit merely for reference to national legislation.

In addition to the field of legal fusions, measures for the protection of employees should also be laid down in the case of acquisition of undertakings by other methods such as those provided for by the Dutch 'fusie code' (Merger Code).

It is also necessary:

(a) To adopt the European Company Statute which would ensure that employees of branches do actually participate in the supervising of the management of the parent company, and which provides for the possibility of concluding collective agreements between employees and administrative organs in the European Company.

Adoption of the fifth Directive would guarantee analagous rights at the level of the individual companies.

(b) Harmonization of labour law in order to guarantee real participation in the Works Council of the parent company for employees of companies which are members of a group.

In addition, the Commission is aware of the legal problem raised by the need for appropriate representation of employees' interest vis-à-vis a company which no longer takes it decisions independently but complies with those of the group of which it forms part. In the course of the coordination of the law on groups of companies which it is at present undertaking, the Commission will examine the question as to what measures will have to be adopted in this field.

The provision of information for, and the participation of employees in cases where either the parent company or any of the member undertakings of the group are situated outside the Community raise substantial problems to which the Commission's departments are seeking adequate solutions.

C. The maintenance of competition

Most multinational undertakings are of considerable size and control substantial sections of markets. They are more able than other companies to restrict competition and to abuse dominant positions. It is therefore desirable in their case to devote special attention to ensuring that the rules on competition shall be respected.

This may be achieved by the following means:

(a) the adoption of the draft Regulation under Articles 87 and 235 establishing the incompatibility of merger operations making it possible to obstruct effective competition with the Common Market and laying down the obligation to give prior notice of merger operations involving undertakings or groups thereof with a turnover in excess of 1,000,000,000 units of account.

(b) active surveillance by the Commission in accordance with Articles 85 and 86 of oligopolistic situations.

D. Purchasing of undertakings

The increasingly frequent purchasing of competitor undertakings with or without the latters' consent justifies the drawing up and application of a certain code of obligations concerning the ways in which such operations are to be carried out.

(a) it is desirable in the Commission's view to adopt Community rules concerning public take-over bids, and the preparation of such rules has been undertaken.

(b) the Commission is also of the opinion that a system for the rapid sharing of information and for coordination should be established as

238

between the national authorities which supervise stock-exchange operations, in order that the latter may assess, on the basis of a complete knowledge of the facts, the often very extensive operations mounted simultaneously in several different countries by large companies. Such coordination ought in particular to allow a number of good conduct rules on stock-exchange operations to be drawn up and to ensure that these are respected.

(c) objective rules regarding the conditions to be satisfied by investment and take-over operations if these are to comply with the economic and social aims of the Community should be drawn up and applied by joint agreement by the Member States.

E. Equality of conditions of reception

According to the information available to the Commission, not all third countries are as liberal in the conditions which they grant to foreign companies as the Member States of the Community. The restrictions in question apply to the right of establishment, financing opportunities and conditions, the right of foreigners to hold capital in or directorships of companies, the sending-back of profits to the home country, or arise from the applications of national anti-trust provisions, etc.

At the present time various important changes are in cause. The disturbances in the international monetary system, in particular changes in exchange rates, substantially affect the cost of investment as between the large economic groupings. At the same time, the attitude of trade unions in the United States might lead the American government to encourage foreign investment in that country. Finally, it has until now been and continues to be difficult to judge the possible consequences of Japan's new open policy with regard to foreign investments.

Under these conditions only a general approach can be outlined, detailed measures of which will have to be adopted at a later stage.

In any event the Community's aim in this field as in others is not to apply restrictive or discriminatory measures but to make liberalization measures more widespread.

In order to eliminate existing discriminatory situations as well as those which might arise from the unilateral application by the Community of the various measures described in this document, it will in the Commission's view be necessary:

(a) to hold meetings, and, if the necessary conditions here fulfilled, to negotiate on specific problems concerning above all the United States and Japan. During negotiations with certain countries the opportunity should be taken to tackle the problem of the tax facilities granted by these countries;

(b)   to aim at the general adoption of most of the measures envisaged in this document throughout the industrialized countries, in other words as far as possible in the Member States of the OECD;

(c)   to obtain guarantees in the specialized organizations of the UN (GATT, UNCTAD, UNID) to the effect that the provisions, which the Community may adopt unilaterally in order to ensure that the operations of multinational companies of Community origin shall correspond with the economic and social objectives of the developing countries, shall not operate to the latters' disadvantage.

F.   Conditions of establishment of multinational companies in developing countries

A frequently substantial proportion of investment in developing countries is made by multinational undertakings. The economic and financial power of the latter may, in certain cases, result in substantial imbalances in the economic development of the developing country concerned, without necessarily being compatible with its long-term development aims.

The Community, particularly concerned as to the future of these countries, and desirous that an effective framework shall be created for balanced and mutually beneficial economic cooperation with them, will make every effort to ensure that investments by multinational undertakings of Community origin shall be closely compatible with the economic and social aims of the host countries.

Under this heading, the following measures, which would be especially effective, should be adopted:

(a)   The appropriate application of the economic and social provisions included in the proposals, concerning a system of guarantees for investments in third countries, which the Commission has submitted to the Council;

(b)   The objective application of Community rules concerning transfer prices and licence fees;

(c)   A development cooperation policy conceived in such a ways as to encourage those private investments best suited to the priorities of the host country, and to govern within the framework of long-term agreements, the conditions of reception of such investments, and possibly detailed rules for implementation in cases of the transfer of ownership of industrial installations.

G.   Better provision of information

In the Commission's view there exists a simple means of assuaging the fears felt in many quarters and at the same time of throwing light on the operations of multinational undertakings.

This would amount to the most widespread possible distribution of an annual report containing straight-forward information on large national and multinational undertakings in order to allow all interested parties to arrive at their own judgement of the policies carried on by the various undertakings.

This information should, *inter alia*, include the following:

(i) funds invested, re-invested, and transferred to the country of origin;

(ii) the origin and composition of the capital;

(iii) the number of jobs created and abolished;

(iv) declared profits and taxes paid, as percentages of the turnover;

(v) expenditure on research and income from licences.

The above would be broken down into the country where the parent company is established and all other branches of the group.

A substantial part of this information is already publicly available but is of relative interest in that it is not included in international comparative statistics, or else is not sufficiently compatible. The proposals at hand or in the course of preparation as regards company accounts and publicity should contribute towards attaining the necessary degree of clarity and compatibility, which at the present time continues to be lacking in some countries or in the case of certain types of company, the economic and social importance of which can no longer justify the degree of secrecy with which they surround themselves.

In order to be effective such action requires the support of the authorities in the Member States and in other States willing to cooperate, as well as the collaboration of multinational undertakings themselves.

IV Conclusion

The mechanism constituted by the action set out above obviously cannot be established in one operation. Certain types of action already figure in formal proposals from the Commission which could rapidly be adopted by the Council. Others on the contrary will probably require many meetings of national experts in order to draw up the detailed rules required for their implementation. The process will take several years to complete.

In order to ensure coherent realization, according to the degree of priority accorded to each, of the types of action set out above, which fall within different Community policies, the Commission requests the Council to adopt the draft resolution in Annex I attached hereto, thus recording its agreement with the aims and principles expounded in this document, and its undertaking to participate actively in their implementation.

DRAFT RESOLUTION OF THE COUNCIL ON THE
MEASURES TO BE TAKEN BY THE COMMUNITY
IN ORDER TO RESOLVE THE PROBLEMS RAISED
BY THE DEVELOPMENT OF MULTINATIONAL
UNDERTAKINGS

The Council of the European Communities

Having regard to the communication of November 1973 from the
Commission on the problems raised by the development of multinational undertakings;

Whereas international economic interpretation may help to promote
a more equitable distribution of labour and of technological knowledge
in the world, and to harmonize social conditions;

Whereas nevertheless the size of the phenomenon gives rise to concern, in particular in the fields of employment, competition, tax
evasion, disturbing movements of capital, the security of the supply of
certain raw materials, and the economic independence of the developing countries; whereas the Community institutions must therefore take
the necessary initiatives to ensure that multinational undertakings in
their operations shall respect the economic and social aims of the
Community;

Whereas the Community must participate fully in international discussions concerning certain problems of world-wide importance which
would be begun within the framework of the various international
organizations, for the seeking of resolutions in a spirit of reciprocity.

Whereas measures which may be adopted at the present time are
concerned with problems which are not specific to multinational undertakings alone; whereas such measures fall in the different policies
adopted or being developed by the Community in accordance with the
Treaty of Rome;

(i) Confirms its intention to act within the time limits laid down in
the various programmes in particular as regards the proposals concerning large-scale dismissals, protection of existing rights of employers
in the case of merger or rationalization, the guaranteeing of investments
in third countries, internal company mergers, the European Company
Statute, the structure of S.E.'s and the supervision of mergers;

(ii) Considers that decisions have to be taken in particular in the
fields set out above and notes the Commission's intention to submit as
soon as possible proposals concerning the following:

    (a) The protection of employees in the case of the take-over of
        companies;

(b) The laying down of Community rules in particular concerning stock exchange operations and on the origins of funds for investment.

(c) Cooperation between and amalgamation of national authorities responsible for the supervision of stock exchange operations;

(d) International assistance and cooperation measures in the fields of information, monitoring, and tax recovery, and in particular the drawing up of a joint schedule of transfer prices and licence fees;

(e) A body of law on groups of companies;

(f) The collection of adequate information on the international activity of undertakings.

INTERVIEW WITH ETIENNE DAVIGNON,
EEC COMMISSIONER FOR INDUSTRIAL
AFFAIRS, ON EEC POLICY TOWARDS MULTI-
NATIONAL COMPANIES
(as appeared in *Multinational Service*, fortnightly, no.10, 25 May 1977)

MULTINATIONAL SERVICE: The European Commission has recently decided to create a new office dealing with policy towards multinational companies. Why did you feel a need to create it and what do you see as its main role?

DAVIGNON: 'If the Commission wants to be a political body which senses what people wish to see happen and thus has to keep in contact with governments and business, then we at the Commission must be organised so as to develop our own thinking on these matters. "Multinationals" is now a slogan and we are not that interested in slogans. All the same, in organising an industrial policy, you have to take account of who your opposite numbers in the negotiation are, and your opposite numbers — today as they were yesterday — are the big companies who have grouped themselves or whose activities reach beyond frontiers. Realisation of this is particularly important when you are in a period of recession, a period of industrial restructuring, when you want to know, for example, the policy of a company on investments — information which cannot necessarily be acquired by contacting just one of the wheels in the multinational's mechanism. You need an overall view of the multinational's policy. In the same way we need to organise ourselves to have a global view of multinationals in the context of our industrial policy'.

MULTINATIONAL SERVICE: Are you saying that the creation of a new multinationals' office is to facilitate a dialogue with multinational companies, and so it is an open-oriented office?

DAVIGNON: 'It's exactly that. In reorganising the whole department that falls under my responsibility [the combined industrial and internal market departments — ed.] we've taken that as one of the guidelines. We want to have an open shop, an open window for consultations with the industrialists, so that one of our priorities in formulating our suggestions, policies and actions will be the priorities of the people concerned by them — one of the priorities, mind you, not the exclusive priority . . .'.

MULTINATIONAL SERVICE: What are the priority issues for the MNC office? And do you not feel that, despite this openness, with the pressures increasing for intervention in the international economy, the

Commission itself will have to assume a more interventionist posture on certain matters?

DAVIGNON: 'I don't like the word interventionism. It is too readily misinterpreted. You can be labelled an interventionist simply because you talk to people, and likewise if you make no such contacts you become an ideal political leader. If that's the case, I certainly should not like to belong to the second category. But both thorough-going dirigisme and total freedom are equally exaggerated and unreal postures in today's world, and we in the Commission want to be between the two extremes.

'As to the main focuses of our policy on multinationals, they are as follow: first, investments — some sort of harmonisation of investments is needed in our industrial policy — things like the Japanese are doing, a sort of strategy enabling you to be ahead of events rather than running behind them to know for example where increased competition is going to come from and thus be able to organise yourself to meet it without succumbing to protectionism. Obviously you have to meet people who decide on investments if you want to organise yourself to meet that competition. Second, — and there's nothing new in this — we must work on dominant positions and ensuring fair competition — which is clearly threatened by dominant positions. The third element concerns the social part of our policy: here it should be clear that you can't avoid being subject to Community rules or national rules which the Community thinks should be implemented by having a legal status which permits you to run through loopholes. There again, that's not interventionism, it's simply being fair. . . . These, I think, are the three big chapters on which we have business to do with multinationals'.

MULTINATIONAL SERVICE: One of the fears expressed by business circles is that in placing the multinationals' office in the company law department of your services, you have taken the company regulation and thus restrictive option towards multinationals. Is this a justifiable fear?

DAVIGNON: 'What I've said above proves that that is not correct. It is just one of the elements . . . . Fundamentally why we wanted to create an MNC policy unit was to respond to the three priorities I've mentioned; we want them to be active in helping us develop our policy, which means cooperation on their side in what I call the growth pattern, the active pattern, of our policy: the overall elements of investment, trade policy, — dialogue on these sort of issues. The other thing is that if MNCs become more and more involved in our various activities, might well receive help to do so, in return we're going to be sure that the policy will be sustained . . . . The help that we're giving them is creating an internal EEC market for these companies, particularly the bigger ones for whom it's more important, for example by getting rid of barriers. In return, we're entitled to some consistency in the way in which multinationals react to the needs of that market. Moreover, you can't pursue this sort of policy without a minimum of transparency. . . . If the Commission has to explain what it does, and if governments explain what they do, then there is the need for business to do the same thing. And to be sure of this transparency, there must be some rules — not more in the EEC than in the USA and Japan or elsewhere, but not less either — and obviously when you're operating within a multi-state framework, there are more loopholes in legislation'.

MULTINATIONAL SERVICE: From what you've said, the Commission's multinationals' policy is an inherent part of its overall industrial policy. EEC industrial policy has been criticised in the past by those outside the Community for being too inward looking. Do you feel that a certain amount of benevolent discrimination is needed to encourage EEC multinationals in the face of competition from their often stronger American counterparts?

DAVIGNON: 'I don't think you should have an overall policy of granting preference to what is European, simply because it's European. If you adopt that sort of policy, then obviously the next step is that even if it's inefficient, and doesn't meet the needs of the consumer, you would still give it preference. Clearly, if we adopted that sort of approach we would be reacting neither to the reality of Europe nor to the reality of what Europeans want. That is one extreme. The other extreme is to say we don't care who produce the goods as long as we have them — thereby ignoring considerations such as dependence, creation of unemployment, and competitive aspects on third markets. This extreme would in my view be just as silly. Nobody does that. What we're trying to do is something in between, and that is always difficult since it will seem not protective enough for some and to others excessively protective.

'Of course we've got to pursue a policy of public purchasing, just like the US does. A great number of advantages for the USA derive from the enormous purchasing markets provided by defence and space — markets which are of course de facto reserved for US industry and even legally so in some cases (the Buy American Act, etc.). What we in Europe must try to do is to give the same type of guarantees to our own companies as other big companies have — not more, not less. This means that if they come up with the products you're asking for, then you will buy, and if they don't, you'll buy elsewhere. But if they do, they must know that they will then have a market of sufficient size to provide them with the opportunity of becoming competitive on third markets . . . '.

MULTINATIONAL SERVICE: Turning to the European position on multinationals in the international framework: do you feel that the voluntary guidelines for MNCs agreed in the OECD can be improved upon in talks in the UN on a code of conduct? Is there a need for more legally binding provisions?

DAVIGNON: 'Well let me answer that by way of an example. We are very worried about the fact that the development of new minerals is coming on very slowly, and our impression is that because of lack of investments we might very well be in a bad situation in the not too distant future because needs will have increased, the minerals will be there, but the necessary investment will not have been made suf-ficiently ahead of time, and so we will run into difficulties. So we've been trying to find out why these investments have not been made. Our first impression was that there simply wasn't the money — but we now have the impression that this is not so, that the money would be avail-able provided you had a system which provided the necessary confidence. You need confidence because of the length of time these investments take to mature, and the investor must have confidence in the country where he's investing. Lack of confidence is a typical political and legal problem which is hindering financial, industrial and economic development. If we could meet this problem by creating rules which would be compulsory for everybody involved, then I think you would have a system of regulation which would be in the interest of all parties. There, I think, would be an area for the improvement you talked of. I give this example because one tends to get the impression that regulations are only in the interest of one party — the state — and against the interest of the business community. I think this is quite wrong. The business community has also an interest in certain types of regulations, so that it knows what the rules of the game are . . . '.

MULTINATIONAL SERVICE: So there is a value for binding inter-national arrangements providing that the arrangements are balanced in their requirements?

DAVIGNON: 'Exactly, it's not a one-way street, it's not a witch-hunt . . . . As I've indicated above, it is in the interests of all parties that some things should be binding. But there's bound to be some dif-ferences though. For instance you're not going to have the situation of a large industrialised country following exactly the same rules for investment as a developing country would. Obviously the conditions are not exactly the same — in an industrialised country it is much more economic rather than political considerations which are the motivating factors. You can't have identical rules for diverse situations.

'We at the Commission are glad, for example, that the resolution on multinationals adopted recently by the European Parliament [see Appendix I(f)] refers to a number of separate approaches — there is reference to the OECD, a reference to the continuation of the Commission's own work, and to a third level, the international level. What the Commission would not have liked [from the Parliament — ed.] is a resolution calling for us to go down a one-way street: that sort of initiative would not have met the diversity of the aspects of the problems we have on the multinationals question'.

I(c) COMMUNITY LAW AND CODES OF CONDUCT
FOR MULTINATIONAL ENTERPRISES
(internal EEC Commission policy paper 22 December 1978)

I The continued development of multinational enterprises: the benefits and the causes for concern

(a) The development of cross-frontier activities by enterprises is a
significant and positive part of our economic system which, despite
current difficulties, is still based on principles of free competition and
free trade. Enterprises are thus faced with the necessity of finding
markets and developing a profitable combination of the factors of
production in a world environment which is competitive, in some
sectors increasingly so. This necessity leads, and may even oblige,
enterprises to reach out beyond the national frontiers of their country
of origin to seek new markets and to achieve a combination of factors
which is closer to the optimum. The fundamental economic result of
this process is of great significance to everyone and should not be
forgotten: a more efficient use of scarce resources upon which real
increases in our standard of living, and even perhaps its maintenance,
depend. Enterprises, developing multinationally, are thus a vital
element in the process of economic and technical innovation which is
the foundation of the Community's prosperity. Improvements in our
own welfare, and in the welfare of countries less developed than ours,
depend to a substantial degree on the contributions which multinational enterprises will make in the future.

(b) At the same time, while recognizing the benefits which we derive
from the activities of multinational enterprises, we cannot ignore the
fact that they also cause concern to many who are affected by their
operations, both in the Member States and outside. This concern is
perhaps most apparent as regards the attitudes of certain developing
countries, which incidentally are frequently sources of raw materials
and markets of considerable importance to us. The main cause of the
concern about multinationals is essentially the perception that multinational enterprises, by reason of their scale and their range of choice,
may be less subject to national constraints, and less sensitive to national
and local pre-occupations and needs, than enterprises which are
national or local in character.
For example, in establishing a combination of production factors
which approaches the optimum as closely as possible, multinationals
have a tendency to specialise the functions of particular establishments
in different countries, notably to achieve economies of scale. The trend

is more obvious in some sectors than in others, and the degree and nature of the specialisation depend in large measure on technical factors. In some cases, one finds specialisation as regards components, which are then assembled into the end product at a limited number of establishments. This kind of integrated production, and the specialisation that it entails, appears to be increasing in the automobile and electronics industries, for example. In other cases, one finds specialisation according to a particular product, or family of related products. But whatever type of specialisation occurs, the result is often that a given establishment, even of a considerable size, has a limited function and depends for its future on decisions taken, or at least co-ordinated and approved, at the centre. A change in circumstances or priorities can put in question the activities of that establishment. Moreover, in spite of its size and importance for the local economy, the establishment, not being a complete and autonomous enterprise, cannot easily separate itself from the multinational enterprise and become an independent, viable enterprise in its own right.

This vulnerability of the local establishment, which is associated with, indeed is a reflection of the scale, resources and relatively wide range of choice of the multinational enterprise taken as a whole, causes natural unease among those who have responsibilities with regard to the communities where the enterprises' establishments are located. Even a nation State of some size may feel itself on unfamiliar and insecure ground when confronted by an enterprise which has an apparently extensive range of possibilities open to it, and, in addition, superior resources (financial, technical and human) organised on a world-wide basis. And it should not be a surprise that others who deal with these enterprises, as suppliers, customers, shareholders, employees, trade unions or competitors, should also express concern from time to time, and that these concerns should be transmitted through political institutions as demands for new regulations, national, Community and international.

(c)   The fact that the activities of multinationals are clearly beneficial, but at the same time a challenge to existing institutions explains the ambivalence of much of the comment and criticism which is expressed concerning their operations. Even those developing countries which are foremost in criticizing multinationals often seem to recognize by their concrete behaviour towards these enterprises the special contribution which they can make to economic and social progress in the third world. As is frequently the case in international politics, it is as important to watch what the protagonists actually do as it is to listen to what they say.

In addition, of course, the two aspects of the activities of multinational enterprises are of crucial importance in determining the kind of policy which the Member States and the Community should adopt.

II The nature of Community policy and law on multinational enterprises

(a) Objectives

Community policy is a reflection of the two aspects of multinational activities to which reference has been made, namely, the resulting benefits and the challenged posed to existing institutions. First, the Community has sought to remove obstacles to the cross-frontier activities of enterprises within the Community. Second, at the same time, it has sought to secure the adoption of appropriate legal rules to regulate the problems which are likely to arise as a result of those activities. The policies of the Community in general and of the Commission in particular are thus in no sense a crusade either for or against multinationals. Rather they constitute an attempt to create a balanced legal framework for their operations.

(b) Major components in the legal framework

(1) The right of establishment The right of establishment for enterprises formed under the laws of the Member States, arising directly from the Community Treaty (Articles 52 to 58), is the foundation for the development of multinational activities in the EEC. The Member States have agreed to introduce no new restrictions on the right of establishment in their territories of enterprises from other Member States (Article 53). Existing obstacles are to be progressively abolished (Article 52). This right of establishment is of great importance, not least because Article 53 requires no further implementation through Community legislation. Enterprises can benefit from it directly, normally by setting up a subsidiary, but sometimes in a more dramatic fashion by simply setting up a branch. For example, the large Ford car plant at Genk in eastern Belgium is owned and operated by Ford AG of Germany, and not by any of Ford's companies in Belgium. It is incidentally a prime example of cross-frontier integrated production with massive liner-trains ensuring an almost continuous two-way flow of material between Genk and Ford AG's main plant near Cologne.

Of course, barriers to more integrated industrial and commercial activity through exercise of the right of establishment were considerable when the Community Treaty was signed and despite their 'progressive' removal, remain real to this day. The Commission has achieved

252

some notable successes in some areas and continues to make substantial efforts in areas where success has so far eluded it.

(2) Removal of barriers to more integrated industrial and commercial activity

(a) For example, in the area of technical standards which, by their diversity can create real obstacles to more integrated forms of production and commerce, considerable progress has been made. Over 100 directives have already been adopted, 39 in the automobile sector alone. In fact, sufficient progress has now been made in this particular sector that the Community is approaching the point at which it should be able to adopt the final directives required for full introduction of EEC type approval procedures, so that in future, vehicles complying with the harmonized requirements can be sold freely throughout the Community. Such a system will facilitate the operation of the internal market for vehicles and is of potentially great significance for the development of a strong Community industry which can compete on the world market. The major obstacle which remains is the reticence of some Member States to introduce a system which they fear might benefit non-Community car producers more than our own industry. This reticence, of course, derives from the fierce competition which our industry has recently faced, notably from Japan. The Commission's view is that the Community has more to gain than it has to lose from the creation of a single vehicle market, and that the problem of our relationship with external competitors is a more general one to be dealt with in the more appropriate context of general agreements on trade (GATT). In that context, of course, the need for adequate reciprocity and for rules to avoid the damaging effects of unfair competition remain of paramount importance. It is to be hoped, therefore, that remaining doubts will be overcome and that the work on coordination of technical standards in the automobile sector, which has already produced substantial results and benefits, will in the foreseeable future reach its logical conclusion. And, of course, in other sectors this technical, unglamorous but very important work proceeds, slowly but steadily eroding the existing obstacles to more integrated business activity in the Community.

(b) As regards fiscal obstacles, less progress has been made and, as a result, the differing tax systems of the Member States may well prevent an enterprise from conducting cross-frontier operations in the most sensible and efficient manner. The Commission has made a series of proposals to tackle the problems, but the difficulties are real. For specific fiscal devices not only play different roles in the tax systems of the Member States, but each device forms part of a complex whole. A change in one component frequently implies changes elsewhere in the system. And changes which alter the distribution of the burden of taxation are to say the least politically sensitive. As a further complication, tax devices are frequently used not only for genuinely fiscal purposes, but to achieve social and economic goals which are of considerable importance and sensitivity in the Member States, but which unfortunately may differ from one State to another. This matrix of difficulties which explains why fiscal harmonization takes so long and is so arduous, should be borne in mind when evaluating the progress which has been made, or rather not been made, to date.

The proposed directive on the fiscal treatment of cross-frontier mergers is a good example. Proposed originally in 1969, the directive has for its primary objective the desirable goal of removing the fiscal disincentive to cross-frontier mergers which arises since the absorption of one company by another is often treated at present as a realization of any capital gains which have or are deemed to have occurred as regards the assets of the company being absorbed. Nearly 10 years of negotiations have been necessary to prepare this measure for consideration at ministerial level in the Council, and while this is now likely to take place in the spring of 1979, important obstacles remain, notably the desire of the German government to exempt from the directive, as is the case under existing German tax law, all operations having as one of their effects for loss or reduction of the co-determination rights of the employees in an absorbed company. In other words, an important social goal which is protected by the German taxation system continues to threaten the chances of adopting a Community harmonisation measure, which as regards its general purpose meets with the approval of nearly all concerned.

There is no easy solution to this type of conflict. Rather we must have the tenacity to persevere, and the imagination to find compromises which will enable objections to be overcome without sacrificing important goals both as regards the construction of the European Community and the fundamental economic and social policies of the Member States. Of course, it is easier to say than it is to achieve, but it is unrealistic to think that, at the Community's present stage of development, any other kind of approach will produce more rapid results. The Commission will thus continue to press for the adoption of appropriate measures as regards fiscal harmonisation though in the knowledge that the programme is a long term one. Measures already proposed, in addition to the directive on cross-frontier mergers, concern the fiscal treatment of dividends distributed by a subsidiary in one Member State to its parent in another; the harmonisation of company taxation and of withholding taxes on dividends; and the elimination of double taxation in connection with the adjustment of transfers of profits between associated enterprises. A detailed examination of these measures would not be within the scope of this speech, though further mention of fiscal harmonization must be made in the context of the subject which now follows, namely, the creation and application of Community rules to deal with the problems created by the increasing cross-frontier activities of business enterprises.

(3) Maintenance of competition as part of the counter-balance to the facilitation of cross-frontier activities The first element in the counter-balance is of great importance, but can be dealt with briefly since it is an aspect of Community law and policy which is well-known and the subject of intensive study and explanation elsewhere: that is, the rules designed to preserve free competition. Besides the continued application of the provisions of the Treaty, notably Articles 85, 86 and 92 to 94, the Commission is concerned to develop Community competition law to meet contemporary needs, for example, by proposing and continuing to press for the adoption of a regulation on merger control at Community level.

Of course, the period of economic transition through which we have been passing in the last few years has posed special problems for the application of competition policy. Structural weaknesses have become apparent or have been aggravated following reductions in demand accompanied by increased pressure from imports. The role of the Commission has been to promote structural change within a socially acceptable framework. It has consistently refused to accept the tempting but illusory view that enterprises can protect themselves from the need to carry out necessary structural changes simply by coming to terms with their competitors or by seeking excessive protection from national authorities. Such practices tend to spill over into related sectors 'downstream' and the problems become more widespread rather than less. Accordingly, it is essential that intervention in the market for social reasons, which in certain cases may be unavoidable and indeed necessary, must take place only in the context of a plan for restoring competitivity in the sector concerned and in the Community economy as a whole. The high costs of poorly adapted structures cannot be supported indefinitely.

(4) Co-ordination of company and tax laws as a second major component of the counter-balance The second major component in the counter-balance to the facilitation of cross-frontier activities by enterprises is the co-ordination of company and tax laws. Substantial differences between the company and tax laws of the Member States may not simply constitute obstacles to efficient cross-frontier activity by enterprises. They may also constitute an occasion, perhaps even the cause, of enterprises so arranging their affairs that while their own

interests are apparently well-served, the legitimate interests of those who have dealings with them may be less well respected. It is obvious, for example, that widely diverging tax rates applicable to corporate profits are a major contributory factor in causing certain multinational enterprises to adopt internal 'transfer prices' which are not economically justifiable and which can damage the interests of other persons, for example, minority shareholders and employees of subsidiaries in the relatively high tax rate countries. Similarly, the location of important parts of the multinational enterprise in jurisdictions with rudimentary disclosure requirements can limit improperly the effect of disclosure requirements contained in the laws of other States in which the multinational is established.

Harmonization of the corporate tax systems and rates of the Member States to which reference has already been made, will make a major contribution to the solution of the transfer pricing problem. Of course, experience suggests that it will be some years before such harmonization can be achieved and in the meantime other less ambitious measures can be usefully taken, such as the directive adopted towards the end of 1977 on mutual assistance by the competent authorities of the Member States in the field of direct taxation. This measure, which came into force on 1 January 1979, aims to combat tax evasion arising from cross-frontier transactions by ensuring a more complete flow of information between the tax authorities of the Member States which should enable those authorities to make more accurate assessments of taxes on income and capital. In the context of multinational enterprises, this concerns in particular corporation and capital gains taxes. It is probably significant that the first step has been taken in the area of information where the problems of reaching an agreement are less acute than is the case when an attempt is made to agree common substantive rules. In addition, of course, the operations of multinational enterprises are complex and frequently shielded from public scrutiny. In these circumstances, it makes good sense to begin by seeking to illuminate the problems by increasing the quantity and quality of the information available to those concerned, a theme which is being developed further in the context of the company law programme.

A start was made as long ago as 1968 when the first company law directive was adopted in which the Member States agreed to set up common disclosure procedures for companies with limited liability. They also were able to agree on a basic list of items which should be disclosed using these procedures, including a company's annual accounts. A further step forward was taken in July 1978 when the Council adopted the fourth company law directive which regulates in some detail the form and content of the information to be contained in the annual accounts of individual companies. This directive in turn prepares the way for the adoption of the seventh directive on group accounts which will have a particular impact on multinational enterprises since these are normally organised as groups of companies. Negotiations are well under way in Council on this matter, and its relatively rapid adoption seems possible, for the Member States would like to implement the fourth directive together with, or at least knowing the contents of, the seventh directive on group accounts. Legislation to implement the fourth directive must be adopted by July 1980, so a great effort is being made to agree the seventh directive during the course of 1979.

The major problem posed by the seventh directive is the manner in which a group of companies should be defined for the purposes of drawing up group accounts. Member States with group accounting requirements in their laws divide into two schools of thought. The older school bases the definition exclusively on the legal power of one enterprise, the parent, to control another, for example, by its possession of more than 50 per cent of the voting capital. The United Kingdom, as you know, is a member, indeed almost the leading spokesman of this school of thought. The other school argues for a definition which does not limit itself to cases where there is a legal power of control, but which includes all cases in which one undertaking exercises in fact a dominant influence over another so that both are managed on a unified basis. This school of thought's major protagonist is Germany, but similar approaches are favoured by France and Denmark. The Commission too in its proposals has adopted an approach based on the general concepts of dominant influence and unified management. The task ahead is to see whether this approach can be refined to meet the main objections of its critics, that is, that the definition is insufficiently certain, and that the concept of dominant influence is inappropriate in the context of relations between enterprises in different countries. This will be the main subject for discussion in the months ahead, and there are reasons to expect a degree of convergence since preliminary discussions have shown that there is a broad measure of agreement as to the substance of the matter. We may well find that the issue is one of method rather than principle. If so, rapid agreement may well be possible. In any event, even if agreement on a uniform definition proves too difficult, the Commission will insist that rules be adopted which will ensure equivalence and comparability as regards the systems in force in all Member States.

Once the seventh directive has been adopted, the Community will have a comprehensive, common framework for disclosure by enterprises. The annual accounts of individual companies, and the group accounts for the enterprise as a whole, supplemented where appropriate by sub-group accounts relating to particular sectors of the group, will ensure a basic transparency for the operations of multinational enterprises. This will apply both to Community multinationals, and to the Community operations of multinationals from third countries. In addition, it is anticipated that the framework will be developed and supplemented as time goes on in the light of experience as to its operation. The fourth directive sets up a contact committee procedure designed to facilitate this process by enabling the Commission and the Member States to discuss priorities and problems in advance of the making of formal proposals for new legislation. In this way, it is hoped that the formal legislative process can be speeded up, and focussed on problems of common concern.

Increased transparency as to the operations of multinationals seems to the Commission to be the most sensible approach. This view is based not only on the pragmatic assessment already given that Member States have less difficulty in agreeing common rules on disclosure of information than they do as regards substantive rules of behaviour. It is also based on the conclusion that adequate disclosure will in itself tend to prevent many abuses. In addition, where publicity alone is not sufficient, it is nevertheless the essential first step towards further reasonable regulation. Physicians must base their prescribed treatment on as accurate a diagnosis as practicable of the ailment, or face claims for professional negligence. Legislators should observe a similar discipline if they are to avoid the justified criticism that like some insane surgeon, they are trying to operate in the dark.

(c) General characteristics of Community measures

An analysis of the Community measures dealt with above reveals that they have certain general characteristics which should be emphasized.

First, given the special nature of the European Community as an international institution, invested as it is with particular legislative powers, the measures have a legally binding character. Directives adopted at Community level are translated by the legislatures of the Member States into laws, enforced through their traditional institutions.

Second, wherever possible, the measures have not been made specifically applicable to multinational enterprises, but framed more generally. This policy has been adopted for several reasons. In the first place, multinational enterprises are very difficult to define legally; a difficulty that is increasing as their forms become more varied and complex. The traditional majority participation in equity capital is increasingly being supplanted, particularly in the developing countries, by joint ventures, minority participations, licensing arrangements and management contracts. In addition, the Commission has consistently taken the view that it is important to avoid unjustified discrimination against multinational enterprises. Legislation applying to multinationals only would be more likely to result in such discrimination. Finally, on close examination, many problems turn out not to be in their nature confined to multinationals, though frequently the problem may manifest itself more intensively where a multinational is involved. Unjustifiable transfer prices can be used, for example, to transfer profits from one member of a group to another within the same country as a tactic to resist a demand for large wage increases in a highly profitable group member. Similarly, the accounts of individual companies may have limited value in the absence of group accounts, irrespective of whether or not the group is multinational. Accordingly, the best solution is often a general one which may nevertheless have a particular significance for multinational enterprises, as indeed is the case with the seventh directive on group accounts.

Finally, all Community measures have necessarily a Community scope. We cannot legislate for companies with their seats in Detroit or Tokyo, but only for the affiliates of such companies which are within our collective jurisdiction. For this reason, other measures need to be taken at the international level.

III   Codes of conduct for multinational enterprises

(a)   *Codes of conduct as useful supplements to the Community's internal legislative programme*

For the European Community, codes of conduct for multinational enterprises have their own special contribution to make.

Clearly, we have an interest in ensuring that European multinationals do not suffer a competitive disadvantage by having to observe standards that from their point of view are substantially more onerous than those observed by our competitors in the industrialized countries and in the developing world. Codes of conduct adopted within the framework of the OECD and the UN will make this possibility less likely.

Second, as countries which must import substantial quantities of raw materials and trade with the rest of the world to survive, we must seek to preserve a positive investment climate both within the Community and outside, particularly in developing countries. Mutually agreed standards as to the behaviour of multinationals in developing countries and as to host countries' treatment of multinationals have an important part to play in ensuring balanced economic development in which the interests of all partners are respected. This aspect of the problem is of particular importance as regards the work going in various agencies of the UN.

Finally, we have the special problem of Southern Africa. Reasons of principle and interest, given our numerous relationships with black Africa, require that the Member States respond in a positive way to the aspirations of black Africans who wish to seen an end to *apartheid* in its present form. At the same time, South Africa is a sovereign State with which we have long established economic and cultural links. The Community Code on South Africa enables us to take positive action within the limits of what is feasible. It seeks to ensure that the presence of Community firms in South Africa will, in so far as is possible given the nature of South Africa's legal system, benefit the black population and hasten the end of *apartheid*. The response of European firms to the Code will be the decisive factor in the Code's future credibility. The follow-up procedures are of crucial importance in this connection, and it is to be hoped that the reports which Community firms will make in accordance with Article 7 of the Code will be prepared with sufficient seriousness that they will enable the Community to defend its policy in the UN and elsewhere. Community firms operating in South Africa will be doing themselves no service if they do not make the most of the opportunity which the Code gives them to demonstrate the beneficial effects of their presence.

(b) The need for balance

As was the case concerning the Community's internal programme, codes of conduct for multinationals must adopt a balanced approach which recognizes both the positive and potentially negative aspects of multinational activities. The European Community Code on South Africa is an obvious example, since it seeks to reinforce the positive contribution which Community firms can make to the lives of black South Africans. The same goal is being pursued in the UN where the Commission is concerned to co-ordinate the positions of the Member States in the Intergovernmental Working Group on a Code of Conduct on Transnational Corporations. In pursuit of this goal, the Member States and the Commission have consistently supported the view that the Code should not only contain provisions as to the comportment of multinationals, but also standards as to the treatment of multinational enterprises by host countries, dealing, for example, with such issues as equal treatment of multinational and national enterprises, nationalisation, compensation and jurisdiction. Only a balanced approach of this kind will ensure the acceptability of the UN Code to the Member States of the European Community.

(c) The limitations of codes

In the Commission's view, and those of the Member States, codes of conduct are likely to be non-binding in character for the foreseeable future, that is, they will not give rise to legal obligations. Many reasons can be given for this conclusion some of which have already been touched upon. The more obvious include the difficulty of defining multinationals; the inherent vagueness of many of the obligations which developing countries wish to impose (for example, 'transnational corporations should support the development efforts of the countries in which they operate'); the diversity of existing national laws; and the divergent interests of the negotiating parties. All make it difficult to envisage the conclusion of a traditional convention giving rise to legal obligations in the foreseeable future. One possible exception to the general rule relates to accounting standards and disclosure, but even in this case, our experience at Community level suggests that a multi-lateral convention would take a long time to negotiate.

Given their non-binding character, Codes are not likely to resolve all difficult cases. Even where there are implementation procedures envisaged by the Code itself, as in the OECD Guidelines, the outcome will often depend on imponderable factors such as the degree of political support which is exerted in particular cases. The result of the Badger Case is illustrative. The American parent finally agreed to pay a much larger amount of redundancy and other payments owed to employees of its Belgian subsidiary, which it had put into liquidation, than the employees would have received in the ordinary winding-up of the Belgian company. But this result was achieved only as a result of high level political intervention, and the considerable influence brought to bear by a number of American multinationals who did not wish to see their general reputation damaged by the behaviour of one enter-prise. But one cannot expect similar leverage to be available in all cases. The dissatisfaction recently expressed by the Trade Union Advisory Committee as to the effects of the OECD Guidelines, while perhaps somewhat naive, does underline the limitations which are inherent in the concept of non-binding international codes of conduct.

These limitations underline the importance of the Community's internal legal regime and legislative programme. Since we have the means to create a binding legal framework for all enterprises, multi-nationals included, in the European Community, we are not driven to rely exclusively on codes of conduct. Community law and codes at the international level complement each other and should not be con-sidered as alternatives. Situations of the kind found in the Badger Case, for example, can as far as Community enterprises are concerned be better dealt with through Community law. One of the major items on the Commission's programme for future legislation is a proposed directive on relations between affiliated enterprises which will suggest how such problems might indeed be solved. Codes of conduct for multinationals which have their own special contribution to make at international level, are from the Community's internal point of view unnecessary and second best.

IV Conclusions

To sum up:

(a) Community law and codes of conduct are complementary parts of the Community's approach to multinationals;

(b) both need to be developed in a balanced fashion which recognizes the positive as well as the negative features of the activities of multinational enterprises;

(c) priority should be given to increased transparency which may well solve many problems in itself, and in any case is the necessary basis for further regulation.

I(d) 'COMPANIES WHICH ARE MEMBERS OF A GROUP'
(Appendix to EEC's 'Green Paper' on 'Employee Participation and Company Structure', November 1975)

Companies which are members of a group

The suggestion has been made that whatever the general desirability of forms of employee participation, special rules are required if it is desired to apply the systems to companies which operate according to coordinated policy as a group, particularly if the group includes companies which are incorporated in different States. There is indeed little doubt that special rules are required, and that the problem is complex, because there are a variety of situations which have to be considered. As indicated towards the beginning of this paper, preparatory work on a proposal for a directive coordinating the laws of the Member States in relation to groups of companies has been going on for some time, and it is in that context that proposals for Community legislation affecting companies incorporated in the Member States will be made. However, certain general considerations can appropriately be stated here. Moreover, the proposed Statute for European Companies contains provisions to deal with the problem when a European Company is a member of a group. These provisions embody certain principles which are capable of a more general application.

The emergence of groups of legally distinct companies and firms which operate according to certain centrally determined policies has been one of the most significant modern developments as regards the structure of large industrial and commercial enterprises in the Community, and indeed throughout the world. However, with a few exceptions, company laws generally take little account of the reality of this situation. The group companies remain legally independent and separate entities, while in practice they operate in a coordinated fashion. Situations may then arise in which the requirements of group policy have harmful effects on an individual group company. Such situations may entail unfortunate consequences for the employees of that company among others. Concern about the problems arising from the activities of groups of companies has been mounting in recent years, and interested groups have begun to make proposals, for example, the recent proposal of the Executive Committee of the European Trade Union Confederation for the passing of legislation to require the creation of an institution for the information and consultation of a group's employees at group level.[1]

1 Resolution of the Executive Committee of the European Trade Union Confederation of 6 February 1975.

The main requirement therefore is the creation of legal systems which recognize the reality of group situations and permit groups to operate according to centrally coordinated policy, but subject to rules which safeguard the legitimate interests of those concerned, in particular minority shareholders, creditors and employees.

As far as employee participation is concerned, the major problem is that of ensuring that a parent company, if it wishes, can have sufficient control over the affairs of its subsidiaries to enable the group to operate according to a coordinated policy, when systems of employee participation have been introduced which impose legal constraints on the freedom of action of the management of a subsidiary. This problem exists even in the case of a group made up of companies incorporated within a single legal system. Situations of conflict may arise, for example, if the management of a subsidiary can take certain decisions only with the consent of employees' representatives, or with the approval of a supervisory body which the parent company cannot in practice be sure of controlling. Accordingly, where employee participation in the supervisory body of a subsidiary takes a form which leaves shareholders' representatives in a clear majority, the problem should not normally arise. However, the problem does arise where a majority of the members of the supervisory body are not appointed or dismissed by the shareholders, as under the Netherlands law of 1971, or in a situation where employees and shareholders appoint equal numbers of members, or in a system with a co-opted final third such as that proposed in the revised European Companies Statute.

In the Netherlands, the exercise of coordinated policy in a group cannot normally be endangered by the application of the legal provisions on employee participation with regard to supervisory bodies. For subsidiaries are exempted from those provisions once they have been applied by the parent company. The Dutch legislator has deemed it sufficient that in group situations this form of employee participation should be effectively implemented at group level only. However, if the parent company does not have employee participation in the appointment of its supervisory body, because it is the holding company of a group with a majority of its employees abroad, a matter considered further below, then the employees of a subsidiary in the Netherlands will participate in the appointment of the supervisory body of the subsidiary. But in this particular case, the coherent functioning of the group has been ensured by providing that the management of the subsidiary can be appointed and dismissed, not by its supervisory body, but by the general assembly of shareholders, i.e. the parent company. It should be pointed out, however, that this provision does not solve the problems of a possible conflict between the parent company and the supervisory body of the subsidiary. The parent company will not be able to impose its views on a subsidiary with regard to a management decision for which the supervisory body has withheld its legally required approval.

It seems questionable whether subsidiaries should be exempted generally from systems of employee participation as to the composition of their boards. In group situations, decisions may be and are taken at the level of the subsidiary on matters which are of immediate interest to the employees of that subsidiary, without there being any intervention by the parent company. In principle therefore, the employees should have their say in the decision making, both at group level and at the subsidiary's level. This participation should probably also relate to the appointment of the management of the subsidiary. Once it is accepted that employees should participate in the appointment of the directors of an individual company through their representation in the supervisory board, then the same should apply in group situations. This of course may create problems for the functioning of the group, but these can be solved by less far reaching devices than exempting the subsidiary completely from the legal regime or preserving the right of the parent company to appoint the management of the subsidiary through the general meeting of shareholders.

In the revised European Companies Statute, it has been provided that an enterprise which wishes to be able to direct the affairs of one or more dependent companies constitutes a group in which the parent can give binding instructions to the subsidiary, provided that instructions for decisions which require the approval of the subsidiary's supervisory board and which have not been so approved, are given by a parent which is organized in such a way that the interests of employees of the group are protected at group level in a manner which is the same as or at least equivalent to that required of the subsidiary. For example, if the parent is itself a European Company, measures requiring the approval of the subsidiary's supervisory board can be made the subject of a binding instruction, if such approval is refused, provided they have been approved by the supervisory board of the parent. It should be recalled that according to the revised proposal, employees' representatives on the supervisory board of a parent European Company are to be elected by the employees of all the members of the group, including those of the parent company itself. If, on the other hand, the parent is formed under national law then such binding directions can be given to a subsidiary European Company only if the interests of the employees of the European Company, and of any other companies controlled through the European Company, are protected at the level of the parent company in a manner equivalent to that required where the parent is itself a European Company.

In Germany, a solution has been adopted which is in one respect on similar lines. An enterprise which has negotiated a contract of domination with a company, in a case in which that company's supervisory board has not consented to a particular decision, may give a binding instruction to that company's board of management which the board must carry out even against the wishes of its supervisory board. But this solution solves the problem of ensuring that the dominant enterprise has sufficient control in a way which can result in the participation of employees being substantially weakened, and indeed, if the dominant undertaking does not have a supervisory board to which employees elect representatives, it can be completely eliminated.

The most hopeful line of approach as far as a Community directive on groups of companies is concerned thus seems to be one based on the principle that a parent company incorporated in a Member State should be able to give binding instructions to a subsidiary which is part of a group operating according to a coordinated business policy, provided that legal forms of employee participation in the subsidiary have equivalent counterparts at group level which have given the necessary approval. In concrete terms, this means that a group supervisory body, and perhaps a representative institution for the employees of the group, have to be organized in a way which permits the employees of the group to participate in the decision making at group level in a manner which is at least equivalent to the way in which the employees of a subsidiary participate in its decision making. If such institutions do not exist, the parent will have to accept the risk of a subsidiary going its own way. However, since the decisions which require the consent of employees' representatives, unlike those requiring the approval of a supervisory board, to a great extent concern only the internal and local affairs of the subsidiary, the necessity for a group level representative institution may well be less acute than for a group supervisory body. Indeed a strong argument can be made that certain matters may be of such essentially local significance that a group representative institution should not have the power to overrule a local institution, for example, as to the settlement of a social plan in the case of a closure. Accordingly, the revised European Companies Statute confines the powers of a group works council to issues which concern the group or a number of undertakings within the group.

A second problem concerns those multinational groups of companies which are based in the Community but have a number of subsidiaries outside the Community. The argument has been made that in view of its multinational role, the parent company should not be required to have a system of employee participation which would be confined to employees situated in the Member State in which it was incorporated, or at most to employees within the boundaries of the Community. It is argued that to do so would be to interfere improperly with the international character of the group and thereby place it under a serious disadvantage as compared with groups based outside the Community.

Indeed, the law of the Netherlands appears to have been based on this view, and excludes from the mandatory provisions as to employee participation in the appointment of the supervisory body, all Netherlands holding companies of international groups with most of their employees abroad. On the other hand, German law does not provide for such an exception, and employees' representatives are appointed to the supervisory bodies of certain companies which are the parent companies of large, multinational groups.

The European Companies Statute provides that a European Company which is a holding company must have members on its supervisory board elected by the employees of the parent company and of all its subsidiaries within the Community. Employees of subsidiaries outside the Community cannot participate. To permit them to do so was considered to be impossible for a number of legal, political and practical reasons. In particular, there seemed to be a real danger of producing conflicts with the laws and policies of States who are not members of the Community in which a subsidiary might be incorporated. The solution proposed is admittedly not perfect, but neither are the alternatives, and the choice involves a delicate balancing of relative advantages and disadvantages.

As far as Community legislation is concerned, a relatively clear political choice has to be made.

On the one hand, the economic and social importance of multinational groups based in the Community can be regarded as so great, that they should be exempted from a regime which is ultimately to apply to all other large and medium-sized companies, on the ground that they would be put at a serious disadvantage as compared with multinationals based outside the Community. But the logical extension of the argument in favour of their exemption is that no regulation of European multinational groups which has an effect on their competitive position should be undertaken until multinationals can be regulated on a world-wide basis. Such regulation is not likely to happen very quickly, and it is extremely doubtful whether the Community should content itself with waiting to see what develops.

On the other hand, the economic and social importance of multinational groups can be seen as a particular reason for ensuring that there is some regulation of their activities. Moreover, Community legislation, applying as it will to nine countries with integrated markets, seems a peculiarly appropriate method for such regulation. Finally, the representation of employees, and perhaps of other general interests alos, seems to be in itself a desirable form of regulation as far as multinational groups based in Europe are concerned, for it will ensure that the broader implications of certain important decisions, such as decisions on major investments, are taken into account.

Furthermore, to exempt certain companies incorporated in a Member State on the ground that they are the parent companies of multinational groups with most of their employees outside the Community, would be to discriminate unfairly between enterprises and between employees. A large company which is the parent of a multinational group operating mostly within the Community would be subject to a regime of employee participation, while a similar enterprise, also active within the Community, but having most of its activities outside, would not. This hardly seems fair either to the multinational group operating mostly within the Community, or to the employees of the group operating mostly outside. Moreover, there would perhaps be an unfortunate incentive for European multinationals to transfer activities to countries outside the Community and so gain exemption.

Finally, reference should be made to the problem of those companies inside the Community which are subsidiaries of parent companies outside the Community. It is not at present possible, legally or politically, for the Community to require such parent companies to implement systems of employee participation, but of course the subsidiary will be subject to a regime and as regards the employee participation, the parent will be in the same position as any other controlling shareholder.

I(e) CODE OF CONDUCT FOR COMPANIES WITH SUBSIDIARIES, BRANCHES OR REPRESENTATION IN SOUTH AFRICA
(Adopted by EEC Foreign Ministers, September 1977)

1   Relations within the undertaking

a)   Companies should ensure that all their employees irrespective of racial or other distinction are allowed to choose freely and without any hindrance the type of organisation to represent them.

b)   Employers should regularly and unequivocally inform their employees that consultations and collective bargaining with organisations which are freely elected and representative of employees are part of company policy.

c)   Should black African employees decide that their representative body should be in the form of a trade union, the company should accept this decision. Trade unions for black Africans are not illegal, and companies are free to recognise them, and to negotiate and conclude agreements with them.

d)   Consequently, the companies should allow collective bargaining with organisations freely chosen by the workers to develop in accordance with internationally accepted principles.

e)   Employers should do everything possible to ensure that black African employees are free to form or to join a trade union. Steps should be taken in particular to permit trade union officials to explain to employees the aims of trade unions and the advantages of membership, to distribute trade union documentation and display trade union notices on the company's premises, to have reasonable time off to carry out their union duties without loss of pay and to organise meetings.

f)   Where works or liaison committees already operate, trade union officials should have representative status on these bodies if employees so wish. However, the existence of these types of committee should not prejudice the development or status of trade unions or of their representatives.

2   Migrant labour

a)   The system of migrant labour is, in South Africa, an instrument of the policy of apartheid which has the effect of preventing the individual from seeking and obtaining a job of his choice: it also causes grave

269

social and family problems.

b)   Employers have the social responsibility to contribute towards ensuring freedom of movement for black African workers and their families.

c)   In the meantime employers should make it their concern to alleviate as much as possible the effects of the existing system.

3   Pay

Companies should assume a special responsibility as regards the pay and conditions of employment of their black African employees. They should formulate specific policies aimed at improving their terms of employment. Pay based on the absolute minimum necessary for a family to survive cannot be considered as being sufficient. The minimum wage should initially exceed by at least 50 per cent the minimum level required to satisfy the basic needs of an employee and his family.

4   Wage structure and black African advancement

a)   The principle of 'equal pay for equal work' means that all jobs should be open to any worker who possesses suitable qualifications, irrespective of racial or other distinction, and that wages should be based on a qualitative job evaluation.

b)   The same pay scales should be applied to the same work. The adoption of the principle of equal pay would, however, be meaningless if black African employees were kept in inferior jobs. Employers should therefore draw up an appropriate range of training schemes of a suitable standard to provide training for their black African employees, and should reduce their dependence on immigrant white labour.

5   Fringe benefits

a)   In view of their social responsibilities, undertakings should concern themselves with the living conditions of their employees and families.

b)   For this purpose company funds could be set aside for use

    — in the housing of black African personnel and their families; in transport from place of residence to place of work and back;

— in providing leisure and health service facilities;

— in providing their employees with assistance in problems they encounter with the authorities over their movement from one place to another, their choice of residence and their employment;

— in pension matters;

— in educational matters;

— in improving medical services, in adopting programmes of insurance against industrial accidents and unemployment, and in other measures of social welfare.

6   Desegregation at places of work

In so far as it lies within their own competence, employers should do everying possible to abolish any practice of segregation, notably at the workplace and in canteens, sports activities, education and training. They should also ensure equal work conditions for all their staff.

7   Reports on the implementation of the code of conduct

a)   Parent companies to which this code is addressed should publish each year a detailed and fully documented report on the progress made in applying this code.

b)   The number of black Africans employed in the undertaking should be specified in the report, and progress in each of the six areas indicated above should be fully covered.

c)   The governments of the Nine will review annually progress made in implementing this code. To this end a copy of each company's report should be submitted to their national government.

I(f) EUROPEAN PARLIAMENT RESOLUTION
ON MNCs (16 APRIL 1977) — DRAFT CODE OF
PRINCIPLES FOR MULTINATIONAL ENTERPRISES
(US Congress/European Parliament, September 1976)

Resolution on principles to be observed by enterprises
and governments in international economic activitiy

The European Parliament

— confirming its resolutions on Community industrial policy (Doc. 277/73),[1] the control of concentrations between undertakings (Doc. 362/73),[2] the second (Doc. 264/73),[3] third (Doc. 290/74),[4] and fifth (Doc. 243/76),[5] reports on competition policy, and on the communication from the Commission of the European Communities to the Council on multinational undertakings and Community regulations (Doc. 292/74),[6]

— having regard to the report of the Committee on Economic and Monetary Affairs (Doc. 547/76), and referring to the declarations by the governments of the OECD Member States on international investments and multinational undertakings and the 'Draft Code of Principles for multinational enterprises and governments', drawn up by the European Parliament delegation for relations with the United States Congress, and annexed to this resolution as a working document,

— having regard to the need to promote the viability and competitiveness of undertakings of all sizes within the Community,

— having regard to the fact that international undertakings have a beneficial effect on productivity, technology and management methods while, on the other hand, there are no international legal regulations to solve the problems caused by their size, massive liquid resources and centralization of economic power,

— having regard to the need to ensure equal opportunities and prevent descrimination in competition between national and international undertakings,

1. Applauds the establishment by the OECD of international guidelines for the conduct of governments and international undertakings based on voluntary implementation of the rules adopted but stresses that binding and legally-enforceable norms must gradually be laid down for international undertakings and a framework for their activities

defined in one or more international agreements;

2   Calls on the Council and Commission to establish one or more international legally-binding agreements through negotiations with the parties concerned — governments and international organizations and undertakings;

3   Feels that these negotiations should use as a basis the declarations by the governments of the OECD Member States on international investments and multinational undertakings and take into account as working document the 'Draft Code of Principles for multinational enterprises and governments' annexed to this resolution;

4   Notes, however, that such international negotiations are only likely to succeed if, at the same time, appropriate measures are taken at Community level and calls on the Council, therefore, to adopt without delay the proposals submitted by the Commission and supported by Parliament and expects the Commission to submit as soon as possible all the proposals called for by the European Parliament in its resolution of 12 December 1974[6] but not yet presented;

5   Instructs its Committee on Economic and Monetary Affairs to follow the development of these matters with a view to drawing up, where appropriate, a further report;

6   Instructs its President to forward this resolution and its Annex to the Council and Commission.

Notes

1   OJ No C 23, 8.3.1974, p.10.
2   OJ No C 23, 8.3.1974, p.19.
3   OJ No C 11, 7.2.1974, p.8.
4   OJ No C 140, 13.11.1974, p.65.
5   OJ No C 238, 11.10.1976, p.35.
6   OJ No C 5, 8.1.1975, p.37.

Delegation from the European Parliament for
the relations with the United States Congress
Washington DC, 19—23 September 1976

A draft code of principles for multinational
enterprises and governments

Draftsmen: Mr Erwin Lange, *European Parliament*
Mr Sam Gibbons, *United States Congress*

Preface

We, as representatives of the European Parliament and the United
States Congress, urge agreement to the principles embodied in this
code.

We do so with the knowledge that other groups and organizations
have undertaken useful work in this area, but that little progress has
been made toward establishing a framework of law and responsibility
for multinational enterprises and governments.

We hope that this code will prove to be a fruitful effort toward that
end, and that it will serve as the basis for needed changes in national
laws, government practices, international agreements, and the policies
of multinational enterprises.

Introductory remarks

1   The internationalization of production is a logical consequence of
the development of our economies. As such, it is a positive phenomenon, contributing to economic growth and increasing prosperity.

2   Nonetheless, the organization of operations beyond national
borders by multinational enterprises may lead to undesirable concentrations of economic power and to conflicts with national policy
objectives.

3   Therefore, it is appropriate to seek to encourage the positive contributions which multinational enterprises can make to economic and
social progress and to minimize and resolve the difficulties and
problems which may arise from their operations.

4   Just as it is normal for firms increasingly to carry on activities beyond the frontiers of their own country, so it is normal and necessary for an international framework to be set up for these international activities, obliging the firms in question to respect certain basic rules and at the same time offering them the necessary legal security.

5   Economic integration, as embodied in multinational enterprises, has stolen a march on politics, for which in most cases the national frontiers remain the relevant framework. Although far-going economic interdependence can be a useful stimulus toward political integration, it is nevertheless, essential in international relations too for public policies to take precedence over economics; that is, the framework in which the multinational enterprise operates must be under political control. This condition is not being met at present. Accordingly, certain rules need to be laid down in an international agreement.

6   The problems connected with the activities of multinational enterprises can no longer be dealt with only in a national context and cannot yet be solved on a work scale. Agreements on multinational enterprise activity among industrial nations would represent a great step forward. The delegations of the United States Congress on the one hand and that of the European Parliament on the other can in the first instance help to bring about an agreement between the United States and the European Community, to which Japan, Canada, and other industrial countries may later accede.

General framework

7   International agreements are to be concluded initially between the United States and the European Community.

8   The agreements are to have the force of law in all nations which are parties to them and are to impose legally binding obligations on firms based in or operating in those countries.

9   For purposes of this code, multinational enterprises (MNEs) are defined as companies of private, State, or mixed ownership operating in different countries and so linked that one can exercise a significant influence over others.

10   These international agreements are to be implemented and enforced through the mutual cooperation of the governments which are parties and through existing institutions of international law.

11   If mutual cooperation and existing international institutions fail to adequately implement and enforce the agreements, an international secretariat may be established to administer these agreements. In

establishing a secretariat, due regard is to be given to the population and economics of the government parties involved.

12   Governments which are parties to these agreements are to treat multinational enterprises according to international law and are to deal with conflicts of national laws as they affect multinational enterprises.

13   During the time prior to the completion of these agreements, the governments which are to be parties shall enter into temporary agreements under which the provisions of this code are to be followed. These transition agreements shall provide for efforts toward harmonization of national legislation to reach compliance with the provisions of this code in anticipation of the permanent agreements.

Explanatory note: From the outset the governments which are to be parties to the international agreements should consult and conclude agreements on administrative aid and on the mutual recognition and enforcement of court judgments, etc., in order to acquire a measure of control over the international activities of these enterprises until effective international agreements have been worked out. Better cooperation among government authorities in this transition period will do much to prevent the circumvention of national laws and policies.

Information

14   Every multinational enterprise is to publish a yearly report.

15   The following information, broken down by specific operations (lines of business) and countries of establishment, is to be published in this report:

(a)   the financial and operational structure of the enterprise;

(b)   the financial and personal links with other concerns;

(c)   the funds invested, reinvested, and transferred to the home country of the enterprise;

(d)   the origin and composition of capital, existing and new;

(e)   the number of employees, jobs created, jobs abolished, and host-country nationals working at various levels of the enterprise;

(f)   the balance sheet and profit and loss account, including gross sales;

(g)   the total amount of taxes paid, broken down to show the amount of each type of tax paid and the amount of each type paid to each individual taxing authority;

(h)   expenditures on research and development;

(i)   income from royalties, licenses, and management contracts;

(j)   such other reasonable information as is requested by government authorities.

Due regard is to be given to legitimate reasons for firms to preserve the confidentiality of certain business information. Governments are to agree on safeguards and penalties to prevent the inappropriate and indiscriminate use of information provided by multinational enterprises and other enterprises.

16 Multinational enterprises of significant size are to use a system of standardized annual accounts and reports. This system is to be established pursuant to international agreement.

Competition

17 All information relevant to the operation of a multinational enterprise, including information in the hands of its establishments abroad, shall be accessible to antitrust bodies. National antitrust bodies are to exchange information and mutually support each other in investigations of restrictive practices, and are to be able to take joint action against abuses of power.

Explanatory note: Multinational enterprises, like other large enterprises, frequently have technical or financial advantages over their competitors, giving them a certain position of power. Competition policy should be aimed at checking abuse of this position. To achieve this, much more intensive cooperation is essential between antitrust authorities of the United States and the European Community. Controlling multinational enterprises is made more difficult by the problems of implementation than by shortcomings in national legislation. The antitrust bodies are frequently unable to prove abuse by a multinational enterprise because the necessary evidence is in the hands of another of its establishments abroad, creating the need for free access to information.

18 Multinational enterprises are to avoid action which would adversely affect competition, such as price fixing, restricting the freedom of operation of licensees, acquiring interests in competitively significant enterprises, or engaging in restrictive cartels of agreements. They are to cooperate with government competition enforcement authorities and to provide information requested by these authorities.

Investment policy

19 Multinational enterprises are to report planned investments to government authorities in the countries where the investments are to be made.

20 The governments of nations that are parties to these agreements are to promulgate regulations governing open bids for total or partial takeovers of existing firms. Such regulations are to provide that

adequate prior information be given to government officials, to officials, workers, and shareholders of the firms to be taken over, and to trade unions.

Explanatory note: More than half of all direct investments abroad involve takeovers of existing firms rather than new, direct investments. Policy considerations dictate greater restrictions over such takeovers of existing firms.

21 The international agreements are to harmonize existing national investment regulations, including guaranteeing, in the event of foreign takeovers of firms, protection of jobs, investment policies, maintenance of national management, maintenance of research activities, and a certain share of exports. The agreements, while recognizing national policy objectives, are to minimize distortions to trade and investment, to harmonize incentives and disincentives, and to avoid discrimination based on country of origin.

Explanatory note: Regulations currently in effect in Canada, Belgium, and Britain provide certain guarantees in the event of foreign takeovers of firms.

Fiscal policy

22 Multinational enterprises are to provide government tax authorities with the information necessary for a correct determination of taxes due. Multinational enterprises may not use the distortion of transfer prices and other practices which alter their tax base or contravene national tax laws or policies.

23 Accounting practices of multinational enterprises and tax policies of governments are to reflect the principle that taxes are to be paid in the country where the income is earned. Dividend and interest income are to be taxed to shareholders and investors by their respective governments. Government authorities may disregard third party holding companies and other entities used to hold income and thereby avoid taxation by taxing this income directly to shareholders as though it were received currently.

24 Government authorities are to:

(a) upgrade present efforts to facilitate the enforcement of national tax laws and policies by entering into tax treaties or other international agreements providing for the comprehensive mutual exchange of information and assistance. Adequate staff support is to be provided for these efforts. Tax authorities of several governments may engage in simultaneous or joint audits of selected enterprises;

(b)   seek to harmonize the withholding tax on portfolio investment in the various countries;

(c)   seek to harmonize other national tax laws, especially those affecting foreign investments;

(d)   take steps to combat the abuse of agreements for the avoidance of double taxation.

25   International agreements are to provide for common actions against enterprises that misuse tax havens. For purposes of this paragraph, tax havens are defined as countries or areas with many or all of the following characteristics: low taxes, little or no exchange control, bank secrecy, no exchange of fiscal data with foreign authorities, a developed banking system, and political stability. The agreements are to provide for coordinated international action against such enterprises, such as denial of the right to open new facilities in the countries that are parties to these agreements, or denial of tax deductions for payments to tax haven countries in computing tax due to any of the countries which are parties to the agreements, or elimination of the withholding tax on portfolio investment for all investors except those giving tax haven countries as their residence.

26   The agreements are to provide for establishment of effective international mechanisms for the settlement of tax disputes.

27   The agreements are to provide for the elimination of undue secrecy surrounding reporting of income earned by banks and others in all countries.

Explanatory note: Such secrecy is not justified and is harmful to the legitimate revenue interests of all countries.

28   The agreements are to provide for coordinated action by government tax authorities instead of unilateral corrective action. Such coordinated action may include penalties for violations of principles established by the agreements and of special agreements among the various countries.

Explanatory note: Unilateral corrective action in tax areas such as financial secrecy, determination of transfer prices, or action against tax-haven holding companies could result in flights of capital to other countries. This provision envisions coordinated action under these international agreements to prevent adverse consequences which could result from unilateral action and to effectively eliminate the non-taxation of income.

29   Measures for corporate or shareholder tax relief or integration of corporate and personal income-tax systems currently being implemented or studied are to be modified or reconsidered so as to prevent discrimination against foreign shareholders.

Explanatory note: Tax relief or integration measures which discriminate against foreign shareholders are not compatible with the free flow of investment, and thus should be modified or reconsidered.

30   The agreements are to provide for the elimination of discrimination in tax treatment against foreign-based enterprises by governments using any method of tax assessment, including the unitary method.

Explanatory note: Under the unitary method, a multinational enterprise is taxed on the basis of its consolidated profit, and the profit assigned to a particular firm by government tax authorities is based on the firm's sales in a country or State and its assets and employment there. There are some indications that this method of taxing is being administered inequitably with regard to foreign-based enterprises.

31   Transfer prices are defined as the prices applied in transactions which take place within an enterprise. The following provisions applicable to transfer prices of goods apply equally to transfer prices of services, including financial services and payments for the use of technical knowhow, trademarks, and patents.

32   Government authorities are to supervise transfer prices and act against enterprises employing transfer price practices directed at avoiding taxation.

Explanatory note: Transactions within multinational enterprises (between subsidiaries of the same enterprise or between a subsidiary and the parent company) constitute an important part of international trade. Fixing the prices for these operations gives multinationals possibilities that firms with establishments in only one country may not have, and may put multinationals in a position to make more profit. A multinational enterprise can have various reasons for setting a transfer price different from the price applicable to a sale from the firm to another independent firm. An enterprise with operations in various countries seeks to declare the highest possible profit in countries with low taxation levels and to keep declared profit low in countries with high taxation levels. Multinational enterprises may also seek to set transfer prices such that more profit goes to wholly-owned subsidiaries than to firms in which they have only part interest. Multinationals may use transfer price setting to achieve low profits or losses in countries where subsidiaries face important wage negotiations. Stability of currency in the country of establishment, exchange control, and risk of nationalization are also factors here.

33   The agreements are to provide for establishment of rules for transfer pricing and a mechanism for determining appropriate transfer prices.

Explanatory note: Such rules can be based on the arms-length principle, the cost-plus basis, a comparison of reported transfer prices with prices of similar goods delivered during a recent period of time or goods delivered at another location at about the same time, or a comparison of the profit or loss margin on the goods with average profits and losses on similar goods sold by other firms.

34   Governments must apply whatever taxing methods are employed to tax various enterprises on an equitable basis, so as not to discriminate.

Explanatory note: Governments may sometimes tax firms which use transfer pricing by taxing at a figure higher than reported profit where the latter figure is judged too low. Whatever method is employed must be applied in a non-discriminatory manner.

Capital market policy and monetary policy

35   Consideration is to be given to requiring banks, in countries which

are parties to these agreements, to regularly inform the central banks of their countries of domicile of their forward exchange positions. Information is to be supplied monthly and is to cover all capital movements within the enterprise. These regulations are to be expanded to apply to all countries of the European Community and the United States and to all enterprises of significant size.

Explanatory note: It is desirable for monetary authorities to have accurate data on international capital movements. The procedure set forth here follows that currently used in some European countries.

36   Government authorities are to avoid unduly restrictive capital controls and are to consult and cooperate in doing so.

37   Enterprises are to allow residents of host countries to acquire their shares. Agreements can provide that a foreign enterprise having recourse to the capital market in the host country must do so partly through an increase in its equity capital available to host country nationals.

Social policy and labour market policy

38   Multinational enterprises are to afford representatives of the workers the opportunity to hold consultations with management responsible for the policy of the firm. Group works councils or other appropriate labour representatives must be allowed to negotiate directly with the central management. Alternatively, the management of the national firm is to provide the workers with all information relevant to their well-being and working conditions and to act with the necessary autonomy.

Explanatory note: This paragraph focuses on the situation often present where trade unions of a country have to deal with management having only limited powers.

39   As a rule, at least one host country national is to have a seat on the management board of a firm that is part of a multinational enterprise.

40   Enterprises are to inform and consult with workers in good time on matters affecting them. In the event of mass layoffs, workers are to have an important voice in drawing up the labour phase-out plans. Enterprises involved in mergers are to guarantee retention of pension and other acquired rights. In cases of industrial labour disputes, operations carried out in some parts and branches of an enterprise are not to be taken over by other parts or branches of the same enterprise in order to thwart the legitimate and legal objectives of workers.

41   Multinational enterprises are to recognize trade unions, workers' bargaining units, direct representatives of the staffs (works councils), or

other duly constituted workers' organizations as contractual partners in negotiations on wage agreements and the fixing of work conditions of the workers employed in a firm. Steps are to be taken to establish the framework for internationally valid collective bargaining agreements.

42 Multinational enterprises are to observe national and local employment and industrial relations laws, standards, and practices.

43 Multinational enterprises are to avoid discrimination on the basis of sex, age, religion, race, ethnic or national origin, or political activity.

44 Firms are to provide jobs in the host country for host country citizens.

Technology

45 Multinational enterprises are to add to local scientific and technological capabilities and are to permit the dissemination of technological know-how on reasonable terms.

Pernicious political activities

46 Multinational enterprises shall not make or be solicited to make payments in money or other items of value to host government officials, other than for manifest public purposes. Multinational enterprises shall not contribute to political parties or candidates in any way unless such contributions are lawful and details on the amounts and beneficiaries are disclosed in a timely manner.

Explanatory note: This provision is aimed at preventing multinational enterprises from attempting to exercise undue influence over host country policies.

47 Governments are to adopt strong penalties for violations of the foregoing prohibition. Penalties may include any of the following: denial of a business-tax deduction for any such unlawful payments; heavy fines and/or prison sentences, and the denial of normal business-tax treatment and benefits to any business income connected with such unlawful payments.

48 Member governments which have concluded an international agreement covering pernicious political activities are to assume an active role in sharing with other governments involved any information they have on any such activity perpetrated by officials of an enterprise or by government officials.

I(g) COUNTRIES OF ORIGIN OF THE 200 MULTINATIONALS WITH THE HIGHEST TURNOVERS

(Source: EEC Commission survey on MNCs, July 1976)   (Turnover in u.a. millions)

[Author's note: the following 2 pages to be read as a single unit]

First hundred enterprises

Country of origin	1–20		21–40		41–60		61–80		81–100		TOTAL	
	No.	Turnover	No.	Turnover	No.	Turnover	No.	Turnover	No.	Turnover	No.	Turnover
United States	10	161,967	9	54,746	10	37,910	8	28,581	11	32,762	48	315,966
Japan	6	102,560	1	5,734	4	18,171	3	11,105	–	–	14	137,570
FR Germany	–	–	5	29,004	4	22,505	3	10,581	1	2,778	13	64,868
United Kingdom	1	10,929	2	10,457	1	4,261	3	10,910	1	2,746	8	39,303
Netherlands (b)(c)	2	28,558	1	6,406	–	–	–	–	–	–	3	34,964
France	–	–	1	7,707	–	–	1	3,719	5	14,492	7	25,918
Italy (a)	1	13,069	1	5,702	1	4,892	1	3,789	1	3,015	5	30,467
Switzerland	–	–	–	–	–	–	1	3,695	–	–	1	3,695
Sweden	–	–	–	–	–	–	–	–	–	–	–	–
Canada	–	–	–	–	–	–	–	–	–	–	–	–
Denmark	–	–	–	–	–	–	–	–	1	2,880	1	2,880
Belgium	–	–	–	–	–	–	–	–	–	–	–	–
Luxembourg	–	–	–	–	–	–	–	–	–	–	–	–
Australia	–	–	–	–	–	–	–	–	–	–	–	–
Grand Total	20	317,083	20	119,756	20	87,739	20	72,380	20	58,673	100	655,631
EEC	4	52,556	10	59,276	6	31,658	8	28,999	9	25,911	37	198,400
United States	10	161,967	9	54,746	10	37,910	8	28,581	11	32,762	48	315,966
Other Countries	6	102,560	1	5,734	4	18,171	4	14,800	–	–	15	141,265

(a) Including the Pirelli/Dunlop union.
(b) Including Unilever, whose parent company is 50 per cent Dutch and 50 per cent British.
(c) Including the Royal Dutch/Shell Group.

I(g) continued

Second hundred enterprises

Country of origin	101–120		121–140		141–160		161–180		181–200		TOTAL		GRAND TOTAL	
	No.	Turnover	No.	Turnover	No.	Turnover	No.	Turnover	No.	Turnover	No.	Turnover	No.	Turnover
United States	12	29,363	8	17,356	15	30,540	12	22,968	7	12,329	54	112,556	102	428,522
Japan	1	2,439	–	–	1	1,982	1	1,886	2	3,585	5	9,892	19	147,462
FR Germany	2	5,278	2	4,511	2	4,066	4	7,602	–	–	10	21,457	23	86,325
United Kingdom	1	2,397	4	9,120	–	–	2	3,861	4	7,226	11	22,604	19	61,907
Netherlands (b)(c)	1	2,674	1	2,215	1	1,994	–	–	1	1,753	4	8,636	7	43,600
France	1	2,636	3	6,744	1	1,995	1	1,897	1	1,800	7	15,072	14	40,990
Italy (a)	1	2,560	–	–	–	–	–	–	–	–	1	2,560	6	33,027
Switzerland	–	–	–	–	–	–	–	–	1	1,835	1	1,835	2	5,530
Sweden	–	–	1	2,126	–	–	–	–	1	1,720	2	3,846	2	3,846
Canada	–	–	–	–	–	–	–	–	2	3,515	2	3,515	2	3,515
Denmark	–	–	–	–	–	–	–	–	–	–	–	–	1	2,880
Belgium	1	2,421	–	–	–	–	–	–	–	–	1	2,421	1	2,421
Luxembourg	–	–	1	2,297	–	–	–	–	–	–	1	2,297	1	2,297
Australia	–	–	–	–	–	–	–	–	1	1,772	1	1,772	1	1,772
Grand Total	20	49,768	20	44,369	20	40,577	20	38,214	20	35,535	100	208,463	200	864,094
EEC	7	17,966	11	24,887	4	8,055	7	13,360	6	10,779	35	75,047	72	273,447
United States	12	29,363	8	17,356	15	30,540	12	22,968	7	12,329	54	112,556	102	428,522
Other countries	1	2,439	1	2,126	1	1,982	1	1,886	7	12,427	11	20,860	26	162,125

(a) Including the Pirelli/Dunlop union.
(b) Including Unilever, whose parent company is 50 per cent Dutch and 50 per cent British.
(c) Including the Royal Dutch/Shell Group.

I(h) PROPOSAL FOR A COUNCIL DIRECTIVE ON
PROCEDURES FOR INFORMING AND CONSULTING
THE EMPLOYEES OF UNDERTAKINGS WITH
COMPLEX STRUCTURES, IN PARTICULAR TRANS-
NATIONAL UNDERTAKINGS[1]
(Presented to the Council by the Commission on 24 October 1980)

The Council of the European Communities, having regard to the Treaty
establishing the European Economic Community, and in particular
Article 100 thereof, having regard to the proposal from the Commission, having regard to the opinion of the Economic and Social
Committee, having regard to the opinion of the European Parliament,
whereas the Council adopted on 21 January 1974 a Resolution concerning a social action programme;[2]

Whereas in a common market where national economies are closely
interlinked it is essential, if economic activities are to develop in a
harmonious fashion, that undertakings should be subject to the same
obligations in relation to Community employees affected by their
decisions, whether they are employed in the Member State to whose
legislation the undertaking is subject or in another Member State;

Whereas the procedures for informing and consulting employees as
embodied in legislation or practised in the Member States are often
inconsistent with the complex structure of the entity which takes the
decisions affecting them; whereas this may lead to unequal treatment
of employees affected by the decisions of one and same undertaking;
whereas this may stem from the fact that the information and consultation procedures do not apply beyond national boundaries;

Whereas this situation has a direct effect on the operation of the
Common Market and consequently needs to be remedied by approxi-
mating the relevant laws while maintaining progress as required under
Article 117 of the Treaty;

Whereas this directive forms part of a series of directives and proposals for directives in the field of company and labour law;

Has adopted the following directive:

Section I

Scope and definitions

Article 1 This directive relates to:
- procedures for informing and consulting employees employed in a
  Member State of the Community by an undertaking whose

decision-making centre is located in another Member State or in a non-member country (Section II);

— procedures for informing and consulting employees where an undertaking has several establishments, or one or more subsidiaries, in a single Member State and where its decision-making centre is located in the same Member State (Section III).

Article 2 For the purposes of this directive the following definitions shall apply:

(a) *Employees' representatives* The employees' representatives referred to in Article 2(c) of Council Directive 77/187/EEC of 14 February 1977 on the approximation of the laws of the Member States relating to the safeguarding of employees' rights in the event of transfers of undertakings, businesses or parts of business.[3]

(b) *Management* The person or persons responsible for the management of an undertaking under the national legislation to which it is subject.

(c) *Decision-making centre* The place where the management of an undertaking actually performs its functions.

Article 3

1   For the purposes of this directive an undertaking shall be regarded as dominant in relation to all the undertakings it controls, referred to as subsidiaries.

2   An undertaking shall be regarded as a subsidiary where the dominant undertaking, either directly or indirectly

(a)   holds the majority of votes relating to the shares it has issued,

or   (b)   has the power to appoint at least half of the members of its administrative, management or supervisory bodies where these members hold the majority of the voting rights.

Section II

*Information and consultation procedures
in transnational undertakings*

Article 4 The management of a dominant undertaking whose decision-making centre is located in a Member State of the Community and which has one or more subsidiaries in at least one other Member State shall be required to disclose, via the management of those subsidiaries, information to employees' representatives in all subsidiaries employing at least one hundred employees in the Community in accordance with Article 5 and to consult them in accordance with Article 6.

Article 5
1   At least every six months, the management of a dominant undertaking shall forward relevant information to the management of its subsidiaries in the Community giving a clear picture of the activities of the dominant undertaking and its subsidiaries taken as a whole.

2   This information shall relate in particular to:

(a)   structure and manning;

(b)   the economic and financial situation;

(c)   the situation and probable development of the business and of production and sales;

(d)   the employment situation and probable trends;

(e)   production and investment programmes;

(f)   rationalization plans;

(g)   manufacturing and working methods, in particular the introduction of new working methods;

(h)   all procedures and plans liable to have a substantial effect on employees' interests.

3   The management of each subsidiary shall be required to communicate such information without delay to employees' representatives in each subsidiary.

4   Where the management of the subsidiaries is unable to communicate the information referred to in paragraphs (1) and (2) to employees' representatives, the management of the dominant undertaking must communicate such information to any employees' representatives who have requested it to do so.

5   The Member States shall provide for appropriate penalties for failure to comply with the obligations laid down in this article.

Article 6
1   Where the management of a dominant undertaking proposes to take a decision concerning the whole or a major part of the dominant undertaking or of one of its subsidiaries which is liable to have a substantial effect on the interests of its employees, it shall be required to forward precise information to the management of each of its subsidiaries within the Community not later than forty days before adopting the decision, giving details of the grounds for the proposed

decision; the legal, economic and social consequences of such decision for the employees concerned; the measures planned in respect of these employees.

2   The decisions referred to in paragraph (1) shall be those relating to:

(a)   the closure or transfer of an establishment or major part thereof;

(b)   restrictions, extensions or substantial modifications to the activities of the undertaking;

(c)   major modifications with regard to organization;

(d)   the introduction of long-term cooperation with other undertakings or the cessation of such cooperation.

3   The management of each subsidiary shall be required to communicate this information without delay to its employees' representatives and to ask for their opinion within a period of not less than thirty days.

4   Where, in the opinion of the employees' representatives, the proposed decision is likely to have a direct effect on the employees' terms of employment or working conditions, the management of the subsidiary shall be required to hold consultations with them with a view to reaching agreement on the measures planned in respect of them.

5   Where the management of the subsidiaries does not communicate to the employees' representatives the information required under paragraph (3) or does not arrange consultations as required under paragraph (4), such representatives shall be authorized to open consultations, through authorized delegates, with the management of the dominant undertaking with a view to obtaining such information and, where appropriate, to reaching agreement on the measures planned with regard to the employees concerned.

6   The Member States shall provide for appropriate penalties in case of failure to fulfil the obligations laid down in this article. In particular they shall grant to the employees' representatives concerned by the decision the right of appeal to tribunals or other competent national authorities for measures to be taken to protect their interests.

Article 7

1   Where in a Member State a body representing employees exists at a level higher than that of the individual subsidiary, the information provided for in Article 5 relating to the employees of all the subsidiaries thus represented shall be given to that body.

2   The consultations provided for in Article 6 shall take place under the same conditions with the representative body referred to in paragraph (1).

3   A body representing all the employees of the dominant undertaking and its subsidiaries within the Community may be created by means of agreements to be concluded between the management of the dominant undertaking and the employees' representatives. If such a body is created, paragraphs 1 and 2 shall be applicable.

Article 8   Where the management of the dominant undertaking whose decision-making centre is located outside the Community and which controls one or more subsidiaries in the Community does not ensure the presence within the Community of at least one person able to fulfil the requirements as regards disclosure of information and consultation laid down by this directive, the management of the subsidiary that employs the largest number of employees within the Community shall be responsible for fulfilling the obligations imposed on the management of the dominant undertaking by this directive.

Article 9
1   The management of an undertaking whose decision-making centre is located in a Member State of the Community and which has one or more establishments in at least one other Member State shall disclose, via the management of those establishments, information to the employees' representatives in all of its establishments in the Community employing at least one hundred employees in accordance with Article 5 and consult them in accordance with Article 6.

2   The management of an undertaking whose decision-making centre is located in a non-member country and which has at least one establishment in one Member State shall be subject to the obligations referred to in paragraph (1).

3   For the purposes of applying this article, the terms 'dominant undertaking' and 'subsidiary' in Articles 4 to 8 shall be replaced by the terms 'undertaking' and 'establishment' respectively.

Section III

Procedures for informing and consulting the employees of undertakings with complex structures whose decision-making centre is located in the country in which the employees work

Article 10   The management of a dominant undertaking whose decision-making centre is located in a Member State of the Community and which has one or more subsidiaries in the same Member State shall be required, via the management of its subsidiaries, to disclose information to employees' representatives in all subsidiaries employing at least one hundred employees in that State in accordance with Article 11 and to consult them in accordance with Article 12.

Article 11

1 At least every six months, the management of a dominant undertaking shall forward relevant information to the management of its subsidiaries in the Community giving a clear picture of the activities of the dominant undertaking and its subsidiaries taken as a whole.

2 This information shall relate in particular to:

(a) structure and manning;

(b) the economic and financial situation;

(c) the situation and probable development of the business and of production and sales;

(d) the employment situation and probable trends;

(e) production and investment programmes;

(f) rationalization plans;

(g) manufacturing and working methods, in particular the introduction of new working methods;

(h) all procedures and plans liable to have a substantial effect on employees' interests.

3 The management of each subsidiary shall be required to communicate such information without delay to employees' representatives in each subsidiary.

4 Where the management of the subsidiaries is unable to communicate the information referred to in paragraphs (1) and (2) above to employees' representatives, the management of the dominant undertaking must communicate such information to any employees' representatives who have requested it to do so.

5 The Member State shall provide for appropriate penalties in case of failure to fulfil the obligation laid down in this Article.

Article 12

1 Where the management of a dominant undertaking proposes to take a decision concerning the whole or a major part of the dominant undertaking or of one of its subsidiaries which is liable to have a substantial effect on the interests of its workers, it shall be required to

forward precise information to the management of each its subsidiaries within the Community not later than forty days before adopting the decision, giving details of: the grounds for the proposed decision; the legal, economic and social consequences of such decision for the employees concerned; the measures planned in respect of these employees.

2   The decisions referred to in paragraph (1) shall be those relating to:

(a)   the closure or transfer of an establishment or major part thereof;

(b)   restrictions, extensions or substantial modifications to the activities of the undertaking;

(c)   major modifications with regard to organization;

(d)   the introduction of long-term cooperation with other undertakings or the cessation of such cooperation.

3   The management of each subsidiary shall be required to communicate this information without delay to its employees' representatives and to ask for their opinion within a period of not less than thirty days.

4   Where, in the opinion of the employees' representatives the proposed decision is likely to have a direct effect on the employees' terms of employment or working conditions, the management of the subsidiary shall be required to hold consultations with them with a view to reaching agreement on the measures planned in respect of them.

5   Where the management of the subsidiaries does not communicate to the employees' representatives the information required under paragraph (3) or does not arrange consultations as required under paragraph (4), such representatives shall be authorized to open consultations, through authorized delegates, with the management of the dominant undertaking with a view to obtaining such information and, where appropriate, to reaching agreement on the measures planned with regard to the employees concerned.

6   The Member States shall provide for appropriate penalties in the case of failure to fulfil the obligations laid down in this article. In particular, they shall grant to the employees' representatives concerned by the decision the right of appeal to tribunals or other competent national authorities for measures to be taken to protect their interests.

Article 13
1   Where in a Member State a body representing employees, exists at a level higher than that of the individual subsidiary, the information

provided for in Article 11 relating to the employees of all the subsidiaries thus represented shall be given to that body.

2   The consultations provided for in Article 12 shall take place under the same conditions with the representative body referred to in paragraph (1).

3   A body representing all the employees of the dominant undertaking and its subsidiaries within the Community may be created by means of agreements to be concluded between the management of the dominant undertaking and the employees' representatives, unless provision is made for it by national law. If such a body is created, paragraphs 1 and 2 shall be applicable.

Article 14
1   The management of a dominant undertaking whose decision-making centre is located in a Member State of the Community and which has one or more establishments in the same Member State shall be required to disclose, via the management of the subsidiaries, information to the employees' representatives in all its subsidiaries employing at least one hundred employees in accordance with Article 11 and to consult them in accordance with Article 12.

2   For the purposes of applying this Article, the terms 'dominant undertaking' and 'subsidiary' in Articles 10 to 13 shall be replaced by the terms 'undertaking' and 'establishment' respectively.

Section IV

Secrecy requirements

Article 15
1   Members and former members of bodies representing employees and delegates authorized by them shall be required to maintain discretion as regards information of a confidential nature. Where they communicate information to third parties they shall take account of the interests of the undertaking and shall not be such as to divulge secrets regarding the undertaking or its business.

2   The Member States shall empower a tribunal or other national body to settle disputes concerning the confidentiality of certain information.

3   The Member States shall impose appropriate penalties in cases of infringement of the secrecy requirement.

Section V

Final provisions

Article 16   This directive shall be without prejudice to measures to be taken pursuant to Council Directive 75/129/EEC of 17 February 1975 on the approximation of the laws of the Member States relating to collective redundancies[4] and Directive 77/187/EEC or to the freedom of the Member States to apply to introduce laws, regulations or administrative provisions which are more favourable to employees.

Article 17

1   The Member States shall introduce the laws, regulations and administrative provisions necessary to comply with this Directive not later than . . .[5] They shall forthwith inform the Commission thereof.

2   The Member States shall communicate to the Commission the texts of law, regulations and administrative provisions which they adopt in the area covered by this directive.

Article 18   Within two years from the date fixed in Article 17, the Member States shall transmit to the Commission all information necessary to enable it to draw up a report to be submitted to the Council relating to the application of this directive.

Article 19   This directive is addressed to the Member States.

Notes to I(h)

1   OJ C 297 of 15 November 1980.
2   OJ C 13 of 12 February 1974.
3   OJ L 61 of 5 March 1977.
4   OJ L 48 of 22 February 1975.
5   Date to be specified at the time of adoption by the Council.

Appendix II
relating to Part III

II(a) DECLARATION ON INTERNATIONAL IN-
VESTMENT AND MULTINATIONAL ENTERPRISES
(21 June 1976)

The governments of OECD member countries

Considering

- that international investment has assumed increased importance in the world economy and has considerably contributed to the development of their countries;
- that multinational enterprises play an important role in this investment process;
- that co-operation by Member countries can improve the foreign investment climate, encourage the positive contribution which multinational enterprises can make to economic and social progress, and minimise and resolve difficulties which may arise from their various operations;
- that, while continuing endeavours within the OECD may lead to further international arrangements and agreements in this field, it seems appropriate at this stage to intensify their co-operation and consultation on issues relating to international investment and multinational enterprises through inter-related instruments each of which deals with a different aspect of the matter and together constitute a framework within which the OECD will consider these issues:

Declare:

Guidelines for multinational enterprises
I   that they jointly recommend to multinational enterprises operating in their territories the observance of the Guidelines as set forth in the Annex hereto having regard to the considerations and understandings which introduce the Guidelines and are an integral part of them;

294

National treatment

II   (1)   that Member countries should, consistent with their needs to maintain public order, to protect their essential security interests and to fulfil commitments relating to international peace and security, accord to enterprises operating in their territories and owned or controlled directly or indirectly by nationals of another Member country (hereinafter referred to as 'Foreign-Controlled Enterprises') treatment under their laws, regulations and administrative practices, consistent with international law and no less favourable than that accorded in like situations to domestic enterprises (hereinafter referred to as 'National Treatment');

(2)   that Member countries will consider applying 'National Treatment' in respect of countries other than Member countries;

(3)   that Member countries will endeavour to ensure that their territorial subdivisions apply 'National Treatment';

(4)   that this Declaration does not deal with the right of Member countries to regulate the entry of foreign investment or the conditions of establishment of foreign enterprises;

International investment incentives and disincentives

III   (1)   that they recognise the need to strengthen their co-operation in the field of international direct investment;

(2)   that they thus recognise the need to give due weight to the interests of Member countries affected by specific laws, regulations and administrative practices in this field (hereinafter called 'measures') providing official incentives and disincentives to international direct investment;

(3)   that Member countries will endeavour to make such measures as transparent as possible, so that their importance and purpose can be ascertained and that information on them can be readily available;

Consultation procedures

IV   that they are prepared to consult one another on the above matters in conformity with the Decisions of the Council relating to Inter-Governmental Consultation Procedures on the Guidelines for Multinational Enterprises, on National Treatment and on International Investment Incentives and Disincentives;

Review

V   that they will review the above matters within three years with a view to improving the effectiveness of international economic co-operation among Member countries on issues relating to international investment and multinational enterprises;

II(b) ANNEX TO THE DECLARATION OF 21 JUNE 1976
BY GOVERNMENTS OF OECD MEMBER COUNTRIES ON
INTERNATIONAL INVESTMENT AND MULTINATIONAL
ENTERPRISES

Guidelines for multinational enterprises

1.   Multinational enterprises now play an important part in the economies of Member countries and in international economic relations, which is of increasing interest to governments. Through international direct investment, such enterprises can bring substantial benefits to home and host countries by contributing to the efficient utilisation of capital, technology and human resources between countries and can thus fulfil an important role in the promotion of economic and social welfare. But the advances made by multinational enterprises in organising their operations beyond the national framework may lead to abuse of concentrations of economic power and to conflicts with national policy objectives. In addition, the complexity of these multinational enterprises and the difficulty of clearly perceiving their diverse structures, operations and policies sometimes give rise to concern.

2.   The common aim of the Member countries is to encourage the positive contributions which multinational enterprises can make to economic and social progress and to minimise and resolve the difficulties to which their various operations may give rise. In view of the transnational structure of such enterprises, this aim will be furthered by co-operation among the OECD countries where the headquarters of most of the multinational enterprises are established and which are the location of a substantial part of their operations. The guidelines set out hereafter are designed to assist in the achievement of this common aim and to contribute to improving the foreign investment climate.

3.   Since the operations of multinational enterprises extend throughout the world, including countries that are not Members of the Organisation, international co-operation in this field should extend to all States. Member countries will give their full support to efforts undertaken in co-operation with non-member countries, and in particular with developing countries, with a view to improving the welfare and living standards of all people both by encouraging the positive contributions which multinational enterprises can make and by minimising and resolving the problems which may arise in connection with their activities.

4   Within the Organisation, the programme of co-operation to attain these ends will be a continuing, pragmatic and balanced one. It comes within the general aims of the Convention on the Organisation for Economic Co-operation and Development (OECD) and makes full use of the various specialised bodies of the Organisation, whose terms of reference already cover many aspects of the role of multinational enterprises, notably in matters of international trade and payments, competition, taxation, manpower, industrial development, science and technology. In these bodies, work is being carried out on the identification of issues, the improvement of relevant qualitative and statistical information and the elaboration of proposals for action designed to strengthen inter-governmental co-operation. In some of these areas procedures already exist through which issues related to the operations of multinational enterprises can be taken up. This work could result in the conclusion of further and complementary agreements and arrangements between governments.

5   The initial phase of the co-operation programme is composed of a Declaration and three Decisions promulgated simultaneously as they are complementary and inter-connected, in respect of guidelines for multinational enterprises, national treatment for foreign-controlled enterprises and international investment incentives and disincentives.

6   The guidelines set out below are recommendations jointly addressed by Member countries to multinational enterprises operating in their territories. These guidelines, which take into account the problems which can arise because of the international structure of these enterprises, lay down standards for the activities of these enterprises in the different Member countries. Observance of the guidelines is voluntary and not legally enforceable. However, they should help to ensure that the operations of these enterprises are in harmony with national policies of the countries where they operate and to strengthen the basis of mutual confidence between enterprises and States.

7   Every State has the right to prescribe the conditions under which multinational enterprises operate within its national jurisdiction, subject to international law and to the international agreements to which it has subscribed. The entities of a multinational enterprise located in various countries are subject to the laws of these countries.

8   A precise legal definition of multinational enterprises is not required for the purposes of the guidelines. These usually comprise companies or other entities whose ownership is private, state or mixed, established in different countries and so linked that one or more of them may be able to exercise a significant influence over the activities of others and, in particular, to share knowledge and resources

with the others. The degree of autonomy of each entity in relation to the others varies widely from one multinational enterprise to another, depending on the nature of the links between such entities and the fields of activity concerned. For these reasons, the guidelines are addressed to the various entities within the multinational enterprise (parent companies and/or local entities) according to the actual distribution of responsibilities among them on the understanding that they will co-operate and provide assistance to one another as necessary to facilitate observance of the guidelines. The word 'enterprise' as used in these guidelines refers to these various entities in accordance with their responsibilities.

9   The guidelines are not aimed at introducing differences of treatment between multinational and domestic enterprises; wherever relevant they reflect good practice for all. Accordingly, multinational and domestic enterprises are subject to the same expectations in respect of their conduct wherever the guidelines are relevant to both.

10   The use of appropriate international dispute settlement mechanisms, including arbitration, should be encouraged as a means of facilitating the resolution of problems arising between enterprises and Member countries.

11   Member countries have agreed to establish appropriate review and consultation procedures concerning issues arising in respect of the guidelines. When multinational enterprises are made subject to conflicting requirements by Member countries, the governments concerned will co-operate in good faith with a view to resolving such problems either within the Committee on International Investment and Multinational Enterprises established by the OECD Council on 21st January 1975 or through other mutually acceptable arrangements.

Having regard to the foregoing considerations, the Member countries set forth the following guidelines for multinational enterprises with the understanding that Member countries will fulfil their responsibilities to treat enterprises equitably and in accordance with international law and international agreements, as well as contractual obligations to which they have subscribed:

General policies

Enterprises should

1   take fully into account established general policy objectives of the Member countries in which they operate;

2   in particular, give due consideration to those countries' aims and priorities with regard to economic and social progress, including industrial and regional development, the protection of the environment, the creation of employment opportunities, the promotion of innovation and the transfer of technology;

3   while observing their legal obligations concerning information, supply their entities with supplementary information the latter may need in order to meet requests by the authorities of the countries in which those entities are located for information relevant to the activities of those entities, taking into account legitimate requirements of business confidentiality;

4   favour close co-operation with the local community and business interests;

5   allow their component entities freedom to develop their activities and to exploit their competitive advantage in domestic and foreign markets, consistent with the need for specialisation and sound commercial practice;

6   when filling responsible posts in each country of operation, take due account of individual qualifications without discrimination as to nationality, subject to particular national requirements in this respect;

7   not render — and they should not be solicited or expected to render — any bribe or other improper benefit, direct or indirect, to any public servant or holder of public office;

8   unless legally permissible, not make contributions to candidates for public office or to political parties or other political organisations;

9   abstain from any improper involvement in local political activities.

Disclosure of information

Enterprises should, having due regard to their nature and relative size in the economic context of their operations and to requirements of business confidentiality and to cost, publish in a form suited to improve public understanding a sufficient body of factual information on the structure, activities and policies of the enterprise as a whole, as a supplement, in so far as necessary for this purpose, to information to be disclosed under the national law of the individual countries in which they operate. To this end, they should publish within reasonable time limits, on a regular basis, but at least annually, financial statements and other pertinent information relating to the enterprise as a whole, comprising in particular:

(i)   the structure of the enterprise, showing the name and location of the parent company, its main affiliates, its percentage ownership, direct and indirect, in these affiliates, including shareholdings between them;

(ii)   the geographical areas* where operations are carried out and the principal activities carried on therein by the parent company and the main affiliates;

(iii)   the operating results and sales by geographical area and the sales in the major lines of business for the enterprise as a whole;

(iv)   significant new capital investment by geographical area and, as far as practicable, by major lines of business for the enterprise as a whole;

(v)   a statement of the sources and uses of funds by the enterprise as a whole;

(vi)   the average number of employees in each geographical area;

(vii)   research and development expenditure for the enterprise as a whole;

(viii)   the policies followed in respect of intra-group pricing;

(ix)   the accounting policies, including those on consolidation, observed in compiling the published information.

Competition

Enterprises should, while conforming to official competition rules and established policies of the countries in which they operate,

1   refrain from actions which would adversely affect competition in the relevant market by abusing a dominant position of market power, by means of, for example,

(a)   anti-competitive acquisitions,

(b)   predatory behaviour toward competitors,

(c)   unreasonable refusal to deal,

(d)   anti-competitive abuse of industrial property rights,

*For the purposes of the guideline on disclosure of information the term 'geographical area' means groups of countries or individual countries as each enterprise determines is appropriate in its particular circumstances. While no single method of grouping is appropriate for all enterprises or for all purposes, the factors to be considered by an enterprise would include the significance of operations carried out in individual countries or areas as well as the effects on its competitiveness, geographic proximity, economic affinity, similarities in business environments and the nature, scale and degree of interrelationship of the enterprises' operations in the various countries.

(e) discriminatory (i.e. unreasonably differentiated) pricing and using such pricing transactions between affiliated enterprises as a means of affecting adversely competition outside these enterprises;

2 allow purchasers, distributors and licensees freedom to resell, export, purchase and develop their operations consistent with law, trade conditions, the need for specialisation and sound commercial practice;

3 refrain from participating in or otherwise purposely strengthening the restrictive effects of international or domestic cartels or restrictive agreements which adversely affect or eliminate competition and which are not generally or specifically accepted under applicable national or international legislation;

4 be ready to consult and co-operate, including the provision of information, with competent authorities of countries whose interests are directly affected in regard to competition issues or investigations. Provision of information should be in accordance with safeguards normally applicable in this field.

Financing

Enterprises should, in managing the financial and commercial operations of their activities, and especially their liquid foreign assets and liabilities, take into consideration the established objectives of the countries in which they operate regarding balance of payments and credit policies.

Taxation

Enterprises should

1 upon request of the taxation authorities of the countries in which they operate, provide, in accordance with the safeguards and relevant procedures of the national laws of these countries, the information necessary to determine correctly the taxes to be assessed in connection with their operations, including relevant information concerning their operations in other countries;

2 refrain from making use of the particular facilities available to them, such as transfer pricing which does not conform to an arm's length standard, for modifying in ways contrary to national laws the tax base on which members of the group are assessed.

Employment and industrial relations

Enterprises should, within the framework of law, regulations and prevailing labour relations and employment practices, in each of the countries in which they operate,

1 respect the right of their employees, to be represented by trade unions and other bona fide organisations of employees, and engage in constructive negotiations, either individually or through employers' associations, with such employee organisations with a view to reaching agreements on employment conditions, which should include provisions for dealing with disputes arising over the interpretation of such agreements, and for ensuring mutually respected rights and responsibilities;

2 (a) provide such facilities to representatives of the employees as may be necessary to assist in the development of effective collective agreements,

   (b) provide to representatives of employees information which is needed for meaningful negotiations on conditions of employment;

3 provide to representatives of employees where this accords with local law and practice, information which enables them to obtain a true and fair view of the performance of the entity or, where appropriate, the enterprise as a whole;

4 observe standards of employment and industrial relations not less favourable than those observed by comparable employers in the host country;

5 in their operations, to the greatest extent practicable, utilise, train and prepare for upgrading members of the local labour force in co-operation with representatives of their employees and, where appropriate, the relevant governmental authorities;

6 in considering changes in their operations which would have major effects upon the livelihood of their employees, in particular in the case of the closure of an entity involving collective lay-offs or dismissals, provide reasonable notice of such changes to representatives of their employees, and where appropriate to the relevant governmental authorities, and co-operate with the employee representatives and appropriate governmental authorities so as to mitigate to the maximum extent practicable adverse effects;

7 implement their employment policies including hiring, discharge, pay, promotion and training without discrimination unless selectivity in respect of employee characteristics is in furtherance of established

governmental policies which specifically promote greater equality of employment opportunity;

8   in the context of bona fide negotiations* with representatives of employees on conditions of employment, or while employees are exercising a right to organise, not threaten to utilise a capacity to transfer the whole or part of an operating unit from the country concerned in order to influence unfairly those negotiations or to hinder the exercise of a right to organise;

9   enable authorised representatives of their employees to conduct negotiations on collective bargaining or labour management relations issues with representatives of management who are authorised to take decisions on the matters under negotiation.

Science and technology

Enterprises should

1   endeavour to ensure that their activities fit satisfactorily into the scientific and technological policies and plans of the countries in which they operate, and contribute to the development of national scientific and technological capacities, including as far as appropriate the establishment and improvement in host countries of their capacity to innovate;

2   to the fullest extent practicable, adopt in the course of their business activities practices which permit the rapid diffusion of technologies with due regard to the protection of industrial and intellectual property rights;

3   when granting licences for the use of industrial property rights or when otherwise transferring technology do so on reasonable terms and conditions.

---

*Bona fide negotiations may include labour disputes as part of the process of negotiation. Whether or not labour disputes are so included will be determined by the law and prevailing employment practices of particular countries.

II(c) DECISION OF THE COUNCIL ON INTER-
GOVERNMENTAL CONSULTATION PROCEDURES
ON THE GUIDELINES FOR MULTINATIONAL
ENTERPRISES (21 June 1976)

The Council,

Having regard to the Convention on the Organisation for Economic
Co-operation and Development of 14th December, 1960 and, in
particular, to Articles 2(d), 3 and 5(a) thereof;
 Having regard to the Resolution of the Council of 21st January,
1975 establishing a Committee on International Investment and
Multinational Enterprises and, in particular, to paragraph 2 thereof
[C(74)247(Final)] ;
 Taking note of the Declaration by the Governments of OECD
Member countries of 21st June, 1976 in which they jointly recom-
mend to multinational enterprises the observance of guidelines for
multinational enterprises;
 Recognising the desirability of setting forth procedures by which
consultations may take place on matters related to these guidelines;
 On the proposal of the Committee on International Investment and
Multinational Enterprises;

Decides:

1   The Committee on International Investment and Multinational
Enterprises (hereinafter called 'the Committee') shall periodically or at
the request of a Member country hold an exchange of views on matters
related to the guidelines and the experience gained in their application.
The Committee shall periodically report to the Council on these
matters.

2   The Committee shall periodically invite the Business and Industry
Advisory Committee to OECD (BIAC) and the Trade Union Advisory
Committee to OECD (TUAC) to express their views on matters related to the guidelines and shall take account of such views in its
reports to the Council.

3   On the proposal of a Member country the Committee may decide
whether individual enterprises should be given the opportunity, if they
so wish, to express their views concerning the application of the guidelines. The Committee shall not reach conclusions on the conduct of
individual enterprises.

4   Member countries may request that consultations be held in the Committee on any problem arising from the fact that multinational enterprises are made subject to conflicting requirements. Governments concerned will co-operate in good faith with a view to resolving such problems, either within the Committee or through other mutually acceptable arrangements.

5   This Decision shall be reviewed within a period of three years. The Committee shall make proposals for this purpose as appropriate.

II(d) DECISION OF THE COUNCIL
ON NATIONAL TREATMENT (21 June 1976)

The Council,

Having regard to the Convention on the Organisation for Economic Co-operation and Development of 14th December, 1960 and, in particular, Articles 2(c), 2(d), 3 and 5(a) thereof;

Having regard to the Resolution of the Council of 21st January, 1975 establishing a Committee on International Investment and Multinational Enterprises and, in particular, paragraph 2 thereof [C(74)247(Final)] ;

Taking note of the Declaration by the Governments of OECD Member countries of 21st June, 1976 on national treatment;

Considering that it is appropriate to establish within the Organisation suitable procedures for reviewing laws, regulations and administrative practices (hereinafter referred to as 'measures') which depart from 'National Treatment';

On the proposal of the Committee on International Investment and Multinational Enterprises;

Decides:

1   Measures taken by a Member country constituting exceptions to 'National Treatment' (including measures restricting new investment by 'Foreign-Controlled Enterprises' already established in their territory) which are in effect on the date of this Decision shall be notified to the Organisation within 60 days after the date of this Decision.

2   Measures taken by a Member country constituting new exceptions to 'National Treatment' (including measures restricting new investment by 'Foreign-Controlled Enterprises' already established in their territory) taken after the date of this Decision shall be notified to the Organisation within 30 days of their introduction together with the specific reasons therefore and the proposed duration thereof.

3   Measures introduced by a territorial subdivision of a Member country, pursuant to its independent powers, which constitute exceptions to 'National Treatment', shall be notified to the Organisation by the Member country concerned, insofar as it has knowledge thereof, within 30 days of the responsible officials of the Member country obtaining such knowledge.

4   The Committee on International Investment and Multinational Enterprises (hereinafter called 'the Committee') shall periodically review the application of 'National Treatment' (including exceptions thereto) with a view to extending such application of 'National Treatment'. The Committee shall make proposals as and when necessary in this connection.

5   The Committee shall act as a forum for consultations, at the request of a Member country, in respect of any matter related to this instrument and its implementation, including exceptions to 'National Treatment' and their application.

6   Member countries shall provide to the Committee, upon its request, all relevant information concerning measures pertaining to the application of 'National Treatment' and exceptions thereto.

7   This Decision shall be reviewed within a period of three years. The Committee shall make proposals for this purpose as appropriate.

II(e) DECISION OF THE COUNCIL ON INTERNATIONAL INVESTMENT INCENTIVES AND DISINCENTIVES
(21 June 1976)

The Council,

Having regard to the Convention on the Organisation for Economic Co-operation and Development of 14th December, 1960 and, in particular, Articles 2(c), 2(d), 2(e), 3 and 5(a) thereof;

Having regard to the Resolution of the Council of 21st January, 1975, establishing a Committee on International Investment and Multinational Enterprises and, in particular, paragraph 2 thereof [C(74)247(Final)] ;

Taking note of the Declaration by the Governments of OECD Member countries of 21st June, 1976 on international investment incentives and disincentives;

On the proposal of the Committee on International Investment and Multinational Enterprises;

Decides:

1   Consultations will take place in the framework of the Committee on International Investment and Multinational Enterprises at the request of a Member country which considers that its interests may be adversely affected by the impact on its flow of international direct investments of measures taken by another Member country specifically designed to provide incentives or disincentives for international direct investment. Having full regard to the national economic objectives of the measures and without prejudice to policies designed to redress regional imbalances, the purpose of the consultations will be to examine the possibility of reducing such effects to a minimum.

2   Member countries shall supply, under the consultation procedures, all permissible information relating to any measures being the subject of the consultation.

3   This Decision shall be reviewed within a period of three years. The Committee on International Investment and Multinational Enterprises shall make proposals for this purpose as appropriate.

II(f) RECOMMENDATION OF THE COUNCIL ON THE DETERMINATION OF TRANSFER PRICES BETWEEN ASSOCIATED ENTERPRISES (16 May 1979)

'The Council,

Having regard to Article 5(b) of the Convention on the Organisation of Economic Co-operation and Development of 14th December, 1960;

Having regard to the Declaration of 21st June, 1976 adopted by the Governments of OECD Member Countries on International Investment and Multinational Enterprises and the Guidelines annexed thereto;

Considering that transactions between associated enterprises (i.e. between parent and subsidiary enterprises or enterprises under common control) may take place under conditions differing from those taking place between independent enterprises;

Considering that the prices charged in such transactions between associated enterprises (usually referred to as transfer prices) should, nevertheless, for tax purposes be in conformity with those which would be charged between independent enterprises (usually referred to as arm's length prices) as provided in Article 9(1) of the OECD Model Double Taxation Convention on Income and on Capital;

Considering that problems with regard to transfer prices in international transactions arise mostly between the various entities of multinational enterprises and assume special importance in view of the substantial volume of such transactions;

Having regard to the considerations in the Report referred to above regarding the methods to be followed for the correct determination of transfer prices for goods, technology, trademarks and services and of interest rates on loans between associated enterprises;

Having regard to the need to achieve consistency in the approaches of tax authorities, on the one hand, and of associated enterprises, on the other hand, in the determination of transfer prices for the purposes of ensuring correct taxation of profits and avoidance of double taxation;

I   Recommends the Government of Member countries:

1   that their tax administrations take into account, when reviewing, and if necessary, adjusting transfer prices between associated enterprises for the purposes of determining taxable profits, the considerations and methods set out in the Report referred to above for arriving at arm's length prices when goods, technology, trademarks and

services are provided or supplied or loans granted between associated enterprises;

2   that they give the Report referred to above publicity in their country and have it translated, where appropriate, into their national language(s);

3   that they develop further co-operation between their tax administrations, on a bilateral or multilateral basis, in matters pertaining to transfer pricing;

II   **Instructs** the Committee on Fiscal Affairs:

1   to pursue its work on issues pertinent to transfer pricing and to the assessment of taxable profits of associated enterprises in general;

2   to report periodically to the Council on the results of its work in these matters together with any relevant proposals for improved international co-operation.'

II(g) RECOMMENDATION OF THE COUNCIL CONCERNING ACTION AGAINST RESTRICTIVE BUSINESS PRACTICES AFFECTING INTERNATIONAL TRADE INCLUDING THOSE INVOLVING MULTINATIONAL ENTERPRISES
(Adopted on 20 July, 1978)

[The Representative for Turkey abstained]

The Council,

Having regard to Article 5(b) of the Convention on the Organisation for Economic Co-operation and development of 14th December, 1960;

Having regard to the Declaration on International Investment and Multinational Enterprises adopted by the Governments of OECD Member countries on 21st June, 1976;

Having regard to the Report of the Committee of Experts on Restrictive Business Practices of 10th February, 1977 on the restrictive business practices of multinational enterprises;

Considering that restrictive business practices may have harmful effects on international trade whether they emanate from purely national or from multinational enterprises;

Considering that the restrictive business practices of multinational enterprises do not differ in form from those operated by purely national enterprises but that they may have a more significant impact on trade and competition due to the fact that multinational enterprises generally tend to wield greater market power, that they play a relatively greater role in the process of national and international concentration and that the restrictive business practices they engage in have more often an international character;

Recognising that, in the present state of international law and of the laws on restrictive business practices of Member countries, control of practices affecting international trade, including those involving multinational enterprises, raises many difficulties, especially in assembling necessary information held outside the jurisdiction of the country applying its law, in serving process and in enforcing decisions in relation to enterprises located abroad.

Recognising that the solution to these difficulties cannot at present be found in an international convention establishing control of restrictive business practices affecting international trade owing mainly to the still differing attitudes adopted by countries towards restrictive business practices and in particular to their varying national legislations in this field.

Considering, however, that the difficulties in controlling restrictive business practices affecting international trade, including those involving multinational enterprises, may be alleviated by simultaneous efforts in the fields of national legislation on restrictive business practices and of international co-operation, particularly within the OECD framework, it being understood that such co-operation should not in any way be construed to affect the legal positions of Member countries, in particular with regard to such questions of sovereignty and extraterritorial application of laws concerning restrictive business practices as may arise;

I **Recommends** the Governments of Member countries to consider the following action:

(1) to adopt new or supplement existing measures on restrictive business practices so as to prohibit or control effectively, such practices, particularly:

(a) actions adversely affecting competition in the relevant market by abusing a dominant position of market power by means of, for example,

- anti-competitive acquisitions;
- predatory behaviour toward competitors;
- unreasonable refusal to deal;
- anti-competitive abuse of industrial property rights;
- discriminatory (i.e. unreasonably differentiated) pricing and using such pricing transactions between affiliated enterprises as a means of affecting adversely competition outside these enterprises.

(b) cartels or other restrictive agreements which without justification adversely affect or eliminate competition;

(2) to develop, consistent with established rules of international law and taking international comity into account appropriate national rules to facilitate investigation and discovery by their respective competition authorities of relevant information within the control of an enterprise under investigation, where such information is located outside their respective national territories and when its provision is not contrary to the law or established policies of the country where the information is located;

(3) to allow, subject to appropriate safeguards, including those relating to confidentiality, the disclosure of information to the

competent authorities of Member countries by the other parties concerned, whether accomplished unilaterally or in the context of bilateral or multilateral understandings, unless such co-operation or disclosure would be contrary to significant national interests;

(4) to facilitate, through conclusion of or adherence to bilateral or multilateral agreements or understandings, mutual administrative or judicial aid in the field of restrictive business practices;

(5) whilst vigorously enforcing their legislation on restrictive business practices, to make use as far as possible of the OECD procedures on co-operation between Member countries in the field of restrictive business practices affecting international trade so as to facilitate consultation and resolution of problems.

II Instructs the Committee of Experts on Restrictive Business Practices

to keep under review this Recommendation and to report to the Council when appropriate.

II(h) REVIEW OF THE OECD GUIDELINES
ON MULTINATIONAL ENTERPRISES
(as agreed by OECD Ministers meeting in Council, Paris, 13–14 June,
1979)

I   General orientation of the Review

A convenient starting point for a review of the Guidelines is the statement in paragraph 6 of their introductory part which remains the basis
for the exercise. Paragraph 6 states that: 'the Guidelines are recommendations jointly addressed by Member countries to multinational
enterprises operating in their territories. These Guidelines, which take
into account the problems which can arise because of the international
structure of these enterprises, lay down standards for the activities of
these enterprises in the different Member countries. Observance of the
Guidelines is voluntary and not legally enforceable. However, they
should help to ensure that the operations of these enterprises are in
harmony with national policies of the countries where they operate
and to strengthen the basis of mutual confidence between enterprises
and States'.

There appears to be a general willingness on the part of multinational
enterprises to apply the Guidelines and, although the present Review is
taking place a relatively short time since these instruments were
adopted, a process of acceptance and use of the Guidelines is under
way. A full assessment of the extent to which the behaviour of multinational enterprises is in accord with that recommended by the
Guidelines will call for a longer period of experience. Meanwhile, an
increased and continuing effort is needed to bring the Guidelines to the
attention of the large number of multinational enterprises operating in
OECD Member countries, to explain their role and purpose and to
encourage their integration into management thinking and practice.
Users of the Guidelines should be able to benefit from a stable framework for the future. Consequently, except in one instance where an
addition to the Guidelines appeared to be desirable in the light of
special circumstances not foreseen at the time of the drafting of the
Guidelines, no changes in the text are proposed in this report. This fact
should also be of value in reinforcing the credibility of the Guidelines.

Given the above considerations, the major emphasis of this Review
of the Guidelines is on improving their implementation at both the
national and international levels. There is, first, a need for increased
promotional and educational efforts to increase the awareness,
understanding, acceptance and use of the Guidelines by the enterprises
to whom they are directed as well as by their employees and the

general public. Second, there is the need to ensure that there are appropriate facilities and procedures at the national and, in particular, the international levels to handle matters and issues that may arise as the Guidelines are applied within the Member countries. Recommendations directed at improving implementation in both these areas are developed in the following chapters.

The fact that the Guidelines must at one and the same time be of practical relevance in the specific contexts in which each enterprise operates and yet retain an overall applicability for the OECD area with its diversity of legal systems and national practices leads inevitably to a formulation in fairly general terms of the principles contained in each of the Guidelines. Experience at the national and international levels has revealed the existence of areas of uncertainty as to the meaning of certain provisions of the Guidelines which is due in part to the general wording utilised. After considering these areas of uncertainty, the Committee has decided it would be useful to seek to develop explanatory comments in response to some of the questions which have been raised. These comments, which are to be found in Section IV, should not be considered as modifying the Guidelines. Their purpose is to explain in more detail the meaning of the existing provisions in order to provide guidance to the parties concerned when using the Guidelines.

II   Relationship between the Guidelines and
      negotiations in other International Fora

While addressed to enterprises operating in Member countries — where most of the parent companies of MNEs are located — the Guidelines have a de facto influence extending beyond the OECD area. As stated in *paragraph 3* of the Introduction to the Guidelines, Member countries are aware of the interests of non-Member countries in this regard and confirm their willingness to contribute in co-operative efforts with these countries in all matters dealt with in the OECD Ministerial Declaration on International Investment and Multinational Enterprises. Member countries continue to support and to participate actively in negotiations on related issues in other international fora.

Since 1976, other international organisations have taken up various issues related to the activities of MNEs. The Governing Body of the International Labour Organisation has agreed to a Tripartite Declaration of Principles concerning Multinational Enterprises and Social Policy. In the framework of the United Nations, a Code of Conduct relating to the activities of MNEs is being negotiated whilst, as part of the UNCTAD negotiations, an international Code of Conduct for the transfer of technology and multilateral principles and rules concerning restrictive business practices are envisaged. In ECOSOC work is underway on an international agreement to prevent corrupt practices in connection with international commercial transactions.

There is clearly a link between these negotiations in other international bodies and the OECD Guidelines, although there is no necessary symmetry between them. Thus the results of the OECD's work, being the first to be made public and to be applied, have had an impact on work going on elsewhere, either on specific subjects covered by one of the OECD Guidelines or on the general approach adopted. At the same time, the context of negotiations in other fora differs from that which prevails inside the group of OECD countries so that each set of international negotiations has its own specificity.

The ILO Tripartite Declaration, which OECD Member countries as well as business and trade union representatives have supported, has a different geographical scope than the Guidelines. Also, while the OECD Guidelines cover all major aspects of corporate behaviour, the ILO Declaration sets out principles only in the fields of employment, training, conditions of work and industrial relations which governments, employers and workers, as well as multinational enterprises, are recommended to observe. Wherever these principles refer to the behaviour expected from enterprises, they parallel the OECD Guidelines and do not conflict with them. They can, therefore, be of use in relation to the OECD Guidelines to the extent that they are of a greater degree of elaboration. It must, however, be borne in mind that the responsibilities for the follow-up procedures of the OECD Guidelines and of the ILO Declaration are institutionally separate.

III   Action by Member governments and by business and labour representatives

The Member governments took steps after 1976 to promote better knowledge and understanding of the Guidelines. Some promotional efforts reported to the Organisation include dissemination of the Guidelines in national languages, speeches by government officials, letters to representatives of individual companies and to business and labour organisations and acts or resolutions of parliamentary bodies. Beyond these initial efforts, a few governments have undertaken — either on their own behalf or jointly with business organisations — surveys of MNE adherence to the Guidelines and for this purpose have sent questionnaires to a representative number of multinational enterprises operating on their territory.

In many Member countries special arrangements have been made either by setting up new mechanisms or adapting already existing procedures, such as inter-ministerial groups or advisory committees, for exchanging views on a regular basis with the parties concerned on matters related to the Guidelines and other parts of the 1976 instruments. Some governments have reported that they take into account the Guidelines when determining their policies. The Guidelines have also been used on occasions as points of reference at the national or bilateral level with respect to the activities of multinational enterprises.

Business and labour organisations have also been active in promoting the Guidelines. Acting through BIAC and in statements issued at the national level, business organisations in Member countries have expressed their support of the 1976 instruments and recommended that their constituent enterprises observe the Guidelines. The business community has made considerable efforts to disseminate and to promote the Guidelines and to identify and to seek to resolve problems which may arise in their application through the organisation of seminars and workshops and through the elaboration of comments and annotations on different chapters of the Guidelines. BIAC has established a special Committee on Multinational Enterprises to co-operate in the work of the OECD Committee on International Investment and Multinational Enterprises and its Working Groups. This Committee has carried out an enquiry among a number of firms operating in OECD countries on the extent to which the Guideline on disclosure of information is being implemented and on the problems met with in using it.

Labour organisations, through TUAC, considered the Guidelines in 1976 as an initial important step taken by the OECD Member governments and they subsequently have undertaken a major effort to distribute and promote the Guidelines widely to employee representatives at the national and local level, who in turn have referred to the Guidelines on a number of occasions in negotiations with multinational enterprises. TUAC has set up a Working Group on Multinational Enterprises which is co-ordinating TUAC work on matters related to the Guidelines, in particular, preparing for the exchanges of views between TUAC and the Committee and its Working Group on the Guidelines and considering and, where necessary, passing on to the Committee questions and problems encountered in the application of the Guidelines, especially with respect to the chapter on Employment and Industrial Relations.

IV   Review of each chapter of the Guidelines

Proceeding chapter by chapter, the Report does not intend to deal exhaustively with all points in the Guidelines. Rather, stress is given to those aspects which have given rise to questions and where the Committee was able to gather experience through its consultation procedures and from the information provided by governments and the advisory bodies, BIAC and TUAC. Where relevant, the work of other OECD Committees is also taken into account. The resulting emphasis on certain chapters should not obscure the fact that the Member governments view the Guidelines as a comprehensive set of standards of good practice for firms which should be seen as a balanced whole.

Introductory part (paragraphs 1—11)

As stated in Section I of the 1976 Declaration, these introductory considerations and understandings form an integral part of the Guidelines and are necessary for a proper comprehension of the nature of the whole exercise. Some points in this regard merit underlining now that the exercise has entered the operational phase.

Paragraph 6 of the Introduction is central to the understanding of the purpose and the nature of the Guidelines. These Guidelines take into account the problems which can arise because of the international structure of multinational enterprises by laying down standards for the activities of these enterprises and, where relevant, of national enterprises in the different Member countries. They constitute, together with the other parts of the 1976 Declaration, a key element of a favourable investment climate by providing a stronger basis of mutual confidence between enterprises and States. While observance of the Guidelines is voluntary and not legally enforceable, they carry the weight of a joint recommendation by OECD governments addressed to MNEs which represent their firm expectation for MNE behaviour. The Guidelines received the support of organisations representing the business community, and a considerable number of major enterprises have publicly stated their acceptance. The Guidelines are also being used as a point of reference by workers' organisations. The follow-up action provided in the Decision on Intergovernmental Consultation Procedures on the Guidelines is designed to enhance their effectiveness and Section V of this chapter sets out further recommendations in this regard.

As is stated in *paragraph 7* of the Introduction to the Guidelines every State retains the right to prescribe the conditions under which multinational enterprises operate within its national jurisdiction subject to international law and the international agreements to which

318

it has subscribed. Multinational enterprises are subject to the laws of these countries, and the Guidelines are no substitute for national laws. Their role, rather, is to introduce, where relevant, supplementary standards of behaviour of a non-legal character, in particular with respect to the international scope of operations of these enterprises.

Paragraph 8 deals with two aspects of importance to the application of the Guidelines as a whole. First, it reflects the understanding of the Committee of what is meant by the term 'multinational enterprise'. Paragraph 8 is couched in non-legal language and the experience of the Committee has demonstrated the merits of such a flexible approach with an enumeration of some guiding criteria rather than a precise definition which would fit less well the diversity of situations found in the real world. The Guidelines are addressed to entities which can be considered as 'enterprises' (private, state, mixed) 'established in different countries and so linked that one or more of them may be able to exercise a significant influence over the activities of others and, in particular, to share knowledge and resources with the others'. These criteria cover a broad range of multinational activities and arrangements, which can be based on equity participation according to the traditional approach to international direct investment, but the same result could be achieved by other means not necessarily including an equity capital element. Second, paragraph 8 notes that the various entities, which include parent companies, local subsidiaries, as well as intermediary levels of the organisations, are expected to co-operate and to provide assistance to one another as necessary to facilitate the observance of the Guidelines, taking into account the degree of autonomy or of dependence of each entity in practice. To the extent that parent companies actually exercise control over the activities of their subsidiaries they have a responsibility for the observance of the Guidelines by those subsidiaries.

It should be noted that in applying the Guidelines, it is not necessary in every instance to seek to determine whether or not the nature of contractual links of a non-equity character between separate entities leads to the conclusion that such entities viewed collectively constitute an MNE within the meaning of the Guidelines. *Paragraph 9* of the introduction clearly states that the Guidelines, wherever relevant, 'reflect good practice for all. Accordingly, multinational and domestic enterprises are subject to the same expectations in respect of their conduct wherever the Guidelines are relevant for both'.

While arising out of the text of *paragraph 8*, the question as to what extent observance of the Guidelines implies responsibilities for the parent companies and/or for the subsidiaries, respectively, is important to the Guidelines as a whole. Considering, first, non-financial responsibilities, the Committee noted that one area in the Guidelines where the parent company clearly is being addressed directly concerns the chapter on Disclosure of Information, which refers to the publication of 'a sufficient body of factual information on the structure, activities and policies of the enterprises as a whole' that is, information which must be gathered and prepared by the parent company. In other areas such as competition and taxation, where it may be important for the specific purposes of the relevant chapters of the Guidelines to obtain a full picture of the operations of the enterprise as a whole, enterprises, including parent companies, should co-operate with national authorities, inter alia, by providing information. The chapter on Employment and Industrial Relations, particularly in its paragraphs 3, 6 and 9, also raises matters germane to the criteria for assessing the respective degrees of responsibility of parents and subsidiaries for facilitating observance of the Guidelines, which are considered at more length in relation to that particular chapter.

The Committee also considered the question whether good practice in conformity with observance of the Guidelines should, in some instances, lead parent companies to assume certain financial obligations of their subsidiaries. The Committee has found that this question raises difficult and complex problems in view of the principle embodied in national laws of all Member countries of limited legal liability of companies. The Committee wishes to underline that the Guidelines, according to their nature described in paragraph 38 above, introduce, where relevant, supplementary standards of non-legal character and thus do not set standards which could be seen as superseding or sub-stituting for national laws governing corporate liability, which are part of the legal basis on which companies operate. For this reason, in the view of the Committee, the behaviour recommended by the Guide-lines in this context cannot be seen in a legal framework and does not imply an unqualified principle of parent company responsibility. None-theless, the Committee has noted that parent companies on a voluntary basis have assumed in certain cases such financial responsibility for a subsidiary. The Committee considers generalization in this area difficult, but the question of such responsibility as a matter of good management practice — in light of such factors as e.g. aspects of the relationship between the parent company and the subsidiary and the conduct of the parent company — consistent with observance of the Guidelines, could arise in special circumstances. The question of assumption of responsibility, for example, could be of particular relevance in the circumstances set out in paragraph 6 of Guidelines on Employment and Industrial Relations relating to important changes in the operations of a firm and the co-operation as to the mitigation of resulting adverse effects.

General policies

Paragraphs 1 and 2 of this chapter of the Guidelines recommend MNEs 'to take fully into account the established general policy objectives of the Member countries in which they operate' and, in particular, 'to give due consideration to those countries' aims and priorities'. Paragraph 2 identifies a number of areas of aims and priorities. Specific cases have shown that these provisions are of particular relevance when a local subsidiary of an MNE is to be closed down. In this context a prudent company would be well advised to seek any necessary clarification of government policies through advance consultations with the government concerned. In the view of the Committee, paragraphs 1 and 2 of this chapter of the Guidelines do not affect the right of the enterprise to reach decisions with respect to cutting back or terminating operations in a given plant. But they indicate certain considerations which should be given due weight in making such a decision. If a firm does proceed in this manner, then it clearly follows that the nature of the final decision will be influenced by the considerations set out in paragraphs 1 and 2 whilst respecting the firm's own judgement.

If MNEs are to take fully into account Member countries' policy objectives and aims as stated in paragraphs 1 and 2, it is understood that governments make such aims and objectives as clear, stable and understandable to management as possible. Where host countries' national legislation or the general framework of their policies may affect disinvestment, *paragraph 7* of the Introduction of the Guidelines is of relevance. Although the right of each state to prescribe the conditions under which multinational enterprises operate within its jurisdiction remains unaffected, such laws, regulations and policies are subject to international law and international agreements and should respect contractual obligations to which a country has subscribed. It also means that these laws, regulations and policies will be consistent with member country responsibilities to treat enterprises equitably.

The question has been raised whether *paragraphs 4 and 5* of the General Policies chapter have special relevance in cases where the decision to close down a subsidiary and to transfer its activities abroad concerns a subsidiary that can be considered still to be a profitable one. Consideration of this question demonstrated to the Committee how difficult it can be in practice to decide whether a particular entity is profitable or not. Accounting data differ according to differences in valuation and the accounting standards that are adopted and widely diverging estimates can be made, in particular, of the future profitability of the subsidiary. When there is clear evidence of the profitability of a subsidiary, this calls for special consideration by a company when it is contemplating the closure of that subsidiary, although other factors may be of importance and this cannot restrict the right of the company to reach its decision. Paragraphs 4 and 5, read together, can be understood to be in favour of a certain degree of integration of the component entities of an MNE into the economic context of the countries in which they operate. On the other hand, the insertion of the words 'consistent with the need for specialisation and sound commercial practices' in paragraph 5 was intended to provide for giving due consideration to the interests of an MNE as a whole, as well as the situation of any of its entities. The Guidelines do not call for the freezing of the existing structures of multinational enterprises nor do they infringe the freedom of MNEs to take decisions to divest in the furtherance of global strategies judged to be in the best interests of the firm as a whole. But this freedom is circumscribed according to national law and contractual obligations entered into by firms and affected by paragraphs 1 and 2 of the chapter on General Policies as described above.

Disclosure of information

'The complexity of these multinational enterprises and the difficulty of clearly perceiving their diverse structures, operations and policies sometimes give rise to concern' (paragraph 1 of Introduction to the Guidelines). The purpose of the chapter on Disclosure of Information was to give greater transparency to the activities of MNEs through the publication of a greater volume of information, 'presented in a form suited to improve public understanding'. In the opinion of the business community also, as conveyed to the Committee notably by BIAC, this is an area where management should make best efforts to show results. Here again, however, it must be recognised that the time which has elapsed since the summer of 1976 when the Guidelines were made public is fairly short — in fact, two accounting years — for implementing any changes needed to bring the practice of companies into line with the chapter on disclosure.

On the basis of information available to the Committee, it can be seen that progress has been achieved by a number of large companies whose annual or other published reports reflect all or most of the disclosure standards of the Guidelines. However, the observance of these disclosure standards to date appears to be considerably less widespread among the medium and smaller sized MNEs, which may be due to their relative size in the economic context of their operations and to cost. Even among the larger firms there are considerable differences according to the home country of the parent, reflecting historical differences in prevailing practices. Thus, the Committee believes that significant further efforts will be needed to encourage wide observance of the recommended standards.

In its discussions with BIAC and through the reports it received from Member governments, the Committee noted a number of concerns some enterprises expressed with respect to this chapter, some of which reflect difficulties of adjustments while others reveal problems of a more conceptual nature. The following comments refer to the problem areas that have been identified:

(a)   Some enterprises considered that the disclosure of certain types of information (cf. operating results by geographical area) may result in competitive disadvantages, especially for firms which have only one or a few customers in a particular country or region. In this regard, the Guidelines on disclosure contain a certain number of qualifications which make allowances for the specific situations of companies in the context of their operations. These qualifications, however, are not intended, other than in very exceptional circumstances, as complete or permanent exemptions from certain disclosure standards and should be invoked only for valid reasons.

(b)   Reference was also made by enterprises to cost and time factors involved in changing or supplementing existing reporting practices, in particular, for smaller companies with limited international experience. As cost and the relative size of the company are specifically mentioned as qualifications in the chapter on Disclosure of Information, the Guidelines provide the necessary degree of flexibility for the adjustment of reporting practices over a reasonable period of time.

(c)   Certain enterprises also referred to the diversity of national reporting and accounting requirements with respect to the items contained in the disclosure guidelines. The recommendations in the chapter, as explicitly stated in the text, were intended to supplement, where necessary, the disclosure and reporting requirements laid down by national law to increase public understanding 'on the structure, activities and the policies of the enterprises as a whole'. National requirements which are less comprehensive should not prevent MNEs from taking action under the Guidelines. Given the present absence of internationally-agreed accounting standards, such reports concerning the enterprises as a whole will usually follow the accounting principles generally accepted in the country in which the parent company or a controlling entity at the intermediary level is domiciled. For the use of such information it is important, according to item (ix) of the chapter on Disclosure of Information, that companies state the accounting principles which have been used.

(d)   Problems were also raised with respect to segmentation of information. In particular, a number of firms expressed doubts as to whether disclosure by 'geographical area' was always the most appropriate method of segmentation. These problems of geographical breakdown should, however, not be exaggerated. As explained in the footnote to the text, the Guidelines leave some degree of flexibility for companies to determine the most appropriate geographical breakdown. This may be an issue where the interests of some users of the published data differ in some cases from those of the enterprises, which may find a line of business approach more useful for internal purposes. It has to be emphasized, however, that the Guidelines reflect the value Member governments place on geographical segmentation of information.

The Committee is presently exploring the ways and means of improving comparability or achieving harmonisation of the accounting concepts referred to in the Disclosure of Information Guidelines. For this purpose, inter alia, an ad hoc technical Working Group on Accounting Standards has been set up and is conducting a survey on the accounting requirements, standards and practices in Member countries which are of particular relevance to the Guidelines so as to be in a position to advise the Committee, by the autumn of 1979, on the feasibility of OECD undertaking further work in this area.

Meanwhile, the Committee is aware that the standards laid down by the OECD for disclosure go beyond actual practice in most Member countries and that adjustment to these standards in some cases presents difficulties and costs. Nevertheless, the Committee believes these standards are reasonable and are sufficiently flexible. It confirms the importance which Member countries attach to the objectives of this chapter of the Guidelines and reiterates its view that companies which have not yet taken steps to observe the disclosure Guidelines, making due allowances for adjustment difficulties, should make every effort to reflect in their next annual published accounts the Disclosure of Information Guidelines. It invites governments and the business community to undertake further promotional and educational efforts so as to enhance the effectiveness of the Guidelines in this area and, in recognition of the fundamental importance of this chapter of the Guidelines, intends to pay continuing attention to this matter.

Competition

The restrictive business practices of multinational enterprises do not differ in form from those operated by purely national enterprises but may have a more significant impact on trade and competition due to the fact that multinational enterprises generally tend to wield greater market power, that they play a relatively greater role in the process of national and international concentration and that the restrictive business practices they engage in have more often an international character.

The text of the chapter on Competition of the Guidelines reflects the major areas of concern shared by Member governments where MNEs are involved and represents a common approach to competition problems by countries in the OECD area. Already this chapter of the Guidelines has proved to be useful to several governments which have referred to it when dealing with international cartels or with problems related to securing information on restrictive business practices of MNEs.

It is recognised that guidelines dealing with complex legal and economic concepts, such as abuse of a dominant position, adverse effects on competition and unreasonably differentiated pricing policies, are not sufficient in themselves to provide precise rules for business executives to follow in specific circumstances. Under the national law of various countries, these concepts have been given meaning through interpretation by the competent tribunals. This is why supporting action by Member governments at national level is needed, together with complementary arrangements and agreements for inter-governmental co-operation.

Thus, the Committee of Experts on Restrictive Business Practices, in its report on Restrictive Business Practices of Multinational Enterprises published in 1977, has put forward proposals for follow-up action at the national and international level. Most of these proposals are incorporated in the Recommendation of the OECD Council of 20th July, 1978 which is annexed to the present report (pp. 311–12)*. This Recommendation invites governments, inter alia, to adopt new or to supplement existing measures on restrictive business practices with particular emphasis on those areas covered by the competition Guidelines.

The Committee of Experts on Restrictive Business Practices is at present engaged in a study of the obstacles to, and jurisdictional issues involved in, the collection of information abroad necessary for the control of restrictive business practices (including those obstacles and issues related to the effects doctrine where it is applied) and of forms of international co-operation in this connection. The Committee welcomes this initiative, which should lead to a greater degree of inter-governmental co-operation in an important area of direct relevance to OECD activities concerning MNEs.

Financing

No particular issues in the area covered by the chapter on Financing

*Appendix II(g).

have been brought to the attention of the Committee. It should be noted, however, that an ad hoc Working Party (subsequently dissolved) examined the role of multinational enterprises in short-term capital movements and reported to the Committee in autumn 1976. The principal conclusion of the Group was that a common reporting system on such capital movements did not appear feasible at that time. Nevertheless, the Committee does note that in recent years significant short-term capital flows have been experienced which have no doubt included among their diverse components flows generated by MNEs. This issue merits continuing attention and it is under consideration in other fora.

Taxation

This Guideline, notably the recommendation in its first paragraph relating to supplying national tax authorities in one country, upon request, with relevant information concerning the operations of related entities in other countries, has been welcomed by national tax authorities as a useful supplement to the means they already have at their disposal for securing information on activities of MNEs abroad.

The OECD Committee on Fiscal Affairs has just completed a comprehensive report on the subject of the determination of transfer prices between associated enterprises. In carrying out its work, the Committee on Fiscal Affairs held consultations with both BIAC and TUAC. The main objective of the report is to set out as far as possible the considerations to be taken into account and to describe, where possible, generally agreed practices in determining such prices for tax purposes. In its report, the Committee expresses the hope that 'the report will not only help tax officials to approach more effectively the problems presented to them by the transfer prices of multinational enterprises but will also help the enterprises themselves by indicating ways in which mutually satisfactory solutions may be found to those tax problems'. The OECD Council has approved the report for publication together with a Recommendation which states, inter alia, that governments of Member countries are recommended 'that their tax administrations take into account, when reviewing and, if necessary, adjusting transfer prices between associated enterprises for the purposes of determining taxable profits, the considerations and methods set out in the Report referred to above for arriving at arm's length prices when goods, technology, trademarks and services are provided or supplied, or loans granted, between associated enterprises'. The Committee on International Investment and Multinational Enterprises shares the expectation of the Committee on Fiscal Affairs that the report will be of help to MNEs and recommends it to their attention.

To date, this is the chapter of the Guidelines to which the Committee has devoted most time. This fact is a reflection both of the importance and complexity of the subject matter covered by the employment and industrial relations Guidelines and of the wishes of some governments and of trade unions (represented by TUAC) to seek further clarification of the precise scope and intent of these guidelines.

*(i)   Right of employees to be represented by trade unions and other bona fide organisations of employees (paragraphs 1 and 2)** Paragraph 1 provides that MNEs should 'respect the right of their employees to be represented by trade unions and other bona fide organisations of employees'. The conditions under which these rights are exercised are a matter of national laws, regulations and practices. Thus it was agreed during the drafting of the Guidelines that they would not seek to indicate what organisations in a specific sense should represent employees for collective bargaining or what criteria should be used for the selection of such organisations. It remains, however, that paragraph 1 does provide expressly for management engaging in constructive negotiations with employee representatives on employment conditions and the provision of paragraph 2 adds that enterprises are expected to co-operate with representatives of employees for the specific purposes stated in paragraphs 1 and 2. Thus, the thrust of these provisions of the Guidelines is towards having management adopt a positive approach towards the activities of trade unions and other bona fide organisations of employees of all categories and in particular, an open attitude towards organisational activities within the framework of national rules and practices.

While not explicitly addressing the issue, the Guidelines imply that the management of MNEs should adopt a co-operative attitude towards the participation of employees in international meetings for consultation and exchanges of views among themselves provided that the functioning of the operations of the enterprises and the normal procedures which govern relationships with representatives of the employees and their organisations are not thereby prejudiced.

The Committee has not considered the question of the conduct of collective bargaining at an international level, for which there are no real examples, although there has been some development of trade union efforts to co-ordinate approaches to multinational enterprises on a cross-country basis. The question has been raised, however,

*Unless otherwise stated, paragraphs cited in this section refer to the chapter of the Guidelines on Employment and Industrial Relations.

whether the Employment and Industrial Relations Guideline could put obstacles in the way of recognition by the management of an MNE, in agreement with the national trade unions it has recognised and consistent with national laws and practices, of an International Trade Secretariat as a 'bona fide organisation of employees' referred to in paragraph 1 of the Guidelines. It is the Committee's view that no such obstacle exists or was intended in the Guidelines.

(ii) Provision of information to employees (paragraphs 2 and 3) Provision of information to employees is usually dealt with under national systems of labour relations or, more recently, by legislation and is an area where national diversity is great. Given this diversity, the Guidelines, nevertheless, make some very relevant recommendations in this area.

Attention is drawn, in particular, in this connection to paragraph 2(b) which calls for the provision to employees of 'information which is needed for meaningful negotiations on conditions of employment'. The word 'meaningful' has to be applied, of course, to the circumstances of each case; but it is a term which will be of operational value to persons experienced in labour relations. Again, paragraph 3 speaks of the provision of information, where this accords to local law and practice, enabling representatives of employees to obtain 'a true and fair view of the performance of the entity or, where appropriate, the enterprise as a whole'. A list of items which would be covered by this wording would not be practicable as it would differ from one country to another. This is particularly the case where information on future plans of the enterprise is concerned. As is known, this is still a very controversial area of industrial and social policy in a number of OECD Member countries. Consequently, recourse has to be made to the introduction to the Guidelines referring to the framework of national laws, regulations and practices. Within such a framework, however, and subject to legitimate interests of business confidentiality, management is encouraged by this paragraph to adopt an open and co-operative attitude to the provision of information to employees relevant to the objective of this paragraph, which could include information on future plans.

Reference is made to paragraph 8 of the Introduction to the Guidelines in which the responsibilities of the various entities within a multinational enterprise are described. If an entity in a given country is not able to provide information to the employees in accordance with paragraph 2(b) and 3, the other entities of the enterprise are expected to co-operate and assist one another as necessary to facilitate observance of the Guidelines. Since representatives of employees may experience difficulties in obtaining such information at the national level, this provision of the Guidelines introduces a useful supplementary standard in this respect.

(iii) Changes in operations (paragraph 6) The management decisions, to which the term 'changes in their operations', in paragraph 6 refers, would cover, in addition to the closure of an entity, which is specifically mentioned in the text, other measures 'which would have major effects upon the livelihood of employees'. The key notions in this paragraph of the Guidelines are the 'reasonable notice' to be given of such changes and actions by management and co-operation with employee representatives and appropriate governmental authorities 'so as to mitigate to the maximum extent practicable adverse effects'.

It has seemed to the Committee that there is a link between these two notions. The notice given has to be sufficiently timely for the purpose of mitigating action to be prepared and put into effect; otherwise, it would not meet the criterion of 'reasonable'. It would be in conformity with the general intention of this paragraph, in the light of the specific circumstances of each case, if management were able to provide such notice prior to the final decision being taken.

(iv) Unfair influence in bona fide negotiations with employees (paragraph 8) Paragraph 8 refers to threats 'to utilise a capacity to transfer the whole or part of an operating unit from the country concerned in order to influence unfairly bona fide negotiations with representatives of employees'. The Committee recalled that this paragraph as drafted was meant to cover only operations involving existing plant and equipment. Nevertheless, future investments, such as replacement of equipment or the introduction of new technology may be crucial to the survival of the enterprises in the medium and long-term and thus may be of interest in this context.

An important issue with respect to paragraph 8 is the distinction between legitimate provision of information and threats designed to influence unfairly negotiations with employees. It was recognised that the term 'unfair' was the key notion in this context. A distinction should be made between information given to employees on the likely consequences for the future of the firm as a going concern of the eventual outcome of such negotiations and threats which would be an unfair use of the management's negotiating power. If certain demands in the view of management have serious implications on the economic viability of this enterprise, it would be appropriate to point this out to employee representatives in the course of negotiations. Yet, management in such instances should be prepared to provide information in order to support this claim.

The Committee also considered the question whether the transfer of employees from a foreign affiliate in order to influence unfairly bona fide negotiations with employee representatives on conditions of employment would be contrary to standards set out in the Employment and Industrial Relations chapter and more particularly to paragraph 8. In the view of the Committee, such behaviour, while not specifically mentioned in the Guidelines, certainly would not be in conformity with the general spirit and approach underlying the drafting of the Employment and Industrial Relations chapter. Accordingly, it is recommended that enterprises should definitely avoid recourse to such practices in the future. The Committee, therefore, proposes that this recommendation, which does not imply a major change of the Guidelines, should be made explicit in the text of paragraph 8 by the following addition (amended language in italics):

> 'Enterprises should within the framework of law, regulations and prevailing labour relations and employment practices, in each of the countries in which they operate,
>
> In the context of bona fide negotiations* with representatives of employees on conditions of employment, or while employees are exercising a right to organise, not threaten to utilise a capacity to transfer the whole or part of an operating unit from the country concerned *nor transfer employees from the enterprises' component entities in other countries* in order to influence unfairly those negotiations or to hinder the exercise of a right to organise.

(v) Access to decision makers (paragraph 9)   When negotiations or collective bargaining are proceeding in the context of any parent subsidiary relationship, there is clearly a possibility that the subsidiary may not be fully empowered to negotiate and to conclude an agreement. There may be special problems in the case of a subsidiary which is situated in one country whilst the parent company is situated in another. The purpose of the text of paragraph 9 was to lay stress on the access of employee representatives to management representatives 'who are authorised to take decisions on the matters under negotiation'. This is the key consideration and the management of an MNE should see that it is observed in the circumstances of each case.

There is also paragraph 8 of the Introduction to the Guidelines which is germane to the matter discussed under paragraph 9 of the Employment and Industrial Relations Guidelines. This text recalls that 'the

---

*Bona fide negotiations may include labour disputes as part of the process of negotiation Whether or not labour disputes are so included will be determined by the law and prevailing employment practices of particular countries.

330

Guidelines are addressed to the various entities within the multinational enterprise (parent companies and/or local entities) according to the actual distribution of responsibilities among them on the understanding that they will co-operate and provide assistance to one another as necessary to facilitate observance of the Guidelines'. Parent companies, therefore, are expected to take the necessary organisational steps to enable their subsidiaries to observe the Guidelines, inter alia, by providing them with adequate and timely information and ensuring that their representatives who carry out negotiations at the national or local level have sufficient authority to take decisions on the matters under negotiation.

Science and technology

To date the several issues under this chapter which have been brought to the Committee's attention have related to research and development activities undertaken outside the country of the parent company of a multinational group — which it is widely feared in host countries will remain the poor relation in the overall research and development activities of the group unless positive action is taken by top management to spread such activities more widely geographically — and to the diffusion of technologies. It is the intent of paragraph 1 of this chapter that, within the limits of economic feasibility and other relevant circumstances, MNEs should consider seriously the steps they can take to distribute their research and development activities more widely among the countries in which they operate and thereby contribute to the innovative capacity of host countries. These matters are, of course, also of considerable importance to home countries and indeed in some Member countries trade unions have expressed concern about the potential domestic effects of transfers of proprietary technology from home to host countries. Paragraphs 2 and 3 of the same chapter of the Guidelines urge MNEs to encourage a rapid diffusion of the results of their research and development activities on reasonable terms and conditions.

Aside from the consideration in this Committee of issues arising under the Science and Technology chapter of the Guidelines, the Organisation's work in this area is centred in the Science and Technological Policy Committee's ad hoc Policy Group on Multinational Enterprises which is studying the effects of MNEs on the national scientific and technological potential of countries in which they operate. Of particular note are three case studies nearing completion by that Group which examine these effects in three industrial sectors, namely, pharmaceuticals, computers and food processing.

V   Follow-up procedures for the Guidelines

The national level

The effectiveness of the Guidelines, that is, the extent to which they are known, understood and accepted by multinational enterprises and integrated into management thinking and practices depends crucially upon action taken at the national level. Effective follow-up procedures can be of various kinds. While significant efforts in this regard have been made since 1976, this Review has revealed a need to strengthen such efforts.

It is recommended that governments, the business community and workers' organisations undertake further promotional and educational activities to make more widely known the content of the Guidelines and the manner in which they are to be implemented. A special effort in this regard is required with enterprises which are partly or wholly state-owned. Further promotional action is also needed with regard to those areas where awareness and understanding of the Guidelines may not yet be sufficiently advanced such as smaller enterprises and the service sector.

The Committee welcomes the fact that a number of individual multinational enterprises have stated publicly that they support and subscribe to the Guidelines. Such statements can have an important reinforcing effect on obtaining wider recognition and acceptance of the Guidelines. Consequently it is recommended to all enterprises concerned that they indicate publicly their acceptance of the Guidelines, preferably in their annual reports. Furthermore, enterprises are invited to include in their subsequent annual reports brief statements on their experience with the Guidelines, which may contain mention of steps taken with respect to their observance as well as any difficulties experienced in this respect. Such statements would be particularly useful with respect to the chapter on Disclosure of Information.

Member governments will henceforth submit every two years reports to OECD on experience and pertinent developments at the national level in all matters related to the Guidelines. These reports will enable the Committee on International Investment and Multinational Enterprises to assess the extent of acceptance and observance of the Guidelines, the action taken within OECD Member countries by governments, business and labour organisations, and the companies themselves to give effect to them, and the areas where problems are being encountered.

Member governments which have not already done so will provide facilities for handling enquiries and for discussions with the parties concerned on matters relating to the Guidelines. They intend to inform the business community, employee organisations and other interested parties of the appropriate contact point(s) within the government for enquiries on matters related to the Guidelines. The Committee believes that such facilities, existing examples of which are listed in Annex I, could usefully contribute to the solution of problems relating to the Guidelines which may arise and that, in any event, as a general principle such prior contacts and discussions at the national level should take place before matters are raised at the international level.

The international level

The intergovernmental consultation procedures provided by the 1976 Decision have the objective of ensuring that an effective forum exists in which Member governments may exchange views on all matters related to the Guidelines and the experience gained in their application and receive periodically the views on these matters of business and labour organisations through the two advisory bodies, BIAC and TUAC. The Committee is of the opinion that these procedures have generally worked well during the initial three-year period but that this experience should be put to use to introduce certain improvements during the next phase.

The Committee wishes to acknowledge the great benefit it has derived from the frequent contacts it has had with the two advisory bodies, BIAC and TUAC. Paragraph 2 of the 1976 Decision on Inter-governmental Consultation Procedures reflects the important role BIAC and TUAC are expected to play in the application of the Guidelines. Accordingly, these bodies were provided with the opportunity to express directly to the Committee their views on matters related to the Guidelines. In the understanding of the Committee, the presentation of such views is not limited to periodic consultations; rather, BIAC and TUAC may communicate their views to the Committee at any time.

The Committee and its Working Group on the Guidelines have been fortunate in finding a general willingness on the part of BIAC and TUAC to take a pragmatic and informal approach to the discussion of matters of common interest. As a result, in addition to the periodic consultations between the Committee and the two advisory bodies as are provided for in the 1976 Decision which up to now have been held once a year, a new approach has evolved, based upon more frequent exchanges of views of an informal character between the Working Group on the Guidelines and the two advisory bodies and upon contacts between the secretariats of the OECD and of these bodies. These contacts have proved to be valuable in clarifying issues and in instituting the practice of informal exchanges of views on matters of common interest. Some important results of these contacts are reflected, inter alia, in the explanatory material included in this report on certain questions which have arisen with respect to the scope and meaning of some parts of the Guidelines. The discussions of the Committee on substantive issues relating to the follow-up of the Guidelines have also benefited from these informal contacts, and the Committee expects that they will become a permanent feature of its procedures. The Committee and its Working Group on the Guidelines will take a positive attitude to requests by the advisory bodies for holding an exchange of views on any matter related to the Guidelines. The following amendment to paragraph 2 of the 1976 Decision on Intergovernmental Consultation Procedures on the Guidelines is accordingly proposed to make this understanding more explicit (amended language in italics):

> 2. The Committee shall periodically invite the Business and Industry Advisory Committee to OECD (BIAC) and the Trade Union Advisory Committee to OECD (TUAC) to express their views on matters related to the Guidelines. *In addition, exchanges of views with the advisory bodies on these matters may be held upon request by the latter.* The Committee shall take account of such views in its reports to the Council.

The Committee has had exchanges of views on a number of cases submitted by governments and the advisory bodies, relating either to alleged non-conformity with provisions of the Guidelines or illustrating problem areas regarding their application. These submissions have proved to be useful in permitting the Committee to gain experience with the Guidelines. The possibility of making such submissions should continue to be open to the advisory bodies as well as to governments but an attempt should be made first to settle the questions involved at the national level and, when appropriate, such efforts should be pursued at the bilateral level, i.e. involving the governments concerned. Where issues related to the Guidelines are identified by governments and/or one of the advisory bodies, the matter may be raised with the Committee. In that event, the government(s) and the parties concerned should be informed in advance of the issues and the points involved.

In connection with such submissions, the Committee feels it important to reaffirm the principle set out in paragraph 3 of the 1976 Decision, which states that 'the Committee shall not reach conclusions on the conduct of individual enterprises'. There were good reasons for this restriction in 1976, in particular, that the Committee was not seen as a judicial or quasi-judicial forum, and those reasons still remain valid today. The Committee, therefore, has avoided drawing any conclusions as to the conformity or non-conformity of a certain behaviour with the

Guidelines but has used the details of the specific cases as illustration of issues arising under the Guidelines. This approach has proved to be useful for the purpose of clarifying the meaning of the Guidelines in the light of specific problems and resulted in the explanatory comments included in the present report.

An important element in the Committee's work as described in paragraph 84 is the identification of issues relating to the application of the Guidelines. It would be detrimental to the credibility of the exercise if the Committee were to content itself with discussing only problems in the abstract, using for that purpose purely hypothetical situations. At the same time, in avoiding purely hypothetical discussions, it would be unfair if issues brought to the Committee's attention contained allegations regarding enterprise behaviour concerning the Guidelines without the enterprise which is subject to such allegations being informed when matters of interest to it are likely to be discussed and of the possibility open to it to state its views. In order to get a complete and fair understanding of circumstances relevant to the application of the Guidelines, the Committee welcomes the presentation of views by an enterprise concerned. It will not request an enterprise to make such a presentation but enterprises who wish to present their views without the necessity of government sponsorship may do so. Such views could be communicated through BIAC, government delegations or directly to the Committee itself. Accordingly, the following amendment of paragraph 3 and a new paragraph 4 of the Decision on Intergovernmental Consultation Procedures on the Guidelines is proposed:

> 3. If it so wishes, an individual enterprise will be given the opportunity to express its views either orally or in writing on issues concerning the Guidelines involving its interests.

> 4. The Committee shall not reach conclusions on the conduct of individual enterprises.

Earlier in this report the Committee underlined the importance to the credibility of the Guidelines of its being able to provide clarification where this is found to be needed in the light of specific situations. In proposing that its report should be published, the Committee intends that the explanatory comments it has developed on issues which have been raised over the past three years will be made available to those directly concerned and to the general public. For the future, the Committee intends to respond in a timely manner to further requests for clarifications. Where such responses are possible, they will be given to the interested parties, as appropriate, through informal contacts or in the context of formal consultations as well as in the periodic reports of the Committee to the Council. In order to reflect the Committee's role in clarifying the Guidelines, the following addition to paragraph 1 of the Decision on Intergovernmental Consultation Procedures on the Guidelines is proposed after the first sentence of this paragraph:

> The Committee shall be responsible for clarification of the Guidelines. Clarification will be provided as required.

The Committee recognises the desirability of keeping the interested parties and the general public informed of its activities on matters relating to the Guidelines as well as on the other parts of the 1976 Declaration. One possible vehicle for providing this information, as well as reporting on any further explanatory comments on the Guidelines which the Committee may find it necessary to develop, could be the periodic reports by the Committee to the Council called for in the Decision on Intergovernmental Consultation Procedures. The Committee intends to submit a report to the Council in 1982 with the recommendation that it should be published.

The Committee recommends that it would be appropriate for the next formal review of the Guidelines and the related Decision to be undertaken within five years. This provision of a five-year review period, which is somewhat longer than the initial three-year review period, would have the advantage of providing a stable framework for the implementation of the Guidelines and would allow adequate time for the follow-up procedures set out in this section to develop. As is noted in the following chapters, the Committee recommends that the review of other elements of the 1976 Declaration and the other two related Decisions should also be held at the same time. It should be understood, however, that this provision does not preclude the possibility of the Organisation subsequently deciding, on the basis of future developments, to review and/or make certain modifications to these instruments before the end of the five-year period should this prove necessary.*

---

*The timetable set out above will involve the following action by governments and by the Committee:

September 1981	Follow-up reports by governments
June 1982	Mid-term report by the IME Committee to Council at permanent delegation level
September 1983	Follow-up reports by governments dealing also, as required, with matters related to the next review
June 1984	Follow-up and report by the IME Committee for the Review by Ministerial Council of the Declaration and Decisions on International Investment and Multinational Enterprises.

II(i) TUAC STATEMENT FOR THE MID-TERM REPORT ON THE OECD GUIDELINES FOR MULTINATIONAL ENTERPRISES
(submitted to Governments, 14 October 1981)

I General comments

1   In connection with the 1982 mid-term report on the experiences with the OECD's Guidelines for Multinational Enterprises, two general issues have to be raised before a detailed examination of the Guidelines is made. The first one concerns the role of Guidelines (or Codes of Conduct) in discussing international economic policy. The mid-term report has to be seen against a broader background where one crucial question is the governments' real commitment to instruments covering the activities of multinational enterprises.

2   For a number of years the OECD's Ministerial Council has affirmed in its Communiqués the member countries' commitment to the necessary work for a United Nations Code of Conduct for Multinational Enterprises. It has been evident that the OECD Guidelines have served as a basis for the governments of industrialised democracies in discussions in the United Nations. The IME Committee has also been the focal point for these governments' preparations for the United Nations negotiations which should lead into a code of conduct reflecting the basic economic and social interests of both developing and developed countries.

3   The Communiqué of the Ministerial Council of 16—17 June, 1981, dropped specific references to the United Nations' work on a Code of Conduct. It endorsed the OECD's continuing efforts to facilitate international private capital flows, noting the 'significant and particularly effective role of direct investment, which carries with it the advantages of technical, managerial and marketing expertise'. The work of the United Nations in the areas of international investment, the transfer of technology and restrictive business practices was seen by the OECD's Ministers in this light, together with the familiar stress on the 'importance of an appropriate investment climate' (paragraph 28 of the Communiqué). The reliance on and promotion of private international capital flows was even more marked in the Communiqué of the Ottawa Summit.

4   The rapid internationalization of production brings about changes which call for increased attention by governments. It is generally accepted that multinational enterprises play an important role in world development. Their impact can be beneficial, if certain conditions are

fulfilled, but it can be detrimental to host and also home countries. This view is reflected in the Declaration on International Investment and Multinational Enterprises and the Guidelines of the OECD. In the present economic situation it is still more important that this balanced attitude, which has been a cornerstone of the activities that international organisations have in the Seventies undertaken regarding multinational enterprises is maintained. Trade unions are worried that there would be a shift towards more permissiveness, less monitoring or control, and in general, away from the need to eliminate the negative consequences of the activities of multinational enterprises.

5   If recent government statements signify a shift in policy, this has far-reaching implications on any further discussions on Guidelines for the behaviour of multinational enterprises. It would reverse commitments made since the adoption of the OECD Guidelines, in 1976, and it would seriously impair the credibility of any measures to implement them. Consequently, the first requirement of a report on the experiences with the Guidelines is that the Council of the OECD, at Ministerial level, reaffirms its commitment to them and other instruments which cover the activities of multinational enterprises.

6   The second basic observation of TUAC concerns the importance of Guidelines for the trade unions. Trade unions have been among the foremost proponents of efficient codes of conduct for the activities of multinational enterprises, also for the over-all economic interests of our societies. This does not mean that unions see these instruments as the main, let alone only way to keep in check the abuses these companies may commit. In a number of industrial sectors, and regarding several companies, trade unions have coped successfully with problems caused by multinational enterprises through their own action, by negotiations or otherwise. In several OECD countries, trade unions have obtained successful results in negotiations with multinational enterprises, as with national ones, without having to seek additional support from the Guidelines even though they would have been relevant. However, this does not mean that the Guidelines would not be useful in these sectors, or with such enterprises, especially where the issues under negotiation have an international dimension.

7   There are, however, differences between sectors, individual enterprises, and also countries. There are areas where rapid internationalization or rationalisation cause abrupt changes which affect the position of the workers. Problems have come up in banking, insurance, and on the whole in the service sectors, the role of which has recently also been underlined by the OECD, together with the persistent problems in all sectors of multinational enterprises following anti-union policies. With the growth of the service sector, unionization is

also increasing, and some multinationals attempt to counter this trend. When multinationals use the argument that workers lack the desire to organise, they hide the fact that consequent anti-union practices have in many cases contributed to a relatively weaker position of the workers in certain sectors, enterprises and/or countries. This has been demonstrated among others by the Citibank case.

8   Furthermore, in a period of economic recession, with closures and transfers of capital and production from one country to another or threats to do so, the multinational employer is in a qualitatively different and much stronger bargaining position than the national firms. In this context anti-union activities take on a new scope, when they are tied to the availability of investment capital. This is exemplified by the fact that multinationals include an assessment of the strength of unions in evaluations on the investment climate in various countries. A negative attitude towards trade unions is all the more regrettable as an orderly system of industrial relations should be in everyone's interests.

9   For the trade unions, codes of conduct are instruments which can supplement the activities they can by right undertake to defend their members' interests when the employer's action is determined by the multinational strategy of a company. These instruments rely strongly on the political will of governments which have drawn them up, in particular as decisions by a multinational enterprise do not only affect the workers directly concerned but the whole economic and social situation of the community where production is located. The member governments of the OECD did not adopt the Guidelines for Multi-national Enterprises solely because of pressure from the trade unions, but because of concerns on the control of their own economic and social future.

10   The overwhelming majority of their provisions of the Guidelines refer to interests of the member countries of the OECD. Thus e.g. the section on General Policies does not contain a single reference to trade unions. The section on Disclosure of Information does not speak about information to the workers but of information which presumably is necessary to governments in their monitoring the effects of the activities of multinational enterprises. The Guidelines are important for the trade unions, but compliance with them by multinational enter-prises is also of broader national interest. This has been demonstrated by the fact that some governments have supported the union views on cases involving this section of the Guidelines.

11   If governments base their policies for economic development on increased freedom of movement for multinational enterprises then the bargaining position of unions will not be the only one to be weakened. The even more serious result will be a growing uncertainty of the

future economic and social perspectives of our societies. A review on the efficiency of the OECD Guidelines on Multinational Enterprises is incomplete, if this question is not seriously tackled.

II   The experience of trade unions

12   TUAC has conducted a survey among its affiliates, together with inputs from the International Trade Secretariats. This survey covered four broad areas: (a) Experiences with national contact points; (b) National legislative or administrative action; (c) Employer action; and (d) Action by the unions themselves. The conclusions concerning each of these sections are based on the responses received, and they are followed by a section which singles out the Guidelines that have shown to be of the most concern to the trade unions.

National contact points

13   The main achievements of the national contact points seem so far to have been to translate the Guidelines and disseminate them to employers and trade union organisations. In some countries they have been made available only upon request. There are instances where the results of the 1979 Review of the Guidelines have been less publicised than the Guidelines originally were (Japan), although the review set out the implementation procedure, including the establishment of national contact points. Only in relatively few countries have the unions been consulted on the terms of reference of the contact points and/or directly involved in their work (Denmark, Finland, Netherlands, Belgium, Sweden). No such interaction is reported in other countries, including some major ones (United Kingdom, France, Germany, Italy). In some countries, the unions have reported difficulties in even locating the contact point (Ireland). There is no uniformity in the approach national contact points have to trade unions, and their terms of reference vary considerably. The relationship between the procedure of the national contact points and established national legislation and practice on certain items has to be further clarified. Also, co-operation between different governments bodies remains on the whole insufficient.

14   Active assistance in solving cases arising under the Guidelines has been forthcoming only in few countries (again Denmark, Finland, Netherlands, Sweden). In these countries, the contact points have also discussed with both trade unions and the employers their participation in the IME Committee. In some countries, contact points have indicated their willingness in the future to involve trade unions,

although this has not yet been the case (Italy). But in most countries, the contact points have been more passive, at best giving minimum response when a case has been brought to their attention. In some countries, the contact points have remained as letter-boxes when requests have been made to them, and they have not even taken action when approached by other governments. In some cases only the necessity to prepare the national contributions to the mid-term report has led the national contact point into contacting the trade unions (United Kingdom, Austria).

15   To the knowledge of TUAC, in no country have the national contact points taken up an issue on their own initiative. Even in countries where the contact points have been comparatively active they have not engaged in collecting data on the observance of the Guidelines by the multinational enterprises (Netherlands). But some contact points have, in sending out the Guidelines to multinationals, requested them to reply on their compliance with them (Italy, Japan). The fact that national contact points are active only in relatively few countries can seriously distort the evaluation of the effectiveness of the Guidelines, as silence by many countries including large ones, might be taken as an indication that they do not have the same kind of problems others have dealt with.

National legislative or administrative action

16   There is no evidence that legislation or administrative measures would anywhere have been adopted as a result of the OECD's decisions on multinational enterprises. In some countries, legislation has been developed on matters which are touched upon in the Guidelines, such as control over the ownership of jointstock and limited liability companies and employees' representation in such companies (Denmark), and laws on co-operation in enterprises which widen the obligations of employers to negotiate (Finland). But even in these cases the legislative action has not been as a direct result of the Guidelines. On the other hand, in one country (United Kingdom) the contact point has responded to a request to give its views on the effect of retrospective legislation on the recognition provision of the Guidelines, after some provisions of the 1975 Employment Protection Act were amended and repealed. Consequently, even though some national contact points have included this in their terms of reference, there is no evidence to show that the governments would have taken the Guidelines as a frame of reference in developing national legislation or other instruments.

17   The proposal by the EEC Commission for draft directives for

information and consultation rights for trade unions in multinational enterprises has received broad support from TUAC affiliates in that area. This proposal builds on, and is complementary to, the OECD Guidelines and the ILO Declaration on Multinational Enterprises and Social Policy.

Employer action

18   In a number of countries, multinational enterprises have stated in their annual reports that they know the Guidelines and respect them. The wording of such statements has usually been vague. In the food and beverage sector, a multinational like Nestlé claims that its management policies 'are inspired by' the Guidelines, and Unilever 'remain supporters' of them. No example of reporting on the observance of the Guidelines has been recorded (e.g. what a multinational has done in connection with rationalisations or plant closures, how and when was information given to the employees, and how did the enterprise co-operate in mitigating adverse effects).

19   General statements on the Guidelines are reported from countries such as Belgium, United Kingdom, the Netherlands and Sweden. In the majority of member countries, the multinational enterprises do not seem to have made such statements of support. In any event such statements are not general practice. The view of TUAC affiliates is that even when this kind of general statements are made, they are not worth much, as they do not contain any information which would be useful for the trade unions in their dealings with the enterprises.

20   The provisions of the OECD Guidelines have come up in negotiations between trade unions and multinational enterprises, as a result of pressure by the unions. In Denmark, a multinational (Telerent, owned by the British firm Granada) agreed to sign a collective agreement with the union organising workers in the field after a conflict where the OECD Guidelines also were evoked. In Finland, there have been negotiations on items, such as conditions of work, which are covered by the Guidelines. Some effects of a threat to take up a contentious matter with the national contact point have been noted in Italy. In Sweden, some multinationals have initiated 'discussions' with the unions. There is also information, understandably not very precise, on cases where employers have agreed to negotiations with real decision makers on the condition that such compliance with the Guidelines not be made public. A specific case is that of Japan where overseas investment is one of the subjects of the labour-management consultation system.

21   In some instances multinationals have refused the invitation to

discussions on a specific case, when the unions have requested the national contact point to issue such an invitation. Refusals were made by KLM and Philips, in the Netherlands, in the cases on the European Airline Groupings and the closure of a subsidiary of Philips in Finland.

22   It is impossible to reach the conclusion that multinational enterprises would have modified their behaviour due to the Guidelines. No such modifications have been noted by TUAC affiliates, unless one considers positive the absence of further conflicts with an enterprise whose activities have been taken up under the Guidelines (Hertz in Denmark). The national unions which have reported changes in some enterprises' behaviour have ascribed this to the result of trade union action.

23   On disclosure of information, a recent survey conducted by the trade unions in Germany concluded that major multinational enterprises do not take seriously the requirements to publish information on their activities. The survey covered 35 enterprises, of which in the beginning of 1981 only 2 published their operating results by geographical area, 9 enterprises published statements on the sources and uses of funds by the enterprise as a whole, 12 published employment data, and none disclosed information on policies followed in respect of intra-group pricing. A Swedish study concluded that information on items which are in the Guidelines but not required by national legislation is insufficiently reported by the companies. This concerned particularly sales and investments by geographical area, R & D expenditure and intra-group pricing. Foreign-owned companies were noted to report better on R & D expenditure, operating results and sales by geographical area and also intra-group pricing than Swedish owned companies which, however, had a better performance on employment data.

24   TUAC's expectations as to the activities of national employers' organisations are based on the view that once BIAC has expressed its support to the Guidelines, and engaged in promotional activities, this should naturally be effectively carried out by its constituent parts. Employers' federations have made general statements of support in the Nordic countries, United Kingdom, the Netherlands, Germany, and the United States. In France, the employers' federation has after some hesitation also gone on the record with a cautious statement of support for the Guidelines. But in most cases their activities seem to have limited themselves to making the Guidelines better known through disseminating them to their members and the publishing of newspaper articles. Their recommendations have also been accompanied by cautions that time is needed for enterprises to adapt themselves to the Guidelines. Such qualifications can serve as an alibi for not doing any-

thing, and they are all the more strange as the Guidelines have been in existence since 1976, and as they were drafted in sufficiently clear language. It seems that the calls of employers' federations have not been heeded to by the overwhelming majority of the multinational enterprises, which have often criticised or even rejected the positions of the employers' central organisations.

25   There are, however, cases where national employers' federations have attempted to hinder a wider applicability of the Guidelines. Thus, in Sweden the employers' federation issued a circular forbidding enterprises from signing agreements with the unions which would have included the observation of the Guidelines. Similar action has been taken by national employers' organisations in the United States. These examples have contributed to the trade unions' concern that at the national level, not only individual enterprises but even employers' federations are reluctant to follow up decisions that international employers' organisations have accepted and supported. At least in one case (Viggo in Sweden), the employers' organisation engaged itself in directly misleading informative activities once the IME Committee had reached its conclusions.

26   There does not seem to be any noticeable difference between the behaviour of private and state-owned multinational enterprises. Although problems concerning multinationals in most peoples' minds are related to the private sector, totally or partially state owned enterprises have been involved in the follow-up procedures. In the light of the case of the European Airlines Groupings, it is not possible to say that state-owned enterprises would behave any better than private ones.

Action by trade unions

27   Throughout the follow-up process, TUAC and its affiliates have been the main actors keeping the issues alive. All clarifications have come about due to cases presented by the trade unions. The cases trade unions have brought up to the OECD, through TUAC, in the period since 1979 have all been discussed by the national contact points. Thus, the procedure established by the review of the Guidelines has been observed. Written clarifications have been received to two submissions, those on British Oxygen Corporated International and its Swedish subsidiary Viggo, and on the case of the European Airlines Groupings. By and large these replies have upheld the view of TUAC on these cases. In reconfirming these clarifications in the mid-term report, OECD's Council should in particular spell out the clarification TUAC received on the Philips case: this was given orally in consultation with

the IME Committee on 12 March, 1981.

28   The trade unions have launched a number of activities to make the Guidelines better known and to inform their members on how to use them. Such activities have included the publishing of handbooks and negotiators' guides on the Guidelines. There have been bilateral union contacts, including fact-finding missions to establish co-operation between unions in the home and host countries (examples of this were the Philips case and co-operation between Japanese and U.S. unions). Such contacts have also led into solidarity action. In several countries, special courses have been arranged for those who are in charge of negotiations with multinational enterprises. The Guidelines have also become a standard item in the normal trade union education pro-grammes in many countries. Further material has been published in the trade union press and other publications. The aim has been to in particular familiarise the shop stewards with the Guidelines as much as possible.

29   In some countries, items included in the Guidelines have been introduced in the process of collective bargaining. The trade unions maintain that one of the most efficient ways of making the Guidelines work is to have an assurance of their observance in collective agree-ments. This approach has, however, met with strong employer opposition. The reasons for this opposition have been difficult to understand.

Main paragraphs for further review

30   The experiences gained so far by trade unions permit to single out a number of paragraphs where further action is needed. The ensuing commentaries may call for either action by national authorities, further clarification of the Guidelines, or revision of them.

31   Cases where the Guidelines have been evoked have almost exclusively concerned two sections, i.e. Disclosure of Information and Employment and Industrial Relations. It is also obvious that in the future, these two areas call for considerable work. Multinational enter-prises should be obliged to follow the requirements contained in the Guidelines on the Disclosure of Information. Even though the data required should be easily available, this section is widely ignored. In particular the data on employment, restructuring, investments and disinvestments should be published. The concept of 'geographical area' is too vague: in order to be useful, the information should be published country by country. This section of the Guidelines is particularly important because if its requirements are not observed, the intentions underlying key paragraphs of the Employment and Industrial Relations

Guidelines cannot be realised.

32   Virtually all of the Employment and Industrial Relations Guidelines have come up in different conflicts. Of these, the first one, the respect of the right of employees to be represented by trade unions, remains violated on a large scale. Recent examples of this have been given by foreign enterprises that have invested in the United States (among others Sharp and Bosch corporations), in Japan (IBM), and in the United Kingdom (Conoco, and the case of Citibank which was already in 1978 submitted to the OECD, without tangible results). Some multinational enterprises respect their workers right to be unionized at home but not abroad. One such example is Toshiba, which for its operations in the United States hired a local consultant firm specializing in anti-union practices. The case was solved through bilateral U.S.–Japanese union co-operation. The above-mentioned events are not submitted by TUAC to the OECD as cases, but they are illustrations of a persistent and widespread malpractice.

33   The Citibank case has shown the limits of the follow-up measures as no action has been taken against an outright and clearly recognised violation of this Guideline. If the Guidelines cannot assist in putting an end to anti-union practices, i.e. if paragraph 1 of the Employment and Industrial Relations Guidelines is not honoured, it is difficult to convince trade unions of the real value of their other provisions.

34   Some multinationals (in particular a multinational bank established in Denmark) have refused to negotiate with the workers in the national language. This is contrary to paragraph 2(a) of the Employment and Industrial Relations Guidelines, and thought could be given to explicitly require that management negotiates with the representatives of the workers in their own language.

35   Apart from the issue of union recognition, most cases reported to TUAC concern paragraphs 2, 3, 5, 6 and 9 of the Employment and Industrial Relations Guidelines, indicating that in this area major problems remain. For example, of the ten cases taken up by the trade unions in the Netherlands since June, 1979, all touched upon paragraphs 3, 6 and 9.

36   The partial answer which the IME Committee gave in December, 1980, on paragraph 9, with also reference to paragraph 8 of the Introduction to the Guidelines, should be expanded. TUAC expects that the following points, contained in the oral answer given by the IME Committee on 12 March, 1981, would be included in the mid-term report:

— Paragraph 9 of the Employment and Industrial Relations Guidelines is also destined to prevent a situation where management says that it cannot negotiate with the representatives of the workers.

- The representatives of the workers have the right to be informed on who at the end of the day is authorised to take decisions on the matters under negotiations.

- If it becomes clear that the representatives of management conducting negotiations do not have the authority to take decisions on the matters under negotiations, the enterprise concerned has acted contrary to the Guidelines.

37 The principle of access to real decision makers presupposes that the companies give the necessary information on their decision-making structure in general. As this obligation is not expressedly covered by the existing Guidelines, they should be revised to include it. This could be done by either amending paragraph 3 of the Employment and Industrial Relations Guidelines so that it covers also the decision making structure of the enterprise, or including the requirement to give this information under point (i) of the Guidelines on Disclosure of Information.

III Concluding observations

38 In making a survey on the experiences of affiliated trade union organisations regarding the Guidelines, TUAC also asked for general observations on their effectiveness. The views expressed in paragraphs 6−9 of this document cover some of these, as also does the section on national contact points (paragraphs 13−15). In way of conclusions, some specific issues can be underlined.

39 Cases are not always brought up by the unions to the national contact points or the IME Committee, even when the Guidelines clearly are relevant and also are used as an argument in negotiations. One reason is that the procedure in national contact points, and the IME Committee, takes a long time, although it has always been broadly accepted that where labour matters are concerned, procedures have to be speedy, as vital interests of a large number of people are directly concerned. Conclusions on the behaviour of a specific multinational enterprise are rarely made. It is to be noted that the terms of reference of regrettably many national contact points do not include the possibility of reaching conclusions on the behaviour of individual multinationals. Unions naturally first rely on their own bargaining strength. The implementation procedure of the Guidelines comes often up only when bargaining has ended, i.e. when the case itself is closed but when unions feel that it has highlighted aspects which need further discussion and action, to prevent similar cases in the future.

40   Trade unions consider that the direct value of the Guidelines is limited, not only because of the cumbersome and unrewarding implementation procedure, but also because the voluntary nature of the Guidelines hinders any efficient implementation when a company is reluctant to comply with them. For instance in a recent case in Sweden, concerning the decision of Goodyear to close down production, no negotiations with the real decision makers took place despite involvement by the Minister of Industry. In the case of Citibank, the national contact point in the United Kingdom has justified its lack of action by the fact that the Guidelines are voluntary.

41   TUAC has consistently seen the Guidelines as one step towards effective rules and regulations covering the activities of multinational enterprises. Its expectation after the 1979 Review was that the then introduced procedure would make the voluntary Guidelines more efficient. Despite some positive developments, the over-all feeling of the trade unions now is one of disappointment.

42   Responses given by the IME Committee since the 1979 review to TUAC submissions have, on the whole, been positive, even though they have not been followed by national action − which in itself weakens the credibility of the follow-up action at the OECD level. It is particularly important to continue work on the whole problem of the access to real decision makers. Trade unions also note with satisfaction that in some countries, national authorities have engaged both themselves and the unions in the attempt to implement the Guidelines. But these countries are few, and the limitations are soon recognised.

43   The reasons for the trade unions' disappointment should be evident. There is no significant change in the behaviour of the multinational enterprises. National authorities lack the initiative to monitor their activities, and they have not themselves taken up any cases where multinationals have violated the numerous provisions of the Guidelines that deal with over-all national interests. With some exceptions contact points have been passive. The mid-term report should conclude that all contact points should live up to the expectations spelled out in the Report of the 1979 Review. The TUAC views on how these contact points should function have been spelled out during earlier consultations with the IME Committee, e.g. on 6 March, 1980. The implementation of the Guidelines has proved to be too slow and bureaucratic to be of immediate use in practical situations. Finally, national legislation or administrative practice have not been developed further along the lines indicated by the Guidelines.

44   TUAC has seen the Guidelines as an element in an evolving process, supplementing national rules and regulations and assisting in

heir further development. Such an evolution is all the more necessary
1 a period of recession, with rising levels of unemployment. The
ctivities of multinational enterprises should not aggravate the
conomic situation and cause more unemployment, in particular as
hese enterprises have the means to provide for stability in the fields of
mployment and industrial relations. But this calls for a revitalization
·f the process introduced in 1976 and continued in 1979, instead of
bandoning the control of significant parts of the economic and social
evelopment of our societies to multinational enterprises. TUAC
eaffirms its conviction that there is an urgent need for international
o-operation by governments to ensure that the multinational enter-
·rises observe minimum standards and accept a frame of co-operation
vhich is beneficial to all concerned.

Appendix III
principally relating to Part IV

III(a)   INTERNATIONAL LABOUR ORGANISATION
TRIPARTITE DECLARATION OF PRINCIPLES CON-
CERNING MULTINATIONAL ENTERPRISES AND
SOCIAL POLICY
(adopted by the Governing Body of the International Labour Offic
November 1977)

The Governing Body of the International Labour Office;
    Recalling that the International Labour Organisation for many yea
has been involved with certain social issues related to the activities o
multinational enterprises;
    Noting in particular that various Industrial Committees, Region.
Conferences, and the International Labour Conference since the mic
1960s have requested appropriate action by the Governing Body in th
field of multinational enterprises and social policy;
    Having been informed of the activities of other international bodie
in particular the UN Commission on Transnational Corporations an
the Organisation for Economic Co-operation and Developmer
(OECD);
    Considering that the ILO, with its unique tripartite structure, i
competence, and its longstanding experience in the social field, has a
essential role to play in evolving principles for the guidance of goverr
ments, workers' and employers' organisations, and multination:
enterprises themselves;
    Recalling that it convened a Tripartite Meeting of Experts on th
Relationship between Multinational Enterprises and Social Policy i
1972, which recommended an ILO programme of research and study
and a Tripartite Advisory Meeting on the Relationship of Multination:
Enterprises and Social Policy in 1976 for the purpose of reviewing th
ILO programme of research and suggesting appropriate ILO action i
the social and labour field;
    Bearing in mind the deliberations of the World Employment Cor

ference;

Having thereafter decided to establish a tripartite group to prepare a Draft Tripartite Declaration of Principles covering all of the areas of ILO concern which relate to the social aspects of the activities of multinational enterprises, including employment creation in the developing countries, all the while bearing in mind the recommendations made by the Tripartite Advisory Meeting held in 1976;

Having also decided to reconvene the Tripartite Advisory Meeting to consider the Draft Declaration of Principles as prepared by the tripartite group;

Having considered the Report and the Draft Declaration of Principles submitted to it by the reconvened Tripartite Advisory Meeting;

Hereby approves the following Declaration which may be cited as the Tripartite Declaration of Principles concerning Multinational Enterprises and Social Policy, adopted by the Governing Body of the International Labour Office, and invites governments of States Members of the ILO, the employers' and workers' organisations concerned and the multinational enterprises operating in their territories to observe the principles embodied therein.

1   Multinational enterprises play an important part in the economies of most countries and in international economic relations. This is of increasing interest to governments as well as to employers and workers and their respective organisations. Through international direct investment and other means such enterprises can bring substantial benefits to home and host countries by contributing to the more efficient utilisation of capital, technology and labour. Within the framework of development policies established by governments, they can also make an important contribution to the promotion of economic and social welfare; to the improvement of living standards and the satisfaction of basic needs; to the creation of employment opportunities, both directly and indirectly; and to the enjoyment of basic human rights, including freedom of association, throughout the world. On the other hand, the advances made by multinational enterprises in organising their operations beyond the national framework may lead to abuse of concentrations of economic power and to conflicts with national policy objectives and with the interest of the workers. In addition, the complexity of multinational enterprises and the difficulty of clearly perceiving their diverse structures, operations and policies sometimes give rise to concern either in the home or in the host countries, or in both.

2   The aim of this Tripartite Declaration of Principles is to encourage the positive contribution which multinational enterprises can make to

economic and social progress and to minimise and resolve the difficulties to which their various operations may give rise, taking into account the United Nations resolutions advocating the Establishment of a New International Economic Order.

3   This aim will be furthered by appropriate laws and policies, measures and actions adopted by the governments and by co-operation among the governments and the employers' and workers' organisations of all countries.

4   The principles set out in this Declaration are commended to the governments, the employers' and workers' organisations of home and host countries and to the multinational enterprises themselves.

5   These principles are intended to guide the governments, the employers' and workers' organisations and the multinational enterprises in taking such measures and actions and adopting such social policies, including those based on the principles laid down in the Constitution and the relevant Conventions and Recommendations of the ILO, as would further social progress.

6   To serve its purpose this Declaration does not require a precise legal definition of multinational enterprises; this paragraph is designed to facilitate the understanding of the Declaration and not to provide such a definition. Multinational enterprises include enterprises, whether they are of public, mixed or private ownership, which own or control production, distribution, services or other facilities outside the country in which they are based. The degree of autonomy of entities within multinational enterprises in relation to each other varies widely from one such enterprise to another, depending on the nature of the links between such entities and their fields of activity and having regard to the great diversity in the form of ownership, in the size, in the nature and location of the operations of the enterprises concerned. Unless otherwise specified, the term 'multinational enterprise' is used in this Declaration to designate the various entities (parent companies or local entities or both or the organisation as a whole) according to the distribution of responsibilities among them, in the expectation that they will co-operate and provide assistance to one another as necessary to facilitate observance of the principles laid down in the Declaration.

7   This Declaration sets out principles in the fields of employment, training, conditions of work and life and industrial relations which governments, employers' and workers' organisations and multinational enterprises are recommended to observe on a voluntary basis; its provisions shall not limit or otherwise affect obligations arising out of ratification of any ILO Convention.

352

General policies

8   All the parties concerned by this Declaration should respect the sovereign rights of States, obey the national laws and regulations, give due consideration to local practices and respect relevant international standards. They should respect the Universal Declaration of Human Rights and the corresponding International Covenants adopted by the General Assembly of the United Nations as well as the Constitution of the International Labour Organisation and its principles according to which freedom of expression and association are essential to sustained progress. They should also honour commitments which they have freely entered into, in conformity with the national law and accepted international obligations.

9   Governments which have not yet ratified Conventions Nos. 87, 98, 111 and 122 are urged to do so and in any event to apply, to the greatest extent possible, through their national policies, the principles embodied therein and in Recommendations Nos. 111, 119 and 122.* Without prejudice to the obligation of governments to ensure compliance with Conventions they have ratified, in countries in which the Conventions and Recommendations cited in this paragraph are not complied with, all parties should refer to them for guidance in their social policy.

10   Multinational enterprises should take fully into account established general policy objectives of the countries in which they operate. Their activities should be in harmony with the development priorities and social aims and structure of the country in which they operate. To this effect, consultations should be held between multinational enterprises, the government and, wherever appropriate, the national employers' and workers' organisations concerned.

11   The principles laid down in this Declaration do not aim at introducing or maintaining inequalities of treatment between multinational and national enterprises. They reflect good practice for all. Multinational and national enterprises, wherever the principles of this Declaration are relevant to both, should be subject to the same expectations in respect of their conduct in general and their social practices in particular.

---

*Convention (No.87) concerning Freedom of Association and Protection of the Right to Organise; Convention (No.98) concerning the Application of the Principles of the Right to Organise and to Bargain Collectively; Convention (No.111) concerning Discrimination in Respect of Employment and Occupation; Convention (No.122) concerning Employment Policy; Recommendation (No.111) concerning Discrimination in Respect of Employment and Occupation; Recommendation (No.119) concerning Termination of Employment at the Initiative of the Employer; Recommendation (No.122) concerning Employment Policy.

12 Governments of home countries should promote good social practice in accordance with this Declaration of Principles, having regard to the social and labour law, regulations and practices in host countries as well as to relevant international standards. Both host and home country governments should be prepared to have consultations with each other, whenever the need arises, on the initiative of either.

Employment

Employment promotion

13 With a view to stimulating economic growth and development, raising living standards, meeting manpower requirements and overcoming unemployment and underemployment, governments should declare and pursue, as a major goal, an active policy designed to promote full, productive and freely-chosen employment.[1]

14 This is particularly important in the case of host country governments in developing areas of the world where the problems of unemployment and underemployment are at their most serious. In this connection, the general conclusions adopted by the Tripartite World Conference on Employment, Income Distribution and Social Progress and the International Division of Labour (Geneva, June 1976) should be kept in mind.[2]

15 Paragraphs 13 and 14 above establish the framework within which due attention should be paid, in both home and host countries, to the employment impact of multinational enterprises.

16 Multinational enterprises, particularly when operating in developing countries, should endeavour to increase employment opportunities and standards, taking into account the employment policies and objectives of the governments, as well as security of employment and the long-term development of the enterprise.

17 Before starting operations, multinational enterprises should wherever appropriate, consult the competent authorities and the national employers' and workers' organisations in order to keep their manpower plans, as far as practicable, in harmony with national social development policies. Such consultation, as in the case of national enterprises, should continue between the multinational enterprises and all parties concerned, including the workers' organisations.

---

1 Convention (No.122) and Recommendation (No.122) concerning Employment Policy.
2 ILO, World Employment Conference, Geneva, 4–17 June 1976.

18   Multinational enterprises should give priority to the employment, occupational development, promotion and advancement of nationals of the host country at all levels in co-operation, as appropriate, with representatives of the workers employed by them or of the organisations of these workers and governmental authorities.

19   Multinational enterprises, when investing in developing countries, should have regard to the importance of using technologies which generate employment, both directly and indirectly. To the extent permitted by the nature of the process and the conditions prevailing in the economic sector concerned, they should adapt technologies to the needs and characteristics of the host countries. They should also, where possible, take part in the development of appropriate technology in host countries.

20   To promote employment in developing countries, in the context of an expanding world economy, multinational enterprises, wherever practicable, should give consideration to the conclusion of contracts with national enterprises for the manufacture of parts and equipment, to the use of local raw materials and to the progressive promotion of the local processing of raw materials. Such arrangements should not be used by multinational enterprises to avoid the responsibilities embodied in the principles of this Declaration.

Equality of opportunity and treatment

21   All governments should pursue policies designed to promote equality of opportunity and treatment in employment, with a view to eliminating any discrimination based on race, colour, sex, religion, political opinion, national extraction or social origin.[1]

22   Multinational enterprises should be guided by this general principle throughout their operations without prejudice to the measures envisaged in paragraph 18 or to government policies designed to correct historical patterns of discrimination and thereby to extend equality of opportunity and treatment in employment. Multinational enterprises should accordingly make qualifications, skill and experience the basis for the recruitment, placement, training and advancement of their staff at all levels.

23   Governments should never require or encourage multinational enterprises to discriminate on any of the grounds mentioned in paragraph 21, and continuing guidance from governments, where

1   Convention (No.111) and Recommendation (No.111) concerning Discrimination in Respect of Employment and Occupation; Convention (No.100) and Recommendation (No.90) concerning Equal Remuneration for Men and Women Workers for Work of Equal Value.

appropriate, on the avoidance of such discrimination in employment is encouraged.

Security of employment

24   Governments should carefully study the impact of multinational enterprises on employment in different industrial sectors. Governments, as well as multinational enterprises themselves, in all countries should take suitable measures to deal with the employment and labour market impacts of the operations of multinational enterprises.

25   Multinational enterprises equally with national enterprises, through active manpower planning, should endeavour to provide stable employment for their employees and should observe freely-negotiated obligations concerning employment stability and social security. In view of the flexibility which multinational enterprises may have, they should strive to assume a leading role in promoting security of employment, particularly in countries where the discontinuation of operations is likely to accentuate long-term unemployment.

26   In considering changes in operations (including those resulting from mergers, take-overs or transfers of production) which would have major employment effects, multinational enterprises should provide reasonable notice of such changes to the appropriate government authorities and representatives of the workers in their employment and their organisations so that the implications may be examined jointly in order to mitigate adverse effects to the greatest possible extent. This is particularly important in the case of the closure of an entity involving collective lay-offs or dismissals.

27   Arbitrary dismissal procedures should be avoided.[1]

28   Governments, in co-operation with multinational as well as national enterprises, should provide some form of income protection for workers whose employment has been terminated.[1]

Training

29   Governments, in co-operation with all the parties concerned, should develop national policies for vocational training and guidance, closely linked with employment.[2] This is the framework within which multinational enterprises should pursue their training policies.

1   Recommendation (No.119) concerning Termination of Employment at the Initiative of the Employer.
2   Convention (No.142) and Recommendation (No.150) concerning Vocational Guidance and Vocational Training in the Development of Human Resources.

30   In their operations, multinational enterprises should ensure that relevant training is provided for all levels of their employees in the host country, as appropriate, to meet the needs of the enterprise as well as the development policies of the country. Such training should, to the extent possible, develop generally useful skills and promote career opportunities. This responsibility should be carried out, where appropriate, in co-operation with the authorities of the country, employers' and workers' organisations and the competent local, national or international institutions.

31   Multinational enterprises operating in developing countries should participate, along with national enterprises, in programmes, including special funds, encouraged by host governments and supported by employers' and workers' organisations. These programmes should have the aim of encouraging skill formation and development as well as providing vocational guidance, and should be jointly administered by the parties which support them. Wherever practicable, multinational enterprises should make the services of skilled resource personnel available to help in training programmes organised by governments as part of a contribution to national development.

32   Multinational enterprises, with the co-operation of governments and to the extent consistent with the efficient operation of the enterprise, should afford opportunities within the enterprise as a whole to broaden the experience of local management in suitable fields such as industrial relations.

Conditions of work and life

Wages, benefits and conditions of work

33   Wages, benefits and conditions of work offered by multinational enterprises should be not less favourable to the workers than those offered by comparable employers in the country concerned.

34   When multinational enterprises operate in developing countries, where comparable employers may not exist, they should provide the best possible wages, benefits and conditions of work, within the framework of government policies.[1] These should be related to the economic position of the enterprise, but should be at least adequate to satisfy basic needs of the workers and their families. Where they provide

---

1   Recommendation (No.116) concerning Reduction of Hours of Work.

workers with basic amenities such as housing, medical care or food, these amenities should be of a good standard.[1]

35 Governments, especially in developing countries, should endeavour to adopt suitable measures to ensure that lower income groups and less developed areas benefit as much as possible from the activities of multinational enterprises.

Safety and health

36 Governments should ensure that both multinational and national enterprises provide adequate safety and health standards for their employees. Those governments which have not yet ratified the ILO Conventions on Guarding of Machinery (No.119), Ionising Radiation (No.115), Benzene (No.136) and Occupational Cancer (No.139) are urged nevertheless to apply to the greatest extent possible the principles embodied in these Conventions and in their related Recommendations (Nos. 118, 114, 144 and 147). The Codes of Practice and Guides in the current list of ILO publications on Occupational Safety and Health should also be taken into account.[2]

37 Multinational enterprises should maintain the highest standards of safety and health, in conformity with national requirements, bearing in mind their relevant experience within the enterprise as a whole, including any knowledge of special hazards. They should also make available to the representatives of the workers in the enterprise, and upon request, to the competent authorities and the workers' and employers' organisations in all countries in which they operate, information on the safety and health standards relevant to their local operations, which they observe in other countries. In particular, they should make known to those concerned any special hazards and related protective measures associated with new products and processes. They, like comparable domestic enterprises, should be expected to play a leading role in the examination of causes of industrial safety and health hazards and in the application of resulting improvements within the enterprise as a whole.

38 Multinational enterprises should co-operate in the work of international organisations concerned with the preparation and adoption of international safety and health standards.

---

1 Convention (No.110) and Recommendation (No.110) concerning Conditions of Employment of Plantation Workers; Recommendation (No.115) concerning Workers' Housing; Recommendation (No.69) concerning Medical Care; Convention (No.130) and Recommendation (No.134) concerning Medical Care and Sickness.
2 The ILO Conventions and Recommendations referred to are listed in 'Publications on Occupational Safety and Health', ILO, Geneva 1976, pp. 1—3.

39   In accordance with national practice, multinational enterprises should co-operate fully with the competent safety and health authorities, the representatives of the workers and their organisations, and established safety and health organisations. Where appropriate, matters relating to safety and health should be incorporated in agreements with the representatives of the workers and their organisations.

Industrial relations

40   Multinational enterprises should observe standards of industrial relations not less favourable than those observed by comparable employers in the country concerned.

Freedom of association and the right to organise

41   Workers employed by multinational enterprises as well as those employed by national enterprises should, without distinction whatsoever, have the right to establish and, subject only to the rules of the organisation concerned, to join organisations of their own choosing without previous authorisation.[1] They should also enjoy adequate protection against acts of anti-union discrimination in respect of their employment.[2]

42   Organisations representing multinational enterprises or the workers in their employment should enjoy adequate protection against any acts of interference by each other or each other's agents or members in their establishment, functioning or administration.[3]

43   Where appropriate, in the local circumstances, multinational enterprises should support representative employers' organisations.

44   Governments, where they do not already do so, are urged to apply the principles of Convention No.87, Article 5, in view of the importance, in relation to multinational enterprises, of permitting organisations representing such enterprises or the workers in their employment to affiliate with international organisations of employers and workers of their own choosing.

45   Where governments of host countries offer special incentives to attract foreign investment, these incentives should not include any limitation of the workers' freedom of association or the right to organise and bargain collectively.

1   Convention No.87, Article 2.
2   Convention No.98, Article 1(1).
3   Convention No.98, Article 2(1).

359

46 Representatives of the workers in multinational enterprises should not be hindered from meeting for consultation and exchange of view among themselves, provided that the functioning of the operations of the enterprise and the normal procedures which govern relationships with representatives of the workers and their organisations are not thereby prejudiced.

47 Governments should not restrict the entry of representatives of employers' and workers' organisations who come from other countries at the invitation of the local or national organisations concerned for the purpose of consultation on matters of mutual concern, solely on the grounds that they seek entry in that capacity.

Collective bargaining

48 Workers employed by multinational enterprises should have the right, in accordance with national law and practice, to have representative organisations of their own choosing recognised for the purpose of collective bargaining.

49 Measures appropriate to national conditions should be taken, where necessary, to encourage and promote the full development and utilisation of machinery for voluntary negotiation between employers or employers' organisations and workers' organisations, with a view to the regulation of terms and conditions of employment by means of collective agreements.[1]

50 Multinational enterprises, as well as national enterprises, should provide workers' representatives with such facilities as may be necessary to assist in the development of effective collective agreements.[2]

51 Multinational enterprises should enable duly authorised representatives of the workers in their employment in each of the countries in which they operate to conduct negotiations with representatives of management who are authorised to take decisions on the matters under negotiation.

52 Multinational enterprises, in the context of bona fide negotiations with the workers' representatives on conditions of employment, or while workers are exercising the right to organise, should not threaten to utilise a capacity to transfer the whole or part of an operating unit from the country concerned in order to influence unfairly those negotiations or to hinder the exercise of the right to organise; nor should they transfer workers from affiliates in foreign countries with a

---

1 Convention No.98, Article 4.
2 Convention (No.135) concerning protection and facilities to be afforded to workers' representatives in the undertaking.

view to undermining bona fide negotiations with the workers' representatives or the workers' exercise of their right to organise.

53 Collective agreements should include provisions for the settlement of disputes arising over their interpretation and application and for ensuring mutually respected rights and responsibilities.

54 Multinational enterprises should provide workers' representatives with information required for meaningful negotiations with the entity involved and, where this accords with local law and practices, should also provide information to enable them to obtain a true and fair view of the performance of the entity or, where appropriate, of the enterprise as a whole.[1]

55 Governments should supply to the representatives of workers' organisations on request, where law and practice so permit, information on the industries in which the enterprise operates, which would help in laying down objective criteria in the collective bargaining process. In this context, multinational as well as national enterprises should respond constructively to requests by governments for relevant information on their operations.

Consultation

56 In multinational as well as in national enterprises, systems devised by mutual agreement between employers and workers and their representatives should provide, in accordance with national law and practice, for regular consultation on matters of mutual concern. Such consultation should not be a substitute for collective bargaining.[2]

Examination of grievances

57 Multinational as well as national enterprises should respect the right of the workers whom they employ to have all their grievances processed in a manner consistent with the following provision: any worker who, acting individually or jointly with other workers, considers that he has grounds for a grievance should have the right to submit such grievance without suffering any prejudice whatsoever as a result, and to have such grievance examined pursuant to an appropriate procedure.[3]

---

1 Recommendation (No.129) concerning Communications between Management and Workers within Undertakings.
2 Recommendation (No.94) concerning Consultation and Co-operation between Employers and Workers at the Level of the Undertaking; Recommendation (No.129) concerning Communications within the Undertaking.
3 Recommendation (No.130) concerning the Examination of Grievances within the Undertaking with a View to their Settlement.

This is particularly important whenever the multinational enterprises operate in countries which do not abide by the principles of ILO Conventions pertaining to freedom of association, to the right to organise and bargain collectively and to forced labour.[1]

Settlement of industrial disputes

58   Multinational as well as national enterprises jointly with the representatives and organisations of the workers whom they employ should seek to establish voluntary conciliation machinery, appropriate to national conditions, which may include provisions for voluntary arbitration, to assist in the prevention and settlement of industrial disputes between employers and workers. The voluntary conciliation machinery should include equal representation of employers and workers.[2]

Geneva, 16 November 1977.

---

1 Convention (No.29) concerning Forced or Compulsory Labour; Convention (No.105) concerning the Abolition of Forced Labour; Recommendation (No.35) concerning Indirect Compulsion to Labour.
2 Recommendation (No.92) concerning Voluntary Conciliation and Arbitration.

List of international labour Conventions and Recommendations
referred to in the Tripartite Declaration of Principles concerning
Multinational Enterprises and Social Policy

Conventions

Convention (No.29) concerning Forced or Compulsory Labour, 1930.
Convention (No.87) concerning Freedom of Association and Protection of the Right to Organise, 1948.
Convention (No.98) concerning the Application of the Principles of the Right to Organise and to Bargain Collectively, 1949.
Convention (No.100) concerning Equal Remuneration for Men and Women Workers for Work of Equal Value, 1951.
Convention (No.105) concerning the Abolition of Forced Labour, 1957.
Convention (No.110) concerning Conditions of Employment of Plantation Workers, 1958.
Convention (No.111) concerning Discrimination in Respect of Employment and Occupation, 1958.
Convention (No.115) concerning the Protection of Workers against Ionising Radiations, 1960.
Convention (No.119) concerning the Guarding of Machinery, 1963.
Convention (No.122) concerning Employment Policy, 1964.
Convention (No.130) concerning Medical Care and Sickness Benefits, 1969.
Convention (No.135) concerning Protection and Facilities to be Afforded to Workers' Representatives in the Undertaking, 1971.
Convention (No.136) concerning Protection against Hazards of Poisoning arising from Benzene, 1971.
Convention (No.139) concerning Prevention and Control of Occupational Hazards caused by Carcinogenic Substances and Agents, 1974.
Convention (No.142) concerning Vocational Guidance and Vocational Training in the Development of Human Resources, 1975.

Recommendations

Recommendation (No.35) concerning Indirect Compulsion to Labour, 1930.
Recommendation (No.69) concerning Medical Care, 1944.
Recommendation (No.90) concerning Equal Remuneration for Men and Women Workers for Work of Equal Value, 1951.
Recommendation (No.92) concerning Voluntary Conciliation and Arbitration, 1951.

Recommendation (No.94) concerning Consultation and Co-operation between Employers and Workers at the Level of the Undertaking, 1952.

Recommendation (No.110) concerning Conditions of Employment of Plantation Workers, 1958.

Recommendation (No.111) concerning Discrimination in Respect of Employment and Occupation, 1958.

Recommendation (No.114) concerning the Protection of Workers against Ionising Radiations, 1960.

Recommendation (No.115) concerning Workers' Housing, 1961.

Recommendation (No.116) concerning Reduction of Hours of Work, 1962.

Recommendation (No.118) concerning the Guarding of Machinery, 1963.

Recommendation (No.119) concerning Termination of Employment at the Initiative of the Employer, 1963.

Recommendation (No.122) concerning Employment Policy, 1964.

Recommendation (No.129) concerning Communications between Management and Workers within the Undertaking, 1967.

Recommendation (No.130) concerning the Examination of Grievances Within the Undertaking with a View to their Settlement, 1967.

Recommendation (No.134) concerning Medical Care and Sickness Benefits, 1969.

Recommendation (No.144) concerning Protection against Hazards of Poisoning arising from Benzene, 1971.

Recommendation (No.147) concerning Prevention and Control of Occupational Hazards caused by Carcinogenic Substances and Agents, 1974.

Recommendation (No.150) concerning Vocational Guidance and Vocational Training in the Development of Human Resources, 1975.

Offprints of the above instruments can be obtained from the Distribution Section, ILO Headquarters, Geneva.

II(b) RESTRICTIVE BUSINESS PRACTICES (UNCTAD) otherwise known as: THE SET OF MULTILATERALLY AGREED EQUITABLE PRINCIPLES AND RULES FOR THE CONTROL OF RESTRICTIVE BUSINESS PRACTICES[1]

Contents

A   Objectives

B   Definitions and scope of application

C   Multilaterally agreed equitable principles for the control of restrictive business practices

D   Principles and rules for enterprises, including transnational corporations

E   Principles and rules for States at national, regional and subregional levels

F   International measures

G   International institutional machinery

The United Nations Conference on Restrictive Business Practices,

Recognizing that restrictive business practices can adversely affect international trade, particularly that of developing countries, and the economic development of these countries,

Affirming that a set of multilaterally agreed equitable principles and rules for the control of restrictive business practices can contribute to attaining the objective in the establishment of a new international economic order to eliminate restrictive business practices adversely affecting international trade and thereby contribute to development and improvement of international economic relations on a just and equitable basis,

Recognizing also the need to ensure that restrictive business practices do not impede or negate the realization of benefits that should arise from the liberalization of tariff and non-tariff barriers affecting international trade, particularly those affecting the trade and development of developing countries,

---

1   The Set of Principles and Rules was adopted by the United Nations Conference on Restrictive Business Practices as an annex to its resolution of 22 April 1980.

Considering the possible adverse impact of restrictive business practices, including among others those resulting from the increased activities of transnational corporations, on the trade and development of developing countries,

Convinced of the need for action to be taken by countries in a mutually reinforcing manner at the national, regional and international levels to eliminate or effectively deal with restrictive business practices, including those of transnational corporations, adversely affecting international trade, particularly that of developing countries, and the economic development of these countries,

Convinced also of the benefits to be derived from a universally applicable set of multilaterally agreed equitable principles and rules for the control of restrictive business practices and that all countries should encourage their enterprises to follow in all respects the provisions of such a set of multilaterally agreed equitable principles and rules,

Convinced further that the adoption of such a set of multilaterally agreed equitable principles and rules for the control of restrictive business practices will thereby facilitate the adoption and strengthening of laws and policies in the area of restrictive business practices at the national and regional levels and thus lead to improved conditions and attain greater efficiency and participation in international trade and development, particularly that of developing countries, and to protect and promote social welfare in general, and in particular the interests of consumers in both developed and developing countries,

Affirming also the need to eliminate the disadvantages to trade and development which may result from the restrictive business practices of transnational corporations or other enterprises, and thus help to maximize benefits to international trade and particularly the trade and development of developing countries,

Affirming further the need that measures adopted by States for the control of restrictive business practices should be applied fairly, equitably, on the same basis to all enterprises and in accordance with established procedures of law; and for States to take into account the principles and objectives of the Set of Multilaterally Agreed Equitable Principles and Rules,

Hereby agrees on the following Set of Principles and Rules for the control of restrictive business practices, which take the form of recommendations:

A Objectives

Taking into account the interests of all countries, particularly those of developing countries, the Set of Multilaterally Agreed Equitable Principles and Rules are framed in order to achieve the following objectives:

1 To ensure that restrictive business practices do not impede or negate the realization of benefits that should arise from the liberalization of tariff and non-tariff barriers affecting world trade, particularly those affecting the trade and development of developing countries;

2 To attain greater efficiency in international trade and development, particularly that of developing countries, in accordance with national aims of economic and social development and existing economic structures, such as through:

    (a) The creation, encouragement and protection of competition;

    (b) Control of the concentration of capital and/or economic power;

    (c) Encouragement of innovation;

3 To protect and promote social welfare in general and, in particular, the interests of consumers in both developed and developing countries;

4 To eliminate the disadvantages to trade and development which may result from the restrictive business practices of transnational corporations or other enterprises, and thus help to maximize benefits to international trade and particularly the trade and development of developing countries;

5 To provide a Set of Multilaterally Agreed Equitable Principles and Rules for the control of restrictive business practices for adoption at the international level and thereby to facilitate the adoption and strengthening of laws and policies in this area at the national and regional levels.

B Definitions and scope of application

For the purpose of this Set of Multilaterally Agreed Equitable Principles and Rules:

(i) Definitions

1 'Restrictive business practices' means acts or behaviour of enterprises which, through an abuse or acquisition and abuse of a dominant

position of market power, limit access to markets or otherwise unduly restrain competition, having or being likely to have adverse effects on international trade, particularly that of developing countries, and on the economic development of these countries, or which through formal, informal, written or unwritten agreements or arrangements among enterprises, have the same impact.

2   'Dominant position of market power' refers to a situation where an enterprise, either by itself or acting together with a few other enterprises, is in a position to control the relevant market for a particular good or service or group of goods or services.

3   'Enterprises' means firms, partnerships, corporations, companies, other associations, natural or juridical persons, or any combination thereof, irrespective of the mode of creation or control or ownership, private or State, which are engaged in commercial activities, and includes their branches, subsidiaries, affiliates, or other entities directly or indirectly controlled by them.

(ii) Scope of application

4   The Set of Principles and Rules applies to restrictive business practices, including those of transnational corporations, adversely affecting international trade, particularly that of developing countries and the economic development of these countries. It applies irrespective of whether such practices involve enterprises in one or more countries.

5   The 'principles and rules for enterprises, including transnational corporations' apply to all transactions in goods and services.

6   The 'principles and rules for enterprises, including transnational corporations' are addressed to all enterprises.

7   The provisions of the Set of Principles and Rules shall be universally applicable to all countries and enterprises regardless of the parties involved in the transactions, acts or behaviour.

8   Any reference to 'States' or 'Governments' shall be construed as including any regional groupings of States, to the extent that they have competence in the area of restrictive business practices.

9   The Set of Principles and Rules shall not apply to intergovernmental agreements, nor to restrictive business practices directly caused by such agreements.

C Multilaterally agreed equitable principles for the control of restrictive business practices

In line with the objectives set forth, the following principles are to apply:

(i)   General principles

1   Appropriate action should be taken in a mutually reinforcing manner at national, regional and international levels to eliminate, or effectively deal with, restrictive business practices, including those of transnational corporations, adversely affecting international trade, particularly that of developing countries and the economic development of these countries.

2   Collaboration between Governments at bilateral and multilateral levels should be established and, where such collaboration has been established, it should be improved to facilitate the control of restrictive business practices.

3   Appropriate mechanisms should be devised at the international level and/or the use of existing international machinery improved to facilitate exchange and dissemination of information among Governments with respect to restrictive business practices.

4   Appropriate means should be devised to facilitate the holding of multilateral consultations with regard to policy issues relating to the control of restrictive business practices.

5   The provisions of the Set of Principles and Rules should not be construed as justifying conduct by enterprises which is unlawful under applicable national or regional legislation.

(ii)   Relevant factors in the application of the Set of Principles and Rules

6   In order to ensure the fair and equitable application of the Set of Principles and Rules, States, while bearing in mind the need to ensure the comprehensive application of the Set of Principles and Rules, should take due account of the extent to which the conduct of enterprises, whether or not created or controlled by States, is accepted under applicable legislation or regulations, bearing in mind that such laws and regulations should be clearly defined and publicly and readily available, or is required by States.

(iii) Preferential or differential treatment
for developing countries

7   In order to ensure the equitable application of the Set of Principles and Rules, States, particularly developed countries, should take into account in their control of restrictive business practices the development, financial and trade needs of developing countries, in particular of the least developed countries, for the purposes especially of developing countries in:

(a)   Promoting the establishment or development of domestic industries and the economic development of other sectors of the economy, and

(b)   Encouraging their economic development through regional or global arrangements among developing countries.

D   Principles and rules for enterprises, including transnational corporations

1   Enterprises should conform to the restrictive business practices laws, and the provisions concerning restrictive business practices in other laws, of the countries in which they operate, and, in the event of proceedings under these laws, should be subject to the competence of the courts and relevant administrative bodies therein.

2   Enterprises should consult and co-operate with competent authorities of countries directly affected in controlling restrictive business practices adversely affecting the interests of those countries. In this regard, enterprises should also provide information, in particular details of restrictive arrangements, required for this purpose, including that which may be located in foreign countries, to the extent that in the latter event such production or disclosure is not prevented by applicable law or established public policy. Whenever the provision of information is on a voluntary basis, its provision should be in accordance with safeguards normally applicable in this field.

3   Enterprises, except when dealing with each other in the context of an economic entity wherein they are under common control, including through ownership, or otherwise not able to act independently of each other, engaged on the market in rival or potentially rival activities, should refrain from practices such as the following when, through formal, informal, written or unwritten agreements or arrangements they limit access to markets or otherwise unduly restrain competition, having or being likely to have adverse effects on inter-

national trade, particularly that of developing countries, and on the economic development of these countries:

(a) Agreements fixing prices, including as to exports and imports;

(b) Collusive tendering;

(c) Market or customer allocation arrangements;

(d) Allocation by quota as to sales and production;

(e) Collective action to enforce arrangements, e.g. by concerted refusals to deal;

(f) Concerted refusal of supplies to potential importers;

(g) Collective denial of access to an arrangement, or association, which is crucial to competition.

4   Enterprises should refrain from the following acts or behaviour in a relevant market when, through an abuse[1] or acquisition and abuse of a dominant position of market power, they limit access to markets or otherwise unduly restrain competition, having or being likely to have adverse effects on international trade, particularly that of developing countries, and on the economic development of these countries:

(a) Predatory behaviour towards competitors, such as using below-cost pricing to eliminate competitors;

(b) Discriminatory (i.e. unjustifiably differentiated) pricing or terms or conditions in the supply or purchase of goods or services, including by means of the use of pricing policies in transactions between affiliated enterprises which overcharge or undercharge for goods or services purchased or supplied as compared with prices for similar or comparable transactions outside the affiliated enterprises;

(c) Mergers, takeovers, joint ventures or other acquisitions of control, whether of a horizontal, vertical or a conglomerate nature;

1 Whether acts or behaviour are abusive or not should be examined in terms of their purpose and effects in the actual situation, in particular with reference to whether they limit access to markets or otherwise unduly restrain competition, having or being likely to have adverse effects on international trade, particularly that of developing countries, and on the economic development of these countries, and to whether they are:

(a) Appropriate in the light of the organizational, managerial and legal relationship among the enterprises concerned, such as in the context of relations within an economic entity and not having restrictive effects outside the related enterprises;

(b) Appropriate in light of special conditions or economic circumstances in the relevant market such as exceptional conditions of supply and demand or the size of the market;

(c) Of types which are usually treated as acceptable under pertinent national or regional laws and regulations for the control of restrictive business practices;

(d) Consistent with the purposes and objectives of these principles and rules.

(d)   Fixing the prices at which goods exported can be resold in importing countries;

(e)   Restrictions on the importation of goods which have been legitimately marked abroad with a trademark identical with or similar to the trademark protected as to identical or similar goods in the importing country where the trademarks in question are of the same origin, i.e. belong to the same owner or are used by enterprises between which there is economic, organizational, managerial or legal interdependence and where the purpose of such restrictions is to maintain artificially high prices;

(f)   When not for ensuring the achievement of legitimate business purposes, such as quality, safety, adequate distribution or service:

   (i)   Partial or complete refusals to deal on the enterprise's customary commercial terms

   (ii) Making the supply of particular goods or services dependent upon the acceptance of restrictions on the distribution or manufacture of competing or other goods;

   (iii) Imposing restrictions concerning where, or to whom, or in what form or quantities, goods supplied or other goods may be resold or exported;

   (iv) Making the supply of particular goods or services dependent upon the purchase of other goods or services from the supplier or his designee.

E   Principles and rules for States at national, regional and subregional levels

1   States should, at the national level or through regional groupings, adopt, improve and effectively enforce appropriate legislation and implementing judicial and administrative procedures for the control of restrictive business practices, including those of transnational corporations.

2   States should base their legislation primarily on the principle of eliminating or effectively dealing with acts or behaviour of enterprises which, through an abuse or acquisition and abuse of a dominant position of market power, limit access to markets or otherwise unduly restrain competition, having or being likely to have adverse effects on

their trade or economic development, or which through formal, informal, written or unwritten agreements or arrangements among enterprises have the same impact.

3   States, in their control of restrictive business practices, should ensure treatment of enterprises which is fair, equitable, on the same basis to all enterprises, and in accordance with established procedures of law. The laws and regulations should be publicly and readily available.

4   States should seek appropriate remedial or preventive measures to prevent and/or control the use of restrictive business practices within their competence when it comes to the attention of States that such practices adversely affect international trade, and particularly the trade and development of the developing countries.

5   Where, for the purposes of the control of restrictive business practices, a State obtains information from enterprises containing legitimate business secrets, it should accord such information reasonable safeguards normally applicable in this field, particularly to protect its confidentiality.

6   States should institute or improve procedures for obtaining information from enterprises, including transnational corporations, necessary for their effective control of restrictive business practices, including in this respect details of restrictive agreements, understandings and other arrangements.

7   States should establish appropriate mechanisms at the regional and subregional levels to promote exchange of information on restrictive business practices and on the application of national laws and policies in this area, and to assist each other to their mutual advantage regarding control of restrictive business practices at the regional and subregional levels.

8   States with greater expertise in the operation of systems for the control of restrictive business practices should, on request, share their experience with, or otherwise provide technical assistance to, other States wishing to develop or improve such systems.

9   States should, on request, or at their own initiative when the need comes to their attention, supply to other States, particularly developing countries, publicly available information, and, to the extent consistent with their laws and established public policy, other information necessary to the receiving interested State for its effective control of restrictive business practices.

F   International measures

Collaboration at the international level should aim at eliminating or effectively dealing with restrictive business practices, including those of transnational corporations, through strengthening and improving controls over restrictive business practices adversely affecting international trade, particularly that of developing countries, and the economic development of these countries. In this regard, action should include:

1   Work aimed at achieving common approaches in national policies relating to restrictive business practices compatible with the Set of Principles and Rules.

2   Communication annually to the Secretary-General of UNCTAD of appropriate information on steps taken by States and regional groupings to meet their commitment to the Set of Principles and Rules, and information on the adoption, development and application of legislation, regulations and policies concerning restrictive business practices.

3   Continued publication annually by UNCTAD of a report on developments in restrictive business practices legislation and on restrictive business practices adversely affecting international trade, particularly the trade and development of developing countries, based upon publicly available information and as far as possible other information, particularly on the basis of requests addressed to all member States or provided at their own initiative and, where appropriate, to the United Nations Centre on Transnational Corporations and other competent international organizations.

4   Consultations:

   (a)   Where a State, particularly of a developing country, believes that a consultation with another State or States is appropriate in regard to an issue concerning control of restrictive business practices, it may request a consultation with those States with a view to finding a mutually acceptable solution. When a consultation is to be held, the States involved may request the Secretary-General of UNCTAD to provide mutually agreed conference facilities for such a consultation;

   (b)   States should accord full consideration to requests for consultations and, upon agreement as to the subject of and the procedures for such a consultation, the consultation should take place at an appropriate time;

   (c)   If the States involved so agree, a joint report on the consultations and their results should be prepared by the States involved and, if they so wish, with the assistance of the UNCTAD secretariat, and be made available to the Secretary-General of UNCTAD for inclusion in the annual report on restrictive business practices.

5   Continued work within UNCTAD on the elaboration of a model law or laws on restrictive business practices in order to assist developing countries in devising appropriate legislation. States should provide necessary information and experience to UNCTAD in this connexion.

6   Implementation within or facilitation by UNCTAD, and other relevant organizations of the United Nations system in conjunction with UNCTAD, of technical assistance, advisory and training programmes on restrictive business practices, particularly for developing countries:

(a)   Experts should be provided to assist developing countries, at their request, in formulating or improving restrictive business practices legislation and procedures;

(b)   Seminars, training programmes or courses should be held, primarily in developing countries, to train officials involved or likely to be involved in administering restrictive business practices legislation and, in this connexion, advantage should be taken, *inter alia*, of the experience and knowledge of administrative authorities, especially in developed countries, in detecting the use of restrictive business practices;

(c)   A handbook on restrictive business practices legislation should be compiled;

(d)   Relevant books, documents, manuals and any other information on matters related to restrictive business practices should be collected and made available, particularly to developing countries;

(e)   Exchange of personnel between restrictive business practices authorities should be arranged and facilitated;

(f)   International conferences on restrictive business practices legislation and policy should be arranged;

(g)   Seminars for an exchange of views on restrictive business practices among persons in the public and private sectors should be arranged.

7   International organizations and financing programmes, in particular the United Nations Development Programme, should be called upon to provide resources through appropriate channels and modalities

for the financing of activities set out in paragraph 6 above. Further-more, all countries are invited, in particular the developed countries, to make voluntary financial and other contributions for the above-mentioned activities.

G   International institutional machinery

(i)   Institutional arrangements

1   An Intergovernmental Group of Experts on Restrictive Business Practices operating within the framework of a Committee of UNCTAD will provide the institutional machinery.

2   States which have accepted the Set of Principles and Rules should take appropriate steps at the national or regional levels to meet their commitment to the Set of Principles and Rules.

(ii)   Functions of the Intergovernmental Group

3   The Intergovernmental Group shall have the following functions:

(a)   To provide a forum and modalities for multilateral consul-tations, discussion and exchange of views between States on matters related to the Set of Principles and Rules, in parti-cular its operation and the experience arising therefrom;

(b)   To undertake and disseminate periodically studies and re-search on restrictive business practices related to the provisions of the Set of Principles and Rules, with a view to increasing exchange of experience and giving greater effect to the Set of Principles and Rules;

(c)   To invite and consider relevant studies, documentation and reports from relevant organizations of the United Nations system;

(d)   To study matters relating to the Set of Principles and Rules and which might be characterized by data covering business transactions and other relevant information obtained upon request addressed to all States;

(e)   To collect and disseminate information on matters relating to the Set of Principles and Rules to the over-all attainment of its goals and to the appropriate steps States have taken at the national or regional levels to promote an effective Set of Principles and Rules, including its objectives and principles;

(f) To make appropriate reports and recommendations to States on matters within its competence, including the application and implementation of the Set of Multilaterally Agreed Equitable Principles and Rules;

(g) To submit reports at least once a year on its work.

4   In the performance of its functions, neither the Intergovernmental Group nor its subsidiary organs shall act like a tribunal or otherwise pass judgement on the activities or conduct of individual Governments or of individual enterprises in connexion with a specific business transaction. The Intergovernmental Group or its subsidiary organs should avoid becoming involved when enterprises to a specific business transaction are in dispute.

5   The Intergovernmental Group shall establish such procedures as may be necessary to deal with issues related to confidentiality.

(iii) Review procedure

6   Subject to the approval of the General Assembly, five years after the adoption of the Set of Principles and Rules, a United Nations Conference shall be convened by the Secretary-General of the United Nations under the auspices of UNCTAD for the purpose of reviewing all the aspects of the Set of Principles and Rules. Towards this end, the Intergovernmental Group shall make proposals to the Conference for the improvement and further development of the Set of Principles and Rules.

III(c) DRAFT INTERNATIONAL CODE OF CONDUCT ON THE TRANSFER OF TECHNOLOGY[1]

Preamble[2]

[The Contracting Parties] *   [The Participating Countries] **

1   *Recognizing* the fundamental role of science and technology in the socio-economic development of all countries, and in particular, in the acceleration of the development of the developing countries,

2   *Believing* that technology is key to the progress of mankind and that all peoples have the right to benefit from the advances and developments in science and technology in order to improve their standards of living,

3   *Bearing in mind* relevant decisions of the General Assembly and other bodies of the United Nations, in particular UNCTAD, on the transfer and development of technology,

4   *Recognizing* the need to facilitate an adequate transfer and development of technology so as to strengthen the scientific and technological capabilities of all countries, particularly the developing countries, and to co-operate with the developing countries in their own efforts in this field as a decisive step in the progress towards the establishment of a new international economic order,

5   *Desirous* of promoting international scientific and technological co-operation in the interest of peace, security and national independence and for the benefit of all nations,

6   *Striving* to promote an increase of the international transfer of technology with an equal opportunity for all countries to participate irrespective of their social and economic system and of their level of economic development,

7   *Recognizing* the need for developed countries to grant special treatment to the developing countries in the field of the transfer of technology,

8   *Drawing attention* to the need to improve the flow of technological information, and in particular to promote the widest and fullest flow of information on the availability of alternative technologies, and

---

1   In the present text (April 1981), the following key is used to identify the source of each element of the composite draft: Group of 77 text: *; Group B text: **; text of Group D and Mongolia: ***.
2   Text transmitted by the President to the Conference at its 7th meeting.

on the selection of appropriate technologies suited to the specific needs of developing countries,

9 *Believing* that a Code of Conduct will effectively assist the developing countries in their selection, acquisition and effective use of technologies appropriate to their needs in order to develop improved economic standards and living conditions,

10 *Believing* that a Code of Conduct will help to create conditions conducive to the promotion of the international transfer of technology, under mutually agreed and advantageous terms to all parties,

11 *Affirming* the benefits to be derived from a universally applicable Code of Conduct and that all countries should [ensure] */*** [encourage] *** that their enterprises, whether private or public, [shall conform] */*** [follow] ** in all respects to the provisions of this Code,

12 [*Convinced* that an international legally binding instrument is the only form capable of effectively regulating the transfer of technology,] *

13 [*Agree* on the adoption of this international legally binding Code of Conduct on the transfer of technology] *

[*Hereby set forth* the following Code of Conduct consisting of guidelines for the international transfer of technology:] **

[This universally applicable Code of Conduct on the international transfer of technology is established.] ***

Chapter 1 Definitions and scope of application[1]

1.1 For the purposes of the present Code of Conduct:

(a) 'Party' means any person, either natural or juridical, of public or private law, either individual or collective, such as corporations, companies, firms, partnerships and other associations, or any combination thereof, whether created, owned or controlled by States, Government agencies, juridical persons, or individuals, wherever they operate, as well as States, Government agencies and international, regional and subregional organizations, when they engage in an international transfer of technology transaction which is usually considered to be of a com-

---

1 Text transmitted by the President to the Conference at its 12th meeting, as revised in the text submitted by the President to the Conference at its 14th meeting, by which provisions 1.1 (d) and (e), as well as footnotes 4 and 5 of TD/CODE TOT/20 were deleted. It is understood that the term 'technology acquiring country' should be used instead of 'country of the acquiring party' in all the chapters of the Code.

mercial nature. The term 'party' includes, among the entities enumerated above, incorporated branches, subsidiaries and affiliates, joint ventures or other legal entities regardless of the economic and other relationships between and among them.[1]

(b) 'Acquiring party' means the party which obtains a licence to use or to exploit, purchases or otherwise acquires technology of a proprietary or non-proprietary nature and/or rights related thereto in a transfer of technology.

(c) 'Supplying party' means the party which licenses, sells, assigns or otherwise provides technology of a proprietary or non-proprietary nature and/or rights related thereto in a transfer of technology.

1.2 Transfer of technology under this Code is the transfer of systematic knowledge for the manufacture of a product, for the application of a process or for the rendering of a service and does not extend to the transactions involving the mere sale or mere lease of goods.

1.3 Transfer of technology transactions are arrangements between parties involving transfer of technology, as defined in paragraph 1.2 above, particularly in each of the following cases:

(a) The assignment, sale and licensing of all forms of industrial property, except for trade marks, service marks and trade names when they are not part of transfer of technology transactions;

(b) The provision of know-how and technical expertise in the form of feasibility studies, plans, diagrams, models, instructions, guides, formulae, basic or detailed engineering designs, specifications and equipment for training, services involving technical advisory and managerial personnel, and personnel training;

(c) The provision of technological knowledge necessary for the installation, operation and functioning of plant and equipment, and turnkey projects;

(d) The provision of technological knowledge necessary to acquire, install and use machinery, equipment, intermediate goods and/or raw materials which have been acquired by purchase, lease or other means;

(e) The provision of technological contents of industrial and technical co-operation arrangements.

---

1 Group B accepts inclusion of this sentence subject to agreement to be reached on qualifications relating to the application of the Code to the relations of these entities in relevant parts of the Code.

[1.4 The Code of Conduct shall apply to international transfer of technology transactions which occur when technology is transferred across national boundaries between the supplying party and the acquiring party or when a transfer of technology transaction is entered into between parties which do not reside or are not established in the same country. This Code does not prevent States from deciding to extend its application to all transactions which take place between parties which are resident of or established in the same country. including the case where either party is a branch, subsidiary or affiliate, or is otherwise directly or indirectly controlled by a foreign entity.] [1]

1.5 The Code of Conduct is universally applicable in scope and is addressed to all parties to transfer of technology transactions and to all countries and groups of countries, irrespective of their economic and political systems and their levels of development.

1.6 [Bilateral and multilateral agreements between States on the transfer of technology for meeting socio-economic needs of development, in accordance with the chapters on objectives and principles and special treatment, should be consistent with the Code.] [2]

---

1   This issue is still outstanding. The text of the draft provision in TD/CODE TOT/14 reads as follows:

[The Code of Conduct shall apply to international transfer of technology transactions which occur when technology is transferred across national boundaries between the supplying party and the acquiring party or when a transfer of technology transaction is entered into between parties which do not reside or are not established in the same country, as well as between parties which are resident of or established in the same country, if at least one party is a branch, subsidiary or affiliate or is otherwise directly or indirectly controlled by a foreign entity and the technology transferred has not been developed in the technology acquiring country by the supplying party, or when it otherwise acts as an intermediary in the transfer of foreign owned technology.] */***

[The Code of Conduct applies to international transfer of technology transactions which occur when technology is transferred across national boundaries between the supplying party and the acquiring party. States may also apply, by means of national legislation, the principles of the Code of Conduct to transactions which take place between parties within their national boundaries.] **

The Chairman of Working Group 1 had prepared a compromise text, which was included in a footnote to the draft provision in TD/CODE TOT/14. The Chairman's text states:

'The Code of Conduct shall apply to international transfer of technology transactions which occur when technology is transferred across national boundaries between the supplying party and the acquiring party or when a transfer of technology transaction is entered into between parties which do not reside or are not established in the same country. States may also decide to extend the application of the Code of Conduct to transactions which take place between parties which are resident of or established in the same country, if at least one party is a branch, subsidiary or affiliate or is otherwise directly or indirectly controlled by a foreign entity and the technology transferred has not been developed in the technology acquiring country by the supplying party, or when it otherwise acts as an intermediary in the transfer of foreign owned technology.'

2   The text in brackets has been proposed by the Group of 77. Groups B and D are in favour of deleting paragraph 1.6.

Chapter 2   Objectives and principles[1]

2.   The Code of Conduct is based on the following objectives and principles:

2.1 *Objectives*

(i)   To establish general and equitable standards on which to base the relationships among parties to transfer of technology transactions and governments concerned, taking into consideration their legitimate interests, and giving due recognition to special needs of developing countries for the fulfilment of their economic and social development objectives.

(ii)   To promote mutual confidence between parties as well as their governments.

(iii) To encourage transfer of technology transactions, particularly those involving developing countries, under conditions where bargaining positions of the parties to the transactions are balanced in such a way as to avoid abuses of a stronger position and thereby to achieve mutually satisfactory agreements.

(iv) To facilitate and increase the international flow of technological information, particularly on the availability of alternative technologies, as a prerequisite for the assessment, selection, adaptation, development and use of technologies in all countries, particularly in developing countries.

(v)   To facilitate and increase the international flow of proprietary and non-proprietary technology for strengthening the growth of the scientific and technological capabilities of all countries, in particular developing countries, so as to increase their participation in world production and trade.

(vi) To increase the contributions of technology to the identification and solution of social and economic problems of all countries, particularly the developing countries, including the development of basic sectors of their national economies.

(vii) To facilitate the formulation, adoption and implementation of national policies, laws and regulations on the subject of transfer of technology by setting forth international norms.

(viii) To promote adequate arrangements as regards unpackaging in terms of information concerning the various elements of the technology to be transferred, such as that required for technical, institutional and financial evaluation of the transaction, thus avoiding

---

1   Text transmitted by the President to the Conference at its 12th meeting, as revised in the text submitted by the President to the Conference at its 14th meeting.

undue or unnecessary packaging.
(ix) To specify restrictive [business] practices from which parties to technology transfer transactions [shall] [should] refrain.
(x) [To set forth an appropriate set of responsibilities and obligations of parties to transfer of technology transactions, taking into consideration their legitimate interests as well as differences in their bargaining positions.]¹

2.2 *Principles*

(i) The Code of Conduct is universally applicable in scope.
(ii) [States may employ all appropriate means of facilitating and regulating the transfer of technology, in a manner consistent with their international obligations and taking into consideration the legitimate interests of all parties concerned.]²

bis The Principles of sovereignty and political independence of States (covering, *inter alia*, the requirements of foreign policy and national security), and sovereign equality of States, should be recognized in facilitating and regulating transfer of technology transactions.
(iii) States should co-operate in the international transfer of technology in order to promote economic growth throughout the world, especially that of the developing countries. Co-operation in such transfer should be irrespective of any differences in political, economic and social systems; this is one of the important elements in maintaining international peace and security and promoting international economic stability and progress, the general welfare of nations and international co-operation free from discrimination based on such differences. Nothing in this Code may be construed as impairing or derogating from the provisions of the Charter of the United Nations or actions taken in pursuance thereof. It is understood that special treatment in transfer of technology should be accorded to developing countries in accordance with the provisions in this Code on the subject.
(iv) The separate responsibilities of parties to transfer of technology transactions, on the one hand, and those of governments when not acting as parties, on the other, should be clearly distinguished.
(v) Mutual benefits should accrue to technology supplying and recipient parties in order to maintain and increase the international flow of technology.

---

1 Text awaiting outcome of the negotiations on chapter 5.
2 Subject to review at the next session of the Conference. The Group of 77 considers the language of this principle superseded by the agreement reached at the second session of the Conference on the chapter on national regulation of transfer of technology transactions (chapter 3).

(vi) Facilitating and increasing the access to technology, particularly for developing countries, under mutually agreed fair and reasonable terms and conditions, are fundamental elements in the process of technology transfer and development.

(vii) Recognition of the protection of industrial property rights granted under national law.

(viii) Technology supplying parties when operating in an acquiring country should respect the sovereignty and the laws of that country, act with proper regard for that country's declared development policies and priorities and endeavour to contribute substantially to the development of the acquiring country. The freedom of parties to negotiate, conclude and perform agreements for the transfer of technology on mutually acceptable terms and conditions should be based on respect for the foregoing and other principles set forth in this Code.

Chapter 3   National regulation of transfer of technology transactions[1]

3.1   In adopting, and in the light of evolving circumstances making necessary changes in laws, regulations and rules, and policies with respect to transfer of technology transaction, States have the right to adopt measures such as those listed in paragraph 3.3 of this chapter and should act on the basis that these measures should:

(i)   Recognize that a close relationship exists between technology flows and the conditions under which such flows are admitted and treated;

(ii)   Promote a favourable and beneficial climate for the international transfer of technology;

(iii)   Take into consideration in an equitable manner the legitimate interests of all parties;

(iv)   Encourage and facilitate transfers of technology to take place under mutually agreed, fair and reasonable terms and conditions having regard to the principles and objectives of the Code;

(v)   Take into account the differing factors characterizing the transactions such as local conditions, the nature of the technology and the scope of the undertaking;

(vi)   Be consistent with their international obligations.

3.2   Measures adopted by States including decisions of competent administrative bodies should be applied fairly, equitably, and on the

---

1   Text transmitted by the President to the Conference at its 12th meeting.

same basis to all parties in accordance with established procedures of law and the principles and objectives of the Code. Laws and regulations should be clearly defined and publicly and readily available. To the extent appropriate, relevant information regarding decisions of competent administrative bodies should be disseminated.

3.2.1 Each country adopting legislation on the protection of industrial property should have regard to its national needs of economic and social development, and should ensure an effective protection of industrial property rights granted under its national law and other related rights recognized by its national law.

3.3 Measures on regulation of the flow and effects of transfer of technology, finance and technical aspects of technology transactions and on organizational forms and mechanisms may deal with:

Finance

(a)   Currency regulations of foreign exchange payments and remittances;

(b)   Conditions of domestic credit and financing facilities;

(c)   Transferability of payments;

(d)   Tax treatment;

(e)   Pricing policies;

Renegotiation

(f)   Terms, conditions and objective criteria for the renegotiation of transfer of technology transactions;

Technical aspects

(g)   Technology specifications and standards for the various components of the transfer of technology transactions and their payments;

(h)   Analysis and evaluation of transfer of technology transactions to assist parties in their negotiations;

(i)   Use of local and imported components;

Organizational forms and mechanisms

(j)   Evaluation, negotiation, and registration of transfer of technology transactions;

(k) Terms, conditions, duration, of transfer of technology transactions;

(l) Loss of ownership and/or control of domestic acquiring enterprises;

(m) Regulation of foreign collaboration arrangements and agreements that could displace national enterprises from the domestic market;

(n) The definition of fields of activity of foreign enterprises and the choice of channels, mechanisms, organizational forms for the transfer of technology and the prior or subsequent approval of transfer of technology transactions and their registration in these fields;

(o) The determination of the legal effect of transactions which are not in conformity with national laws, regulations and administrative decisions on the transfer of technology;

(p) The establishment or strengthening of national administrative mechanisms for the implementation and application of the Code of Conduct and of national laws, regulations and policies on the transfer of technology;

(q) Promotion of appropriate channels for the international exchange of information and experience in the field of the transfer of technology.

Chapter 4   [The regulation of practices and arrangements involving the transfer of technology] [Restrictive business practices] [Exclusion of political discrimination and restrictive business practices] [1]

Section A [2]

In furtherance of the objectives of this Code, particularly to avoid practices which [unreasonably] ** restrain trade [and] **/*** [or] * adversely affect the international flow of technology, particularly as such practices hinder the economic and technological development of acquiring countries, parties to technology transfer transactions [shall] */*** [should] ** refrain from the following practices [or practices having similar effects] * [in licensing patents or know-how or trade marks associated with patents or know-how] ** [unless the

---

1 Text submitted by the Chairman of the Second Committee to the Conference at its 12th meeting.
2 In view of continuing negotiations on the chapter, no attempt has been made to number the provisions of this chapter consistently with the other chapters.

practice is] **/*** [subject to exceptions or justifications in the following provisions or reasonable] ** [in an individual case] ** [.] * [,] ** [Whether a restrictive practice listed below is] * [consistent with the objectives of this Code in an individual case] */*** [which] *** [should be examined in terms of its purpose and effect in the actual situation,] */*** taking into account [its appropriateness in] */*** [all] ** the relevant circumstances, including those prevailing at the inception of the arrangement [and its acceptability under pertinent national or regional laws or regulations for control of restrictive practices] *.

[Practices and restrictions between commonly owned enterprises should be examined in the light of the rules, exceptions and factors applicable to all transfer of technology transactions. Such practices may be considered as not contrary to the provisions of the Code when they are otherwise acceptable and which do not adversely affect the transfer of technology] *. [Recognizing that restrictions for the purpose of rationalization or reasonable allocation of functions between parent and subsidiary or among enterprises belonging to the same concern will normally be considered not contrary to this chapter unless amounting to an abuse of a dominant position of market power within the relevant market, for example unreasonable restraint of the trade of a competing enterprise] **.

Section B (List of practices)

1   [Exclusive] ** *Grant-back provisions*   Requiring the acquiring party to transfer or grant back to the supplying party, or to any other enterprise designated by the supplying party, improvements arising from the acquired technology, on an exclusive basis [or] * without offsetting consideration or reciprocal obligations from the supplying party, or when the practice will constitute an abuse of a dominant market position of the supplying party.

2   *Challenges to validity*   [Unreasonably] ** requiring the acquiring party to refrain from challenging the validity of patents and other types of protection for inventions involved in the transfer or the validity of other such grants claimed or obtained by the supplying party, recognizing that any issues concerning the mutual rights and obligations of the parties following such a challenge will be determined by the appropriate applicable law and the terms of the agreement to the extent consistent with that law.[1]

1   The spokesmen for the regional groups noted that their acceptance of agreed language which makes reference to the term 'applicable law' is conditional upon acceptable resolution of differences in the group texts concerning applicable law and national regulation of this Code.

3 *Exclusive dealing* Restrictions on the freedom of the acquiring party to enter into sales, representation or manufacturing agreements relating to similar or competing technologies or products or to obtain competing technology, when such restrictions are not needed for ensuring the achievement of legitimate interests, particularly including securing the confidentiality of the technology transferred or best effort distribution or promotional obligations.

4 *Restrictions on research* [Unreasonably] **/*** restricting the acquiring party either in undertaking research and development directed to absorb and adapt the transferred technology to local conditions or in initiating research and development programmes in connection with new products, processes or equipment.

5 *Restrictions on use of personnel* [Unreasonably] ** requiring the acquiring party to use personnel designated by the supplying party, except to the extent necessary to ensure the efficient transmission phase for the transfer of technology and putting it to use or thereafter continuing such requirement beyond the time when adequately trained local personnel are available or have been trained; or prejudicing the use of personnel of the technology acquiring country.

6 *Price fixing* [Unjustifiably] ** imposing regulation of prices to be charged by acquiring parties in the relevant market to which the technology was transferred for products manufactured or services produced using the technology supplied.

7 *Restrictions or adaptations* Restrictions which [unreasonably] ** prevent the acquiring party from adapting the imported technology to local conditions or introducing innovations in it, or which oblige the acquiring party to introduce unwanted or unnecessary design or specification changes, if the acquiring party makes adaptations on his own responsibility and without using the technology supplying party's name, trade or service marks or trade names, and except to the extent that this adaptation unsuitably affects those products, or the process for their manufacture, to be supplied to the supplying party, his designates, or his other licensees, or to be used as a component or spare part in a product to be supplied to his customers.

8 *Exclusive sales or representation agreements* Requiring the acquiring party to grant exclusive sales or representation rights to the supplying party or any person designated by the supplying party, except as to subcontracting or manufacturing arrangements wherein the parties have agreed that all or part of the production under the tech-

388

nology transfer arrangement will be distributed by the supplying party or any person designated by him.

9   *Tying arrangements*   [Unduly]** imposing acceptance of additional technology, future inventions and improvements, goods or services not wanted by the acquiring party or [unduly]** restricting sources of technology, goods or services, as a condition for obtaining the technology required when not required to maintain the quality of the product or service when the supplier's trade or service mark or other identifying item is used by the acquiring party, or to fulfil a specific performance obligation which has been guaranteed, provided further that adequate specification of the ingredients is not feasible or would involve the disclosure of additional technology not covered by the arrangement.

10   *Export restrictions*   [Unreasonable]** restrictions which prevent or [substantially]**/*** hinder export by means of territorial or quantitative limitations or prior approval for export or export prices of products or increased rates of payments for exportable products resulting from the technology supplied [,unless justified]**/*** [, for instance,]** [to prevent export of such products to countries where they are protected by the supplying party's industrial property rights]**/*** [or where relevant know-how has retained its confidential character]** [, or where the supplying party has granted]**/*** [an exclusive right]*** [a licence]** [to use the relevant technology]**/***.

11   *Patent pool or cross-licensing agreements and other arrangements* Restrictions on territories, quantities, prices, customers or markets arising out of patent pool or cross-licensing agreements or other international transfer of technology interchange arrangements among technology suppliers which unduly limit access to new technological developments or which would result in an abusive domination of an industry or market with adverse effects on the transfer of technology, except for those restrictions appropriate and ancillary to co-operative arrangements such as co-operative research arrangements.

12   *Restrictions on publicity*   Restrictions [unreasonably]** regulating the advertising or publicity by the acquiring party except where restrictions of such publicity may be required to prevent injury to the supplying party's goodwill or reputation where the advertising or publicity makes reference to the supplying party's name, trade or service marks, trade names or other identifying items, or for legitimate reasons of avoiding product liability when the supplying party may be

subject to such liability, or where appropriate for safety purposes or to protect consumers, or when needed to secure the confidentiality of the technology transferred.

13 *Payments and other obligations after expiration of industrial property rights* Requiring payments or imposing other obligations for continuing the use of industrial property rights which have been invalidated, cancelled or have expired, recognizing that any other issue, including other payment obligations for technology, shall be dealt with by the appropriate applicable law and the terms of the agreement to the extent consistent with that law.[1]

14 *Restrictions after expiration of arrangement* Restrictions on the use of the technology after the expiration or termination of the arrangement [,unless the technology is still legally protected, or has not entered the public domain] **/*** [or after the know-how has lost its secret character] * independently of the acquiring party.

15 [*Limitations on volume, scope, etc.*] */*** [Unreasonable] *** [Restrictions on the scope, volume and/or capacity of production] */*** [and/or field of activity] *.

16 [*Use of quality controls*] */*** [Use by the supplying party of quality control methods or standards not needed or not wanted by the acquiring party, except] */*** [to meet the requirement of a guarantee or] *** [when the product bears a trade mark, service name or trade name of the supplying party] */***.

17 [*Obligation to use trade marks*] */*** [Requirement to use a particular trade mark, service name or trade name when using the technology supplied] */*** [; the supplying party, however, has the right to request that its name be mentioned on the product] ***.

18 [*Requirement to provide equity or participate in management*] */*** [Obliging the acquiring party to provide equity capital or to allow the supplying party to participate in the management of the acquiring party as a condition to obtaining the technology] */***.

19 [*Unlimited or unduly long duration of arrangements*] */*** [Unlimited or unduly long duration of transfer of technology arrangements] */***.

---

1 See footnote on p.387.

20 [*Limitations upon use of technology already imported*] * [Limitations upon the diffusion and/or further use of technology already imported.] *

Section C [Exceptions] */***

[Notwithstanding] */*** [the provisions] *** [section 4.3] * [of this chapter transfer of technology transactions or practices and arrangements contained therein shall be deemed]*/*** [non-objectionable] *** [valid] * [if] */*** [, based upon exceptional circumstances,] * [the competent national authorities of the] */*** [acquiring party's] *** [technology acquiring] * [country decide that it is in its public interest] */*** [and that on balance the effect on its national economy will not be adverse] * [and it has no substantial adverse effects in other countries] ***.

Chapter 5 Guarantees/Responsibilities/Obligations[1]

Common provision on negotiating as well as contractual phase

5.1 When negotiating and concluding a technology transfer agreement, the parties [shall] */*** [should] **, in accordance with this chapter, be responsive to the economic and social development objectives of the respective countries of the parties and particularly of the technology acquiring country, and when negotiating, concluding and performing a technology transfer agreement, the parties should observe fair and honest business practices.

Negotiating phase

5.2 In being responsive to the economic and social development objectives mentioned in this chapter each party [shall]*/*** [should] **, take into account the other's request to include in the agreement, to the extent practicable and for adequate consideration, when appropriate, such as the case in which the supplying party incurs additional costs or efforts, items clearly related to the official economic and social development objectives of the country of the requesting party as enunciated by its government. Such items include, *inter alia*, where applicable:

---

1 Text submitted by the Chairman of the Second Committee to the Conference at its 12th meeting.

(a)   Use of locally available resources

(i)   specific provisions for the use for the tasks concerned of adequately trained or otherwise suitable local personnel to be designated and subsequently made available by the potential technology recipient including managerial personnel, as well as for the training of suitably skilled local personnel to be designated and subsequently made available by the potential technology recipient;

(ii)   specific provisions for the use of locally available materials, technologies, technical skills, consultancy and engineering services and other resources to be indicated and subsequently made available by the potential technology recipient;

(b)   Rendering of technical services   Specific provisions for the rendering of technical services in the introduction and operation of the technology to be transferred;

(c)   Unpackaging   Upon request of the potential acquiring party, the potential supplying party [shall] */*** [should] **, to the extent practicable, make adequate arrangements as regards unpackaging in terms of information concerning the various elements of the technology to be transferred, such as that required for technical, institutional, and financial evaluation of the potential supplying party's offer.

5.3   Fair and honest business practices

When negotiating a technology transfer agreement, the parties should observe fair and honest business practices and therefore:

(a)   Both potential parties

(i)   *Fair and reasonable terms and conditions*   Should negotiate in good faith with the aim of reaching an agreement in a timely manner and upon fair [and reasonable commercial] ** terms and conditions, including agreement on payments such as licence fees, royalties and other consideration; [the price or consideration to be charged should be non-discriminatory] */*** [and no less favourable than the consideration usually required by the supplying party or other technology suppliers for similar technologies under similar circumstances;] *

(ii)   *Relevant information*   Should consider requests to inform each other, to the extent appropriate, about their prior arrangements which may affect the contemplated technology transfer;

(iii) *Confidential information*   Should keep secret, in accordance with any obligation, either legal or contractual, all confidential information received from the other party and make use of the confidential information received from a potential party only for the purpose of evaluating this party's offer or request or for other purposes agreed upon by the parties;

(iv) *Termination of negotiations*   May cease negotiations if, during the negotiations, either party determines that a satisfactory agreement cannot be reached;

(b)   The potential acquiring party

Relevant information   Should provide the potential technology supplier in a timely manner with the available specific information concerning the technical conditions and official economic and social development objectives as well as legislation of the acquiring country relevant to the particular transfer and use of the technology under negotiation, as far as such information is needed for the supplying party's responsiveness under this chapter;

(c)   The potential supplying party

Relevant information

(i)   [shall] */*** [should] ** disclose, in a timely manner, to the potential technology acquiring party any reason actually known to him, on account of which the technology to be supplied, when used in accordance with the terms and conditions of the proposed agreement, would not meet particular health, safety and environmental requirements in the technology acquiring country, already known to him as being relevant in the specific case or which have been specifically drawn to his attention, as well as any serious health, safety and environmental risks known by the supplier associated with the use of the technology and of products to be produced by it;

(ii)   [shall] */*** [should] ** disclose to the potential technology acquiring party, to the actual extent known to him, any limitation, including any pending official procedure or litigation which adversely concerns the existence or validity of the rights to be transferred, on his entitlement to grant the rights or render the assistance and services specified in the proposed agreement;

(iii) *Provision of accessories, spare parts and components* [shall] */*** [should] **, to the extent feasible, take into account the request of the acquiring party to provide it for a period to be specified with accessories, spare parts and components produced by the supplying party and necessary for using the technology to be transferred, particularly where alternative sources are unavailable.

Contractual phase

5.4   The technology transfer agreement [should] ** [shall] */*** contain mutually acceptable contractual obligations, including those relating to payments, and [where in accordance with fair and reasonable commercial practice, should normally provide for] ** [shall be subject to] */*** the following provisions [taking into account the specific circumstances of the individual case] ***. [The specific circumstances of the individual case should be taken into account in the inclusion of the provisions listed and recognition be given to certain circumstances, namely the stage of development of technology, the limitation of the supplying party's resources or the nature of the economic relationship of the parties such as any ongoing or continuous flow of technology between the parties] **;[1]

(i)   Access to improvements   Access by the [parties] **/*** [acquiring party] * for a specified period or for the lifetime of the agreement to improvements to the technology transferred under the agreement;

(ii)   Confidentiality   Respect for the confidentiality [and proprietary nature, and the use only] **/*** [for the purposes and] ** [on terms stipulated in the agreement] **/*** of any trade secrets, secret know-how and all other confidential information received from the other party in connection with the transfer of technology [, provided that this obligation shall] */*** [not extend beyond an adequate lapse of time after the transmission of each item of secret information] * [and after the trade secrets, secret know-how and other confidential information received have entered the public domain independently of the acquiring party] ***;

(iii)   [Dispute settlement arrangements and applicable law] ** [appropriate dispute settlement arrangements, such as impartial fact-finding, and arbitration procedures or choice of judicial forum and choice of applicable law to be followed in connection with the formation, validity, interpretation and the performance of the technology transfer agreement;] **

---

1   Group B suggests that this paragraph should be added to section 5.1. (Common provision on negotiating as well as contractual phase.)

(iv) Description of the technology   The technology supplier's guarantee that the technology meets the description contained in the technology transfer agreement;

(v) Suitability for use   The technology supplier's guarantee that the technology, if used in accordance with the supplier's specific instructions given pursuant to the agreement, is suitable for manufacturing of goods or production of services as agreed upon by the parties and stipulated in the agreement;

(vi) Rights to the technology transferred   The technology supplier's representation that on the date of the signing of the agreement, it is, to the best of its knowledge, not aware of third parties' valid patent rights or similar protection for inventions which would be infringed by the use of the technology when used as specified in the agreement;

(vii) Quality levels and goodwill   The technology recipient's commitment to observe quality levels agreed upon in cases where the agreement includes the use of the supplier's trade marks, trade names or similar identification of goodwill, and both parties' commitment to avoid taking actions primarily or deliberately intended to injure the other's goodwill or reputation;

(viii) [Achievement of predetermined results] */*** [the supplying party's guarantee that the use of the technology will ensure the achievement of a predetermined result under the conditions specified in the agreement;] */***

(ix) Transmission of documentation   The supplying party's commitment that relevant technical documentation and other data required from him for a particular purpose defined in terms directly specified in the agreement will be transferred in a timely manner and as correctly and completely for such purpose as agreed upon.

(x) [Training of personnel] */*** [to provide adequate training to the personnel of the acquiring party, or to the personnel designated by it, in the knowledge and operation of the technology transferred, on terms stipulated in the agreement;] */***

(xi) [Provision of spare parts, components, etc.] */*** [the supplying party shall] */*** [, to the extent possible,] *** supply the acquiring party, as required, with accessories, spare parts, components and other requirements produced by the supplying party and necessary for using the technology transferred, at usual prices and for the period specified

in the agreement;] */***

*(xii) [Consideration for the technology transferred] */***

[(a) The price charged or other consideration made for all elements involved in the transfer of technology transactions, including goods and services in so far as they are part of the transaction, shall be distinctly specified for each item;] */***

[(b) The price charged or other consideration made for the technology transferred shall be explicitly determined or, where this is not possible, all the necessary elements for their determination shall be specified;] */***

[(c) The price or consideration to be charged shall be non-discriminatory] */*** [and no less favourable than the consideration usually required by the supplying party or other technology suppliers for similar technologies under similar circumstances;] *

*(xiii) [Purchase of input] */*** [When the acquiring party has no other alternative than to purchase goods and/or services from the supplying party, or from any enterprise designated by it, prices for such inputs shall be fair and not higher than current world prices for goods or services of the same quality offered on comparable commercial terms and conditions;] */***

*(xiv) [Sale of output] */*** [When the acquiring party sells its output to the supplying party, or to any enterprise designated by it, the price offered for such products shall be reasonable and fair and comparable with current world prices for the goods of the same quality sold on similar commercial terms and conditions;] */***

(xv) Liability [The supplying party shall be liable] */*** [according to the appropriate applicable law] *** [for the loss of, damage or injury to property or persons, arising from the technology transferred or the goods produced by it, provided that the technology is used as specified in the agreement, or in absence of such specification, in a technically correct manner.] */*** [Disposition concerning liability for the non-fulfilment by either party of its responsibilities under the technology transfer agreement.] **

5.5 [Effects of non-fulfilment] *

[The effects of non-fulfilment of the provisions set forth in this chapter shall be governed by the appropriate applicable law.] *

Chapter 6 Special treatment for developing countries[1]

6.1 Taking into consideration the needs and problems of developing countries, particularly of the least developed countries, governments of developed countries, directly or through appropriate international organizations, in order to facilitate and encourage the initiation and strengthening of the scientific and technological capabilities of developing countries so as to assist and co-operate with them in their efforts to fulfil their economic and social objectives, should take adequate specific measures, *inter alia*, to:

(i) facilitate access by developing countries to available information regarding the availabilities, description, location and, as far as possible, approximate cost of technologies which might help those countries to attain their economic and social development objectives;

(ii) give developing countries the freest and fullest possible access to technologies whose transfer is not subject to private decisions;[2]

(iii) facilitate access by developing countries, to the extent practicable, to technologies whose transfer is subject to private decisions;[2]

(iv) assist and co-operate with developing countries in the assessment and adaptation of existing technologies and in the development of national technologies by facilitating access, as far as possible, to available scientific and industrial research data;

(v) co-operate in the development of scientific and technological resources in developing countries, including the creation and growth of innovative capacities;

(vi) assist developing countries in strengthening their technological capacity, especially in the basic sectors of their national economy, through creation of and support for laboratories, experimental facilities and institutes for training and research;

(vii) co-operate in the establishment or strengthening of national, regional and/or international institutions, including technology transfer centres, to help developing countries to develop and obtain the technology and skills required for the establishment, development and enhancement of their technological capabilities including the design, construction and operation of plants;

1 Agreed text prepared in the First Committee and transmitted to the Conference at its 7th meeting, as revised in the text submitted by the President to the Conference at its 14th meeting.
2 The term 'private decision' in the particular context of this chapter should be officially interpreted in the light of the legal order of the respective country.

(viii) encourage the adaptation of research and development, engineering and design to conditions and factor endowments prevailing in developing countries;

(ix) co-operate in measures leading to greater utilization of the managerial, engineering, design and technical experience of the personnel and the institutions of developing countries in specific economic and other development projects undertaken at the bilateral and multilateral levels;

(x) encourage the training of personnel from developing countries.

6.2 Governments of developed countries, directly or through appropriate international organizations, in assisting in the promotion of transfer of technology to developing countries − particularly to the least developed countries − should, as a part of programmes for development assistance and co-operation, take into account requests from developing countries to:

(i) contribute to the development of national technologies in developing countries by providing experts under development assistance and research exchange programmes;

(ii) provide training for research, engineering, design and other personnel from developing countries engaged in the development of national technologies or in the adaptation and use of technologies transferred;

(iii) provide assistance and co-operation in the development and administration of laws and regulations with a view to facilitating the transfer of technology;

(iv) provide support for projects in developing countries for the development and adaptation of new and existing technologies suitable to the particular needs of developing countries;

(v) grant credits on terms more favourable than the usual commercial terms for financing the acquisition of capital and intermediate goods in the context of approved development projects involving transfer of technology transactions so as to reduce the cost of projects and improve the quality of technology received by the developing countries;

[(vi) Omit] [1]

(vii) provide assistance and co-operation in the development and administration of laws and regulations designed to avoid health, safety and environmental risks associated with technology or the products produced by it.

1 The Group of 77 reserves its position on this provision (6.2.(vi)) of the chapter until it has had the opportunity to examine the references to the industrial property system in the final draft of all chapters of the Code. For the original proposal see TD/CODE TOT/1.

6.3 Governments of developed countries should take measures in accordance with national policies, laws and regulations to encourage and to endeavour to give incentive to enterprises and institutions in their countries, either individually or in collaboration with enterprises and institutions in developing countries, particularly those in the least developed countries, to make special efforts, *inter alia*, to:

(i) assist in the development of technological capabilities of the enterprises in developing countries, including special training as required by the recipients;

(ii) undertake the development of technology appropriate to the needs of developing countries;

(iii) undertake R and D activity in developing countries of interest to such countries, as well as to improve co-operation between enterprises and scientific and technological institutions of developed and developing countries;

(iv) assist in projects by enterprises and institutions in developing countries for the development and adaptation of new and existing technologies suitable to the particular needs and conditions of developing countries.

6.4 The special treatment accorded to developing countries should be responsive to their economic and social objectives vis-à-vis their relative stage of economic and social development and with particular attention to the special problems and conditions of the least developed countries.

Chapter 7 International collaboration[1]

7.1 The States recognize the need for appropriate international collaboration among governments, intergovernmental bodies, and organs and agencies of the United Nations system, including the international institutional machinery provided for in this Code, with a view to facilitating an expanded international flow of technology for strengthening the technological capabilities of all countries, taking into account the objectives and principles of this Code, and to promoting the effective implementation of its provisions.

7.2 Such international collaboration between governments at the bilateral or multilateral, subregional, regional or interregional levels may

---

1 Text prepared by the Intergovernmental Group of Experts, as revised in the text submitted by the President to the Conference at its 14th meeting.

include, *inter alia*, the following measures:

(i) Exchange of available information on the availability and description of technologies and technological alternatives;

(ii) Exchange of available information on experience in seeking solutions to problems relating to the transfer of technology, particularly restrictive [business] ** practices in the transfer of technology;

(iii) Exchange of information on development of national legislation with respect to the transfer of technology;

(iv) Promotion of the conclusion of international agreements which should provide equitable treatment for both technology supplying and recipient parties and governments;

(v) Consultations which may lead to greater harmonization, where appropriate, of national legislation and policies with respect to the transfer of technology;

(vi) Promotion, where appropriate, of common programmes for searching for, acquiring and disseminating technologies;

(vii) Promotion of programmes for the adaptation and development of technology in the context of development objectives;

(viii) Promotion of the development of scientific and technological resources and capabilities stimulating the development of indigenous technologies;

(ix) Action through international agreements to avoid, as far as possible, imposition of double taxation on earnings and payments arising out of transfer of technology transactions.

Chapter 8   International institutional machinery[1]

8.1   *Institutional arrangements*

(a) [A Special Committee on the Code established within UNCTAD] [The Committee on Transfer of Technology] will provide the institutional machinery;

(b) The [Special Committee] [Committee on Transfer of Technology meeting in special session with respect to the Code and matters related thereto] [as a special agenda item of its regular sessions or, if necessary, at special sessions of the Committee,] open to all members of

---

1 Text transmitted by the President to the Conference at its 12th meeting, as revised in the text submitted by the President to the Conference at its 14th meeting.

UNCTAD, should meet as often as necessary, but at least once a year. The Committee may create appropriate subsidiary bodies to assist it in its work. Its rules of procedure [at least initially] shall be those of the main committees of the Trade and Development Board.

(c) States which have accepted the Code of Conduct on the Transfer of Technology should take appropriate steps at the national level to meet their commitment to the Code.

8.2 *Functions of the Committee*

8.2.1 The Committee shall have the following functions:

(a) To provide a forum and modalities for consultations, discussion, and exchange of views between States on matters related to the Code, in particular its application and its greater harmonization, and the experience gained in its operations;

(b) To undertake and disseminate periodically studies and research on transfer of technology related to the provisions of the Code, with a view to increasing exchange of experience and giving greater effect to the application and implementation of the Code;

(c) To invite and consider relevant studies, documentation and reports from within the United Nations system, particularly from UNIDO and WIPO;

(d) To study matters relating to the Code and which might be characterized by data covering transfer of technology transactions and other relevant information obtained upon request addressed to all States;

(e) To collect and disseminate information on matters relating to the Code, to the over-all attainment of its goals and to the appropriate steps States have taken at the national level to promote an effective Code, including its objective and principles;

(f) To make appropriate reports and recommendations to States on matters within its competence including the application and implementation of the Code;

(g) To organize symposia, workshops and similar meetings concerning the application of the provisions of the Code, subject to the approval of the Trade and Development Board where financing from the regular budget is involved;

(h) To submit reports at least once a year on its work to the Trade and Development Board.

8.2.2 In the performance of its functions, neither the Committee nor its subsidiary organs may act like a tribunal or otherwise pass judgement on the activities or conduct of individual Governments or of individual parties in connection with a specific transfer of technology transaction. The Committee or its subsidiary organs should avoid becoming involved when parties to a specific transfer of technology transaction are in dispute.

8.2.3 The Committee shall establish such procedures as may be necessary to deal with issues related to confidentiality.

8.3 Review procedure

Subject to the approval of the General Assembly [four] [six] years after the adoption of the Code a United Nations Conference [of Plenipotentiaries] shall be convened by the Secretary-General of the United Nations under the auspices of UNCTAD for the purpose of reviewing all the aspects of the Code [with a view to bringing about its universal application as a legally binding instrument] [including its legal nature] [including the final decision on the legal character of the Code]. Towards this end, the Committee shall make proposals to the Conference for the improvement and further development of the Code, taking into account relevant activity in the field of transfer of technology within the framework of the United Nations system.

8.4 Secretariat

The secretariat for the Committee shall be the UNCTAD secretariat. At the request of the Committee the secretariat shall submit relevant studies, documentation and other information to the Committee. It shall consult with and render assistance, by the relevant services, to States, particularly the developing countries, at their request, in the application of the Code at the national level, to the extent that resources are available.

8.5 General provisions

[The establishment of the Special Committee by the Trade and Development Board shall be subject to the approval of the General Assembly.] The establishment by the Committee of such subsidiary bodies as it may deem necessary shall be subject to the approval of the Trade and Development Board. [Financial requirements in connection with the servicing of the Committee which are to be borne by the United Nations budget shall be subject to approval by the General Assembly.]

Chapter 9 Applicable law and settlement of disputes

[under consideration]

Chapter 10 Other provisions

[to be drafted]

III(d) DRAFT INTERNATIONAL AGREEMENT TO PREVENT AND ELIMINATE ILLICIT PAYMENTS IN INTERNATIONAL COMMERCIAL TRANSACTIONS

Article 1

Each Contracting State undertakes to make the following acts punishable by appropriate criminal penalties under its national law:

'(a) The offering, promising or giving of any payment, gift or other benefit by any person, on his own behalf or on behalf of any other natural or juridical person, to a public official, either directly or indirectly with the intention of inducing such official to perform or refrain from the performance of his duties in connexion with an international commercial transaction.'

'(b) The soliciting, demanding, accepting or receiving, directly or indirectly, by a public official of any payment, gift or other benefit, as consideration for performing or refraining from the performance of his duties in connexion with an international commercial transaction.'

Article 2

'(a) "Public official" means any person whether appointed or elected who, at the national, regional or local level holds a [legislative,] administrative, judicial or military office or who is an employee of a government or of a public or governmental authority or agency or an employee of an entity which provides a public service and which is owned [or controlled] by such a body, and any other person when performing a public function.'

'(b) "International commercial transactions" includes any sale, contract or other business transaction with a national, regional or local Government or any authority or entity referred to in paragraph (a) of this article [and any application for government approval of a sale, contract or business transaction], which under the laws of that State is open to foreign persons or enterprises [or to suppliers of imported goods, services, capital or technology].'

'(c) "Intermediary" means any natural or juridical person who negotiates with or otherwise deals directly or indirectly with a public official on behalf of another natural or juridical person. However, the term does not include any employee of the person on whose behalf the intermediary is acting.']

Article 3

'[(a) Each Contracting State shall ensure that contracts which are entered into by agencies or instrumentalities of its Government for international commercial transactions include a provision that no payment, gift or other benefit which would constitute an offence under article 1 has been or will be offered, promised or given in connexion with the transactions.]

'(b) Each Contracting State shall, in accordance with national and international law, [endeavour to] take all practicable measures [, and particularly administer its national laws and regulations,] for the purpose of preventing the offences referred to in article 1 [involving its own public officials or public officials of another State.] '

Article 4

'(1) Each Contracting State shall take such measures as may be necessary to establish its jurisdiction:

(a) Over the offences referred to in Article 1 when they are committed in the territory of that state,

(b) Over the offence referred to in article 1(b) when it is committed by a public official of that state,

(c) Over the offence referred to in article 1(a) relating to any payment, gift or other benefit in connexion with the negotiation, conclusion, retention, revision or termination of an international commercial transaction when the offence is committed by a national of that State, provided that any element of that offence, or any act abiding or abetting that offence, is connected with the territory of that State.

'(2) This Agreement does not exclude any criminal jurisdiction exercised in accordance with the national law of a Contracting State.'

Article 5

'(1) A Contracting State in whose territory the alleged offender is found, shall, if it has jurisdiction under article 4, paragraph 1, be obliged without exception whatsoever to submit the case to its competent authorities for the purpose of prosecution, [through proceedings in accordance with the laws of that State.] [Those authorities shall take their decision in the same manner as in the case of any ordinary offence under the law of that State.]

'(2) The obligation provided for in paragraph 1 of this article does not apply if the Contracting State has extradited the alleged offender, or if the Contracting State knows that a prosecution has been undertaken in another State, for the same offence and with respect to the same person.'

Article 6

'(1)(a) Each Contracting State shall ensure, under penalty of law, that [persons resident or] entities established in its territory maintain accurate records of payments made by them to an intermediary, or received by them as an intermediary, [for the purpose of securing] [in connexion with] an international commercial transaction.

(b) These records shall include, *inter alia*, the amount and date of any such payment or payments [exceeding $50,000] which are made to an intermediary in a calendar year or which are attributable to a particular international commercial transaction; the name, address, and nationality of the intermediary or intermediaries receiving such payments; [and, to the extent ascertainable by the party concerned, the name and address of any public official who is employed or retained by or has a financial interest in the intermediary.]

'(2) The records maintained pursuant to paragraph 1 of this article shall be made available for the purpose of criminal investigations and proceedings to the competent law enforcement authorities of another Contracting State in accordance with the provisions for mutual judicial assistance in Article 10.'

Article 7

'(a) Each Contracting State shall prohibit its persons and enterprises of its nationality from making any royalty or tax payments to, or from knowingly transferring any assets or other financial resources in contravention of United Nations resolutions to facilitate trade with or investment in a territory occupied by, an illegal minority regime in southern Africa.

'(b) Each Contracting State shall require, by law or regulation its persons and enterprises of its nationality to report to the competent authority of that State any royalties or taxes paid to an illegal minority régime in southern Africa in contravention of United Nations resolutions.

'(c) Each Contracting State shall submit annually, to the Secretary-General of the United Nations, reports on the activities of transnational corporations of its nationality which collaborate directly or indirectly with illegal minority regimes in southern Africa in contravention of United Nations resolutions.] '

Article 8[1]

(a) Each Contracting State recognizes [agrees to ensure that its national law provide] that if bribery or illicit payment are decisive in procuring the consent of a party to a contract relating to an international commercial transaction such party may at its option institute judicial proceedings in order to have the contract declared null and void.]

Article 9

'(a) The Contracting States shall inform each other upon request of measures taken in the implementation of this Agreement.

'(b) Each Contracting State shall biannually furnish, in accordance with its national laws, to the Secretary-General of the United Nations, information concerning its implementation of this agreement. Such information shall include legislation and administrative regulations, as well as general information on judicial proceedings and other measures taken pursuant to such laws and regulations. Where final convictions have been obtained under laws within the scope of this Convention, information shall also be furnished concerning the case, the decision and sanctions imposed in so far as it is not confidential under the national law of the State which provides the information.

'(c) The Secretary-General shall circulate a summary of the information referred to in paragraph (b) of this article to the Contracting States.'

Article 10

'1   Contracting States shall afford one another the greatest measure of assistance in connexion with criminal investigations and proceedings brought in respect of the offences [referred to in article 1] [within the scope of this Convention whether committed by natural or juridical persons] . The law of the State requested shall apply in all cases.

1 Several representatives pointed out that this article had not been discussed at the fourth, fifth and resumed fifth sessions.

'2   Mutual assistance shall, *inter alia*, include, as far as permissible under the law of the State requested [and taking into account the need for preserving the confidential nature of documents and other information transmitted to appropriate law enforcement authorities] :

'(a) Production of documents or other information, taking of evidence and service of documents, relevant to investigations or court proceedings;

'(b) Notice of the initiation and outcome of [any public] criminal proceedings concerning an offence referred to in article 1, to other Contracting States which may have jurisdiction over the same offence according to article 4.

'3   Contracting States shall upon request enter into negotiations towards the conclusion of bilateral agreements with each other to facilitate the provision of judicial assistance in accordance with this article. [Such agreements shall, *inter alia*, make provision for the taking of evidence and conduct of interviews under the law of the Contracting States.]

'4   The provisions of this article shall not affect obligations under any other treaty, bilateral or multilateral, which governs or will govern in whole or in part mutual assistance in criminal matters.'

Article 11

'1   The offences referred to in article 1 shall be deemed to be included as extraditable offences in any extradition treaty existing between Contracting States. Contracting States undertake to include the said offences as extraditable offences in every extradition treaty to be concluded between them.

'2   If a Contracting State which makes extradition conditional on the existence of a treaty receives a request for extradition from another Contracting State with which it has no extradition treaty, it [may at its option] [shall] consider this Convention as the legal basis for extradition in respect of the offence. Extradition shall be subject to the other conditions provided by the law of the requested State.

'3   Contracting States which do not make extradition conditional on the existence of a treaty [shall] [may at their option] recognize the offence as an extraditable offence between themselves subject to the conditions provided by the law of the requested State.

'4   The offence shall be treated, for the purpose of extradition between Contracting States, as if it had been committed not only in the place in which it occurred but also in the territories of the States

408

required to establish the jurisdiction in accordance with article 4, paragraph 1.'

Article 12[1]

'(a) Any dispute between Contracting States concerning the interpretation or application of this Agreement shall be settled by bilateral consultations unless it is freely and mutually agreed by all States concerned that other peaceful measures be sought on the basis of sovereign equality of States.

'[(b) Any dispute between Contracting States concerning the interpretation or application of this Agreement which cannot be settled through bilateral consultations, shall, at the request of either Contracting State be submitted to an *ad hoc* arbitral tribunal for settlement in accordance with the applicable principles and rules or public international law.] '

Article 13

Alternative 1

'(a) This Agreement shall enter into force [30 days] after the receipt by the depository of the Xth instrument of ratification, [acceptance or approval] or accession.

Alternative 2

'In respect of articles 'a' to 'n', this Agreement shall enter into force [30 days] after the receipt by the depository of the Xth instrument of ratification, [acceptance or approval] or accession. In respect of articles 'o' to 'z', this Agreement shall enter into force [30 days] after the receipt by the depository of the "X + Yth" instrument of ratification, [acceptance or approval] or accession.

'(b) The depository for this Agreement shall be the Secretary-General of the United Nations.'

---

1 Several representatives pointed out that this article had not been discussed at the fourth, fifth and resumed fifth sessions.

Article 14[1]

'(a) Any Contracting State may at the time of its signature, ratification, [acceptance or approval] or accession, enter [a] reservation[s] with respect to the following articles:

'(b) . . .

'(c) . . .

'(d) No reservation shall be permitted in respect of any provisions of this Agreement other than those referred to in paragraph 1 of this article.

'(e) Any reservation entered at the time of signature shall be subject to confirmation at the time of ratification, [acceptance or approval] or accession.

'(f) The entry and confirmation of any reservation in accordance with paragraphs (a) and (e) respectively of this article shall be communicated in writing to the depository.

'(g) A reservation shall take effect from the time of the entry into force of the present Agreement with respect to the reserving State.'

---

[1] Several representatives pointed out that this article had not been discussed at the fourth, fifth and resumed fifth sessions.

III(e) CONCLUDED PROVISIONS OF A UN CODE OF CONDUCT: ACTIVITIES OF TRANS-NATIONAL CORPORATIONS

A. General and political

Respect for national sovereignty and observance of domestic laws, regulations and administrative practices

1   Transnational corporations should/shall respect the national sovereignty of the countries in which they operate and the right of each State to exercise its [full permanent sovereignty] [in accordance with international law] [in accordance with agreements reached by the countries concerned on a bilateral and multilateral basis] over its natural resources [wealth and economic activities] within its territory.

2   [Transnational corporations] [Entities of transnational corporations] [shall/should observe] [are subject to] the laws, regulations [jurisdiction] and [administrative practices] [explicitly declared administrative practices] of the countries in which they operate. [Entities of transnational corporations are subject to the jurisdiction of the countries in which they operate to the extent required by the national law of these countries.]

3   Transnational corporations should/shall respect the right of each State to regulate and monitor accordingly the activities of their entities operating within its territory.

Adherence to economic goals and development objectives, policies and priorities

4   Transnational corporations should/shall [endeavour to] carry on their activities in conformity with the [declared] [established] development policies, objectives and priorities [established by] the countries in which they operate. [Consistent with their financial, technological and managerial resources and capabilities] [Consistent with the nature, purpose and extent of their business operations] [entities of] transnational corporations should [endeavour to] make a positive contribution towards the achievement of [established] [declared] economic development goals of the countries in which they operate at the national and, where appropriate, the regional level within the framework of regional integration programmes. Transnational corporations should/shall [be prepared to] engage in consultations and co-operate with governmental authorities in the countries in which they operate

411

with a view to maximizing their contributions to the development process thereby establishing mutually beneficial relations with these countries.

5   Informal consultations will be pursued at a later stage.

Adherence to socio-cultural objectives and values

6   Transnational corporations should/shall respect the social and cultural objectives, values and traditions of the countries in which they operate. While economic and technological development is normally accompanied by social change, transnational corporations should/shall avoid practices, products or services which cause detrimental effects on cultural patterns and socio-cultural objectives as determined by Governments. For this purpose, transnational corporations should/shall respond positively to requests for consultations from Governments concerned.

Respect for human rights and fundamental freedoms

7+8   Transnational corporations should/shall respect human rights and fundamental freedoms in the countries in which they operate. In their social and industrial relations, transnational corporations should/shall not discriminate on the basis of race, colour, sex, religion, language, social, national and ethnic origin or political or other opinion. Transnational corporations should/shall conform to government policies designed to extend equality of opportunity and treatment.

9   In accordance with the efforts of the international community towards the elimination of *apartheid* in South Africa and its continued illegal occupation of Namibia,

[(a) Transnational corporations shall progressively reduce their business activities and make no further investment in South Africa and immediately cease all business activities in Namibia;

(b) Transnational corporations shall refrain from collaborating directly or indirectly with that régime especially with regard to its racist practices in South Africa and illegal occupation of Namibia to ensure the successful implementation of United Nations resolutions in relation to these two countries.]

Transnational corporations operating in southern Africa

(a) Should respect the national laws and regulations adopted in pursuance of Security Council decisions concerning southern Africa;

(b) Should within the framework of their business activities engage in appropriate activities with a view to contributing to the elimination of racial discrimination practices under the system of *apartheid.*] [1]

Non-interference in internal political affairs

10 Transnational corporations should/shall not interfere [illegally] in the internal [political] affairs of the countries in which they operate [by resorting to] [They should refrain from any] [subversive and other [illicit]] activities [aimed at] undermining the political and social systems in these countries.

11 Transnational corporations should/shall not engage in activities of a political nature which are not permitted by the laws and established policies and administrative practices of the countries in which they operate.

Non-interference in intergovernmental relations

12 Transnational corporations should/shall not interfere in [any affairs concerning] intergovernmental relations [, which are the sole concern of Governments] .

13 Deleted.

14–15 Discussion was postponed. [2]

Abstention from corrupt practices

16 Discussion was postponed.

---

1 This paragraph has been referred to in previous working papers as 'non-collaboration by transnational corporations with racist minority régimes in southern Africa'. The Group will consider at subsequent sessions whether to include a separate heading regarding this paragraph.
2 See Appendix III(f) for Chairman's formulation.

B Economic, financial and social

Ownership and control

17 Transnational corporations should/shall so allocate [endeavour so to allocate] their decision-making powers among their entities as to enable them to contribute to the economic and social development of the countries in which they operate.

18 To the extent permitted by national laws, policies and regulations of the country in which it operates, each entity of a transnational corporation [consistent with its legal status and obligations] should/shall co-operate with the other entities so as to enable each entity to meet effectively the requirements established by the laws, policies and regulations of the country in which it operates.

19 (ex-19 and 20) Transnational corporations shall/should co-operate with Governments and nationals of the countries in which they operate in the implementation of national objectives for local equity partici- pation and for the effective exercise of control by local partners as determined by equity, contractual terms in non-equity arrangements or the laws of such countries.

21 Transnational corporations should/shall carry out their personnel policies in accordance with the national policies of each of the countries in which they operate which give priority to the employment and promotion of its [adequately qualified] nationals at all levels of management and direction of the affairs of each entity so as to enhance the effective participation of its nationals in the decision-making process.

22 Transnational corporations should/shall contribute to the managerial and technical training of nationals of the countries in which they operate and facilitate their employment at all levels of manage- ment of the entities and enterprises as a whole.

Balance of payments and financing

23 Transnational corporations should/shall carry on their operations in conformity with laws and regulations and with full regard to the [declared] policy objectives of the countries in which they operate, particularly developing countries, relating to balance of payments, financial transactions and other issues dealt with in the subsequent paragraphs of this section.

24 (ex-28) Transnational corporations should/shall respond positively to requests for consultation on their activities from the

Governments of the countries in which they operate, with a view to contributing to the alleviation of pressing problems of balance of payments and finance of such countries.

25 (ex-24) [As required by government regulations and in furtherance of government policies] [Consistent with the purpose, nature and extent of their operations] transnational corporations should/shall contribute to the promotion of exports and the diversification of exports [and imports] in the countries in which they operate and to an increased utilization of goods, services and other resources which are available in these countries.

26 Transnational corporations should/shall be responsive to requests by Governments of the countries in which they operate, particularly developing countries, concerning the phasing over a limited period of time of the repatriation of capital in case of disinvestment or remittances of accumulated profits, when the size and timing of such transfers would cause serious balance-of-payments difficulties for such countries.

27 (ex-25) Transnational corporations should/shall not, [contrary to prudent financial practices], engage in short-term financial operations or transfers [short-term financial transactions] nor defer or advance foreign exchange payments, including intra-corporate payments, in a manner which would increase currency instability and thereby cause serious balance-of-payments difficulties for the countries concerned.

28 (ex-26) [In respect of their intra-corporate transactions,] transnational corporations should/shall not impose restrictions on their entities, [beyond generally accepted commercial practices] regarding the transfer of goods, services and funds which would cause serious balance-of-payments difficulties for the countries in which they operate.

29 (ex-27) When having recourse to the money and capital markets of the countries in which they operate, transnational corporations should/shall not [beyond generally accepted financial practices] engage in activities which would have a significant adverse impact on the working of local markets, particularly by restricting the availability of funds to other enterprises [than international corporations]. When issuing shares with the objective of increasing local equity participation in an entity operating in such a country, or engaging in long-term borrowing in the local market, transnational corporations shall/should consult with the Government of the country concerned upon the request on the effects of such transactions on the local money and capital markets.

Transfer pricing

30   (ex-29—30) In respect of their intra-corporate transactions, transnational corporations should/shall not use pricing policies that are not based on relevant market prices, or, in the absence of such prices, the arm's length principle, which have the effect of modifying the tax base on which their entities are assessed or of evading exchange control measures [or customs valuation regulations] [or which [contrary to national laws and regulations] adversely effect economic and social conditions] of the countries in which they operate.

Taxation

31   (ex-32b) Transnational corporations should/shall not, contrary to the laws and regulations of the countries in which they operate, use their corporate structure and modes of operation, such as the use of intra-corporate pricing which is not based on the arm's length principle, or other means, to modify the tax base on which their entities are assessed.

Competition and restrictive business practices

32   (ex-33)   (a) Transnational corporations shall conform to the laws and regulations relating to restrictive business practices in the countries in which they operate and consult and co-operate with the competent authorities of those countries in charge of controlling restrictive business practices.

(b) Transnational corporations shall refrain from restrictive business practices adversely affecting international trade, particularly that of developing countries and the economic development of these countries.

(c) Transnational corporations in their intra-group transactions and in their dealings with other enterprises shall/should adhere to the relevant provisions of The Set of Multilaterally Agreed Equitable Principles and Rules for the Control of Restrictive Business Practices, adopted by the General Assembly in its resolution 35/63 of 5 December 1980, and in particular refrain from the practices listed in section D thereof containing principles and rules for enterprises including transnational corporations.]

[For the purposes of this Code, the relevant provisions of The Set of Multilaterally Agreed Equitable Principles and Rules for the Control of Restrictive Business Practices adopted by the General Assembly in its resolution 35/63 of 5 December 1980 shall/should apply in the field of restrictive business practices.]

Transfer of technology

33 (ex-34) Discussion was postponed pending developments in UNCTAD.

Employment and labour[1]

Consumer protection

36 Transnational corporations shall/should carry out their operations, in particular production and marketing, in accordance with national laws, regulations, administrative practices and policies concerning consumer protection of the countries in which they operate. Transnational corporations shall/should also perform their activities, with due regard to relevant international standards, so that they do not cause injury to the health or endanger the safety of consumers or bring about variations in the quality of products in each market which would have detrimental effects on consumers.

37 Transnational corporations shall/should, in respect of the products and services which they produce or market or propose to produce or market in any country, supply to the competent authorities of that country on request or on a regular basis, as specified by these authorities, all relevant information concerning:

> Characteristics of these products or services which may be injurious to the health and safety of consumers including experimental uses and related aspects;

> Prohibitions, restrictions, warnings and other public regulatory measures imposed in other countries on grounds of health and safety protection on these products or services.

38 Transnational corporations shall/should disclose to the public in the countries in which they operate all appropriate information on the contents and to the extent known, on possible hazardous effects of the products they produce or market in the countries concerned by means of proper labelling, informative and accurate advertising or other appropriate methods. Packaging of their products should be safe and the contents of the product should not be misrepresented.

39 Transnational corporations shall/should be responsive to requests from Governments of the countries in which they operate and be prepared to co-operate with international organizations in their efforts to develop and promote national and international standards for the

---

1 See below, p.423.

protection of the health and safety of consumers and to meet the basic needs of consumers.

Environmental protection

40 Transnational corporations shall/should carry out their activities in accordance with national laws, regulations, administrative practices and policies relating to the preservation of the environment of the countries in which they operate and with due regard to relevant international standards. Transnational corporations shall/should, in performing their activities, take steps to protect the environment and where damaged to restore it [qualification will be elaborated later] and should make efforts to develop and apply adequate technologies for this purpose.

41 Transnational corporations shall/should in respect of the products, processes and services they have introduced or propose to introduce in any country supply to the competent authorities of that country on request or on a regular basis, as specified by these authorities, all relevant information concerning:

> Characteristics of these products, processes and other activities including experimental uses and related aspects which may harm the environment and the measures and costs necessary to avoid or at least to mitigate their harmful effects;

> Prohibitions, restrictions, warnings and other public regulatory measures imposed in other countries on grounds of protection of the environment on these products, processes and services.

42 Transnational corporations shall/should be responsive to requests from Governments of the countries in which they operate and be prepared where appropriate to co-operate with international organizations in their efforts to develop and promote national and international standards for the protection of the environment.

C Disclosure of information

43 Transnational corporations should disclose to the public in the countries in which they operate by appropriate means of communication, clear, full and comprehensible information on the structure, policies, activities and operations of the transnational corporation as a whole. The information should include financial as well as non-financial items and should be made available on a regular annual basis, normally within six months and in any case not later than 12 months from the

418

end of the financial year of the corporation. In addition, during the financial year, transnational corporations should wherever appropriate make available a semi-annual summary of financial information.

The financial information to be disclosed annually should be provided where appropriate on a consolidated basis together with suitable explanatory notes and should include, *inter alia*, the following:

1   A balance sheet;
2   An income statement, including operating results and sales;
3   A statement of allocation of net profits or net income;
4   A statement of the sources and uses of funds;
5   Significant new long-term capital investment;
6   Research and development expenditure.

The non-financial information referred to in the first subparagraph should include, *inter alia*:

1   The structure of the transnational corporations, showing the name and location of the parent company, its main entities, its percentage ownership, direct and indirect, in these entities, including shareholdings between them;

2   The main activity of its entities;

3   Employment information including average number of employees;

4   Accounting policies used in compiling and consolidating the information published;

5   Policies applied in respect of transfer pricing.

The information provided for the transnational corporation as a whole should as far as practicable be broken down:

—   By geographical area or country, as appropriate, with regard to the activities of its main entities, sales, operating results, significant new investments and number of employees;

—   By major line of business as regards sales and significant new investment.

The method of breakdown as well as details of information provided should/shall be determined by the nature, scale and interrelationships of the transnational corporation's operations, with due regard to their significance for the areas or countries concerned.

The extent, detail and frequency of the information provided should take into account the nature and size of the transnational corporation as a whole; the requirements of confidentiality and effects on the transnational corporation's competitive position as well as the cost involved in producing the information.

The information herein required should, as necessary, be in addition to information required by national laws, regulations and administrative practices of the countries in which transnational corporations operate.

44 Transnational corporations should/shall supply to the competent authorities in each of the countries in which they operate, upon request or on a regular basis as specified by those authorities, and in accordance with national legislation, all information required for legislative and administrative purposes relevant to the activities and policies of their entities in the country concerned.

Transnational corporations should/shall, to the extent permitted by the provisions of the relevant national laws, regulations, administrative practices and policies of the countries concerned, supply to competent authorities in the countries in which they operate, information held in other countries needed to enable them to obtain a true and fair view of the operations of the transnational corporation concerned as a whole in so far as the information requested relates to the activities of the entities in the countries seeking such information.

The provisions on paragraph 48 concerning confidentiality shall apply to information supplied under the provisions of this paragraph.

44a With due regard to the relevant provisions of the ILO Tripartite Declaration of Principles concerning Multinational Enterprises and Social Policy and in accordance with national laws, regulations and practices in the field of labour relations, transnational corporations should/shall provide to trade unions or other representatives of employees in their entities in each of the countries in which they operate, by appropriate means of communication, the necessary information on the activities dealt with in this code to enable them to obtain a true and fair view of the performance of the local entity and, where appropriate, the corporation as a whole. Such information should/shall include, where provided for by national law and practices, *inter alia*, prospects or plans for future development having major economic and social effects on the employees concerned.

Procedures for consultation on matters of mutual concern should/shall be worked out by mutual agreement between entities of transnational corporations and trade unions or other representatives of employees in accordance with national law and practice.

Information made available pursuant to the provisions of this paragraph should be subject to appropriate safeguards for confidentiality so that no damage is caused to the parties concerned.[1]

---

1 Para 44a was accepted as concluded on the basis that it would be the sole reference in the Code to the subject of consultations discussed therein.

Treatment of transnational corporations

*General treatment of transnational corporations
by the countries in which they operate*

45 States have the right to regulate the entry and establishment of transnational corporations including determining the role that such corporations may play in economic and social development and prohibiting or limiting the extent of their presence in specific sectors.

46 Transnational corporations should receive [fair and] equitable [and non-discriminatory] treatment [under] [in accordance with] the laws, regulations and administrative practices of the countries in which they operate [as well as intergovernmental obligations to which the Governments of these countries have freely subscribed] [consistent with their international obligations] [consistent with international law].

47 Consistent with [national constitutional systems and] national needs to [protect essential/national economic interests,] maintain public order and to protect national security, [and with due regard to provisions of agreements among countries, particularly developing countries,] entities of transnational corporations should be given by the countries in which they operate [the treatment] [treatment no less favourable than that] [appropriate treatment.] accorded to domestic enterprises under their laws, regulations and administrative practices [when the circumstances in which they operate are similar/identical] [in like situations]. [Transnational corporations should not claim preferential treatment nor the incentives and concessions granted to domestic enterprises of the countries in which they operate.] [Such treatment should not necessarily include extension to entities of transnational corporations of incentives and concessions granted to domestic enterprises in order to promote self-reliant development or protect essential economic interests.]

47a [Endeavouring to assure the clarity and stability of national policies, laws, regulations and administrative practices is of acknowledged importance. Laws, regulations and other measures affecting transnational corporations should be publicly and readily available. Changes in them should be made with proper regard to the legitimate rights and interests of all concerned parties, including transnational corporations.]

[to be deleted]

48 (ex-51) Information furnished by transnational corporations to the authorities in each of the countries in which they operate contain-

421

ing [legitimate business secrets] [confidential business information] should be accorded reasonable safeguards normally applicable in the area in which the information is provided, particularly to protect its confidentiality.

49[1]

50 (ex-51 (b)) [In order to achieve the purposes of paragraph 22 relating to managerial and technical training and employment of nationals of the countries in which transnational corporations operate, the transfer of those nationals between the entities of a transnational corporation should, where consistent with the laws and regulations of the countries concerned, be facilitated.]

[to be deleted]

51 [Transnational corporations should be able to transfer freely and without restriction all payments relating to their investments such as income from invested capital and the repatriation of this capital when this investment is terminated, and licensing and technical assistance fees and other royalties, without prejudice to the relevant provisions of the 'Balance of payments and financing' section of this Code and, in particular, its paragraph 26.]

[to be deleted]

Nationalization and compensation

52[2]

Jurisdiction

53—56[3]

Intergovernmental co-operation

57 [It is acknowledged] [States agree] that intergovernmental co-operation is essential in accomplishing the objectives of the Code.

58 [States agree that] intergovernmental co-operation should be established or strengthened at the international level and, where appropriate, at the bilateral, regional and interregional levels [with a view to

---

1 See reference to employment and labour on p.423.
2 See Appendix III(f), pp. 424—5.
3 Ibid.

promoting the contribution of transnational corporations to their developmental goals, particularly those of developing countries, while controlling and eliminating their negative effects] .

59 States [agree to] [should] exchange information on the measures they have taken to give effect to the Code and on their experience with the Code.

60 States [agree to] [should] consult on a bilateral or multilateral basis, as appropriate, on matters relating to the Code and its application [in particular on conflicting requirements imposed on transnational corporations by the countries in which they operate and issues of conflicting national jurisdictions] [in particular in relation to conflicting requirements imposed by parent companies on their entities operating in different countries] and with respect to the development of international agreements and arrangements on issues related to the Code.

61 (ex-60) States [agree to] [should] take into consideration the objectives of the Code as reflected in its provisions when negotiating bilateral or multilateral agreements concerning transnational corporations.

62 [States agree to co-operate, within the framework of regional groupings, for making appropriate arrangements to assess the effectiveness of the application of the Code in the region.]

[To be deleted or to be considered under the part of the Code related to implementation]

63 (ex-49) States [agree not to use] [should not use] transnational corporations as instruments to intervene in the internal or external affairs of other States [and agree to take appropriate action within their jurisdiction to prevent transnational corporations from engaging in activities referred to in paragraphs 10 to 12 of this Code.]

Employment and labour[1]

For the purposes of this Code, the principles set out in the Tripartite Declaration of Principles concerning Multinational Enterprises and Social Policy, adopted by the Governing Body of the International Labour Office, should apply in the field of employment, training, conditions of work and life and industrial relations.

---

1 To be placed in one of the introductory substantive parts of the Code.

III(f)   CHAIRMAN'S FORMULATIONS ON THE PARTS OF THE CODE NOT YET CONCLUDED

Activities of transnational corporations

A   General and political

Adherence to economic goals and development objectives, policies and priorities
5   Transnational corporations should, as all parties to contracts freely entered into, respect and adhere to such contracts. In the absence of contractual clauses providing for review or renegotiation, transnational corporations should respond positively to requests for review or renegotiation of contracts concluded with Governments or governmental agencies in circumstances marked by duress, or clear inequality between the parties, or where the conditions upon which such a contract was based have fundamentally changed, causing thereby unforeseen major distortions in the relations between the parties and thus rendering the contract unfair or oppressive to either of the parties. Aiming at ensuring fairness to all parties concerned, review or renegotiation in such situations should be undertaken in accordance with applicable legal principles and generally recognized legal practices.

Non-interference in intergovernmental relations
14   Transnational corporations, in pursuing their corporate interests, should not request Governments to act on their behalf in any manner that exceeds normal diplomatic representation or other regular intergovernmental communication and, in particular, in any manner that amounts to the use of coercive measures of an economic and political character.

15   Transnational corporations shall/should exhaust available means provided by local laws in host countries. When applicable, other agreed means for resolving disputes, including the submission of international legal claims, may be used.

Treatment of transnational corporations

B   Nationalization and compensation

52   In the exercise of their sovereignty, States have the right, acting in the public interest, to nationalize property in their territory. Fair

and equitable treatment of transnational corporations by the countries in which they operate includes payment of just compensation in the event of nationalization or other taking of their property, such government action being undertaken under due process of law, in accordance with national laws, regulations and administrative practices without discrimination between enterprises in comparable situations and with full regard to international obligations and contractual undertakings to which States have freely subscribed.

C   Jurisdiction

53   Entities of transnational corporations are subject to the jurisdiction of the countries in which they operate.

54   Disputes between a State and a transnational corporation, which are not amicably settled between the parties, are subject to the jurisdiction of the courts and other authorities of that State and are to be submitted to them, except for disputes which the State has agreed to settle by arbitration or by other methods of dispute settlement.

55   The validity of clauses providing for selection of applicable law or of the forum for settlement of disputes or for commercial arbitration in contracts between private parties, at least one of which is an entity of a transnational corporation, is to be determined by the national law of the countries concerned.

56   Where the exercise of jurisdiction over transnational corporations and their entities by more than one State may lead to conflicts of jurisdiction, adoption by the States concerned of mutually acceptable principles and procedures, bilaterally or multilaterally, for the avoidance or settlement of such conflicts, on the basis of respect for the interests of the States concerned and relevant international obligations, serves to improve the relations among States and between States and transnational corporations.

Introductory part

Preamble

Conscious of the world-wide growth of transnational corporations, the diversity of their operations, their role in the utilization of capital, technology and human resources, their impact on international relations and their influence on the development process of the countries in which they operate, particularly developing countries,

Noting that the advances made by transnational corporations in organizing their operations beyond the national framework may lead to abuse of concentrations of economic power and to conflicts with national policy objectives,

Recognizing that transnational corporations can bring substantial benefits to the countries in which they operate by contributing to the efficient use and development of the resources of those countries,

Noting that the nature, influence and growth of transnational corporations has caused concern in the countries in which they operate and led to action towards the regulation and monitoring of those corporations,

Considering that the complexity of operations and the international structure of transnational corporations may render national measures ineffective,

Noting that the economic situation of developing countries makes them particularly sensitive to the impact of the activities of transnational corporations and may put them at a disadvantage in their dealings with such corporations,

Recognizing the need to associate effectively the activities of transnational corporations with the efforts to establish the new international economic order, thereby also contributing to the achievement of the individual and collective self-reliance of developing countries,

Bearing in mind relevant decisions of the General Assembly pertaining to the activities of transnational corporations,

Recalling Economic and Social Council resolutions 1721 (LIII), 1908 (LVII) and 1913 (LVII) on the impact of transnational corporations on the development process and on international relations, which led to the establishment of the Commission on Transnational Corporations as a subsidiary body of the Council to deal with the entire range of issues related to the activities and operations of transnational corporations,

Recalling also the Decisions of the Commission on Transnational Corporations, approved in Council decision 180 (LXI), which assigned highest priority to the formulation of a code of conduct and established the Intergovernmental Working Group on a Code of Conduct to elaborate and submit to the Commission and the Council a final draft of a code of conduct,

Referring to work done by other bodies of the United Nations system relevant to transnational corporations, in particular to the International Labour Organisation Tripartite Declaration of Principles Concerning Multinational Enterprises and Social Policy, the Set of Multilaterally Agreed Equitable Principles and Rules for the Control of Restrictive Business Practices, adopted by the General Assembly in resolution 35/63, and the work of the United Nations Conference on an International Code of Conduct on the Transfer of Technology, of the Intergovernmental Working Group on the Problem of Corrupt Practices and the Committee on Illicit Payments, pursuant to Council resolution 2041 (LXI) and of the Intergovernmental Working Group of Experts on International Standards of Accounting and Reporting, pursuant to Council resolution 1979/44,

Convinced that a universally adopted and effective Code of Conduct establishing international standards concerning the activities and treatment of transnational corporations will usefully supplement national measures and provide a framework for international co-operation among States on issues relating to transnational corporations,

Have agreed to adopt this Code of Conduct.

Objectives

The objectives of the Code of Conduct are:

1   To establish international standards and arrangements, supplementing national measures and forming an integrated whole where all parts are related to one another, with a view to reducing and resolving the difficulties to which the activities of transnational corporations may give rise and promoting the contribution of transnational corporations to economic and social progress in the countries in which they operate;

2   To facilitate co-operation among States on issues relating to transnational corporations and alleviate difficulties stemming from the transnational character of those corporations and the multiplicity of national laws and policies relating to them;

3   To reassert the principle of respect by transnational corporations for the national sovereignty, laws and regulations of the countries in which they operate, and for the established policies of those countries and the right of States to regulate and accordingly monitor the activities of transnational corporations;

4   To proscribe subversion, interference in the internal affairs of States and other inadmissible activities by transnational corporations which aim to undermine the political and social systems of the countries in which they operate;

5   To reassert the principle that when applying their national laws, regulations and administrative practices to entities of transnational corporations under their jurisdiction, the countries concerned remain committed to any applicable international obligations;

6   To help create conditions conducive to the promotion of mutually beneficial relations between transnational corporations and the

countries in which they operate, under which the laws, regulations and administrative practices of those countries would be equitably applied and the ability of transnational corporations to make efficient use of their capabilities maintained, so as to allow them to contribute fully to the economies of those countries;

7   To help ensure that the activities of transnational corporations are carried out in conformity with and contribute to established development policies of the countries in which they operate, giving due recognition to the special needs of developing countries;

8   To contribute to strengthening the negotiating capacity of developing countries in their dealings with transnational corporations;

9   To improve the understanding of the nature, structure and effects of transnational corporations by all parties concerned by establishing standards for the disclosure of information by transnational corporations;

10   To make adequate arrangements for the effective implementation of the Code of Conduct at the national, regional and international levels, including procedures for revising and supplementing the Code as required in the light of experience and evolving circumstances, thus giving the Code an evolutionary character;

11   To establish a focal point for international arrangements and agreements relating to transnational corporations in close co-operation with other bodies within the United Nations system.

Definitions and scope of application

1   The term 'transnational corporation' as used in this Code means a commercial enterprise, comprising entities in two or more countries, regardless of the legal form and the fields of activity of these entities, which operates under a system of decision-making permitting coherent policies and a common strategy and in which the entities are so linked, by ownership or otherwise, that one or more of them may be able to exercise a significant influence over the activities of others, and, in particular, to share knowledge, resources and responsibilities with the others.

2   The Code applies to all enterprises having those characteristics, including State-owned or State-controlled enterprises, in so far as they pursue activities dealt with in the Code.

3   The term 'entities' in the Code means both parent entities — that is, entities which are the main source of influence over others — and other entities.

428

4 The term 'transnational corporation' in the Code refers to the enterprise as a whole and/or its various entities according to the actual distribution of responsibilities among them, on the understanding that entities will co-operate and provide assistance to one another as necessary to facilitate observance of the Code.

5 The term 'home country' means the country in which the parent entity is located. The term 'host country' means a country in which an entity other than the parent entity is located.

6 The term 'country in which a transnational corporation operates' means a country in which an entity of a transnational corporation conducts substantial operations. The term includes home as well as host countries.

7 The Code is universally applicable in and open to adoption by all States, regardless of their political and economic systems and their level of development.

8 Any reference in the Code to 'States', 'countries' or 'Governments' includes regional groupings of States to the extent that they have power to take action in matters relating to transnational corporations.

Implementation of the Code of Conduct

1 Governments agree that action at the national and international levels is essential in accomplishing the objectives of the Code.

Action at the national level

2 In order to support and promote the application of the Code at the national level Governments will:

(a) Publicize and disseminate the Code and, as appropriate, reports relevant to the Code prepared by the Commission on Transnational Corporations, through official policy statements and other means, with a view to ensuring that transnational corporations, trade unions and others concerned are fully aware of them;

(b) Review the application of the Code within their territories;

(c) Make appropriate administrative and institutional arrangements to review the application of the Code and to deal with any related issues and difficulties;

(d) Report to the Commission on Transnational Corporations every second year, or upon its request, on the action taken at the national level to promote the Code and the experience gained from its application, the form and structure of such reports to be recommended by the Commission;

(e) Take the Code fully into account when introducing, implementing and reviewing laws, regulations and administrative practices relevant to the application of the Code with a view to facilitating the observance of the Code;

(f) Take no action contrary to the objectives of the Code.

Action at the international level

3 In order to increase the effectiveness of the Code, to enhance consistency in its application and to alleviate difficulties related to its application, Governments will:

(a) Co-operate at the bilateral, regional and other multilateral levels, as appropriate, by:

> (i) Exchanging information related to the application of the Code;
>
> (ii) Engaging in consultations at the request of another Government specific issues on the application of the Code relating to the Governments concerned, including difficulties arising from conflicting requirements on transnational corporations;
>
> (iii) Taking fully into consideration the relevant provisions of the Code when negotiating bilateral or multilateral agreements concerning issues related to the Code;
>
> (iv) Promoting the application of the Code within the framework of regional arrangements in which Governments participate;

(b) Making full use of the United Nations institutional machinery, the structure and functions of which are described below.

Institutional machinery

4 The United Nations institutional machinery for the application of the Code at the international level will consist of the Commission on Transnational Corporations, which may establish the subsidiary bodies and specific procedures it deems necessary for the effective discharge of its functions in this respect, and the United Nations Centre on Transnational Corporations, which will act as the secretariat to the Commission.

5   The Commission will:

(a)   Periodically or at the request of a Government discuss matters related to the Code. The Commission may invite representatives of transnational business, trade unions, consumer organizations and other interested groups to express their views on such matters. If agreed by all Governments engaged in consultations on specific issues related to the application of the Code, such consultations may be held within the Commission;

(b)   Periodically review the application of the Code, such reviews being based on reports submitted by Governments and supplemented by documentation from non-governmental organizations and United Nations organizations and specialized agencies performing work relevant to the Code, as well as by studies prepared for this purpose by the Centre upon the request of the Commission. The timing and procedures of the reviews are to be determined by the Commission. The first review will be made not earlier than two years and not later than three years after the adoption of the Code;

(c)   Provide, upon the request of a Government, clarification of the provisions of the Code in the light of actual situations in which the applicability and implications of the Code have been the subject of intergovernmental consultations. The Commission may also decide to provide clarification at the request of non-governmental organizations represented in the Commission. Transnational business, trade unions, consumer organizations and other interested parties may request clarification through Governments or non-governmental organizations represented in the Commission. The Commission should endeavour to respond in a timely manner to requests for clarification. In clarifying the provisions of the Code, the Commission shall not draw conclusions concerning the conduct of the parties involved in the situation which led to the request for clarification. The clarification is to be restricted to issues illustrated by such a situation. The detailed procedures regarding clarification are to be determined by the Commission;

(d)   Recommend, as and when appropriate, revision of the Code in the light of experience gained in its application and evolving circumstances, including developments in other United Nations organizations and specialized agencies performing work relevant to the Code. Having regard to the importance of stability and consistency to the effectiveness of the Code, recommendations for its revision will not be made during the initial period of five years after its adoption, unless justified by exceptional circumstances or as a consequence of developments in other international forums to which reference is made in the Code;

(e)   Consider, under its general mandate to promote the exchange of views between, *inter alia*, transnational business and trade unions, steps aimed at encouraging an exchange of views regarding the application of the Code between individual transnational corporations and business organizations on the one hand and trade union representatives of the various entities of a transnational corporation on the other hand;

(f)   Report to the Economic and Social Council the results of its discussions and periodic reviews, the response given to requests for clarification and the recommendations made in regard to revising the Code;

(g)   The Commission will act as the focal international body for all matters related to the Code. It will establish and maintain close contacts with other United Nations organizations and specialized agencies dealing with matters related to the Code and its implementation with a view to co-ordinating steps taken for the promotion and application of the Code. When matters covered by international agreements and arrangements which have been worked out in other United Nations forums specifically referred to in the Code arise, the Commission will forward such matters to the competent bodies charged with the implementation of such agreements or arrangements.

6   The United Nations Centre on Transnational Corporations will:

(a)   Collect and analyse information with regard to the promotion and application of the Code on the basis of reports submitted to the Commission by Governments and documentation supplied to the Commission by non-governmental organizations and other United Nations organizations and specialized agencies;

(b)   Conduct research and surveys concerning the substantive issues relating to the Code as directed by the Commission;

(c)   Provide other assistance as required by the Commission.

Appendix IV
relating to Part V

IV(a)   EUROPEAN ACTION PROGRAMME –
MULTINATIONAL GROUPS OF COMPANIES
(Adopted by the European Trade Union Confederation, June 1977)

**European Action Programme: multinational
groups of companies**

When presenting this programme of action, the European Trade Union
Confederation addresses itself to the EEC and EFTA institutions, as
well as to the governments of their Member States. Although multinational groups raise problems at the world level, the ETUC considers
that in Europe one can start to lay down binding rules. Moreover, it
should be stressed that the demands made in the following chapters
apply to all undertakings and not only to multinational groups.

The 50 largest undertakings in Europe, almost all of which are multinational groups of companies (including some Euro-offices of American
multinationals), realised a total turnover of 180 thousand million
dollars in 1972, with the help of about 6.2 million employees. Their
total investments in the same year amounted to around 15 thousand
million dollars. These figures went up in 1973; these 50 largest undertakings employed about 17 per cent of the total number of workers and
employees in industrial sectors. Of the some 4500 undertakings in the
Member States of the European Community with transnational
activities, more than 1100 undertakings (i.e. about 25 per cent) have
connections with at least five undertakings in other countries (subsidiary companies, interests, associated companies).

One can give an idea of the importance of multinational companies
by saying that a whole series of them have an annual turnover which
far exceeds the annual budget of small States. It is clear that, in such
cases, the political power of the governments of these States is considerably diminished.

The economic power of multinational groups of companies is not statistically neutral. It is wielded non-stop throughout the world. It sets flows of capital, investments, raw materials, semi-finished and finished products in motion across national frontiers and continents, thus exercising considerable influence on the labour market in the countries and regions concerned. This multinational strategy and the decisions it entails often contradict the national tendencies of States in which a multinational group of companies carries out economic activities. This type of strategy, which is dominated primarily by the goal of maximum profits, leaves little room for the economic, social and cultural interests of workers.

It is the law of democratic reasoning that power of any sort must be controlled in order to prevent its abuse. The expansion of the activities of multinational undertakings has created new structures of economic power, which make it easier to abuse this economic power because national laws and regulations no longer guarantee sufficient control of power.

In the past few years, international organisations such as the United Nations, the OECD, the Council of Europe and the ILO have begun to elaborate rules of procedure for multinational groups of companies. Although these first steps are commendable, they alone do not suffice for the establishment of a sound and disciplined basis for the activities of multinational undertakings.

The European Trade Union Confederation is of the opinion that on the basis of the existing legislation in individual countries additional regulations must be laid down, which are legally binding and valid transnationally, for instance in the field of company and fiscal law. This can be done both in the European Community and in EFTA and also through international agreements which would include both EEC *and* EFTA countries.

The European Trade Union Confederation will co-operate with the International Confederation of Free Trade Unions (ICFTU) and the World Confederation of Labour (WCL) and, in its relations with the OECD, the Council of Europe and the ILO will advocate the elaboration of rules of procedure and the application, extension and more effective formulation of any rules of procedure which already exist. The European Trade Union Confederation considers it to be its specific task furthermore to put forward proposals and demands to the EEC and EFTA institutions for legislative initiatives in questions which require concrete and precise rules of procedure.

The demands set out in the following chapters are not directed against multinational groups of companies. They are in fact intended more generally and are based on the consequences observed in the internationalisation of economic activities, in which multinational groups of companies have inevitably come to play a major part.

I   Investments

In the last few years a whole series of shortcomings in the economic system have become evident in Western European countries, whose causes can no longer be remedied by fighting the symptoms. Unusually high unemployment rates coupled with in some cases high inflation rates are the results of structural crises, and the efforts to eliminate these problems have not yet been forceful enough. It would seem that the market economy system is reaching its limits and that its internal forces no longer suffice to guarantee the constant development of the economy and of society.

It can be regarded as certain that particularly during the last economic upswing many undertakings based their decisions on market trends of too short a term and that the long-term expectations had to be disappointed. This assessment is confirmed by the present imbalance which can be observed in the development of the various sectors of the economy.

The essential factors for economic development are technology and investments. To a great extent, technological evolution determines where and how investments and production should be carried out. It is essential to control technological development if one wishes to control economic development. Since technological know-how is constantly changing, it is necessary to finalise an adequate international strategy.

The tight budget situation in the public sectors makes it necessary from the outset to plan investment activities, whereas the investment activities of private undertakings are only co-ordinated to a very minor extent. It is thus urgently necessary to take measures to improve the co-ordination of the investments of private undertakings. As the sum of all decisions concerning investments contributes to determining any community's economic and social development, individual decisions on investments must fit into the framework of orientations, complemented by qualitative criteria. The following criteria, given as examples, could serve as a test for authorising investments or simply for granting public aid:

- regional and structural aspects of the choice of site;
- application of technologies requiring large capital assets or a large volume of labour;
- application of technologies which respect the environment;
- satisfaction of the needs of the community, etc.

Conclusion

1   Governments must create the necessary conditions for the elaboration of guidelines for investment in the important branches of the
economy. For this purpose, the Governments must carry out regular
statistical surveys in individual sectors of the economy — which will
make it possible to make medium-term and long-term forecasts of the
development of demand. The guidelines for investments must be revised
annually on the basis of developments which have in fact taken place
and must be corrected accordingly where necessary. Each Government
must draw up an annual report on those activities, which is to be submitted to Parliament and the employer and employee organisations.

2   Each Government must entrust a special office — already existing
or to be created — to deal with all questions of investment activity
(including investments in the public sector). This office must be
notified of all investments which exceed a certain volume. The investing
undertakings must state:

   — whether and if so which new technologies are involved in the
     planned investment;

   — what effect the investment may have on the employment of
     workers;

   — whether the technology and/or rationalisation which the invest-
     ment is to promote is compatible with the requirements of
     environmental protection and the demands of industrial safety
     in plants.

This office shall have the role of a registration office for investments. It
shall have certain controlling rights, which must be laid down in detail
and shall embrace primarily the observance of statutory regulations.

3   The workers' representatives in the investing undertaking must be
granted a right to information and consultation which is guaranteed by
law and applies during the period in which the decision on investment is
being planned and carried out. Details of the exercise of this right can
be laid down by law or agreed on in a contract. Provision must also be
made for this information and consultation in the availability and utilisation of investment aid of any sort.

4   The Governments and/or national registration offices should
exchange information regularly on the investments effected by multinational groups of companies and on all important concentration
operations.

5   Direct financial aid or tax concessions can only be granted for
investments when investigations have been carried out to determine

whether all the legal requirements connected with the investment are fulfilled. Furthermore, the individual Governments should lay down additional conditions for the granting of any type of aid to investments. The granting of such aid must depend primarily on whether the investment is likely to fulfil social needs (e.g. the maintaining and creation of jobs, respect of the environment, choice of site etc.). The type and volume of aid paid out of public funds can be determined and scaled in proportion to the social value of the investment concerned.

The utilisation of funds for promoting investment must be effectively controlled. If the conditions stipulated for the granting of investment aid, such as the creation of a certain number of new jobs, are not fulfilled in due course, the funds must be repaid accordingly.

6   An office must be set up at the level of EEC and EFTA organs which must be notified of the investments and investment schemes of undertakings in all sectors — which must be defined — which are internationalised to a large extent (such as the aircraft industry, shipyards, data processing, the chemical industry, the electrical industry). In the EEC the procedure for the registration of investments is governed by the provisions laid down in articles 54–56 of the ECSC Treaty.

Statistical surveys must be carried out annually in these branches of the economy, which have yet to be defined; these surveys must make it possible to predict the development of demand, and these predictions can then in turn serve as indicators for the investment activities of undertakings. Provision must be made for trade union participation in this investment planning at EEC and EFTA level.

7   Investigations must be carried out to establish the role which the Economic and Social Councils which already exist or are to be set up can play in investment policy at EEC level and at national, regional and sectoral level. The joint sectoral committees planned at EEC level could be a suitable instrument for monitoring developments on a permanent basis which can have a considerable influence on the willingness to invest and on investment activities.

8   In the case of investments in third countries, the workers' representatives in the investing undertaking must be informed and consulted in good time by the management of the undertaking. Should these investments lead to the transfer of production processes to third countries, Governments and employers must increase their measures for the readaptation of labour in good time so that the structural changes can be overcome more easily.

Guarantees from public funds for investments in third countries must only be granted provided that the investor is prepared and in a position to meet specific social demands in favour of the workers in his employment or in the employment of his agent in the third country, such as are laid down in ILO Conventions nos. 87, 98 and 135.

II   Law pertaining to groups of companies

Groups of companies have become the usual instrument of 'collaboration' between undertakings in all Western European countries. The most important feature of a company group is that of a number of undertakings being so interlinked through unilateral or bilateral interest in the capital of the companies, by means of the same persons serving on management boards or controlling bodies, or through contractual connections, that a dominant company is able to manage all the other economically dependent companies by itself. This single management exists, whether or not the dominant company is located in a country where there are legal provisions on groups of companies, or simply has a 'de facto' presence there.

From the point of view of company law, and particularly by reason of the need to provide suitable protective measures for shareholders and workers in dependent countries and to impose obligations on group management bodies with respect to the disclosure of their activities, it is urgently necessary for legislative provisions governing groups of companies — which should be standardised as far as possible — to be introduced throughout Western Europe. This applies particularly to the Community, because the provisions of the Treaty of Rome already provide for this and the proposal for a Statute for European Companies already contains a chapter headed 'Law pertaining to groups of companies'. This requirement also applies to EFTA institutions; standards of company law, which have also been conceived for application to multinational groups, would not completely fulfil their purpose if they were restricted to only a certain number of Western European countries.

Standardised regulations governing groups of companies must be based on the following principles:

1   Precise definition of the status of groups of companies (central management, dependence of companies within the group, procedure for the establishment of the status of group of companies);

2   Protective measures for shareholders and workers in dependent undertakings of the group of companies;

3   Obligation to prepare and declare consolidated group annual accounts on the basis of standardised rules;

4   Establishment of an information and consultative body for the representatives of workers in all the companies within the group;

5   Representation of workers at the level of governing bodies in dominant companies, where a system of worker representation must be established to enable workers and their trade unions to have an influence on the fixing of the group's objectives and policy, especially in the case of multinational groups of companies.[1]

III Competition policy — concentration of undertakings and domination of the market

All Western European countries have economic control systems which are basically geared to competition, but also contain many features of government planning.

Over and above national legislation, there are standardised regulations on competition in the EEC embraced by both the Treaty of Rome and the European Coal and Steel Community Treaty. In certain other countries legislation on competition is less severe, but even within the Community there is room for considerable improvement, in the opinion of the trade unions.

Regulations on competition are intended primarily to serve the interests of consumers and protect them against the abuse of economic power on markets. In addition, these rules must, in a general sense, prevent the formation of oligopolistic or monopolistic market structures. Cartels must be forbidden in principle and only permitted when they fulfil a purpose which serves the general interest. Dominant market positions held by companies or groups of companies must be prohibited; not only the abuse of such power should lead to legislative intervention.

Appropriate control machinery should be included in legislation on competition to permit the supervision of the process by which concentrations of companies are formed. A complete system of price information and price supervision would guarantee the discontinuance of speculative price fixing.

The ETUC makes the following demands for the creation of an effective policy on competition:

1   Legislation on competition must be based on the principle that all agreements between undertakings or groups of undertakings, or

1   For further information, see the Resolution of the London Congress of the ETUC (April 1976) DEMOCRATISATION OF THE ECONOMY — MULTINATIONAL GROUPS OF COMPANIES.

mutually agreed policies which prevent, restrict or distort competition, are to prohibited. Exceptions to this principle are only to be permitted when an agreement or an agreed policy is obviously in the interests of society at large, workers or consumers. Competition policy in the European Community should make specific provisions allowing undertakings in certain sectors to draw up and carry out sectoral development plans under the control of the authorities and in collaboration with the competent unions.

2   Legislation on competition must guarantee that individual undertakings or groups of undertakings will be prevented from acquiring positions in which they dominate the market. Exceptions to this principle require express authorisation from the competent competition authorities, and this may only be granted when a dominant market position is in the interests of society as a whole, workers and consumers. When an undertaking or group of undertakings already dominates the market effective control must be carried out to ensure that this domination of the market is to the advantage of society as a whole, workers and consumers.

3   Any type of operation which leads to the further concentration of undertakings is to be declared at a centre specially set up for the purpose. Criteria are to be laid down (e.g. turnover, number of employees, capital, balance sheet total, market share), which, when exceeded, shall require that a procedure be initiated for the approval of the planned concentration operation. Authorisation can only be granted when the concentration is proved to be in the interests of society at large, workers and consumers.

4   Workers' representatives in the undertakings concerned must be given the right to advance information and consultation in the event of all concentration proceedings. The managements of the undertakings concerned must be obliged to negotiate with workers' representatives on measures which are favourable to workers, at the proper time and prior to any decision to carry out concentration proceedings, for the purpose of ensuring their employment and the economic and social benefits which they have obtained. A report on the economic justification of the concentration operation is to be made available to workers' representatives in the undertakings concerned; each separate undertaking must deliver a written report on the effects of the concentration operation on the employment of its workers to the workers' representatives and the general meeting of shareholders. These reports would be the basis for informing and consulting with the workers' representatives and for negotiations between management bodies and their workers' representatives.

5   An effort must be made to draw up and institute standardised rules in all EEC and EFTA Member States for the takeover of undertakings. The past and present practice of takeover bids must be abolished, since it is unacceptable that the determining factor in a takeover should be whether individual shareholders believe that the price and conditions of a bid would be profitable to them personally. With the present system of takeover bids, which are frequently used for the exclusion of competitors or for other purposes of market strategy, unjustified takeover prices can endanger the existence of the undertaking which has been taken over and the jobs of its employees. Legal provisions must therefore be laid down which stipulate that the takeover of an undertaking can only be carried out through the normal decisions of the boards of the undertakings concerned, and that workers' right to information, consultation and negotiation must be respected.

6   A well functioning system of price information and supervision must be set up in all countries as part of their competition policy; this system would provide for the introduction of various instruments according to conditions in each individual country. Authorities responsible for competition must possess the right to set up a procedure of price controls in certain economic sectors (particularly those with a high proportion of multinational groups of companies), whereby it can be established within the undertaking itself whether or not prices for individual products are justified.

IV   Taxation and tax controls

The internationalisation of undertakings' business activities is revealed by the growth of multinational groups of companies and brings with it greater uncertainty with regard to the assessment of taxable profits. It can be taken as certain that a considerable volume of tax revenue is denied to tax authorities in the individual countries simply because tax laws, being restricted to national boundaries, have loopholes enabling tax advantages to be gained without, however, recourse to illegal means. Bilateral double taxation agreements are not sufficient to provide any basic remedy for this situation.

A major cause of any attempt to reduce the tax burden by the most diverse means is the fact that there are widely varying systems of corporation tax in the different countries, together with varying tax rates and tax concessions. Another factor which varies is the definition of what constitutes taxable profits.

Opportunities for curtailment of tax liability are provided through differing tax legislation on the offsetting of costs, within multinational groups of companies, for the delivery of materials, goods and services, as well as remuneration for patents and licences, or patent and licence fees.

A further problem is posed by holding companies, which are often founded solely for the purpose of receiving income, in certain countries with favourable tax laws, from several other countries; such income is in the form of dividends, interest on loans, licence fees etc. In this way, countries where such income or profits are earned are deprived of tax revenue.

Finally, the taxation of multinational groups of companies must be looked at in connection with regulations on the preparation and publication of consolidated annual statements of accounts and profit and loss accounts. Particularly important is the question of the principles to be applied to the assessment of fixed and current assets.

In view of the complexity of tax legislation, it will be necessary to propose measures for harmonising tax regulations within the EEC and EFTA and in collaboration with international organisations such as the OECD and the Council of Europe. The tax harmonisation must of course take account of the practice of individual States of granting special tax concessions to undertakings for the achievement of certain objectives within the framework of industrial and regional policy. At the same time, however, the governments of the individual countries must make every effort to ensure that their own tax legislations are so adapted to suit the new conditions created by the spread of the activities of multinational groups of companies. There is a whole range of opportunities for tax manipulation made possible simply because tax legislation varies widely from State to State, from which of course certain States benefit.

The ETUC calls upon governments and institutions in the EEC and in EFTA to make every effort — and as soon as possible — to achieve the following goals:

1   Systems of corporation tax, including tax rates, should be harmonised within a general plan to harmonise all direct and indirect taxes to such an extent that the transfer of money to countries with favourable tax legislation is no longer an attractive speculation. In addition, the term of 'taxable profits' must be clearly defined.

2   The content of existing double taxation agreements must be examined and, if necessary, adjusted to suit present-day conditions and requirements.

Furthermore, there is a need for a system of international tax supervision and control, through which tax authorities in the individual countries can co-operate by providing one another with general information on a permanent basis, as well as information in individual cases on request. This system must embody the right of national tax authorities or other interested parties to apply a control procedure in individual cases. The exchange of information must not be hindered by reason of insubstantial claims that professional or industrial secrecy has to be preserved.

3   In order to ensure that tax authorities can assess taxes on dividends and other capital income without loopholes in tax legislation, a withholding tax should be applied to such income, to be assessed by those liable to tax when making their income tax declaration.

4   A uniform rule for the control of transfer prices within multinational groups of companies (in payment of deliveries of materials, goods or services, patents, licences and patent and licence fees) must be established within the framework of an international system of tax supervision and control (see para. 2). The exchange of information between tax authorities in the individual countries must devote particular attention to transfer prices within multinational groups of companies. It would be an important step forward if there were a single method of calculating for the delivery of goods.

When establishing uniform rules, the possibility of abuse by means of fictitious transfer prices for services (e.g. breakdown of overhead or research costs), the discharge of debts and for patent and licence fees must at all events be reduced. In doubtful cases, tax authorities must have express authority to make appraisals.

5   In the longer term, all governments should work together to eliminate the so-called 'tax havens'. The founding of holding or base companies in countries providing such tax facilities is almost always intended to collect returns from several countries and then pay little or no tax on them. This privilege, which is exploited chiefly by multinational groups of companies, is contrary to the most fundamental rules of tax morality.

By way of immediate measures to be introduced, controls are necessary to guarantee that income which is received centrally is taxed at its place of origin. Such controls can be given effect through an international system of exchange of information between national tax authorities.

A special problem is raised by finance companies which collect untaxed income from several countries and invest it in such a way that it yields still more tax-free income. Even these privileges can be reduced immediately, at least in part, if controls on the taxation of income at its point of origin are introduced through the exchange of information. The introduction of a uniform withholding tax could be the means of obtaining greater justice in the field of taxation.

6   Cross-frontier financial transactions which are not in fact based on a de facto business transaction must be liable to a tax penalty. The work to be undertaken by national tax authorities could be made easier if the burden of proof of the legality of financial transactions, for the purpose of assessing tax liability for returns, could be laid on the person who undertakes or has undertaken such transactions.

V   Capital markets

Although a new regulation for the co-ordinated control of international capital markets is necessary, it is too much to hope that this objective will be achieved within the near future. Collaboration between governments in a world monetary fund could give priority to the preparation of a world-wide system of reporting, which would make it possible for them to follow and analyse the short-term movement of capital on a permanent basis. It is obvious that this would require the constant exchange of information between the competent authorities of the individual States.

Efforts being made to control capital markets must be extended with greater intensity from the national to the international sphere. Collaboration between governments in communities of States such as the EEC and EFTA, as well as in regional governmental organisations such as the OECD and the Council of Europe, must be so designed as to set up compulsory information and control systems regarding the short-term movement of capital in their respective areas, as soon as possible.

Article 72 of the Treaty of Rome provides for a system of information on the movement of capital, which can be expanded later: for instance, to embrace a uniform reporting system between the Member States. The same should be attempted within EFTA. In many cases, however, it will not be sufficient simply to record movements of capital when there are speculative intentions behind the transactions involved.

Co-ordinated trouble-free capital markets are not only of great importance to the economies of the industrialised countries, but also to those of the developing countries, who are even more dependent than the former on the stability of an international monetary system and the capital markets.

The following demands must be made for greater transparency of the international capital markets:

1   In the interests of all States and their economies, uniform and effective control measures must be taken to prevent multinational groups of companies or other structures from effecting short-term movements of capital for speculative purposes which always only bring

advantages to a minority of persons. The principle of the freedom of capital movement becomes the opposite in practice if this freedom becomes compulsion for others.

2   Particular attention must be paid to the role played by banks in international capital movements, and this role must be better controlled by existing or other bank supervision bodies to be created. Banking secrecy must be relaxed at least to the extent where tax authorities and other authorities concerned would be given the information necessary for the fulfilment of their tasks.

3   The communities of States of the EEC and EFTA, the Council of Europe and the OECD, should come to an agreement as soon as possible on widespread co-operation in Europe and amongst all institutions. This co-operation should make provisions for appropriate initiatives both in the individual fields of competence and beyond European frontiers. It should be recommended urgently that the OECD carry out a thorough examination of the operation of the international capital markets.

4   Stricter publicity regulations must be laid down for undertakings, particularly multinational groups of companies (cf II. Law pertaining to groups of companies), in such a way that the information thus given will make it possible to establish facts on the means and method of financing of the undertaking concerned.

VI   The spread of technical knowledge

European multinational groups of companies and European subsidiaries of American groups have played an important part in the spread of technical knowledge throughout the world.

It has been shown over the last 20 years in particular that the Paris Agreement of 1883 on the protection of industrial property has remained an instrument which protects exclusively the interests of those who possess technical knowledge. It is for them to determine what technological innovations are to be introduced and at what price. In most industrialised countries, technological research is carried out by undertakings with a considerable amount of State aid, a factor which provokes the danger of the developing countries being exposed to renewed exploitation by technological forces whose activities are motivated solely by profit.

In order to obtain jobs for their populations, the developing countries are more or less obliged to accept the investment and production plans of multinational groups of companies, although these plans are frequently unsuited to the objectives of these countries, particularly as regards their development needs. Moreover, large and often arbitrary sums of money must be paid for production licences; these are withdrawn from the economy of a developing country and frequently invested in other countries. In such circumstances of dependence it is very difficult, if not impossible, for developing countries to achieve economic independence.

Furthermore, the progressive international division of work is tending to bring technologies to developing countries which are particularly harmful to the environment and also contain hazards for technical industrial accidents.

A means must be found of making it impossible for sellers of technological know-how to be able to dictate conditions. In the long run, further monopolising of private technological interests could be harmful to mankind as a whole. Measures should aim at:

1   The revision of the Paris agreement of 1883 and its replacement by a system of bilateral or multilateral negotiations on fees; in particular, the revision of the duration of patent rights in view of the rapidity of technical advancement.

2   The extensive interpretation of all the regulations of the Lomé Convention, which was concluded between the EEC and the ACP States, in order to guarantee those States all possible advantages as regards the utilisation of technological knowledge.

3   Decisive State influence on the application of new technologies if the State is providing financial aid for technological research.

4   Development of technologies requiring a large volume of labour, whose application is particularly suitable for developing countries.

5   An appeal to multinational groups of companies to include the indigenous population to as wide an extent as possible in the training and further training of qualified personnel and top executives.

6   The establishment of an office in an international organisation, or first of all at the Commission of the EEC and the Secretariat General of EFTA, to which notification of all contracts on the exploitation of patent rights and the payment of licence fees must be given and the contracts submitted.

7   The exertion of influence on developing countries to encourage them to form groups in various regions and come to an agreement on common rules which will make it difficult for those who possess technical knowledge to dictate conditions for investment and for the payment of licence fees to individual developing countries.

446

VII Workers' solidarity rights

The internationalisation of the activities of undertakings in groups of undertakings which are often world-wide has placed workers and their trade unions in a worse position to negotiate in the field of working conditions. Whereas the management of a multinational group of companies can at any time issue instructions which are binding for the entire group of companies, the trade unions' power to negotiate is restricted by legal regulations to national territories. Moreover, individual undertakings which are dependent on the group are not given adequate authority to negotiate by the management of the group of companies.

The situation is made more difficult for workers and their trade unions in that in numerous countries their right to strike is restricted by legislation or jurisdiction. In such companies workers cannot hold sympathy strikes or take measures to boycott multinational groups of companies in the event of serious industrial disputes or the violation of trade union or human rights; the workers' will to international solidarity is thwarted to a considerable extent.

Demands and proposals of the European Trade Union Confederation:

1   In international organisations which deal with the elaboration of rules of procedure for multinational groups of companies, workers' rights to solidarity should be included. The ILO in particular should endeavour to propose international rules in this field.

2   Sympathy strikes and boycott measures should be possible within each defined economic sector, whenever an international trade union organisation, having agreed with its member organisations, calls the strike or calls for certain measures.

3   Governments in EEC and EFTA Member States are called upon:

   (a)   to bring their influence to bear on the international organisations and institutions so that the problem of workers' rights to solidarity is dealt with;

   (b)   to investigate how in their own countries existing legislation or other regulations could be changed in order to legalise workers' international solidarity action.

IV(b)   A CHECK-LIST FOR TRADE UNIONISTS
(Chapter VI of 'Trade Unions and the Transnationals — A Handbook for Negotiators' — ICFTU, November 1979)

Introduction

The purpose of this Check-List is to:

- explain to *trade unionists* how, in their relations with transnationals, they can best take advantage of the progress made in recent years at the international level;

- set out the practical steps to ensure that *employers* fulfil their obligations under the OECD and ILO codes which employer bodies have endorsed at the international level;

- highlight the responsibility of *governments* for making transnationals more accountable at the level of the world-wide corporation through the establishment of transnational information and consultation rights.

Multinational companies — or transnational corporations, as they are now often called — dominate the world economy. Transnationals are today a major feature of international economic and commercial relations, and exchanges in goods and services between the different subsidiaries of one particular transnational may, in volume, exceed trade between sovereign nation states. Trade unions are at present only able to deal with parts of a transnational; they rarely get a chance to influence the activities of the transnational as a whole. The transnational corporation therefore presents a number of special problems which cannot be adequately handled by any one government or trade union organisation. It is for this reason that there has been a growing awareness of the need to devise international instruments capable of dealing with them. To date, official efforts have largely been directed at the drawing-up of voluntary 'codes of conduct', which set out a number of standards which corporations should, in the view of governments, adhere to. Any company which infringes these standards is therefore going against what a large and representative group of governments have agreed are normal business practices, and is likely to be subject to serious adverse publicity.

At this moment, two codes are in operation. One was concluded in 1976 at the Organisation for Economic Development and Cooperation,

448

OECD.[1] It covers a wide range of issues, including employment, industrial relations and minimum standards for reporting data on companies' operations and policies. The second code was approved of a year later by the Governing Body of the International Labour Office, ILO.[2] and lays down detailed requirements for employment and training policies, pay, fringe benefits, health and safety and industrial relations. The two codes are complementary.

Moreover, a world-wide code is now being drawn up by the United Nations. This would deal with all aspects of transnational operations and could therefore become the most important code of all.

The international trade union movement has for long argued for effective controls for transnationals; it recognises the OECD and ILO codes as useful first steps which should be made use of. The ensuing Check-List is intended as a guide to the many trade union officials, at national as well as local level, who have direct dealings and negotiations with transnationals and who may be unaware of the international codes which are available to them. The Check-List takes the form of a number of questions and answers, and aims to inform trade unionists on how best to deal with transnational management.

1   Is the company a transnational?

An obvious question which trade union officials must ask themselves is whether the company they are dealing with is in fact a transnational, i.e. whether it is a subsidiary controlled from abroad or has operations abroad. In a great number of cases the answer is likely that there will be a major transnational component in the company's activities, e.g. ownership of foreign marketing outlets. The annual company reports should provide some indication on whether a company is a transnational; guidance is available from the national trade union centre or the International Trade Secretariats, ITS, to which the union concerned may be affiliated.

2   How can the ILO and OECD codes be used?

There is no substitute for well organised trade unions in all subsidiaries of a transnational. However, the two codes can help with some problems that frequently arise when trade unions have to deal with a

---

1   OECD member countries are: Australia, Austria, Belgium, Canada, Denmark, Finland, France, the Federal Republic of Germany, Greece, Iceland, Ireland, Italy, Japan, Luxembourg, the Netherlands, New Zealand, Norway, Portugal, Spain, Sweden, Switzerland, Turkey, the United Kingdom and the United States. Turkey has, however, abstained from the OECD code.
2   The ILO is a specialised agency of the United Nations and has a world-wide membership. It is tripartite in structure, with equal representation of governments, employers and workers.

transnational, and trade union representatives should be familiar with the detailed provisions of both codes. Here are some examples:

(i) *Union recognition* Both codes endorse the right of employees to be represented by trade unions. The ILO code condemns victimisation for trade union activities. Management is supposed to show a positive attitude to trade union work.

(ii) *Information needed for bargaining* Both codes require management to provide workers' representatives with information needed for meaningful negotiations. This information should, in accordance with local law and practice, include data on the business situation of the transnational as a whole, not only the subsidiary in question.

(iii) *Bargaining and the right to strike* The codes give workers the right to negotiate with the real decision-makers. This could well be head office, rather than local management. The codes specify in this context that management negotiators must be those who are authorised to take decisions on the matters under negotiation.

Both codes say management must not try to influence the course of negotiations — including negotiations during a strike — or an organising drive by threatening to transfer production to another country or bring in strike-breakers from abroad.

(iv) *Wages and workers conditions* The ILO code lays down certain minimum conditions. They should be at least adequate to satisfy the basic needs of the workers and their families. In any case, they must not be worse than those offered by comparable companies in the country.

(v) *Health and safety* The ILO code states that transnationals should ensure the highest standard of safety and health and should provide the unions concerned with information on the standards which they observe in other countries. When new products or processes are introduced, management must inform of any special hazards involved.

(vi) *Closures and mass sackings* Neither code prevents management from closing down a local business or making mass dismissals. But the OECD code says that management must give reasonable notice to representatives of the employees and co-operate with them so as to mitigate 'adverse effects'. This could, for instance, mean that a company must not default on redundancy pay by claiming that the subsidiary it wants to close is bankrupt and that it should use the resources of the parent company to meet its obligations. The experience with the OECD code has found that the parent company has a financial responsibility. The ILO code has a special section on security of employment which goes further. It calls on transnationals to assume a leading role in promoting security of employment. Moreover,

arbitrary dismissals procedures should be avoided.

3   Does the company comply with the codes?

(i)   Company obligations   Trade unionists should establish whether management is aware of the obligations under the respective OECD and ILO codes. It may be that management simply does not know of the existence of the codes. Management may, however, be consciously and deliberately ignoring the code. Trade unionists should be able to point out that international associations of big business such as the Business and Industry Advisory Committee to the OECD, the International Chamber of Commerce and the International Organisation of Employers have frequently said that they have made exhaustive efforts to inform individual companies about the codes. Trade unionists should find out whether the company is disclosing any information about its compliance with the individual provisions of the code. In a majority of cases there will be no such disclosure although the OECD governments have now asked transnationals to indicate their observance of the OECD code, preferably in their annual report.

(ii)   Formalising company compliance   To ensure that management formally complies with the two codes, it is recommended that a clause be written into the appropriate collective agreement which states that:

> Management accepts the provisions set out in the OECD Guidelines on Multinational Enterprises and/or in the ILO Tripartite Declaration on Multinational Enterprises and Social Policy.

4   What information is necessary?

(i)   The information required   If no information about a company's compliance with a particular code is available it is up to the union concerned to demand it. The OECD governments have called on companies to include brief statements in their annual report on their experience with the OECD code, which may contain mention of steps taken with respect to the (1) observance and (2) their experiences. Under the ILO code, moreover, governments will question companies about their compliance and experience and then report back to the ILO. Information should therefore be formally presented in a regular, possibly annual, report published by management and made available to the trade unions. The information provided should be concise and to-the-point and should also deal with future management plans, including investment programmes, research and development projects, plant rationalisations or closures.

Management will often argue that the provision of detailed information would be costly and time-consuming, but unions should not be deterred by this. Nor should unions accept that information be withheld because of its confidential nature. It may, however, sometimes be necessary for unions to agree to keep certain details confidential.

(ii) Formalising information disclosure There should ideally, exist a formal agreement between trade unions and management for the disclosure of information under a particular code. In most countries, a clause could be written into the appropriate collective agreement and could, for example, take the following format:

> Management agrees to the provision to the trade union representatives of regular reports on the company's compliance with the provisions of the OECD Guidelines and/or ILO Tripartite Declaration.

In order to ensure disclosure of specific information when and where required, this clause should be supplemented by a sub-clause, whereby:

> Management agrees to provide, upon request of the trade union representatives, additional information on specific matters relating to the code in question.

5   *What consultation arrangements are necessary?*

Information disclosure on its own is not enough: there must be a possibility for trade unions to consult with management at all levels about the information made available and to pose questions.

(i) Use of established procedures There will normally exist established procedures for trade union/management consultation at local level and these can be used as far as possible. Discussions at local level are by their nature — or by the insistence of management — limited to the operations of the transnational within a particular country. It is therefore necessary to devise a special mechanism for trade unions to discuss with the global corporation its world-wide strategy. A number of International Trade Secretariats, ITS, had established company 'World Councils' in which trade union officials from the various transnational subsidiaries in different countries meet and discuss common problems. As yet, management has refused to consult with these ITS bodies although some headway has recent been made, for example the meeting between the Volkswagen management and the respective International Metalworkers' Federation World Council in 1979. Trade unionists should therefore first seek to discover if any consultative mechanism already exists at global level, such as an ITS World Council.

(ii) Consultation at world level A flexible approach is called for. Not all meetings would require participation of union representatives from each subsidiary. In some cases, the job can be delegated to special trade union committees or regional sub-bodies. What is important is that the trade unions, not management decide who will be on the union delegation. In some cases, consultations could also be undertaken on a tripartite basis, involving home and host governments.

Global consultations do not, as management sometimes claims, mean transnational collective bargaining. While there may be good reason for trade unions and companies to develop a bargaining system involving subsidiaries in more than one country, this is an objective which needs to be pursued separately.

(iii) Formalising consultation As in the case of information disclosure, there should, ideally, be a formal agreement between the trade unions and management. Most national situations will allow for a specific clause to be inserted into the appropriate collective agreement. This could read:

> Management agrees to regular consultations, upon request, with trade union representatives concerning its policy arising from the OECD Guidelines and/or the ILO Tripartite Declaration on the basis of information indicating the company's compliance with the code in question.

To ensure that global consultations will be possible, this clause should be supplemented a specific sub-clause whereby:

> Such consultations may involve meetings between head-office management and trade union representatives from different subsidiaries, including those abroad, as well as representatives from international trade union organisation.

6   What if a company does not respond?

(i) Action at the national level If a company does not respond to the demand of a trade union, the next step must be to involve the responsible national trade union centre. The latter will be in the best position to decide whether to bring a particular case to the attention of the responsible government department (e.g. the department of industry or labour). In this connection, the OECD has recommended the establishment of 'national contact points' within each country which would have the responsibility of coordinating policy towards foreign investment.

(ii) Action at the international level If national action brings no

result, the case can be brought up at the level of the OECD or ILO. This can be done by a national government or by the Trade Union Advisory Committee to the OECD, TUAC, (in the case of the OECD code) or the ICFTU (in the case of the ILO code). There should therefore be consultation between the trade unions directly concerned, the national trade union centre and the TUAC and the ICFTU as well as the responsible ITS (if applicable) on whether to raise a problem about the company's behaviour with regard to a particular code. This will require close co-ordination between all the trade union organisations concerned. There already exist bodies for co-ordination, such as the TUAC Working Group on Multinational Enterprises and the ICFTU/ITS Working Party on Multinational Companies, and a decision to proceed with a complaint should normally be taken in the framework of these bodies.

TUAC views on the occasion of the 1979 review of the OECD Guidelines for Multinational Enterprises:

I   General

1   Both through the Trade Union Advisory Committee and at the national level, the trade unions participated actively in the preparation of the OECD Guidelines for Multinational Enterprises and the related Decisions of the OECD Council in June 1976. TUAC has been involved in consultations with the Committee for International Investments and Multinational Enterprises and, lately, its Working Group on the Guidelines. The trade unions have had a major and in some cases decisive role in bringing cases related to the Guidelines to the attention of the Governments and the OECD. They will continue their active involvement in the follow-up of the Guidelines. A basic demand of TUAC is that the methods for doing this and carrying out the necessary consultations be improved both at the company, national and international levels.

2   The trade unions judge the Guidelines from the point of view of their impact on the real world. Their existence created expectations among the unions who hoped that the climate for their relations with multinational enterprises would change for the better. Evidence of this, after almost three years of experience, still is not forthcoming. There is very little to show that the world of the multinational enterprise has been changed. Furthermore, there is very little evidence that the present voluntary set of Guidelines is being vigorously pursued or that there is effective action to create a framework within which their implementation could be ensured.

3   TUAC underlines that even if its involvement in the follow-up of the Guidelines so far has been active and will continue to be so, it is not primarily for the trade union movement to see to the functioning of the Guidelines. They were agreed upon by Governments, who took upon themselves the responsibility to address them to the multinational enterprises. Consequently, they should also ensure their implementation.

4   Unless the Guidelines are really implemented, the trade union movement will have to seriously consider their usefulness and also any further support to them. As a compromise, TUAC accepted the Guide-

lines in 1976 as a first step. At that time, the trade unions clearly envisaged not only their implementation but also further development. If no change to the better has taken place in the real world due to the Guidelines, what was the use of the whole exercise? And if this remains the verdict, all parties will be confronted with a loss of credibility due to a collapse of the discussions. In 1979, OECD must thus be prepared to take the next step.

5   In the context of the present review process, and also looking beyond it, TUAC attaches importance to the implementation, the interpretation and a revision of the Guidelines. Implementation will have to take place both at the company, national and international levels. Interpretation of the provisions of the Guidelines is a *sine qua non* for any meaningful implementation. And a revision of the text itself is necessary in order to make it conform to general developments in other international organisations as well as to respond to cases that have demonstrated lacunae in the present text itself.

II   Implementation

6   TUAC considers that there is a general failure on the part of multinational enterprises to seriously respond to the Guidelines. The trade unions believe that the Guidelines will prove to be a useful agenda for discussing the problems of multinational enterprises at the company level. The major gap in the operation of the Guidelines today is at that level. Too few companies are taking the Guidelines seriously in their day-to-day operations, and few trade unions are aware of the relevance of the Guidelines.

7   In order to secure the implementation of the Guidelines, the Governments should agree to a number of measures which would put certain well-defined obligations on the enterprises. We propose therefore a three-stage implementation procedure:

(a)   Governments should agree, through national legislation, to put an obligation on multinational enterprises based or operating in their territory, or both, to make annual reports on their policies regarding each of the points covered by the Guidelines.

(b)   Governments should oblige the enterprises to make these reports available to the trade unions and provide that they have the rights and facilities to discuss these reports with the enterprises. These reports would also be available to the representatives of the Governments for similar consultations.

(c) Governments should also agree to report to the OECD on steps taken with regard to the above as well as on experiences gained thereof.

8 Governments should submit annual reports to the OECD, taking fully into account also the views of the trade unions, about any pertinent developments in the countries, including measures taken by the Governments for the implementation and monitoring of the Guidelines. These reports should enable the Committee for International Investments and Multinational Enterprises, as well as TUAC and BIAC, to assess the degree of compliance with the terms of the Guidelines and the action taken by the Governments, the employers organisations, trade unions and the multinational enterprises themselves to give effect to them, as well as possible difficulties and inadequacies.

9 At the same time TUAC reaffirms that it reserves the right to bring up cases to the attention of the Committee. This could take place in the event that national negotiations to settle a question falling within the Guidelines do not lead into results and if the Government concerned is reluctant to bring the question up on the international level. Also successfully settled cases could be brought to the attention of the Committee insofar as they illustrate the working of the Guidelines. Arrangements should be made to have the multinational enterprise concerned be heard and participate in the discussions also on the OECD level.

10 One of the problems of the follow-up hitherto has been the theoretical and legalistic nature of the discussions. In order to explore the issues involved, especially where a specific case is concerned, the facts may have to be assessed through fact-finding procedures. TUAC is favourable to the idea of developing such procedures and feels that it should be self-evident that such fact-finding would fully involve the trade unions as well.

III   Revision

11 The experience of the Guidelines has demonstrated a number of needs to amend their text itself. TUAC fully recognizes that before the questions of implementation and interpretation have been satisfactorily settled, there is little point in suggesting extensive revisions. Redrafting, on the other hand, can come about as a result of the interpretation of the Guidelines or of the practical experiences in their implementation. However, there are some questions which can be addressed already today.

12   There is a clear, demonstrated and recognized gap in paragraph 8 of the employment and industrial relations section of the Guidelines. This concerns the transfer of workers in the case of negotiations or labour conflicts. This can be amended by adding to that paragraph, after the words 'from the country concerned', the following: 'nor transfer workers from affiliates in foreign countries'. In the same paragraph, TUAC considers it an omission not to mention the threat of withholding further investment.

13   In order to make clear the interpretation of the responsibilities of the parent company (see paragraph 19 (a) below), the following sentence should be added to the paragraph 8 of the introductory section of the Guidelines: 'This, however, cannot be interpreted as relieving the parent company and/or the regional management from sharing the responsibility for the policies of any local entity, to the extent they control the policies and decisions or the entity itself'.

14   In the section on disclosure of information, TUAC considers that the subparagraph (vi) could be replaced by the following: 'the average number of employees by geographic area and, as far as practicable, country by country for the enterprise as a whole;'. After this, a new subparagraph could be inserted with the following wording: 'average nominal wages and fringe benefits by geographical area for the enterprise as a whole, converted in the currency of the home country;'.

15   TUAC also considers that the Guidelines should spell out a specific obligation on enterprises to inform the trade unions concerned, and negotiate with them, at an early stage, before final decisions are taken, regarding the economic, social and legal consequences of mergers and other forms of concentration of decision making across the borders within the OECD area. More specifically this concerns the concentration of decision making between companies by the founding of common holding companies, by transfer of activities across borders, by acquiring assets across borders and by concentrating *de facto* decision making power through acquiring assets of another company within the OECD area or also outside the area if enterprises based outside the area carry out activities within the area or affecting it.

IV   Interpretation

16   Unless there is a clear interpretation of the meaning of the Guidelines, the responsibility for observing and implementing them can be evaded. TUAC regrets that despite the discussions on a number of cases by the Committee for International Investments and Multinational Enterprises and its Working Group on the Guidelines, no interpretation

of in particular questions of paramount trade union interest have been given. Unless the Governments agree on the meaning and general purpose of what they have collectively adopted, and say so to all parties concerned, the implementation of the Guidelines is seriously impaired. It is the view of TUAC that, as part of the review process, the report to the OECD Council in June 1979 should give a clear interpretation of the Guidelines. Furthermore, arrangements should be made for the further development of the interpretation process. It is only against this background that TUAC has been prepared to participate in the informal discussions with the Committee's Working Group on the Guidelines.

17 Regarding the interpretation of the Guidelines in their present form, there are a number of questions that have to be dealt with urgently. To the extent they are already discussed by the Working Group on the Guidelines, together with TUAC and BIAC, such discussions will have to serve an interpretation by the Summer of 1979. There are important questions, such as the responsibility of the parent company, which have not yet been discussed, and they will have to be taken up in the review process as well, in consultation with TUAC and BIAC.

18 TUAC does not wish to present an exhaustive list of questions where interpretation is asked for. The cases brought forth by the trade unions hitherto illustrate concerns, and difficulties, that have come up during the first years of experience of the Guidelines. In stressing the need for interpretation, the trade unions are above all concerned about the usefulness of the Guidelines to their own members. Both the Governments and the OECD have recently increasingly solicited the views of the unions and have recognized that the trade unions have a role in following up the Guidelines, both nationally and, through TUAC, internationally. But in the absence of clearer rules and interpretations, the unions, just as Governments, will have to make interpretations nationally themselves. Differences from one country to another in such interpretations only serve confusion and render the Guidelines inefficient.

19 The interest of TUAC at this stage focuses itself above all on the following questions:

(a) *Parent company responsibilities* (paragraphs 6 and 8 of the Guidelines). It must be recognized that the parent company has a responsibility for all areas covered by the Guidelines, and a responsibility to inform the local entity of decisions and strategies affecting it. (See paragraph 13 above).

(b) *Local law and regulations* (introduction to the section on employment and industrial relations). The words 'within the framework of law' etc. should not be interpreted so as to enable the enterprises to take a minimalistic line and abstain from their obligations under the Guidelines merely by referring to the absence of specific national legal obligations. The interpretation should at least correspond to the meaning of 'taking into account national circumstances' in the ILO.

(c) *Recognition of trade unions* (paragraph 1 of the employment and industrial relations section). An unequivocal pronouncement of this is a precondition for the Guidelines being a useful instrument for the trade unions. It should be clarified that this concerns non-manual workers as well, and especially bank employees. The words 'and other bona fide organisations of employees' should be interpreted in a way to cover the International Trade Secretariats.

(d) *Right to trade union consultation within multinational enterprises* (paragraph 2 of the employment and industrial relations section). Necessary facilities must be interpreted in a way to cover facilities for contacts with employees in other parts of the same multinational enterprise. Information, to be meaningful, must include information on the enterprise as a whole. The provisions of the Guidelines must also be interpreted in a way that will not hinder representatives of the International Trade Secretariats to participate in negotiations when necessary.

(e) *Information to employees* (paragraph 3 of the employment and industrial relations section). This information will have to include future plans, in order to give a true and fair view of the entity or the enterprise.

(f) *Obligation to negotiate future plans* (paragraph 6 of the employment and industrial relations section). Such negotiations should be seen as mandatory, and they should be introduced immediately when such changes in operations can be anticipated as would have major effects upon the livelihood of the employees. This paragraph, in the view of TUAC, contains both the obligation to give reasonable notice, i.e. notice as soon as the management becomes aware of an impending situation, and also the obligation to mitigate adverse effects through negotiations. Such negotiations should take place before any final decisions are made, and, whenever necessary, they should enable to alter any decision made without the participation of the representatives of the employees.

(g) The Guidelines should also be recognized to cover such groupings as those of airline companies which regardless of their legal structure or the presence or absence of direct investment by the participating companies function as multi-national enterprises.

20 TUAC notes that there cannot be conflicting interpretations between those of the OECD Guidelines and other relevant instruments, in particular the Tripartite Declaration on Multinational Enterprises and Social Policy, adopted by the ILO Governing Body. As the ILO instrument will also have its own follow-up procedure, it is imperative that OECD Governments, when interpreting the Guidelines, ensure that there are no conflicts with other relevant international instruments.

IV   Conclusions

21 For the trade union movement, the OECD Guidelines were a first step towards more specific, functioning rules of the game. There has been little progress in making them work, and the follow-up has largely been a theoretical exercise on the level of the Committee for International Investment and Multinational Enterprises. The key question now is their implementation on the everyday working level, in the enterprises themselves. Within this implementation process, the crucial element is the creation of a system of information and consultation at both the company, national and international levels.

22 It is obvious that the review of the Guidelines will have to be seen as an on-going process. For this purpose, the OECD Council should provide for another formal review by 1981 at the latest.

23 TUAC has not addressed itself here to the other parts of the Decisions of the OECD Council in 1976. This is mainly due to the fact that the consultations it has been involved in have concerned the Guidelines. On the other hand, regarding the other Decisions, TUAC is still waiting for the first results of the Government deliberations. TUAC will be in due time interested in pronouncing itself on them, and assumes that work on them by the OECD and the Governments will be of an on-going character.

IV(d) INTERNATIONAL BUSINESS' POLICY
POSITION ON THE OECD GUIDELINES ON
MULTINATIONAL ENTERPRISES
(as communicated by BIAC, under the chairmanship of Mr Wagner, at a
meeting with OECD governments on 29 January 1979)

I   The BIAC Statement on the Review

Mr Wagner augmented the written document by a brief oral commentary, indicating that BIAC has worked and continues to work to gain
public acceptance of the Guidelines and that the more probing and
questioning done, the greater the confirmation of the need to live with
the current Guidelines a while before taking them further. BIAC was
therefore of the strong opinion that the Guidelines should remain un-
changed at the present time. BIAC wished to be consulted on the report
and any commentary which CIME would develop for presentation to
the Ministers. BIAC promised to keep up the pressure on firms and
also to continue to identify any problem area brought to light. As to
procedure, Mr Wagner told the Levy Group that BIAC is pleased with
the current combination of formal and informal consultations, but he
stressed the importance that the CIME report on the Review should be
provided to BIAC and BIAC's comments solicited before that report
becomes final.
    Many government delegates expressed their appreciation for the
documents submitted by BIAC and for the continuing efforts to
propagate the Guidelines. Several of them agreed that the time and
experience had been too short to consider changing the text at this
point, and expressed their understanding that we are all engaged in an
educational process − government, business, and labor − and that a
stable text will further this cause.
    In response to numerous questions from government delegates, the
BIAC representatives made the following additional points:

   − that experience with the Guidelines had been of only slightly
     more than two year duration, since they were published in
     November, 1976;

   − that they are Guidelines established by *governments*, and that
     the role of business is to be of assistance and to co-operate;

   − that the next step in our continuing efforts is not yet determined;
     certainly more letters, pamphlets, workshops, seminars, con-
     ferences, etc. should be a part of the process;

— that business will continue to recommend public statements of support of the Guidelines, but does not feel that numbers of declarations are nearly so significant as actual observation — that some firms do not understand any value in a public declaration because it is understood that if the government makes a request and especially if the Organization of Employers supports that request, the businesses accept the recommendation;

— that the 'obstacles' encountered by firms in applying the Guidelines are principally either administrative and will be overcome with time, or have to do with competition which will always be a legitimate concern. A government delegate said that he felt it must be left to the enterprise to decide what information is sensitive;

— that any attempt to make a single or a very few modifications in the text would be the opening of a Pandora's box, that this is unnecessary and would best not be done;

— that it is in the interest of business to observe the Guidelines;

— that, with regard to labor's 'access to decision makers,' any good company's local manager represents the company; that where this is not the case, that company should supplement local management in discussions with labor;

— that stability of the text of the Guidelines would be more important to smaller firms which would be more hesitant to commit themselves to keeping up with all the changes;

— that CIME commentary on the Review if done should not be lengthy but should be limited to clarification of a few points;

— that the fact that only a few complaints of non-compliance had been brought up should indicate that the Guidelines are relatively effective;

— that one should also recognize that the Guidelines have a certain preventative effect;

— that the firms having publicly announced their observance of the Guidelines represent a very large share of economic activity and employment, and that this is more important than the acceptance by large numbers of small firms with minor economic impact;

— that 'voluntary' guidelines are morally binding on those who have agreed to observe them;

— that the recognized 'gap' in the Guidelines with respect to 'strike-breakers' is no longer very important since it has been covered by the ILO Declaration and is most unlikely to recur;

— that with regard to harmonization of accounting standards, BIAC is co-operating in the OECD work; BIAC expressed the hope that greater complexities in accounting would not result.

II The BIAC Progress Report and the Survey on Disclosure

In response to questions from government delegates, the BIAC representatives made the following points:

— that probably the best method for disclosing information is by means of the annual report;

— that breaking down employment figures by geographic area had not been traditional and was not considered useful to firms; but there was no conceptual difficulty and BIAC felt that this would be done in time;

— that the concept of transfer pricing is a very complex one, as has been evidenced by the work of the OECD's Working Party No.6 of the Fiscal Affairs Committee — to which BIAC has contributed. The Levy Group were informed of the existence of a BIAC paper on transfer pricing in the pharmaceutical industry which had been submitted to Working Party No.6. In any event, the Levy Group were assured that the U.S. Law now requires this disclosure and that some U.S. frims had obviously been confused when in response to the Survey, they indicated no disclosure on this point;

— that in BIAC's opinion the argument that disclosure of a certain item was not legally required was not considered a valid one;

— that BIAC had made a straightforward and frank report of the data received to date; that the members of the BIAC Committee present did not control all of those enterprises which had reported; and that time was now needed to talk to the firms in order to better understand some of the arguments made;

— that disclosure requirements are quite difficult at times. For example, it was explained that subsidiaries of German firms in Greece must now prepare four different balance sheets;

— that BIAC would provide a breakdown by country of the 190 firms' figures on which the numerical analysis had been based;

— that BIAC delegates would reflect on the issue of harmonization of accounting standards, and come back;

— that wide-spread observance with the Disclosure Guidelines would come with time.

464

III   The TUAC Statement on the Review

There was little time remaining when this agenda item was introduced. Mr Wagner gave a very brief indication of BIAC's reaction to the document by saying that it was rather ambitious, that although TUAC felt that little or nothing had changed since the Guidelines were published, business was aware of considerable change in the world — increased internationalization, a more troubled climate, with firms more risk-conscious, governments more protective and firms, especially smaller ones very busy just surviving. He made a plea that the burden of business not be increased unnecessarily, while pledging co-operation along whatever lines were decided by government.

In response to questions various BIAC delegates made the following comments:

— that 'threats' to disinvest are not at all a serious problem in the real world;

— that BIAC would consult with businesses to determine whether adding a section on observance of the Guidelines to the consolidated annual report would be considered a burden and would report back;

— that, with regard to what CIME may include in their report on the Review insofar as the chapter on Disclosure is concerned, BIAC has concluded that problems are mostly administrative or competitive — rather than fundamental — and that disclosure will come with time.

IV   Consultation

The members of the BIAC Committee expressed their interest in maintaining the same basic type of consultations as had been the case over the past year — a combination of formal and informal contacts. The BIAC participants indicated their continued willingness to assist and to advise the governments and their strong interest in having the opportunity to comment upon the CIME draft report on the Guidelines at a time when the comments offered could still be taken into consideration in preparing the final version of the Report.

In bringing the session to a close, Mr Levy assured the BIAC participants that in all probability the CIME revised draft report would be made available to them in early February, although the government representatives had to approve that procedure.

IV(e)   GUIDELINES FOR INTERNATIONAL INVESTMENT
(as adopted by the International Chamber of Commerce, 29 November 1972)

I   Investment policies

1   The investor[1]

(a)   Should ensure in consultation with the competent authorities that the investment fits satisfactorily into the economic and social development plans and priorities of the host country.

(b)   Should be prepared in any negotiations with the government of the host country to make known his expectations concerning the expansion of the enterprise, employment and marketing prospects and the financing of its operations.

(c)   Should in appropriate cases, where the government of the host country so wishes, be prepared to enter into contractual arrangements with that government.

(d)   Should, in response to the interest shown by the public of the host country in his activities, take steps to provide relevant information about the operations of the enterprise, subject to any exclusions necessary for competitive reasons.

2   The government of the investor's country

(a)   Should, in the formulation or modification of policies that affect foreign investments by its nationals, take the fullest possible account of the need of investors for stability, continuity and growth in their operations as well as of the general interests of the host country.

(b)   Should seek to enter into binding obligations under international law with other governments either on a bilateral or multilateral basis, in respect of the reciprocal treatment to be accorded to the property, rights, and interests of its nationals.

(c)   Should offer, either nationally or through participation in an international investment insurance agency, guarantee facilities against non-commercial risks encountered by the investor.

---

1   Wherever the circumstances are such that a recommendation addressed to 'the Investor' falls for implementation to the enterprise operating in the host country, it should be regarded as addressed to that enterprise.

466

(d)   Should examine the possibility of providing special aid for relevant economic and social infrastructure projects in developing countries which will facilitate private investment of significance to the economic development of the host country.

3   The government of the host country

(a)   Should in the formulation or modification of policies that affect foreign investments, take the fullest possible account of the need of investors for stability, continuity and growth in their operations.

(b)   Should, with regard to sectors not reserved to domestic ownership, make known to prospective investors its economic priorities and the general conditions that it wishes to apply to incoming direct private investment, and should provide an opportunity for consultation with the private sector during the development of national planning.

(c)   Should make known the treatment that it will accord to the proposed investment and any limitations or financial charges that it will impose.

(d)   Should not discriminate on the grounds of its foreign ownership in the treatment accorded to the enterprise, it being understood that the government has a right to accord special treatment to any enterprise or enterprises, whether domestic or foreign owned, in the interest of the national economy.

(e)   Should, in appropriate cases and where the foreign investor so wishes, be prepared to enter into contractual arrangements with the investor concerned.

(f)   Should be prepared to enter into binding obligations under international law with other governments either on a bilateral or multilateral basis, in respect of the reciprocal treatment to be accorded to the property, rights, and interests of nationals of the other state or states.

II   Ownership and management

1   The investor

(a)   Should, in presenting his investment proposals to the authorities of the host country, examine favourably suitable proposals concerning forms of association with local interests, public or private.

(b)   Should, in developing countries where the necessary institutional facilities exist, offer part of the equity of the subsidiary for purchase or subscription by local investors, wherever this is compatible with the

467

long-term economic interest of the enterprise.

(c) Should encourage local participation in the management of the enterprise, promoting nationals to posts of increasing responsibility and providing the training and experience that are a prerequisite for such promotion.

(d) Should, if he finds himself in a dominant market position, refrain from abuse of that position by actions that are to the detriment of the economy of the host country.

2 The government of the investor's country

Should, in the framework of foreign aid, support financial, educational and other institutions, including those providing managerial training, thus preparing the ground for more local private participation in the financing and management of enterprises established in developing countries.

3 The government of the host country

(a) Should, once the details of the implementation of an investment project have been accepted and the ownership and management structure of the enterprise has been established, refrain subsequently from modifying such arrangements otherwise than through negotiation and agreement.

(b) Should recognise that joint ventures are much more likely to be successful if they are entered into voluntarily and if the terms of the contracts are left to the free negotiation of the parties, and that there may be cases where investments which deserve high priority are only feasible on the basis of total foreign ownership.

(c) Should take appropriate measures, principally by encouraging the creation or development of an effective capital market, to facilitate the purchase of equity in domestic and foreign-owned enterprises by local interests.

(d) In so far as laws or regulations requiring local participation are judged to be necessary, should frame these laws in such a way that the rights of existing enterprises are respected, new investment is not discouraged and flexible application is possible.

(e) Should rely on economic, fiscal and commercial policy measures applying to all business operations, national and foreign, for the exercise of controls in the public interest rather than seek to do this through compulsory governmental participation in the equity or management of enterprises.

(f)   If there is abuse of a dominant market position, should, in preference to the immediate application of restrictive regulations, seek to remedy the situation either by stimulating competition, especially through the encouragement of new investment and the lowering of import tariffs, or, by recommending a change in the investor's practices.

III   Finance

1   *The investor*

(a)   Should, without prejudice to the freedom of transfer of financial resources, where there is government concern about the balance of payments of the host country, take this situation into account in shaping his commercial and other policies.

(b)   Should assist the enterprise to comply with the requirements for disclosure of profits and other financial information imposed generally on companies by the host country.

(c)   Should, when having substantial recourse to local sources of capital, take into account the impact which his requirements may have on the availability of funds to local enterprise.

(d)   Should consider favourably the reinvestment of part of his profits, whether in the enterprise or in other economic activities in the host country which he considers suitable.

2   *The government of the investor's country*

(a)   Should not interfere in the financial management of the enterprise by, for example, insisting upon a given level of remittances in any period unless an adverse balance of payments situation forces it to do so.

(b)   Should remove as speedily as possible any existing restrictions on the outflow of capital in the form of direct investment by companies, and should refrain from introducing new restrictions except where exceptional circumstances make short term regulation necessary.

3   *The government of the host country*

(a)   Should place no restrictions on the remittance of loan interest, redemption payments, service and advisory fees, licence fees, royalties and similar payments except in circumstances where the laws of the country require prior approval of the underlying agreement between payor and payee and such approval has not been obtained.

(b)   Should allow the investor liberty to remit his profit, in particular avoiding the imposition of restrictions not notified at the time of the investment, and should respect any engagements entered into with the investor. Similar conditions should apply to the repatriation of capital, although it is recognised that developing countries may find it necessary to require that remittances be spread over a reasonable period of time.

(c)   Should, if faced with balance of payments difficulties which justify the temporary imposition of restrictions, follow the principles of the International Monetary Fund and the General Agreement on Tariffs and Trade.

(d)   Should, in devising any special exemptions or incentives aimed at attracting foreign investment or encouraging new investment in general, have regard to the need to avoid undue distortion of competition between enterprises operating within its territory, whether domestic or foreign.

(e)   Should allow the unrestricted transfer of the personal savings of the investor's expatriate personnel and the funds necessary to meet pension and family commitments.

(f)   Should, where restrictions on local borrowing are necessary, make them equally applicable to all enterprises without any discrimination as between foreigners and nationals, except that developing countries may in special circumstances be justified in restricting long and medium term borrowing by foreign-owned enterprises.

IV   Fiscal policies

1   The investor

(a)   Should observe the laws and regulations of the host country in relating to the submission of returns, and provision of information in connection with the assessment and collection of taxes.

(b)   Should, to the extent that such information is not available to the enterprise that is under the tax jurisdiction of the host country, be prepared to assist that enterprise to provide justification for its export and import prices.

2   The government of the investor's country

(a)   Should seek to enter into effective arrangements for avoidance of double taxation with capital importing countries.

(b) Should ensure that when, in double taxation arrangements, the host country retains a primary right to tax dividends, interest, royalties, etc. such tax is fully relieved by tax credit or reimbursement according to the legal status or personal circumstances of the beneficiary deriving the income directly or through an intermediate company.

(c) Should ensure that, even in the absence of double taxation arrangements, the aggregate of foreign and domestic tax imposed on income from foreign sources (including, in the case of a dividend from direct investment, the foreign tax on profits underlying the dividends) does not exceed the greater of the foreign tax or the tax imposed on similar income from domestic sources.

(d) Should introduce arrangements, unilaterally if necessary, to avoid any double taxation on the salaries and other incomes of expatriate employees.

(e) Should refrain from frustrating the effects of development reliefs granted by host countries in respect of new investment by affording appropriate matching reliefs.

3   The government of the host country

(a) Should seek to enter into effective arrangements for avoidance of double taxation with capital-exporting countries.

(b) Should ensure that taxes on income are imposed on no more than the net income arising in the host country after deducting all expenses properly attributable thereto incurred within or outside the country, whether such expenses are payable to associated or non-associated enterprises.

(c) Should not impose on enterprises wholly or partially foreign-owned, taxes which are higher or more burdensome than those to which purely domestic enterprises are subject.

(d) Should provide a stable tax system with profits and other income being taxed at rates which do not discourage private investment and enterprise.

V   The legal framework

1   The investor

(a) Should respect the national laws, policies and economic and social objectives of the host country in the same way as would a good citizen of that country, and abide by undertakings given to the government of the host country in connection with the investment.

(b) Should be willing to enter into arrangements for the settlement by international conciliation or arbitration of disputes with the government of the host country.

2   *The government of the investor's country*

Should not seek to interefere with the legal order of the host country by extending the application of its national laws, directives and regulations to the investor's operations in the host country.

3   *The government of the host country*

(a) Should respect the recognised principles of international law, reflected in many international treaties regarding the treatment of foreign property, concerning in particular:

(i)   fair and equitable treatment for such property;
(ii)   the avoidance of unreasonable and discriminatory measures;
(iii) the observance of contractual and other undertakings given to the investor;
(iv)   in the event of expropriation or nationalisation the effective payment, without undue delay, of just compensation.

(b) Should in suitable circumstances enter into arrangements for the settlement by international conciliation or arbitration of disputes with the investor.

(c) Should provide in its national laws for suitable protection for minority share-holdings in those cases where appropriate provisions do not as yet exist.

VI   Labour policies

1   *The investor*

(a) Should make the maximum practicable use of qualified local personnel.

(b) Should co-operate with the host government, labour unions and local educational and vocational training institutions in programs for the upgrading and training of local labour.

(c)   Should, to the extent consistent with the efficient operation of the enterprise, take into account the host government's efforts to create employment opportunities in the localities where they are most needed.

(d)   Should, in all matters directly affecting the interests of labour, to the extent appropriate to local circumstances, consult and co-operate with organisations representing its employees.

(e)   When the necessity for the closure of factories or the laying off of redundant employees becomes apparent, should give adequate advance information, and in consultation with the employees, arrange the timing and conditions of such action in a way that will cause the minimum social damage.

(f)   Should, in fixing wage and salary levels, act as a good employer, participating constructively as a member of national employers associations where these exist, and providing, according to local circumstances, the best possible wages, social benefits, retirement provisions and working conditions within the framework of the government's policies.

2   The government of the investor's country

(a)   Should, in formulating policies aimed at securing full employment, rely on stimulating domestic demand through appropriate economic and social policies, rather than on restrictions on the outflow of direct investment.

(b)   Should consider making available aid for educational and vocational training of local personnel in the skills needed by the enterprise and elsewhere in the economy of the host country, especially if it is a developing country.

3   The government of the host country

(a)   Should seek, in co-operation with investors and with appropriate national and foreign organisations, to assess future needs for skilled employees and to develop adequate programs for technical and managerial training.

(b)   Should permit the employment of qualified foreign personnel where this is needed for the efficient operation of the enterprise or for training purposes.

VII Technology (including inventions, know-how and skills)

1 The investor

(a) Should, whenever practicable, promote the development of the technological capacity of the host country, particularly if it is a developing country, for example by the training of local staff, assistance to educational institutions, and, provided that conditions for efficient research so allow, by establishment in the host country of suitable research activities.

(b) Should, when granting licences for the use of industrial property rights or when otherwise transferring technology, do so on reasonable terms and conditions and with an adequate market area.

(c) Should make the latest suitable technology available in return for appropriate payments, and keep it up to date in accordance with the circumstances of the host country.

(d) Should not, without prejudice to existing contracts, require payment for the use of industrial property rights or technology of no real value to the enterprise.

(e) Should support its investment with appropriate services and advice to ensure the full contribution of the investment to the development of the economy of the host country.

(f) Should co-operate with the government of the host country in examining the impact of his operations on the environment and take steps to minimise damage so far as is economically and technically practical in the local situation.

2 The government of the investor's country

(a) Should, in so far as it has not already done so, accede to relevant international treaties relating to Industrial Property and seek to conclude bilateral agreements that will facilitate the transfer of technology by private enterprises in return for appropriate remuneration.

(b) Should, where applicable, provide assistance to the host country, especially if it is a developing country, with a view to promoting the scientific and educational infrastructure necessary to facilitate the transfer and development of technology.

3 The government of the host country

(a) Should, in the formulation of its policies, take into account the fact that technology is mainly developed by private enterprises in the principal industrial and scientific centres of the world, and that its successful international transfer by such enterprises depends not only upon appropriate compensation being provided but also upon suitable conditions in the receiving country.

(b)   Should facilitate the continuing acquisition on appropriate terms of the additional know-how necessary to sustain competitive efficiency.

(c)   Should, if it wishes to encourage the investor to establish research facilities in its territory, take account of the need for an adequate scientific and educational infrastructure, and of the practical limits to dispersing research activities.

(d)   Should ensure effective legal protection for industrial property rights and encourage freedom of contract for licensing, subject to legislation for preventing abuses of industrial property rights such as failure to put them to use.

(e)   Should, in so far as it has not already done so, accede to relevant international treaties relating to Industrial Property and seek to conclude bilateral agreements that will facilitate the transfer of technology by private enterprises in return for appropriate remuneration.

(f)   Should not impose withholding taxes on licence fees, royalties and payments for services and advice at such a level that they materially increase the cost of the technology, make its transfer difficult, or even prevent it altogether.

VIII Commercial policies

1   The investor

(a)   Should not seek undue protection from competition from imports nor require unjustified guarantees against competition from new manufacturers in the same market.

(b)   Should assist the enterprise in its efforts to develop its export business and should not place any obstacle to such exports unless he is prevented by existing obligations to third parties or by sound economic reasons which he should be prepared to disclose to the government of the host country.

(c)   Should practice fair pricing policies for goods and services in dealings with associated companies which take into consideration the tax, Customs and competition regulations of the countries involved.

(d)   If prices and quality are competitive, should give preference to local sources of supply for components and raw materials, particularly where the host country is a developing country.

2 The government of the investor's country

(a) Should open its frontiers as fully as possible to foreign imports and in particular improve access to its markets for the industrial and agricultural products of developing countries.

(b) Should not seek to extend the application of its national laws, directives and regulations to restrict the exports of the enterprise from the host country to any third market.

3 The government of the host country

(a) Should co-operate in worldwide and regional initiatives towards liberalisation of international trade to the fullest extent that its level of economic development permits and in this connection avoid cost raising policies inconsistent with sound development.

(b) Should not impose export obligations on the enterprise beyond those contractually entered into.

(c) Should permit the enterprise to import the equipment, spare parts, components and materials which it requires for efficient production without undue formalities and without excessive Customs and other duties.

IV(f) EXTORTION AND BRIBERY IN BUSINESS TRANSACTIONS

(recommendations and rules adopted by the International Chamber of Commerce, November 1977)

RECOMMENDATIONS TO GOVERNMENTS

I Affirmation by governments of their commitment against extortion and bribery

Basic criminal statutes of most countries clearly prohibit extortion and bribery. In the interest of gradual harmonisation of standards of criminal legislation in this field, each government should review its statutes to ensure that they effectively prohibit, within its territorial jurisdiction, all aspects of both the giving and the taking of bribes, including promises and solicitation of bribes, as well as so-called facilitating payments to expedite the performance of functions which governmental officials have a duty to perform. Where no such legislation exists, the governments concerned should introduce it; in those countries where corruption is already clearly prohibited, the relevant legislation should be perfected.

Each national government should affirm its commitment to enforce vigorously its legislation in this area.

The ICC recommends that an international treaty be drawn up as a matter of urgency under the aegis of the United Nations so as to induce the various governments to take the necessary measures and to promote cooperation between governments which would facilitate the elimination of corruption. Bodies such as the ICC which have consultative status with the United Nations should be requested to give their views on the content of such a treaty.

Such a treaty should provide for:

(a) the implementation of the governmental measures recommended below;

(b) international cooperation and judicial assistance in dealing with extortion and bribery;

(c) cooperation by all States in the investigation and prosecution of offenders; to this effect, appropriate provisions should be included in all existing or future extradition treaties.

II   National measures

In order to deal with the problem of extortion and bribery, governments should, within the limits of their territorial jurisdiction, take the following measures, if they have not already done so.

A   Preventive measures

1.   Disclosure procedures

(a)   For the sake of transparency and within the limits defined in national legislation, such procedures should provide for periodic reports to an authorized government body of measures taken by governments to supervise government officials involved directly or indirectly in commercial transactions.

(b)   For enterprises engaged in transactions with any government or with any enterprise owned or controlled by government, disclosure procedures should provide for access, upon specific request, by the appropriate government authorities to information as to agents dealing directly with public bodies or officials and as to the payments to which such agents are entitled.

2.   Economic regulations

When laying down any economic regulations or legislation, Governments should, as far as possible, avoid the introduction of systems under which the carrying out of business requires the issue of individual authorisations, permits, etc. Experience shows that, in contrast with a legal framework within which business can operate freely, such systems offer scope for extortion and bribery, since the conclusion of business deals then often depends on decisions taken at a level at which it is almost impossible to ensure effective control and supervision.

3.   Transactions with governments and intergovernmental organisations

Such transactions should be subject to special safeguards to minimize the opportunities for their being influenced by extortion or bribery. The system for awarding government contracts might include disclosure, to an appropriate government entity independent of the one directly concerned in the transaction, of the criteria and conclusions upon which the award is based. The ICC supports the growing practice of making government contracts dependent on undertakings to refrain from bribery, and recommends that such contracts should include appropriate provisions to ensure compliance with international, national or enterprise codes against extortion and bribery.

4. Political contributions The **ICC** recognizes that political contributions are usually legitimate and proper. However, undisclosed political contributions may on occasion serve as a vehicle for extortion and bribery. Therefore, where payments by enterprises to political parties, political committees or individual politicians are permitted by the applicable national legislation, governments should consider, having regard to all the circumstances prevailing within each country, enacting legislation which ensures that such payments are publicly recorded by the payors and accounted for by the recipients.

B   Enforcement measures

Governments should ensure that adequate machinery exists for surveillance and investigation, and should ensure the prosecution with appropriate penalties, of those who, within their territorial jurisdiction, offer, give, demand, solicit or receive bribes in violation of their laws. Governments should periodically publish statistical or other information in respect of such prosecutions.

C   Auditing

Governments, if they have not already done so, should consider the enactment of appropriate legislation providing for auditing by independent professional auditors of the accounts of enterprises which are economically significant.

III   International cooperation and judicial assistance

Pending the establishment of a multilateral treaty under the aegis of the United Nations as recommended under Section I above, States should agree, under appropriate provisions for confidentiality, to exchange through law enforcement agencies relevant and material information for the purpose of criminal investigation and prosecution of cases of extortion and bribery. They should also continue to cooperate bilaterally on matters involving extortion and bribery.

RULES OF CONDUCT TO COMBAT
EXTORTION AND BRIBERY

Introduction

These Rules of Conduct are intended as a method of self-regulation.

Their voluntary acceptance by business enterprises will not only promote high standards of integrity in business transactions, whether between enterprises and public bodies or between enterprises themselves, but will also form a valuable defensive protection to those enterprises which are subjected to attempts at extortion.

Thus, such enterprises will be able to draw attention to the existence of the ICC Panel, the functions of which are outlined in Article 11 hereafter.

The ICC is only too well aware that extortion and bribery cannot be eliminated by a stroke of the pen overnight. Much of the evil, particularly in cases involving minor amounts, is the result of social conditions which may take time to ameliorate. This is also the case with so-called facilitating payments usually in regard to documentation, dock or customs clearances and similar matters, where minor officials in many countries habitually demand payments to supplement often inadequate salaries. The remedy for this state of affairs lies primarily in the hands of governments and, since the greater threat to competition comes from extortion and bribery relating to business transactions, it is not the present intention that the Panel should concern itself with particular instances of facilitating payments.

For the rest it is the hope of the ICC that all business enterprises, whether international or domestic, will faithfully follow the spirit of the Rules of Conduct.

These Rules of Conduct are of a general nature constituting what is considered good commercial practice in the matters to which they relate but without direct legal effect. They do not derogate from applicable local laws, and since national legal systems are by no means uniform, they must be read *mutatis mutandis* subject to such systems.

Basic principle

All enterprises should conform to the relevant laws and regulations of the countries in which they are established and in which they operate, and should observe both the letter and the spirit of these Rules of Conduct.

> For the purposes of these Rules of Conduct, the term 'enterprise' refers to any person or entity engaged in business, whether or not organised for profit, including any entity controlled by a State or a territorial subdivision thereof; it includes, where the context so indicates, a parent or a subsidiary.

Basic rules

Article 1 Extortion

No one may demand or accept a bribe.

Article 2 Bribery

No enterprise may, directly or indirectly, offer to give a bribe in order to obtain or retain business, and any demand for such a bribe must be rejected.

Article 3 'Kickbacks'

Enterprises should take measures reasonably within their power to ensure that no part of any payment made by them in connection with any commercial transaction is paid back to their employees or to any other person not legally entitled to the same.

Article 4 Agents

Enterprises should take measures reasonably within their power to ensure:

(a)   that any payment made to any agent represents no more than an appropriate remuneration for the services rendered by him; and

(b)   that no part of any such payment is passed on by the agent as a bribe or otherwise in contravention of these Rules of Conduct.

Article 5 Financial recording

(a)   All financial transactions must be properly and fairly recorded in appropriate books of account available for inspection by boards and auditors.

(b)   There must be no 'off the books' or secret accounts, nor may any documents be issued which do not properly and fairly record the transactions to which they relate.

Guidelines for implementation

Article 6 Responsibilities of enterprises

The body or individual which or who under the applicable law has the ultimate responsibility for the enterprises with which it or he is concerned should:

(a) take reasonable steps, including the establishment and maintenance of proper systems of control, to prevent any payments being made by or on behalf of the enterprise which contravene these Rules of Conduct.

(b) periodically review compliance with these Rules of Conduct and establish procedures for obtaining appropriate reports for the purposes of such review.

(c) take appropriate action against any director or employee contravening these Rules of Conduct.

Article 7 Auditing

Enterprises should take all necessary measures to establish independent systems of auditing in order to bring to light any transactions which contravene the present Rules of Conduct. Appropriate corrective action must then be taken.

Article 8 Agents

Enterprises should maintain a record of the names and terms of employment of all agents whose remuneration exceeds US $50,000 a year and who are employed by them in connection with transactions with public bodies or State enterprises. This record should be available for inspection by auditors and, upon specific request, by appropriate governmental authorities.

Article 9 Political contributions

Contributions to political parties or committees or to individual politicians may only be made in accordance with the applicable local law and must be accorded such publicity as that law requires.

Article 10 Company codes

These Rules of Conduct being of a general nature, enterprises should, where appropriate, draw up their own codes consistent with the ICC Rules and apply them to the particular circumstances in which their business is carried out. Such codes may usefully include examples and should enjoin employees or agents who find themselves subjected to any form of extortion or bribery immediately to report the same to senior management.

Article 11   Panel

(a)   The ICC is establishing a Panel to interpret, promote and oversee the application of these Rules of Conduct.

(b)   In particular, the Panel will periodically review matters relating to the Rules of Conduct and the experience gained in their application, as well as developments in fighting extortion and bribery in business transactions.

(c)   The Panel may consider the interpretation and the clarification of the Rules of Conduct, and may suggest modifications thereto, as occasion requires.

(d)   The Panel will periodically report to the Council of the ICC on its activities.

(e)   The Panel may, in appropriate circumstances, consider alleged infringements of the Rules of Conduct.

MULTINATIONAL CHARTER
(as adopted by International Confederation of Free Trade Unions,
Mexico, October 1975)

Preamble

1   From an early stage in its history, the labour movement has been
acutely aware of the dangers which the international operations of
capital could beget for the exercise of trade union rights, as well as for
the earnings and job security of the workers. It is now more than 100
years since international solidarity was first proclaimed as a weapon,
not only for the achievement of social justice, but also — more
immediately and concretely — for the defeat of employers' attempts to
break strikes by transferring production abroad. International labour
solidarity was the motive force behind the formation of the first international labour groupings in the third quarter of the nineteenth
century. And today international labour solidarity is being given ever
more concrete shape in the new forms of organisation which our movement is seeking to evolve for meeting the even greater challenge posed
by the activities of multinational companies.

2   What is a multinational company? For trade union purposes, the
simplest definition is one which carries on activities other than
marketing its own products in more than one country. Companies
doing that have, of course, existed for a long time. What is new is the
rapid growth in their number and size, the varied fields into which they
have moved, the use made by some of them of modern technology and
communications in order to set up integrated production facilities sited
in various countries and, above all, the economic, social and political
problems they pose, not only to the trade unions but to many national
governments too. These problems do not arise exclusively from any
misdeeds of the companies (such as those mentioned in the following
two paragraphs). They can be a consequence of their 'normal' industrial, financial and commercial activities and of the private planning in
their own interest which they are often able to impose to the detriment
of public planning in the interest of the community as a whole. They
collect financial resources from all over the world and invest them
where and how it is most profitable to themselves. In so doing they
may in many cases virtually decide whether a country is to expand its
production and employment or alternatively to stagnate. Or again, with
their built-in tendency to boost cash flow and their easy access to
international capital markets, they may have an inherent inflationary

effect, quite apart from any price-hiking possibilities arising from their position of market domination. From the global viewpoint, they are also very largely responsible for perpetuating the world's economic imbalance and further widening the gap between rich and poor nations: two thirds of international investment still goes to the older industrial countries, despite all the brave talk about the multinationals' role in promoting economic growth in the Third World.

3   These companies owe no allegiance to any nation-state. They mostly seek to escape any form of democratic control or social responsibility; they are guided primarily by motives of expansion and profit-maximisation. Conceiving company policies on a world-wide basis, and with production and assembly facilities in many different countries, they can juggle exports and imports by fixing artificial prices for transfers between the parent firm and/or its foreign subsidiaries. They can also manipulate dividends, tax payments and capital movements in ways which often escape the control of national authorities. There is no doubt that some of the financial and trading practices of these companies have had serious repercussions on the implementation of the policies of many governments in respect of the balance of payments, domestic industrial development, inflation and national economic planning in general. Some of these companies, moreover, have used their enormous resources to interfere in the internal political affairs of countries in which they have established subsidiaries; the methods used have ranged from the large-scale bribery of politicians to the active promotion of subversive movements aiming at the overthrow of democratically elected governments.

4   The activities of the multinationals in certain developing countries have given rise to especially sharp criticism from the trade union movement. Profiting from the urgent need of these countries for industrial investment — and, in a predominantly capitalist world economy, there is no visible alternative for the supply of the necessary capital and know-how — the companies have extracted far-reaching concessions which such countries can ill afford to make; tax holidays for up to ten years, exemption from import duties, even the provision of ready-built factories and — most despicable of all from the labour viewpoint — guarantees against trade union interference in the shape of restrictive legislation for ensuring the trouble-free exploitation of vast pools of cheap labour. Add to those incentives the attraction of freedom from the increasingly stringent antipollution and health-protection measures being adopted in the older industrialised countries, and the motives of the companies for investing in some parts of the Third World become clearer. In return the developing countries it is true receive some badly

needed industrial investment — but not necessarily that best suited to their real development needs — some access to scarce foreign currency from increased exports — after deduction of course of profits whose repatriation they have had to guarantee to the companies. And in the final analysis, there is no certainty that the companies will stay once their tax holiday has expired, or increasing trade union pressure — despite all the restrictions — has begun to eat into their super profits. A side effect of the superprofit-making activities of the multinationals in the Third World is the stimulus they give to protectionist feelings and the jeopardising of support for development aid policies among workers in industries affected by unfair competition in the older industrial countries. Another predilection of some multinational companies is for investments in countries with dictatorial regimes, where elementary human and labour rights are systematically flouted.

5   In the absence of coordinated international trade union action, it is obvious that the growth and concentration of international capital must tip the balance of bargaining power in favour of management and against labour. Strikes can be broken by the transfer of production to other factories of the same company; the introduction of industrial democracy can be rendered null and void, if the board of directors on which the workers are granted representation is not autonomous but subject to control from a parent body in another country. Hence the efforts of the international trade secretariats to build up a counter-vailing power to that of the companies, in particular through the creation of world councils representing the workers in the various concerns. The ICFTU recognises the primordial role of the international trade secretariats in strengthening union bargaining capacity vis-à-vis the companies and in seeking to evolve new forms of organisation based on international workers' solidarity in order to meet the multinational challenge.

6   There is general recognition throughout the international labour movement, however, that collective bargaining procedures are not in themselves sufficient for dealing with all the various problems raised by the activities of multinational companies. As in the case of certain other trade union objectives, political action for securing appropriate legislation is also required. The immediate aim of this action is to protect the general interests of the workers and the peoples by imposing social controls on the activities of the companies. Its long-term aim is to substitute for the international division of labour which the multinationals have imposed on the world a more just and humane system of international cooperation under democratic control. We wish to put an end to the frantic competition between nations to secure investment and jobs from the multinationals. Only when industrial

production is geared to satisfying the basic needs of the masses, not the private profit of a few, will it be possible to give really effective aid to the industrial development of the Third World countries. Such development would thus complement that of the industrially advanced countries; it would not have the effect which much multinational investment has at present, of simply transferring jobs from the industrial to developing countries, with consequently higher unemployment in the former. An essential element in the kind of democratic control mentioned above will be the introduction or extension of systems of industrial democracy giving the workers a greater say in economic decision-making at all levels. As for the mechanics of transferring capital and technical know-how to the countries which need them most through channels other than the multinationals, there are vast untapped possibilities in cooperation between countries with a well-developed public sector, as well as in international investment by the cooperative movement with its basic philosophy of production for use rather than profit.

Trade union objectives

7   Recognising the need for a common trade union strategy towards the multinationals, particularly for the attainment of our political objectives, the 10th ICFTU World Congress in July 1972 called for the creation of a joint working party together with the international trade secretariats. Set up in February 1973, the ICFTU/ITS Working Party on Multinational Companies has concentrated its main endeavours on the promotion of legislation, national and international, for controlling the activities of these companies. Our studies of the problems involved have confirmed our belief that national legislation in many cases needs to be complemented — and sometimes even preceded — by international agreements with machinery for supervision and enforcement. This is true where the nature of the practices calling for control is intimately connected with the international character of the multinationals. It is also true in respect of almost any control measures to be applied by small countries whose total budget may be less than one tenth of the annual turnover of some of the huge concerns they have to deal with. Such countries obviously need the moral, material and institutional support of the international community.

8   Ideally, we would have wished to see a general multilateral treaty under United Nations auspices with a new fully-fledged UN agency for supervising its application. It would be the task of this agency to elaborate the international agreements of a social, economic, com-

mercial, technological, fiscal and financial nature required to co-ordinate, complement and reinforce national legislation in the matter. It would do so in close cooperation with other United Nations specialised agencies and regional bodies concerned with particular aspects of the problem. In addition, the agency would provide technical assistance to governments of developing countries to help them in dealing with the companies. Without such an agency, concerned exclusively with multinational company problems and having the power to promote socially useful solutions, the companies will continue to hold their present licence to blackmail the developing countries, to disrupt the economies of the industrial countries, to export pollution and in general to act without regard for trade union rights, the health and job security of the workers, or for the national sovereignty and economic independence of whole peoples. Such an agency would need, moreover, to be based on tripartite representation of governments, workers and employers, as is the ILO, and equipped with a similar complaints procedure.

9   As a possible first step in that direction, the trade unions welcomed the decision of the UN Economic and Social Council to set up a Commission on Transnational Corporations, to be backed up with an Information and Research Centre. Obviously, however, that Commission will never be in a position to elaborate and apply effective social controls on the multinationals unless it finds ways and means of realistically associating the trade union movement with its work.

10   Certain United Nations specialised agencies have for some time been studying various particular aspects of the problem: the ILO (social aspects), UNCTAD (transfer of technology and unfair business practices in developing countries). So, too, have some intergovernmental regional groupings: the six Andean Pact countries of South America have evolved a common policy regarding foreign investment; the European Economic Community has a rather timid project for a very rudimentary code of conduct which has been awaiting the approval of its Council of Ministers for about two years, while the Organisation for Economic Cooperation and Development has been studying the problem in a number of expert committees for some three years without evolving any definite proposals.

11   In all these intergovernmental bodies, as well as in the United Nations, the ICFTU − in cooperation with the international trade secretariats and in support of their action at the level of the various companies − will continue to urge the early adoption of policies which can really control multinational company activities. Pending the creation of an effective international agency with trade union partici-

pation for the control of the multinationals, we believe that they should follow four lines of action: firstly to establish guidelines and machinery for effective cooperation between governments in their relations with multinational enterprises; secondly, to promote co-ordinated national legislation in the various fields where government control is needed; thirdly, to adopt international conventions imposing enforceable standards and rules on the companies; and, finally, to keep under constant review the impact of the multinationals on industrial structures and social and economic development in all countries, as well as on international trade and the international monetary system.

12   We believe that the approach generally adopted by intergovernmental bodies — that is towards a voluntary 'code of conduct' — is too timid and inadequate in face of the challenge posed by the activities of multinational companies. We could accept such a code only as a first step towards binding regulations set out in international conventions to which the governments can give legal force by embodying them in national legislation.

13   An essential element of these conventions would be the establishment of tripartite committees with equal representation of governments, trade unions and employers' organisations. Infringements of the conventions, especially in regard to social standards, would be reported to these committees whose hearings would be public.

14   The conventions would become binding upon ratification by a specified number of states. By the same conventions, the governments would be obliged to adopt common measures in such fields as employment and social policy, capital movements, investment incentives, control of mergers, safeguarding of competition and taxation.

15   Responsibility for the overall promotion and co-ordination of such international agreements would obviously be the task of the United Nations and its Economic and Social Council under which a Commission on Transnational Corporations together with an Information and Research Centre has been set up. We have welcomed the establishment of this Commission, but only as a step in the direction of an international agency with executive powers and with effective trade union participation. Progress towards the conclusion of a global international convention covering all aspects of the problems raised by the activities of multinational companies should not, however, preclude the promotion of regulations covering certain aspects of those problems by UN specialised agencies, or by regional bodies such as the OECD, the European Community or the Andean Pact. The ILO, in particular, has had the question of the social impact of multinational companies on its

agenda since 1968 and the trade union movement is now awaiting some concrete proposals from that quarter.

16   In the advance towards the international control of the activities of multinational companies, we believe a very important role could be played by the UN Information and Research Centre when it becomes operative. Its major priority task will obviously be the elaboration of a global multilateral agreement defining the areas in which binding regulations should be applied. In order to facilitate intergovernmental cooperation, another priority task for the Centre would be a close examination of different industrial sectors in order to assess the degree and pattern of domination by the multinationals; 'ad hoc' working groups could be set up for particular industries. In general, the Centre's studies of the impact of multinationals should be undertaken with the effective tripartite cooperation of governments, trade unions and employers and in close liaison with the appropriate UN specialised agencies; those, for example, concerning the impact on employment and other social problems could obviously not be effectively pursued without the collaboration of the ILO.

17   Another very important and continuing task for the Centre would be the organising of technical assistance projects for developing countries in order to equip their governments better for dealing with the companies.

Trade union proposals for action

18   The ICFTU and the international trade secretariats associated with it, propose that the appropriate intergovernmental organisations take steps for the adoption of international conventions concerning multinational companies on the subjects listed below. The legal form and scope of such agreements are clearly matters for the agencies concerned. As for the content, in the light of trade union experience in dealing with these companies, we believe that our proposals represent the minimum of regulations required. We are ready and willing to discuss them with any intergovernmental agency which is ready to come to grips with the problem of elaborating realistic international social controls on the activities of the multinational companies.

(i)   Public accountability

19   Not only are the trade unions often hindered in their collective bargaining activities by the lack of basic financial information on the

490

operations of the multinationals; the governments of many countries, too, need much more ample and specific data on these operations for purposes of national economic and social planning, as well as for co-operating in the international control of the companies.

20 What is needed is legislation obliging multinational concerns to provide detailed financial accounts and other data not only for the branch in any particular country but also for the parent company. This information should accurately reflect all aspects of production development, including the worldwide breakdown of production operations, profits, cash flow, investment expenditure and projects, capital borrowing, participations, taxes, employment, wages, corporate ownership, etc.

21 Our proposals for the substance of the legislation required in order to enforce public accountability are contained in Appendix I*, to which are attached three further sub-appendices outlining a suggested model form of financial reporting to be required from the companies.

22 In signing an international convention on legislative measures for enforcing public accountability, it is understood that the signatory states would thereby also agree to make the resultant information available to the United Nations and/or appropriate specialised agencies or intergovernmental regional organisations.

23 It is furthermore strongly recommended that, with a view to facilitating the enforcement of those regulations, in order to ensure that the trade unions concerned have the essential information and in the general public interest, governments should appoint special auditors for checking the information supplied by the companies.

(ii) Social obligations of the companies

24 It is clear that multinational companies are expected to comply with the social legislation of every country in which they operate. Any derogations granted by way of investment incentives are obviously socially and economically undesirable and should be expressly forbidden in the international conventions adopted in this field. Furthermore, such companies should be subject to certain additional social obligations not applicable to exclusively domestic concerns. This is not a question of discriminating against the multinationals, but rather of redressing to some extent the balance of power of the companies with their vast international ramifications, on the one hand and, on the other hand, their workers who are limited within a national context, just as indeed are the governments. This is particularly true

*Appendix to ICFTU Charter not included in this extract.

of the developing countries, where trade unions are generally weak, while many of the governments concerned may have national budgets as little as one tenth the size of the annual turnover of some of the companies with which they have to deal.

25 Our proposals for the content of a series of conventions laying down the social obligations incumbent upon the companies are contained in Appendix II*.

Control of international direct investment and takeovers

26 The period since the end of the second world war has been characterised, so far as the international movement of capital is concerned, by an increasingly liberal 'laissez-faire' attitude on the part of most governments. In the OECD area this found expression in a Code of Liberalisation of Capital Movements. In recent years this tendency has also been discernible even in the countries of centrally planned economies. Very few governments, on the other hand, took any steps to safeguard the interests of the labour force which were often jeopardised by the lack of minimum social and labour standards in many of the countries to which investments were freely flowing. This policy of liberalising capital movements provided the essential condition for the mushrooming growth of multinational companies, which undoubtedly contributed a good deal to economic development in many countries. This progress was achieved, however, at the cost of a tremendous concentration of economic power in the hands of a relatively small group of industrial and financial interests, with all the obvious social and political dangers inherent in such a violent upheaval in the balance of social forces.

27 The trade union movement believes that the time has come to call a halt to the unbridled freedom of international investment and to insist that stricter control be imposed with a view to safeguarding the economic independence and national sovereignty of all nations, as well as to ensuring that certain social obligations are attached to such operations. Controls are even more necessary when the international investment involves the takeover of an existing concern. Apart from the social considerations involved, the job security and trade union rights of the workers, for example, such operations may conflict with national economic, industrial and science policies (research workers are usually among the first victims of the rationalisation measures which frequently accompany an international takeover). The trade unions of the OECD countries have already made concrete proposals

*Appendix to ICFTU Charter not included in this extract.

492

for the amendment of the OECD Code of Liberalisation in the sense outlined above. Non-OECD countries, however, are certainly at least as much in need of protection from the effects of uncontrolled foreign economic penetration. This, in fact, is eminently a case for concerted international action: one unfortunate result of isolated national attempts to deal with the situation will be to divert multinational investment to the countries with the least controls.

28   The ICFTU and the international trade secretariats associated with it consequently submit the following elements which they believe should enter into an international convention on the control of foreign direct investment and takeovers.

(a)   Prior authorisation by the competent national authorities shall be required for all inward foreign direct investment or acquisition of existing undertakings, such authorisation only being granted when it is deemed to be in the national interest, after consultation with the trade union movement.

(b)   As a condition for the establishment or acquisition of an undertaking the competent authorities may impose limitations in time or other conditions, reserving for example the right for public participation, with or without the further right to subsequent partial or total ownership.

(c)   Authorisation shall be granted only on condition that the investor agrees to comply fully with the terms of the conventions on social obligations outlined in (ii) above.

(d)   In the case of acquisition of an existing undertaking, the views of the workers concerned shall be an essential factor to be taken into consideration by the competent authorities in deciding if the operation is in the national interest.

(e)   As a guarantee for the fulfilment of the foregoing conditions the investor shall be required to deposit a certain sum (the amount being mutually agreed with the competent authorities in accordance with criteria to be established by international agreement), which may, in particular, be used for the compensation of the workers in the event of subsequent retrenchment or close-down.

(f)   In respect of outward investment, authorisation will, as in the case of inward investment, only be granted on condition the investor complies fully with the terms of the conventions or social obligations outlined in (ii) and such compliance shall furthermore be a condition for benefiting from any outward investment guarantee scheme.

493

(iv) Restrictive business practices and oligopolistic pricing

29 The use of economic power to dominate the market and restrict competition — in the matter not only of prices, but also of conditions for the sale or purchase of goods and services, access to patents and licences, the physical removal of competitors either through mergers or the acquisition of control over rival enterprises and similar cartel practices — was certainly not an invention of the multinational companies. They have been able to use such practices to vastly greater effect, however, thanks to their world-wide ramifications and thus to set up international cartels for the boosting of profits and the building of economic empires.

30 These practices are not only socially and politically undesirable, but also economically disastrous in their long-term effects. There is no doubt that the near-monopoly control of prices administrated by many multinationals has been a major factor in the violent upsurge of inflation which by the mid '70's was rocking the world economy to its very foundations.

31 What is also clear is that purely national legislation has in many respects proved ineffective for controlling the restrictive business practices of the big multinationals. An international convention for the suppression of these practices is urgently required. That convention would also provide the basis for the closer collaboration between the taxation and customs authorities — at regional and world levels — which would certainly be needed to translate the good intentions of such a convention into reality.

32 Our proposals for the main elements of a convention on restrictive business practices and oligopolistic pricing are contained in Appendix III*.

Taxation of the multinationals

33 It is common knowledge, although not always easy to prove in any particular case, that existing tax law and regulations in most countries fail to keep a grip on the slippery — if not strictly illegal — financial practices of some multinational companies. This inadequacy is due to a number of resources and subterfuges which, by the very nature of their structure, are available only to multinational companies in their dealings with national tax authorities. These include: the ability to withhold or give insufficient information on their operations

*Appendix to ICFTU Charter not included in this extract.

outside the national territory; the use of fictitious transfer prices, royalties, debt repayments and the division of overhead expenses between the parent company and/or its branches in various countries; the switching, thanks to the foregoing devices, of the lion's share of total profits to low-tax or tax-haven countries; and, finally, the perfectly legal, but morally indefensible, tax advantages granted as incentives to invest, particularly in developing countries.

34 What may well be necessary in taxing multinational companies would be to take as the basis, not apparent gross profits, but the size of the investment, expenses and the turnover as criteria for arriving at a realistic estimation.

35 We therefore propose that regional and international conventions on the principles and rules for the taxation of multinational companies be elaborated to include the elements set out in Appendix IV*.

(vi) Transfer of technology and the role of multinationals in development

36 Apologists for the multinational companies are wont to harp on the benefits by way of industrialisation they have brought, especially to the developing countries, thanks to the spread of modern technology of which they have a virtual monopoly. What is not usually mentioned is the tremendous cost this has involved, especially to developing countries which can ill afford to pay the exorbitant sums demanded as royalties and patent rights.

37 The instrument whereby patent holders in the rich countries have established their right to exact their pound of flesh from the poor countries is the Paris Convention for the Protection of Industrial Property of 1883. This lays down the principle of temporary monopoly of production and sale to the licence owner or patentee of an industrial process. Most developing countries have refused to sign this convention, but are nevertheless obliged to comply with it, faced as they are with the enormous power of the multinational licence holders. They rightly regard it as an instrument of exploitation whereby they are expected to strengthen the position of foreign firms on their own territories through the payment or royalties unilaterally fixed by the companies themselves.

38 There is no doubt that the Paris Convention, with its santification of technological monopoly, has been instrumental in promoting a tremendous concentration of economic power in the hands of a few powerful companies. The international trade union movement has con-

*Appendix to ICFTU Charter not included in this extract.

sequently called for the drastic revision of the Paris Convention and its replacement by a system of fees to be fixed by negotiation or arbitration.

39   Even where the transfer of technology takes place within the company itself and involves no direct charge on a developing country, this is not necessarily an unmixed blessing. It usually means that an industrial process has been foisted willy-nilly on that country without regard to its real development needs or its national planning objectives. Furthermore, it generally does little to raise the level of technological knowledge in the country, but on the contrary reinforces its economic and technological dependence on monopoly capital.

40   We consequently recommend to the attention of the United Nations and intergovernmental regional bodies the conclusions of the Group of Twenty regarding technology in their report 'The Impact of Multinational Corporations on Development and International Relations'.

41   We also recommend the common regulations evolved by the Andean Group of countries, which seek to render null and void contracts containing clauses which permit the supplier to interfere directly or indirectly in the management of the purchasing company, establish the obligation to transfer to the supplier improvements developed by the purchasing company, establish the obligation to purchase from certain suppliers only, or limit the volume of production.

42   We furthermore recommend, as one possible and obviously socially useful alternative to the transfer of technology by multinationals, the studies which the International Cooperative Alliance is pursuing on the possibility of joint cooperative productive investment in developing countries for the benefit of the workers and peoples concerned.

Short-term capital movements

43   The breakdown in the early 1970s of the international monetary system set up by the Bretton Woods agreement for the stabilisation of exchange rates is one of the main factors behind the present world economic crisis. And there is no doubt that the financial operations of multinational companies have played a big part in the collapse of that system. They were able to do this because of the huge cash flow which they controlled; by the end of 1971 multinational companies and international banks held more than twice the liquid assets of all the

world's central banks and financial institutions put together. Their ability to move these vast sums round the world, switching millions at the lift of a telephone from one currency into another, was used not only for normal commercial transactions but also for purely speculative purposes directed against the principal reserve currencies — the US dollar and the pound sterling. The successive devaluations of these currencies affected not only the two countries directly concerned, but also and perhaps even more acutely a good many developing countries which had a great part of their monetary reserves in those currencies and whose economies were ill-equipped to stand such speculative buffeting.

44   The ICFTU believes that international agreement is essential on a new, stable monetary system and on the co-ordinated control of international capital markets in order to prevent governments losing control of their countries' economies through the actions of speculators, including multinational companies. A fuller analysis of the whole problem of the international monetary system, together with ICFTU proposals for its reform, will be found in the Congress document 'Economic security and social justice: ICFTU policies 1975—78'. Here we are concerned only with the special controls needed to prevent multinational companies abusing their financial power to indulge in currency speculations. Such control would have to be applied also to other firms with international financial ramifications such as insurance companies, building societies and international banks.

45   The ICFTU believes that the International Monetary Fund should take the initiative in preparing guide-lines to assist governments in setting up adequate reporting systems in order to identify financial transactions made by multinational enterprises. In most countries the information is already available on a daily basis through the reporting system of the banks to the national exchange authorities. Some countries, however, have no appropriate reporting systems: even those with such highly developed economies and financial structures as Canada, Germany and the USA, while in Switzerland special legislation would be needed to authorise it.

46   In order to reinforce national reporting systems in this matter international cooperation between the appropriate national authorities would be necessary, just as we have proposed in the matter of taxation controls. Such cooperation should be more immediately feasible on a regional basis, especially where a fully structured intergovernmental regional organisation already exists. In the OECD, for example, the Trade Union Advisory Committee has submitted a proposal in this connection to the Organisation, together with a project of a questionnaire for gathering the required information.

Index

'Ad-hoc Council' 204
Aer Lingus 53
AFL/CIO 197, 206, 207
AKZO 53
Akumu, Dennis 214
Allende, Salvador 116
American Chamber of Commerce 50; EEC Committee in Belgium 204
Arab–Israeli conflict 1973 25
Arbed 53
Atlantic Richfield: sale of *Observer* 154
ATLAS 135
Australia: view of OECD Guidelines 154

Badger International 48: Belgian case under OECD Guidelines 65, 122, 125–8; subsidiary of Raytheon 125
Bank of Tokyo 209

BASF 209
Bekaert Co. 209
Belgium: attitude to MNC control 28–9; enterprise committees 63; nationalised banking in 92; OECD contact point in 145, 146; unions opposed to class collaboration 55
Bénard, André 208, 217
Black and Decker: case under OECD Guidelines 130
Bosch Co.: from standpoint of OECD Guidelines in the US 145
British American Tobacco Co. (BAT) 56: Dutch case under OECD Guidelines 31, 122, 136–7, 146
British Institute of Management (BIM): on worker participation 54
British Leyland 154

498

British Oxygen 56: Swedish case of Viggo AB under OECD Guidelines 122, 137–8, 143, 146
Bullock Report 54
Business organisations: EEC lobby 201–4; OECD lobby 208–12; political organisation 27–8; UN lobby 217–18; versus unions on MNC control 195–8; basic battle lines 196–8; defensive tactics 196

Caborn, Richard 27
Carbonel, V. 209
Carter, Pres. James 182
Chamber of Economic Rights and Duties of States 165
Chaumont, P. 209
CII 94
Citibank–Citicorp: UK case under OECD Guidelines 134–5, 145
Clarke, J.G. 209
Clarke, K.H.J. 209
Coates, J.A.G. 209
Coca Cola 79
Commercial Solvents Co.: anti-trust judgement on 81, 82
Confédération Géneral du Travail (CGT) 55
Confederation of British Industry (CBI) 49, 211
Conoco 145
Continental Group 79: anti-trust judgement on 81, 82, 83
Crean and Co. Ltd, Robert 209
Crean, J.G. 209

Davidow, Joel 177
Davignon, Viscount Etienne 23, 36, 37, 38, 42, 77, 200, 204: takes middle way on MNC control 38, 39
Denmark: view of MNC control 10, 29; worker participation laws 48, 53
Deutscher Gewerkschafts Bund (DGB) 57, 205
Dribbusch, Dr F. 209
Dupont Co. 39, 56, 78

European Airlines Groupings: question of airline organisations as MNCs 135–6
European Centre of Public Enterprise (CEEP) 202
European Commission 23, 36, 39, 57, 66, 103, 204: 'Employee Participation and Company Structure' 64; interventionist vocation 25; MNCs' employment protection programme 58; monopolies list 84–6; on threat of 'bigness' 74; power in anti-trust field 77, 79; powers to control state aid 93
European Economic Community (EEC): and OECD Guidelines 36
anti-trust challenge to MNCs 73–94; Article 86 on monopolies 79–82, 83; battle against size 82–8; crackdown on cartels 89–90; co-operation with US 102–4; EEC control of state aids 93; independence and rapidity of procedure 76–9; power in dealing with private monopolies 79–82; weakness in facing nationalised industries 90–2;

European Economic Community (cont.)
approach to MNC control 9, 12, 19–20;
Council of Ministers 60, 64: draft resolution on MNCs 1973 38
Court of Justice 77–80 *passim*, 92, 94: judgements against cartels 89, 90; judgements against monopolies 81–2; judgements on state aid 93
decade of growth to 1970 19
decade of uncertainty to 1980 19–20; Economic and Social Committee 204
external business policy 98–105: anti-trust co-operation with US 102–4; attitude to international business codes 100–1; 'Code of Conduct for Companies with Subsidiaries, Branches or Representation in South Africa' 101–2, 104; external tariff 99; share of world trade 99; trade deficits 100; trade preferences 99–100; transition to protectionism 99–100;
factors conditioning policy towards MNCs 22–32: diplomatic 23, 32; economic 22, 23–4; institutional 22, 25; national 28–31; political 23, 26–8
fibres cartel 39, 77, 78;
half MNCs' HQs in 23;
labour and company law and MNCs 47, 52, 55–6, 56–64: corporate disclosure and tax exposure 67–8; employee consultation in MNCs 58–63; employment protection rules 51, 58; participation in company boards 63–4, 65; two-tier board structure 64; 'unlimiting' company liability 65–6

MNC control legislation tabled 106–7; national differences about MNC control 10; not comparable to US free market 20–1; policy of public procurement 42–3;
policy towards MNCs 35–44: containment measures 37–8; development 1970–77 35; dirigisme or liberalism? 37, 38–9; discrimination against 37, 43–4; pro-European 37, 39, 42–3
position of MNCs in 21–2; size of market 23; socialisation of economy 21; trade union and business lobbies 198–204; trends in policy towards MNCs 1980–85 12–14; on corporate disclosure 13; on employment protection and industrial democracy 13; on foreign competition 14; on tax evasion and transfer pricing 13;
unemployment in 99
European Foundation for the Economy 204
European League for Economic Co-operation 204
European Parliament 9, 27, 60, 64, 204: code on MNCs agreed with US Congress 9, 74, 103; lobbying at 204; Socialist Group 27
European Trade Union Confederation (ETUC) 57, 197, 198, 201, 202, 203:

European Trade Union Confederation (cont.)
Brussels HQ 26, 27, 197; influence on EEC 198–201: agreement on MNC policy 199–201; supporter of MNC control 26, 27
Exxon 209: refinery case 93
Eyskens, Mark 125

Federation of Danish Industries 209
Fiat 209: representative in Brussels 28; workers' council 54
Finland: view of MNC control 10
Firestone Co. 48, 146: Swiss case under OECD guidelines 136–7
Ford Co. 53, 56, 143, 209: Dutch case under OECD Guidelines 146
France: MNCs' rejection of control in 227; output of nationalised industries 91, 92; socialist experiment 69; view of MNC control 29–30; worker participation in 54–5
Furumi, K. 209

Galbraith, J.K. 49
Gauthier, Dr Aak 120
General and Municipal Workers Union 130
General Agreement on Tariffs and Trade (GATT): Kennedy Round 98; Tokyo Round 99, 166
General Foods 79
General Motors 52–3, 73, 209
Germany (FDR): Bundeskartelamt 75; Codetermination Law 1951 51; industrial democracy in 69; Law on

Codetermination 1976 133; OECD contact point in 145; output of nationalised industries 91, 92; trade unionists on boards in 56; view of MNC control 10, 29; worker participation laws 48, 50–1; works councils 52, 63
Gibbons, Sam 103
Giscard d'Estaing, Pres. Valéry 30, 54
Glättli, Dr H. 209
Greece: EEC employment protection rules and 58; view of MNC control 30
Group B states 151, 165: position on UN code for MNCs 168; views on technology transfer 179–81
Group of 77 151, 163, 164, 165: position on UN code for MNCs 167–8; reasons for restricting MNCs 10, 117; views on technology transfer 179–81
GTE: Belgian case under OECD Guidelines 146
Gundelach, Finn Olav 63

Heinz, H.J. 79
Hertz Rentacar 56: Danish case under OECD Guidelines 29, 122, 124n, 129
Hoffman La Roche 73, 79: anti-trust judgement on 81, 82, 83

ICL 94
IG Metall 132
Imperial Chemical Industries (ICI) 51, 209
Inco Ltd 209
Industrial democracy: EEC legislation for 47; European 50–6

Industrial Business Machines (IBM) 43, 52, 73, 79, 201: EEC anti-trust contest with 87–8, 94; World Trade Corporation subsidiary of 87

International Chamber of Commerce (ICC) 198, 212, 214: 'Guidelines for International Investment' 11, 212; 'International Panel on Extortion and Bribery in International Transactions' 11; lobbying role at UN 217; 'Rules of Conduct to combat Extortion and Bribery' 182; US Council 209

International Chemical and Energy Workers Federation 207

International Federation of Employees and Technicians (FIET) 134, 206;

International Confederation of Free Trade Unions (ICFTU) 27, 32, 117, 154, 197, 198, 206, 212, 213, 214; eight-point programme on MNCs 215–17; 'Handbook for trade union negotiators in MNCs' 206; 'Multinational Charter' 212; on implementation of UN code on MNCs 190–1

International Labour Organisation (ILO) 11, 15, 151, 217: Tripartite Declaration of Principles regarding MNCs and Social Policy 7–8, 11, 12, 15, 27, 100, 117, 151, 155, 164, 166, 171–6, 189, 192, 206, 215; disputes procedure 175; implementation 175–6; main principles 173–6; parties to 172

International Metalworkers Federation 206

International Organisation of Employers 198, 212, 214, 217; code on extortion and bribery 212

International Telephone and Telegraph (ITT) 51, 56, 196: W. German case under OECD Guidelines 133–4

International Textile, Garment and Leather Workers Federation 206

International trade secretariats 206, 207

International Transport Workers' Federation 206

International Union of Food and Allied Workers 207

Investment: Euro-American switch, late 1970s 148–50; outward flows, by countries 149

Ireland: EEC employment protection rules and 58; view of MNC control 30; worker participation 53

Italy: *consigli di fabbrica* 48, 54, 63; OECD contact point in 145; output of nationalised industries 91; resistance to industrial democracy 50, 55; slackening of Christian Democrat grip 69; view of MNC control 30–1

Japan: penetration of EEC markets 99; question of OECD Guidelines in 211; SOHYO union centre 197

Jenkins, Roy 57, 198

Kaaris, P. 209
Kawasaki Co. 73
Kodak Co. 79
KSSU 135

Lands Organisationen 57
Lange, Erwin 103
Lea, David 207, 214
Lennep, Emile van 117
Levinson, Charles 56, 207, 213
Lévy, Philippe 120, 126: report on Badger case 127
Lindgren, H. 209
Litton Industries: Sweda subsidiary case under OECD Guidelines 132
Lockheed Co. 196
Lockwood, R. 209
Lonrho 154
Luxembourg: opposed to financial disclosure 68; view of MNC control 31; worker participation laws 53

Markley, R.W. 209
Massey Ferguson: Motor Iberica subsidiary case under OECD Guidelines 129–30
Mauroy, M. 30, 55
Mensbrugghe, Y. van der 209
Mitterrand, Pres. François 30, 55, 102
Monsanto 39, 51, 78
Multinational companies (MNCs): approach to UN code 217–8; authority in executives' hands 49, 225; challenge of industrial democracy to 46–69; conflict with worker participation laws 51; EEC anti-trust policies and 73–94; EEC approach to control of 9, 12, 19–20; EEC policy towards 35–44; EEC laws on corporate responsibility and 64–8; effect of national trade policies on 99, 100; erosion of local decision-making in 47, 49; factors conditioning EEC policy towards 22–32; hostility towards EEC labour law 56–64; hostility towards worker consultation 49–50; international guidelines for, see OECD Guidelines, ILO Declaration of Principles and UN and UNCTAD codes of conduct; need for advisory councils 229; need to become politically minded 26; number, by country of origin 24;
political constraints 223–4, 227: demand for accountability 224, 225–6; MNCs' attempts to reject 226–7, 228, 229
position in EEC 21–2; problem of responsibility of parent company 65, 66;
public affairs departments, by company 203: need to upgrade 228–9;
trend analysis of policy outlook 1980–5: general trends 11–12; trends at EEC 12–14; trends at OECD 14–15; trends at UN 15–16
trend towards international control 3–4; turnover and assets, worldwide 40–1, 42
Murray, Len 202

National Foreign Trade Council 50
National Panasonic 90
National Union of Bank Employees (NUBE) 134
Nationalised industries: output in EEC countries 91–2; weakness of EEC jurisdiction over 90–2

Nestlé Co. 79
Netherlands: enterprise councils
52, 163; OECD contact point
in 145, 146; view of MNC
control 10, 31, 154; worker
participation laws 48, 52–3
Niklasson Sten 10, 32, 166
Norway: view of MNC control
10

Observer 154
OECD Guidelines for MNCs 7–
8, 9–12 passim, 14, 15, 20,
27, 29, 31, 35, 36, 55, 59, 65,
100, 104, 113–5, 164, 172,
175, 191–2, 187, 204–12
passim, 227:
   assessment of 152–7; anti-
   trust policy 156–7; prospect
   for individual guidelines
   155–7; question of corporate disclosure 156;
   question of MNC parental
   responsibility 156; science
   and technology guideline
   157; selective nature 153;
   views of interested parties
   153–5;
   cases brought under 122,
   125–38; publicity impact
   123;
   counter to UN code 151;
   EEC influence on 20;
   'Employment and Industrial
   Relations' 123–4, 130–5
   passim, 155; governments'
   positions between unions and
   MNCs 142, 144; importance in
   industrial relations 112, 114,
   175; machinery of application
   119–20; MNC view of 143–4,
   154;

paternity of 113: internal
   pressure in West 118–20;
   UN connection 115–8;
political and business impact
   141–57; price for contravention 111; reviewed 1979
   114, 115, 137, 142, 143, 205
   role vis-à-vis developing
   countries 150–2; 'soft law'
   nature of 111–12, 152, 155,
   189; trade union influence on
   20; trade union view of 142–
   3, 152, 154; voluntary nature
   113, 118
Oil Crisis of 1973 116
Organisation for Economic Co-
   operation and Development
   (OECD) 11, 67, 101: Business
   and Industry Advisory Committee (BIAC) 119, 120, 143,
   198, 204, 205, 208–12, 217;
   Committee on International
   Investments and Multinational
   Enterprises (IME Committee)
   120, 125–8, 150, 157, 176;
   Council 7, 113; Decision on
   Investment Incentives and Disincentives 1976 147–8;
   Guidelines for MNCs, see
   OECD Guidelines for MNCs;
   national contact points 144–
   6; question of encouragement
   of investment by 146–50;
   'Recent International Direct
   Investment Trends' 148, 150;
   recommendation on transfer
   pricing 156; Trade Union
   Advisory Committee (TUAC)
   32, 65, 118, 119, 120, 122,
   123, 129, 143, 145, 197, 198,
   104, 204–8; trade union and
   business lobbies 204–12;

504

Organisation for Economic Co-operation and Development (cont.)
trends in policy towards MNCs 1980–85 14–15; working party on multinationals 206, 208
Organisation of African Trade Union Unity (OATUU) 214
Organisation of American States: Resolution on Transnational Enterprises 1978 10
Organisation of Petroleum Exporting Countries (OPEC) 165

Patronat Français 49, 209
Pechiney Ugine Kuhlman 209
Peugeot Co. 154
Philip Morris Co. 93
Philips Co. 31, 48, 53, 56, 146: Finnish case under OECD Guidelines 138, 143, 146; W. German case under OECD Guidelines 132–3
Pioneer Co. 73, 90: heavy EEC fine on 89
Portugal: EEC employment protection rules and 58
Preston, C.K. 209

Radio Luxembourg 53
Raytheon Co.: connection with Badger case 125, 126, 128
Reagan, Pres. Ronald 116, 146, 182
Rebhan, Herman 56
Renault Co. 48
Richard, Ivor 154
Royal Dutch Shell 31, 53, 203, 208, 217

Sahlgren, Dr Klaus 10, 32, 166, 206
Sallier de la Tour, V. 209

Sandoz Co. 209
Schmidt, Helmut 28, 215
Serpette, M. 209
Sharp Co.: from standpoint of OECD Guidelines in the US 145
Siemens 48, 56, 94, 209: Belgian case under OECD Guidelines 130–1; distributes OECD Guidelines 211
Skandinavska Enskildabanken 209
Soviet bloc: position on UN code for MNCs 168; views on technology transfer 179
South Africa: EEC code dealing with 101–2
Spain: EEC employment protection rules and 58
Spencer, Tom: report on worker information and consultation in MNCs 27
Spinelli, Altiero: 'Multinational Undertakings and the Community' 36, 37
Sudreau Commission 54, 55
Sweden: OECD contact point in 146, 147; view of MNC control 10, 154
Switzerland: Berne Declaration 213, 214; view of MNC control 10

Tacke, Dr G. 209
Tapiola Kari 206
Thatcher, Margaret 145, 146
Thomson-Brandt Co. 79
Toshiba Co.: from standpoint of OECD Guidelines in the US 145
Trades Union Congress (TUC) 57, 206, 207; support for worker participation 54

Trades unions: EEC lobbying by 198–201; growth in industrial democracy and 48, 50; influence in politicising MNC issue 26–7; OECD lobbying by 205–8; officials on German boards 56; role as OECD Guidelines watchdog 15, 112, 119, 175; supporters of MNC control 10–11; UN lobbying by 214–18;
versus Western MNCs on MNC control 195–8; basic battle lines 196–8; on the attack 196

Treaty of Rome 19, 21, 35, 36, 75, 91, 92, 93

UN Centre on Transnational Corporations (UNCTC) 10, 164, 166, 168, 182, 206, 214: 'Comprehensive Information System' on MNCs 184–5; research into impact of MNCs 185–6; technical co-operation programmes on MNCs 185

UN Commission on International Trade Law (UNCITRAL) 182

UN Commission on Transnational Corporations 164–5, 168, 185, 191, 214, 216

UN Conference on Trade and Development (UNCTAD) 117, 151:
code of conduct for MNCs 8, 11, 15–16, 36, 117, 151, 157, 166, 189, 215: anti-trust 176–8, 189; transfer of technology 178–81

UN Economic and Social Council 117, 164: code on illicit payments 152, 182–4, 189–90

UN Food and Agricultural Organisation: Industry Co-operative Programme 213, 214

Unilever 31, 53, 79, 203, 209

Union of Industries of the European Community (UNICE) 198, 201–2: membership 201

United Brands 73, 79: anti-trust judgement on 81–2, 83

United Kingdom 69: collective bargaining at plant level 54; effect of joining on EEC 25; Monopolies Commission 75; OECD contact point in 145; output of nationalised industries 91, 92; resistance to industrial democracy 50, 55; shop stewards' committees 63; view of MNC control 10, 31

United Nations (UN) 67:
channels for influence 214; code of conduct for MNCs 7, 8–9, 11, 15, 35, 36, 100, 104, 151, 214; connection with OECD Guidelines 115–18; corporate disclosure 186–7; demand for muted by economic crisis 166–7; implementation 190–2; major issues 168–9; negotiations 167–8; roots of 163–7; trade union influence on 20; voluntary nature 190

'Impact of MNCs on Development and International Relations' report 164, 186; trade union and business lobbying at 212–18

United States of America: changes from investor to country receiving investment 148–50;
Congress: code on MNCs agreed with European Parliament 9, 74, 103;

United States of America
Congress (cont.)
  House of Representatives
  103; suspicious of anti-
  Americanism in European
  MNCs 42
Department of Justice 76, 77,
103
Department of State:
  Advisory Committee on
  Industrial Investment, Tech-
  nology and Development
  145
Foreign Corrupt Practices Act
182; Foreign Trade Commis-
sion 76; Government view of
OECD Guidelines 153, 164;
Securities and Exchange Com-
mission 52, 67, 68; Sherman
Act 83

Vetter, Oscar 202
Volkswagen Co. 48
Vredeling, Henk 52, 68:
  'initiative' on worker consultation 27, 30, 32, 43, 47, 52,
  53, 55, 56, 58, 60, 63, 64,
  65, 67, 69, 112, 142, 154, 226

Wagner, G.A. 208
Warner Lambert: Swedish case
  under OECD Guidelines 131–
  2
Weisglas, Dr M. 209
Williams, Harold M. 68
Wilms-Wright, Carl 215
World Confederation of Labour
  117, 154, 163, 197, 206,
  214
World Federation of Trade
  Unions 214